DIALOGICAL PLANNING
IN A
FRAGMENTED SOCIETY

DIALOGICAL PLANNING
IN A
FRAGMENTED SOCIETY

- CRITICALLY LIBERAL
- PRAGMATIC
- INCREMENTAL

Thomas L. Harper
Stanley M. Stein

Center for Urban Policy Research—CUPR Press
Edward J. Bloustein School of Planning and Public Policy
Rutgers, The State University of New Jersey
New Brunswick, New Jersey

The Credits and Acknowledgments section on pages xiii and xiv constitutes an extension of this copyright page.

Published by the CENTER FOR URBAN POLICY RESEARCH
Edward J. Bloustein School of Planning and Public Policy
Rutgers, The State University of New Jersey
Civic Square • 33 Livingston Avenue
New Brunswick, New Jersey 08901-1982

For purchasing information, contact CUPR PRESS at the above address, by telephone at 732•932-3133, ext. 555, or by e-mail at cuprbook@rci.rutgers.edu

Printed in the United States of America

Library of Congress Cataloging-in-Publication Data

Harper, Thomas L.
    Dialogical planning in a fragmented society : critically liberal, pragmatic, incremental /
  Thomas L. Harper, Stanley M. Stein
        p.   cm.
    Includes bibliographical references and index.
    ISBN-13: 978-0-88285-179-2
    ISBN-10: 0-88285-179-9 (alk. paper)

    1. City planning—Philosophy. I. Stein, Stanley M.   II. Title.
    HT166.H387   2006
    307.1'2'01—dc22

                                                                    2005045406

Cover design: Helene Berinsky

Editing/Typesetting: Arlene Pashman

For Hannah, her great-grandmother Hannah,
and her great-great-grandmother Hannah
— Stanley M. Stein

For my mother Kay, my father Len,
my daughter Rachael, and my son Nicholas Harper
— Thomas L. Harper

About the Authors

THOMAS L. HARPER is professor in the planning program of the Faculty of Environmental Design, University of Calgary. He did graduate work in management at Carnegie-Mellon University and in economics at the University of Chicago and the London School of Economics. He has served as Canadian liaison to the Association of Collegiate Schools of Planning, was president of the Association of Canadian University Planning Programs (ACUPP), and is currently ACUPP's representative to the Global Planning Education Associations Network. He is on the editorial board of the *Journal of Planning Education and Research*, the biennial *Dialogues in Urban and Regional Planning*, and the annual *Canadian Policy and Planning*. A member of the Canadian Institute of Planners, he has consulted for government, community, and private-sector clients and has served on boards and committees for numerous community, social service, educational, and church organizations.

STANLEY M. STEIN is Resident Philosopher, Faculty of Environmental Design, University of Calgary. He holds a doctorate in philosophy from the University of Calgary. In collaboration with Thomas Harper, he has published widely on the practical implications of philosophical and ethical aspects of planning theory, the ethical and economic justifications of government intervention, environmental ethics, and social institutions. In collaboration with other colleagues, he has published work on theories of aesthetics and design as well as architecture theory. Stein has developed an interdisciplinary philosophy of environmental design based on the recognition that all beliefs and concepts are historically contingent: they arise and evolve in response to new issues and problems. Stein maintains that new problems and crises facing society in a contemporary world require reconceptualization of old categories, descriptions, and ways of thinking to generate a new interdisciplinary approach to theory and practice. In this regard, he and his colleagues have worked to apply a neopragmatic approach to the challenges of the twenty-first century. Dr. Stein serves on the editorial board of the *Journal of Planning Education and Research*.

Contents

Preface   xi

Credits and Acknowledgments   xiii

Introduction   xv

I

PLANNING SHOULD GIVE UP THE MODERNIST PARADIGM

1
The Crisis in Modernist Planning   3

2
Modernistic ("Rational") Planning   20

II

PLANNING SHOULD BE PRAGMATIC

3
Two Responses to Modernism: Postmodernism or Neopragmatism   43

4
Out of the Postmodern Abyss: Postmodernist Themes   63

III

PLANNING SHOULD BE CRITICALLY LIBERAL

5
Classical Liberalism and Planning   81

6
A Critical Liberal Perspective   94

7
Pragmatic Incrementalist Planning 118

IV

PLANNING SHOULD RECOGNIZE AN EMERGING WAY

8
A Dialogical Planning Approach 135

9
A Dialogical Planning Approach: Critiques and Questions 157

10
Dialogical Planning in Practice 185

V

PLANNING SHOULD AVOID MODERNIST AND POSTMODERNIST TRAPS

11
The Search for Clear Categories and Universal Principles 213

12
The Radical Paradigm Shift 224

13
The Multicultural Trap (Relativism) 240

14
The Rejection of Theory 254

15
Power, Trust, and Planning 263

16
Conclusion: Key Strengths of Dialogical Planning 282

Endnotes 288

Glossary 303

References 316

Index 335

Preface

This book is the culmination of a critical study of a certain conception of philosophy and its application to planning. The conception of philosophy that links the various chapters is based on what can be referred to as neopragmatism, an approach that has been best expressed or implied in the writing of Hilary Putnam, Richard Rorty, and, in particular, Donald Davidson, John Rawls, and Ludwig Wittgenstein.

The following chapters flow from philosopher Stanley Stein's examination of neopragmatism and his thinking about how this philosophical approach can be useful in the field of environmental design—specifically, how it can be applied to planning procedures and problems. Thomas Harper provided the context for this theoretical application from his academic background in economics and management as well as his practical experience with political decision-making processes, community planning, and economic development, to illustrate the various approaches examined.

The result is a fresh synthesis of ideas—a new approach to thinking about planning theory and its implications for, and relationship with, practice. Philosopher Michael Walzer (1987, 136) has asserted that "Philosophy reflects and articulates the political culture of its time, and politics presents and enacts the arguments of philosophy. . . ." Similarly, the authors view planning theory as planning reflected upon in tranquillity, away from the tumult of battle, and planning practice as planning theory acted out in the confusion of the trenches. Each changes the other in a dynamic way. The authors' hope is that this book will demonstrate the intimate and inextricable link between them.

Credits and Acknowledgments

Many of the chapters in this book incorporate material from earlier publications:

CHAPTER 2

Portions of chapter 2 contain material revised from T. L. Harper and S. M. Stein (1992), The centrality of normative ethical theory to contemporary planning theory. *Journal of Planning Education and Research* 11, 2: 105–16. ©1992 Sage Publications. Used by permission of Sage Publications, Inc.

CHAPTER 3

Portions of chapter 3 contain material revised from T. L. Harper and S. M. Stein (1995), Out of the post-modern abyss: Preserving the rationale for liberal planning. *Journal of Planning Education and Research* 14, 4: 233–44. ©1995 Sage Publications. Used by permission of Sage Publications, Inc.

CHAPTER 4

Portions of chapter 4 contain material revised from T. L. Harper and S. M. Stein (1995), Out of the post-modern abyss: Preserving the rationale for liberal planning. *Journal of Planning Education and Research* 14, 4: 233–44. ©1995 Sage Publications. Used by permission of Sage Publications, Inc.

CHAPTER 5

Portions of chapter 5 contain material revised from T. L. Harper and S. M. Stein (1995), Classical liberal (libertarian) planning theory. In S. Hendler, *Planning ethics: A reader in planning theory, practice and education.* New Brunswick, NJ: Center for Urban Policy Research.

CHAPTER 6

Portions of chapter 6 contain material revised from the following sources:
- T. L. Harper and S. M. Stein (1992), The centrality of normative ethical theory to contemporary planning theory. *Journal of Planning Education and Research* 11, 2: 105–16. ©1992 Sage Publications.
- S. M. Stein and T. L. Harper (2005), Rawls's "Justice as fairness": A moral basis for contemporary planning theory. *Planning Theory* 4, 2. ©2005 Sage Publications.
  — Revised portions of the above two articles are used by permission of Sage Publications, Inc. —

- T. L. Harper and S. M. Stein (1993), Normative ethical theory: Is it relevant to contemporary planning practise? *Plan Canada* 33, 7 (September): 6–12.
- S. M. Stein and T. L. Harper (2000), The paradox of planning in a multi-cultural society: A pragmatic reconciliation. In M. Burayidi, ed., *Urban planning in a multi-cultural society.* Westport, CN: Greenwood Press. Revised and reproduced with permission of Michael A. Burayidi (© Michael A. Burayidi 2000) and Greenwood Publishing Group, Inc., Westport, Connecticut.

CHAPTER 6 (continued)

- Harper, T. L., and S. M. Stein (1995). Contemporary procedural ethical theory and planning theory. In S. Hendler, *Planning ethics: A reader in planning theory, practice and education.* New Brunswick, NJ: Center for Urban Policy Research.

CHAPTER 7

Portions of chapter 7 contain material revised from S. M. Stein and T. L. Harper (1997), Pragmatic incrementalist planning in post-modern society: A normative justification. *Planning Theory* 18: 3–28. Used by permission.

CHAPTER 8

Portions of chapter 8 contain material revised from T. L. Harper and S. M. Stein (1992), The centrality of normative ethical theory to contemporary planning theory. *Journal of Planning Education and Research* 11, 2: 105–16. ©1992 Sage Publications. Used by permission of Sage Publications, Inc.

CHAPTER 9

Portions of chapter 9 contain material revised from S. M. Stein and T. L. Harper (2005), Rawls's "Justice as fairness": A moral basis for contemporary planning theory. *Planning Theory* 4, 2. ©2005 Sage Publications. Used by permission of Sage Publications, Inc.

CHAPTER 11

Portions of chapter 11 contain material revised from the following sources:

- T. Jamal, S. M. Stein, and T. L. Harper (2002), Beyond labels: Pragmatic planning in multi-stakeholder tourism-environmental conflicts. *Journal of Planning Education and Research* 22, 2: 164–77. ©2002 Sage Publications. Used by permission of Sage Publications, Inc.
- S. M. Stein and T. L. Harper (1996), Planning theory for sustainable development. *Geography Research Forum* 16 (December). Used by permission of Editor, *Geography Research Forum.*

CHAPTER 12

Portions of chapter 12 contain material revised from S. M. Stein and T. L. Harper (1996), Planning theory for sustainable development. *Geography Research Forum* 16 (December). Used by permission of Editor, *Geography Research Forum.*

CHAPTER 13

Portions of chapter 13 contain material revised from the following sources:

- S. M. Stein and T. L. Harper (2000), The paradox of planning in a multi-cultural society: A pragmatic reconciliation. In M. Burayidi, ed., *Urban planning in a multi-cultural society.* Westport, CN: Greenwood Press. Revised and reproduced with permission of Michael A. Burayidi (© Michael A. Burayidi 2000) and Greenwood Publishing Group, Inc., Westport, Connecticut.
- S. M. Stein and T. L. Harper (2005), Rawls's "Justice as fairness": A moral basis for contemporary planning theory. *Planning Theory* 4, 2. ©2005 Sage Publications. Used by permission of Sage Publications, Inc.

CHAPTER 15

Portions of chapter 15 contain material revised from S. M. Stein and T. L. Harper (2003), Power, trust and planning. *Journal of Planning Education and Research* 23, 2. Used by permission of Sage Publications, Inc.

Introduction

The planning profession has been in a state of turmoil for several decades as planners in Western liberal democratic societies struggle to adapt to change and fragmentation in their cultural, social, and political contexts. This fragmentation is associated with a change often referred to as the shift from modernism to postmodernism. Some writers see the profession as suspended in the midst of a paradigm shift, unwilling to go back to the old modernist, "rational" paradigm, yet unable to agree on a vision of a new one (Alexander 1984; Beauregard 1991). Sandercock (1998a) has called for a new "postmodern" paradigm; Allmendinger (2001) prescribes a planning for "postmodern times"; others see a new public planning paradigm emerging. Ten years ago, Innes (1995) had the temerity to attach the label "emerging new paradigm" to a variety of views[1] loosely known as "communicative action planning." Well, that brought out the barracudas! Since then, anything remotely associated with this "new paradigm"[2] can expect a barrage of critical commentary.[3]

While most planning theory writers seem to accept the demise of the "old" paradigm, many resist the idea that there is a "new" or even an "emerging" one. Even more resisted is any suggestion that there might be a *dominant* new paradigm. This resistance became very evident at a 1998 planning theory conference in Oxford,[4] where a multiplicity of approaches were represented. However, there did seem to be two main perspectives; these have been labeled as "communicative-pragmatist" and "critical"[5] (Yiftachel 1999).

This diversity of perspectives led some to argue that there is no need for a paradigm: Every planner should devise his or her own paradigm.[6] We don't think such a state of extreme fragmentation is at all workable. We believe that a dramatic change (shift, or whatever you may choose to call it) in the practice of planning has occurred incrementally over the past thirty years. We also believe that the planning profession does require something like a paradigm, at least in some senses of this much-abused term.[7] We do not need a paradigm in the sense of a rigidly fixed set of protocols that govern our profession. We *do* need some shared framework of presuppositions, concepts, values, norms and standards within which planners can do their work and conduct their debates. These shared elements are dynamic, fluid, evolving, in flux . . . but they are still shared. To forestall an unproductive debate, we try to avoid the term "paradigm"; rather, we use "way," "approach," "vocabulary," or "framework" to denote the set of elements (presuppositions, concepts, values, and procedures) that we believe the planning profession should share.

OUR PURPOSE

The purpose of this book is to address the question: "What is the best planning approach for a contemporary liberal democratic society?" We believe that a workable approach for public planning in the contemporary fragmented social and political context should have certain attributes in addition to the *communicatively* rational and *practical action* orientations advocated by Forester (1989; 1993a) and Innes (1995). The approach we have advocated to public planning is first and foremost *liberal* in its normative values (Harper and Stein 1995a) and *neopragmatic* in its philosophical orientation (Harper and Stein 1994; 1996). It is also *critical* in its evaluation of actual institutions (Harper and Stein 1995b) and *incremental* both in its justification and in its practice (Stein and Harper 1997), because we believe these attributes are necessary to get us where we want to go.

We are well aware that these attributes of public planning may have negative overtones for many planners. So we must stress that by *communicative* we do not mean "seeking to persuade at any cost" or "manipulative" or "non-critical" or "ignoring the dark side" or "naive about human nature" or "focusing only on communication and process." By *liberal* we do not mean "wishy-washy," "naive," "noncritical," or "blind to inequalities." By *pragmatic* we do not mean "amoral" or "opportunistic" or "anything goes if it works." By *critical* we do not mean "carpingly negative" or "unengaged," and by *incremental* we do not mean "stuck in the status quo," "noncritical," or "deferential and quiescent."

These negative connotations are not entirely groundless; they are probably rooted in experience. But in our interpretation these attributes do have positive implications, particularly in their interactive combination. Liberalism and incrementalism need critique to avoid complacency and quiescence in the face of power, and to address socially systematic structural distortions (Forester 1993a, 75–7). Critique needs liberalism for its normative orientation. All need pragmatism for justification in the contemporary context. We believe that all of these ideas reinforce and support each other. We will attempt to convey the positive sense in which we intend these terms, because we believe each describes something that is essential to an effective public planning approach that will be appropriate in contemporary liberal democratic societies.[8]

Although we are cautious about labels, in previous publications we have referred to our approach as "critically liberal" or "pragmatically incremental." To avoid the excess baggage of negative connotations, we decided to use the label "dialogical planning" to denote our approach, which attempts to incorporate the above elements. This approach overlaps, in many important respects, with both communicative planning and the "critical" school identified by Yiftachel (1999). We hope that advocates of both approaches can embrace dialogical planning as an extension of their own approach.

One major difference: We developed dialogical planning from a different starting point. While communicative planning begins with Habermas (1984) and the critical school begins with Foucault, we have attempted to incorporate and integrate insights from a variety of Anglo-American "post-analytic" philosophers.[9] We will also argue that our dialogical approach can incorporate useful and valid elements from both modernist and postmodernist perspectives. However, we certainly have no intention of imposing its dominance or hegemony on anyone. We will seek to convince our readers, by giving good reasons and advancing sound arguments, that this is a productive shared approach.

Much of what we advocate is neither novel nor radical. Most contemporary planning theory is (at least implicitly) liberal in its value orientation. Hoch (1984), Blanco (1994), and Verma (1993) have all applied various forms of pragmatism to planning, and Hoch (1984) traces a pragmatic influence on Lindblom (1959), Friedmann (1973), Davidoff (1965), and Grabow and Heskin (1973). Forester advocates a "critical pragmatism" (1993a), and Innes's (1995) depiction of "communicative action" planning sounds very pragmatic. All of these writers presupposed the normative ideals of liberalism in the public realm. All have sought to develop a planning process that better fits the contemporary context.

Most communicative theorists are also "critical," and we have seen that there is an emerging school of Foucauldian "critical" planning theory (Flyvbjerg 1998; Yiftachel 1999). The best of contemporary planning practices frequently exhibit several (and sometimes many) of these attributes but often without an explicit theoretical basis. Our goal is to set forth a firmer normative theoretical grounding for planning that is reflective and incorporates best practices.

WHAT IS PLANNING?

At this point, we should give a general idea of what we mean by "planning." Public planning, first as a reform movement and then as a profession, arose out of desires to improve the horrendous living environments of the nineteenth-century modern industrial city (Friedmann 1987; Sutcliffe 1981). The aim was simply to design better places to live decent and healthy lives. However, planners now perform such a wide range of activities, covering such a wide variety of functions and environments, that the current profession defies easy definition. The traditional focus on the regulation and control of land use and built form has expanded to include urban design, planning for urban functions (housing, transportation, parks, recreation, infrastructure), economic and community development planning, social planning (social service delivery, education, health care), heritage and tourism planning, environmental and resource planning, and corporate/strategic planning, to name only a few. To further complicate matters, many of these functions are also performed by other professionals including policy analysts, public administrators, lawyers, engineers, developers, and architects. So the professional planner is only one of many actors in the process of planning.

Even though planning encompasses such a diversity of activities, we can outline some very general characteristics. In ordinary usage, "planning" often refers to an activity done by individuals, groups, or organizations that involves deciding on a desired future and implementing actions to achieve it. Planning activity entails translating knowledge into action (Friedmann 1987). The knowledge required for planning's mission comes from a variety of professions, fields, and academic disciplines. This means that effective planning is inherently interdisciplinary. Reflective integration and synthesis of knowledge is necessary for successfully translating knowledge into action.

As taught in university planning programs, "planning" focuses primarily on a subsidiary activity often called "public planning." A reflective practitioner might define public planning as having the following general characteristics:

1. It is *normative*: Plans and designs are guided by some vision or ideal of what ought to be; the idea of "betterment" is central.

2. It is *action-oriented*: Plans are not just studies but are intended to be implemented.

3. It is *social*: It is a collective activity that occurs in the public domain.[10]

4. It is *public*: It is undertaken by the government or state—the public entity that claims a geographic monopoly over coercive power.

5. It is *directed outwardly*: The plans made generally apply to persons who are not part of the planner's own organization.[11]

6. It can secure *compliance* by *involuntary* means: Ultimately, public plans are enforced by the coercive powers of the state.

7. It involves the allocation of *tax-funded* resources.

To these attributes, Forester (1993a) would add that:

8. It organizes, directs and *shapes attention* to the desirability and feasibility of public actions, alternatives, and possibilities.

Many of these attributes are implicit in Healey's definition of planning as "managing our coexistence in shared space" (1997, 3), and in Yiftachel's definition as "the public production of space and/or urban habitat" (Yiftachel et al. 2001, 5).[12] In enumerating these characteristics, we are not attempting to identify an "essence" of planning. Few examples of public planning exhibit all of these characteristics, but most examples do exhibit a number of the characteristics. Thus, these attributes form what Wittgenstein (1958, para. 67) calls an overlapping "family of resemblances." At the fringes, we can debate where to draw the line. For example, many observers note an increase in planning in "civil society" that fulfills criteria numbers 1–3 and 8, but generally not numbers 4–7. This may or may not be defined as "public planning": It will depend on the purpose of the definition. Our definition of "planning" will focus primarily on the state activity.

OUR APPROACH

Before we discuss the current crisis in planning and outline the more detailed elements of dialogical planning, we should outline our general approach to planning and planning theory. Rather than starting with a particular philosopher or social theorist and then working out all the implications of applying that writer's thought to planning,[13] we begin with a normative basis and then use writers and ideas that we find useful or helpful. We believe that the most robust and useful approach can be developed by drawing ideas from various sources and applying them pragmatically; that is, we should use a variety of sources as appropriate to our purposes. We want to avoid doctrinal debates about whether our (or anyone else's) interpretation of Habermas—or Foucault or Rawls or Forester or Friedmann or Innes or whomever—is the *correct* one. Each has flaws and weaknesses. We would like to put these aside and focus on the ideas that are useful for our purposes. In an artificially linear format, the basic elements follow.

Public planning is an inherently normative undertaking. We begin with the normative ideals of Enlightenment *liberalism* and liberal democracy. Although these ideals can lead in somewhat different directions, liberal democratic societies share a political commitment to a basic fundamental value: their focus on the *free, equal, and autonomous individual person* as the basic unit of society, the ultimate object of moral concern, and the ultimate source of value.[14] We will assume these values in general and not as they have been implemented in any particular locale (e.g., the United States, the United Kingdom, Canada, Sweden, Australia, Israel).

We adopt a *pragmatic* (or more precisely, neopragmatic[15]) philosophical approach. Some of the implications of this approach follow. We are not interested in unachievable utopias (unless they provide a useful heuristic). To implement normative ideals, we must devise a feasible *incremental* path from here to there. Successful planning requires an understanding of how participants view the meaning of their institutions and actions. Here is where Habermas's "*communicative* rationality" and Walzer's (1987) "critical interpretation" are essential. We recognize that all humans, human knowledge, and social structures/institutions will be flawed, imperfect, and fallible. Thus, we need critical reflection and study of where our institutions in practice fail to meet our normative aims. This is where Habermas's *critical* rationality is required. We also recognize that humans are not always ethical and sometimes (but certainly not always) are manipulative, and that the power of planning is not always exercised benevolently. Here we draw on Habermas's critical idea of *ideological distortion*. And when we look at Habermas's work, we find this distortion can arise from both individuals and social structures or institutions.

Given the societal institutions that we now have as a starting point, our goal is to ascertain the attainable institutions, practices, and processes that are likely to attain the ideal best expressed by John Rawls (2001): to give us the best (fairest) system of cooperation among free and equal, reasonable and rational, persons. Thus, we look for a process that will help us to understand, critique, develop, and reform public institutions, processes, and agencies, and to make decisions and resolve conflicts within these frameworks. Here we turn to Rawls's (2001) process of *Wide Reflective Equilibrium*[16] (WRE) and apply it in a way that incorporates communicative, critical (and other) rationalities. We can use this process both to develop planning theories and processes and to conduct actual planning work.

A WRE process[17] involves seeking *coherence* among (1) our considered judgments; (2) normative theories, or principles; and (3) other background theories. "Background theories" include all the relevant information and knowledge available to us, whether normative or descriptive/predictive, and both internal and external to a culture (see chapters 6 and 13). We try to fit all of the interlocking elements together as an organic whole. The goal is a reflective equilibrium in which all of the above factors are coherent and consistent, giving as much sense as possible to our shared life.

A NORMATIVE FOCUS

The focus of this book is normative procedural planning theory—a particular sort of planning theory that we believe is relevant to contemporary planners. By relevant, we mean planning theory that can help planners to: (1) understand the rapidly changing and turbulent environments (social, political, economic, legal, institutional, professional) in which they attempt to carry out their historic mission—making human environments better places to live; and (2) justify the role and purpose of public planning and plans in our society.

To many practitioners, unfortunately, "relevant planning theory" is an oxymoron (chapter14). They simply do not understand the vocabulary of planning theory and they do not regard learning it as a priority. This is a very dangerous situation. Planners who ignore relevant planning theory do so at their own peril, and a planning profession that attempts to practice without reflective theory in the contemporary turbulent context may be doomed to irrelevance, decline, and perhaps even extinction.

Some will object to our procedural and normative orientation, decrying the contemporary focus of planning theory on "methods, processes, and inter–actions" at the expense of attention to "the substantive nature and consequences of that activity" (Yiftachel et al. 2001, 5). Many authors use the term "planning theory" to encompass either substantive explanatory or descriptive theories of how the city (or the region) functions, or how political processes are dominated by elites, or descriptive accounts of how planners do their work in different contexts. While these theories are helpful to planners in understanding the implications of their plans[18] and the barriers to their effectiveness, our focus will be on a normative account of the *process* or procedures[19] that planners *ought* to follow in carrying out their mandates. This is not to denigrate other varieties of theory, nor to deny them the status of "planning theory." To those who advocate the study of "the power of planning to shape social relations" and the "manifold manifestations of that power" (Yiftachel et al. 2001, 1), we would reply that in order to do this, planning needs good empirical (descriptive/explanatory), interpretive (communicative), and normative (critical) theories. Our explicit focus on the normative is central to raising what Yiftachel calls "critical questions" about the power of planning.

The activity and the profession of planning are inherently normative. We make this assertion on two levels. First, planning is normative in that it deals with what *ought* to be and thus conducts evaluations on that basis. Second, on a deeper level, most of the concepts used by planners are imbued with normative meaning:[20] They have an evaluative and justificatory component beyond the descriptive, explanatory, or predictive.[21] For example, planning is often seen as a "rational" process. The term "rational" is generally seen in a logical or empirical sense. However, as planners use "rational," it has a significant normative content (i.e., it is the way things ought to be done). Because of this connotation, we often use Rawls's (2001) notion of "reasonableness" instead. He uses "reasonable" to mean an acceptance of fair terms of cooperation and a commitment to abide by them, provided everyone else is also similarly committed. This gives "reason-able" a broader normative content than "rational."

The characteristics of public planning outlined earlier have very important implications in a liberal democratic society. If the state makes plans that affect the rights or interests of persons, that can be implemented coercively, and that involve public expenditures, then it is imperative to provide a justification for so doing. Typically, this needs to be a normative (usually a moral) justification. In a pluralistic democratic society, this justification will appeal to basic shared liberal democratic values like individual autonomy, tolerance, equity, fairness, democracy, and the rule of law. Planners must be careful not to let the post-modern celebration of difference fragment this core of shared values.

The normative nature of planning should be kept front and center. Good planning theory involves more than describing and understanding what planners do. Accurate descriptive theory (facts and predictions) is necessary but not enough. Description is preliminary to deciding what *ought* to be done. Knowledge of effective implementation is also necessary but not enough: The last thing we need is planners who are highly skilled at implementing bad ideas. It may be true, as one of our colleagues once commented, that "some of the most successful implementers and entrepreneurs don't justify," but this is a serious problem.

Public planners have a moral obligation to justify what they propose to do. For example, a few years ago, a policy was adopted that local churches in Norway had to be large enough to hold 10 percent of the area's population. As a result, many old churches, some dating back to 1000 A.D., were demolished apparently to make way for new ones that were large enough to satisfy the policy. This seems like a case of very effective implementation, but was it a good thing? Shouldn't we engage in reflective justification *before* action?

WHERE WE GO FROM HERE

In the chapters following, we examine some of the flaws in modernist planning and outline the postmodernist challenge to planning. We summarize some of the intellectual roots of both modernism (Part I) and postmodernism (Part II), critically examine their major themes, and identify some of their implications for planning. We believe that there is a need for a planning approach that avoids the narrow dogma and the oppression of modernism as well as the paradoxes and relativism of postmodernism. In Part II, we begin to show how our alternative nonmodernist philosophical perspective (neopragmatism) can enable planning to respond to this challenge. Developing a dialogical approach requires a reexamination of planning theory and its unresolved debates in the light of issues raised by postmodernist critics of modernity, including deconstructionists, radical feminists, and deep ecologists, as well as other issues raised by critics of the newer communicative approach. We believe that such a dialogical approach will be appropriate and workable for contemporary pluralistic liberal democratic societies in an era of postmodern fragmentation.

In Part III, we outline in more detail, and argue for, other aspects that we believe should be part of a workable and coherent view of any emerging planning approach: it should be *liberal* in its normative presuppositions and *incremental* in its practice and its justification. In Part IV, we summarize the elements of a dialogical approach to planning and briefly look at their antecedents in historical and contemporary planning theory (chapter 8). We also anticipate questions and concerns that may arise concerning our approach (chapter 9) and discuss practical applications of similar approaches (chapter 10).

Finally, in Part V, we look at traps that can vitiate contemporary planners. Most of these traps are postmodernist: the radical paradigm shift (chapter 12), the multicultural trap of relativism (chapter 13), and the focus on power (chapter 15). One is modernist: the search for labels and universal principles (chapter 11). And one—the rejection of theory (chapter 14)—could beset either approach. Although all sections have been significantly updated from the original papers upon which they are partly based, this section includes our more recent work. In particular, chapter 15, in addressing the current trend among planning theorists to focus (excessively in our view) on issues of power, also recapitulates some of our earlier themes, as does the conclusion.

Part I

PLANNING SHOULD GIVE UP
THE MODERNIST PARADIGM

1

The Crisis in Modernist Planning

INTRODUCTION

The idea of planning as a profession—indeed, the very idea of a profession—is a modern idea. Modernism arose out of the intellectual ferment and political upheaval of the eighteenth century at the time of intellectual, social and cultural change now known as the Enlightenment.[1] What is sometimes called the "enlightenment project" has a variety of aspects, including emphases on science, liberalism, and rationality—elements that are often in conflict.[2]

In the premodern world, religion provided an absolute foundation for certain knowledge (truth) and justification of all kinds—empirical, moral, aesthetic, religious. This single foundation gave the premodern worldview unity and coherence. There was a divine order in which everything and everyone had a fixed place that was defined by birth. As Rowland explains, for medieval people:

> The great cathedral of Notre-Dame de Paris was not what it is for us. It was not simply an object, a pile of stone and glass artfully arranged. It was that and much more: it was an extension of their collective existence as humans, or perhaps a *projection* of their being, a reaching up to God by man and a simultaneous reaching down to man by God, as in Michelangelo's *Creation of Adam* in the Sistine Chapel. Men and women wore it . . . like a cloak . . . and it exalted their existence, in ways most of us can no longer even imagine.
> ' (Rowland 1999, 59)

Religion gave a unified meaning to their existence, their experience, their artifacts, their world.

Major upheavals were beginning to crack the foundation of religion by the end of the seventeenth century. Skepticism and the questioning of tradition, custom and authority (that led later historians to call this time the Age of Reason) were turning the medieval world upside down, with the claim that science could provide a new unshakeable foundation for knowledge. By the end of the eighteenth century, advances in scientific knowledge were being applied to technology (leading to the Industrial Revolution). At the same time, the entire social and political order was challenged by radical ideas. The structure of society, the legitimacy of monarchs and aristocrats, and the absolute power of the Roman Catholic Church were all questioned.

Science

Modernism retained the premodern idea that certainty of knowledge and justification are impossible without firm foundations. The huge shift was that science replaced religion as the foundation of knowledge about the world. In some senses, this is the very core of modernism—the enlightenment thinkers' claim that science had replaced premodernism's faith in religion as the certain foundation of knowledge. This did not leave religion with no role, but it did greatly narrow its realm; it no longer provided a legitimation for all knowledge. Thus the unity of the premodern view was eroded.

Science claims to produce an objective understanding through the observation of regularities. The scientific method provides a procedure for determining which regularities are causal. This method specifies a sequence of activities—observation of regularities, generalization, theorizing, hypothesis-testing, establishing scientific laws, uniting theories under general theories—that legitimize or establish empirical knowledge. For modernist enlightenment thinkers, this is the *only* method accepted as legitimate for determining what is true. Science turned out to be very successful in providing explanations that enabled us to manipulate and control the physical world for human purposes. As a result, themes of the "scientific" aspect of modernism include faith in progress through science and technology, and belief in the possibility of objective knowledge about the real world.

Scientism

The success of science led many modernists to expand what they believe the role of the scientific method should be, to claim that all knowledge (religious, social, moral, aesthetic) must be translated and *reduced* to a form that can be investigated using this method. In this worldview, language reflects (mirrors) or represents reality.[3] It is a way of noting relationships in the *real* world. Language that can not be translated into scientific language (so that its claims can be falsified or verified) is meaningless.[4] This misapplication of the scientific method is what Habermas (1984) called *scientism:* the claim that science (and its method) is the only source of knowledge.

In addition to the dominance of scientism, modernism is characterized by *positivism* and *foundationalism.* Positivism is the claim that only empirical knowledge is legitimate; foundationalism is the belief that foundations for universal or certain truth are necessary and can be established. Adherents to scientism apply this perspective to the analysis of social structures, developing *meta-narratives*—universal theories that explain social reality in a deterministic way. For example, Marxism claims that social structures and moral beliefs are determined solely by economic forces. Reflecting the influence of modernism, the investigation of human and social phenomena came to be known as *social science.*

One of the most important results of applying scientism to practical decision making is a bifurcation of fact and value, and of means and ends. Thus, there can be no rationality of ends, but only of means (Meyerson and Banfield 1955, 116). Modernism limits rationality to instrumental rationality (finding the best means to any given end)—a question of fact. Practical decision making is regarded as a technical matter: determining causal relations between means and end, without any evaluation of ends.

The scientism of the modernist worldview is expressed in all realms of life. Ethically, modernism is *utilitarian*—the most scientistic approach to morality, which reduces it to a cost–benefit calculation (see chapter 2). Politically, the modernist form is *representative democracy*, with its sharp bifurcation of politics and administration. Organizationally, the modernist form is *bureaucracy,* with its emphasis on hierarchical structure, routine, and instrumental rationality. All of these taken together form a fairly consistent and coherent worldview (summarized in table 1-2). This worldview still dominates a good deal of institutional planning practice and is increasingly influential in the third world (developing countries) as various "first-world" (Western or Northern) agencies assist it to "modernize" at a frenetic rate.

Efforts to reform any single aspect of modernism that do not recognize the interrelatedness of these various facets tend to get blindsided by them—hence the frustration experienced by many planners when they attempt to implement nonmodernist planning approaches in bureaucratic public organizations within a system of representative democracy.[5]

The pernicious effects of scientism came to full fruition in planning with the dominance of the positivistic *Rational Comprehensive Planning Model* (RCPM).[6] The RCPM unites modernist rationality, ethics, politics, and organizational forms (see chapter 2). When the RCPM was seen as foundational, planning education was primarily a matter of technical training and the focus was on the empirical and the quantitative. The term *planning* came to refer to a cluster of substantively disparate activities traditionally done by many different actors. Planning as a profession claimed not so much a systematic body of substantive knowledge but primarily a common "scientific"

TABLE 1-1

Three Kinds of Rationality (Habermas)

	Instrumental/ Technical Rationality	Communicative Rationality	Critical Rationality
Interest	Empirical	Communicative, Interpretive	Emancipatory
World	Physical	Community	Ethics
Purpose	Control	Understanding people, actions	Emancipation

Source: Adapted from Habermas 1984.

(instrumentally) rational methodology seen as unifying these disparate activities (Branch 1990). The "professional protocol" (Hoch 1994) of planning rested on the planner's role as the technical *expert* within this framework— the one who recommends the best means to ends that are set by politicians and that the planner is expected to accept and implement without question.

Rationality

A second aspect of modernism, as seen in the RCPM, is its faith in rationality. The core idea is that progress comes via rational argument—giving good reasons for what we advocate and what we oppose. Science can (and should) serve human needs and wants, if we go about satisfying them in a rational way. Action toward liberal ideals can, and should, be guided by knowledge (Friedmann 1987). Sandercock characterizes the enlightenment attitude of mind as "dedication to human reason, science and education as the best means of building a stable society of free men on earth" (Sandercock 1998a, 61). Thus, modernism is not only "positivistic, technocentric and rationalistic, . . . with the belief in linear progress, absolute truth, . . . (and) standardization of knowledge," but it also incorporates a faith that the "rational planning of ideal social orders" can achieve equality, liberty, and justice (Harvey 1989, 11–13).

Liberalism

"Equality, liberty, and justice" brings us to the third aspect of modernism— the "liberal" or humanistic aspect—originating in the ideas of John Locke and Thomas Jefferson. The core belief is that the autonomous individual is the appropriate object of moral and political concern.[7] The fundamental common value shared by liberal positions is their focus on the *free, equal, and autonomous individual person* as the basic unit of society, the ultimate object of moral concern, and the ultimate source of value. Specific liberal values include

1. *Equality* of persons—each entitled to inalienable individual rights and to fair, impartial treatment

2. *Liberty*—autonomy or freedom of choice to live a good life, a life worth living

3. *Tolerance*—acceptance and respect for a plurality of conflicting conceptions of the good life

4. Rational, *reflective choice*—critical evaluation of life conceptions

5. Belief in society as a *fair system* of cooperation between free and equal persons

6. The *rule of law*—the impartial application of law to all persons

7. A primary *government role* in protection of liberty

8. *Restrictions* on the coercive powers of government.[8]

There is another view of liberalism influencing our notion of public planning that at times complements the above and at other times is in conflict with it. This is the notion of the *public good*, an idea loosely traced back to Rousseau (1968[1768]). It gives rise to the ideal of the citizenry who participate in social and political action out of a duty that transcends their own self-interest.

The liberal perspective forms the basic value set of a Western liberal democracy. We believe that historically (in Western European, North American, and related cultures), this perspective underlies planning as a reform movement and as a profession. We will assume a commitment to these general liberal political values throughout this book. This leads us to a basic concern with fairness and justice—criteria by which planning systems, policies, plans, and decisions should be judged. As shown later, it is possible to adopt a liberal perspective both as one's private philosophical worldview and, for pragmatic reasons, as a public political consensus. This latter "political liberalism" (Rawls 1993, 2001) is the aspect of modernism that we want to retain and refine. Our aim is to help planners who share this perspective to be able to understand, reflectively apply, justify, and defend it.

Justification

We have already argued that, from a liberal perspective, planning requires legitimation or justification. If a government makes plans that affect the rights or interests of persons and that will be implemented coercively, it must provide a normative justification for so doing. Planning as meaningful, intelligent, social action is normatively impregnated.

The *meaning* of any planner's action (or of any plan) rests on a normative account of the activity of doing planning; thus, a planner soliciting the views of inner-city residents about the impact of proposed density increases in response to growth pressures is playing a particular role as a representative of local government. The planner does this in the context of a society that recognizes certain rights (and limitations on these rights) of individuals and of property owners, one that values democratic procedures in public decision making, and one that expects government to be responsible (to some degree) for preserving the rights and enhancing the well-being of its citizens.

The planner's actions have meaning in the context of a number of *shared frameworks*, e.g., the legal, political, and economic institutions[9] of society; the roles of government that are regarded as *legitimate*; the purpose of public planning; and the mandate of the particular agency or organization.[10] These shared frameworks rest on both empirical and normative assumptions, on political positions that, in turn, can be justified (or not) by normative ethical theories; and on the particular balance between competing normative claims prevailing in society at any particular time.

These normative frameworks specify boundaries (often fuzzy) on which actions are *legitimate* for a public planner and which are not. For example, it would usually be inappropriate for a planner to promise that the views of residents will be the sole determinant of density policy, or to impose on residents the views of the planning department or the interests of the development industry, or the planner's own preferences. On the other hand, it is appropriate for the planner to ensure that all parties are aware of the differential impacts that density policies have on various socioeconomic groups and that all affected groups and individuals have an opportunity to understand the decisions being made and to voice their concerns.

THE CRISIS IN PLANNING

We see contemporary planning as being in a chronic perennial crisis that very much reflects the current crisis in our culture as a whole. This crisis relates to the loss of the modernistic faith in science as the certain foundation for knowledge.

Challenges to the Authority of Science

The dominance of science has been challenged on three levels: from within science, from social science, and from postmodernism. We will outline the first two below and discuss the postmodernist challenge in chapter 3.

The challenge within science came from several quarters. Einsteinian relativity and quantum mechanics (exemplified by the work of Bohr and

Heisenberg) shook the foundations of the Newtonian physics that had held sway for several hundred years. The scientific view had been that Newtonian physics established absolutely true physical laws governing the universe. Then the verification principle was undermined by the recognition that the act of measuring alters the measurement (which means that it cannot be ascertained whether or not the act of investigating actually alters the phenomenon being investigated). Thus, the objective observation assumed by the scientific method is impossible. In addition, Godel demonstrated that no logical system can be proven to be both complete and consistent (Honderich 1995, 320). In order to function, every system thus requires unprovable assumptions. In particular, science assumes that (1) every event has a cause, and (2) the future will be like the past. These assumptions cannot be proven without begging the question;[11] they simply have to be accepted in order to "do science." Contemporary physics now questions even these deeply embedded assumptions.

Kuhn's (1970[1962]) challenge came from applying a social science approach to the study of science as a culture, as a social phenomenon. He studied the history of science to show that scientific progress did not proceed according to the ideal account (i.e., the scientific method). Each discipline or field has a "paradigm," which is roughly: (1) the presuppositions, concepts, and general theories of a field; (2) the accepted procedures in that field; and (3) the constitutive rules of the community/social group that practice in this field and that accept and support these elements. Kuhn makes a distinction between "normal times," when scientists work within an established paradigm, and times of crisis or *paradigm shift*, when the established paradigm is being challenged and ultimately is replaced by a new one.[12]

A Paradigm Shift?

Many observers (Alexander 1984; Beauregard 1989, 1991; Innes 1995; Sandercock 1998) have seen planning as being in the midst of a paradigm shift. In such a time of crisis, planning has often been described as being in a precarious and unstable position with regard to its claims to legitimacy and professional expertise, marginal in its influence on public policy and decision making, and facing an uncertain future.

Hoch (1994) and many others have argued the failure of the modernistic RCPM and its professional protocol to provide practical guidance to practitioners. It has ceased to be a functional paradigm for planning:

> Planners, however, do not use the rational planning model as a guide for their practical planning activity, but rather as a rhetorical protocol to legitimize their activity within the city and county government institutions where planning occurs. (Hoch 1994, 277)

Planners do appeal to this model and its protocol to justify their professional influence but have learned from experience that they can not rely on it as a guide to practical action.

Friedmann (1987) also wrote of the failure of institutional planning:

> Talk to planners, and nine out of ten will describe their work as a "failure" or of "little use." They will say . . . "Our solutions don't work. The problems are mounting. . . . " We are forced to conclude that mainstream planning is in crisis. Knowledge and action have come apart. (1987, 311)

Later he argued that

> We live in an unprecedented time, confronted by unprecedented problems . . . the engineering model of planning that served us during this [two hundred year] period, with its penchant for advance decision making and its claims to superiority . . . is no longer valid and must be abandoned. Friedmann 1993, 482)

Planning will not survive, in his view, unless it adapts to a rapidly changing world. While he later expressed optimism about planning, his optimism relates more to the resurgence of civil society—the non-government, non-corporate part of the public domain (Douglass and Friedmann 1998). He is less optimistic about mainstream, institutional, bureaucratic, state-sponsored public planning.

One aspect of the crisis in planning is that new descriptions of practice are proliferating everywhere (including the planning literature) and are affecting the profession. The way planners talk *is changing* in several ways. The profession is becoming increasingly fragmented into different specializations and different ideological camps. Practitioners may be just as unfamiliar with the talk of some of their practitioner colleagues as they are with the talk of planning theorists. The planning profession and its vocabularies are in a state of flux. Even if practitioners are not talking to planning theorists, they are talking to *someone*, and those they talk to may in turn be talking to (or at least reflecting) theorists of some kind, perhaps even (perish the thought!) some of the same philosophers and thinkers read by planning theorists.

Planners are increasingly influenced and often politically pressured by a cacophony of voices demanding change. On the one hand, strategic planners talk of scenarios, visioning, SWOT,[13] key factors, and similar terms. On the other, free marketeers and management gurus talk of downsizing, efficiency, and "customer satisfaction," influenced by Friedman (1984), Peters and Waterman (1982), and Osborne and Gaebler (1992), among others. In a very different vein, deep ecologists, radical feminists, and community activists draw on the ideas of Foucault (1972), Derrida (1989), and Lyotard (1987) in rejecting modernism and in talking of celebrating difference and otherness, exhorting us to expand the circle of moral concern, urging us to hear and respect all voices. At the same time, communitarians argue that a fair process and the ideal of the autonomous individual[14] are not enough and talk of the revival of civic virtue, character formation, and substantive moral discourse (Sandel 1996). More and more planning is happening outside of the planning profession. "Civil society" is rising in size and influence, often without the aid of planners (Douglass and Friedmann 1998; Innes 1995; Sandercock 1998). The associated vocabulary is also different: There is talk of collaboration, institutional design, social capital, household economies, citizenship, resistance, and transformative politics.

The Nature of the Crisis

We view the crisis in planning as having three dimensions: (1) a crisis of efficacy; (2) a crisis of justification (what Habermas [1984] calls a "crisis of legitimation"); and (3) a crisis of understanding (what Friedmann (1987, 312) calls a "crisis of knowing."[15] We (and many others) see this crisis in planning as reflecting a deeper underlying crisis in society. Essentially, it arises from a realization that traditional forms of justification, when pushed to their limits, dissolve under the pressure. Sharp distinctions, such as reality/appearance, truth/opinion, objectivity/subjectivity, and fact/value cannot be maintained as we once thought they could be. In addition, traditional forms of foundation such as science or religion are incapable of justifying our beliefs and values.

Society has been undergoing a profound change in how we see the world (our conceptual frameworks or paradigms), in how we come to know it (what philosophers call epistemology), and in how we decide what we ought to do (what philosophers call morality or normative ethics). As Friedmann (1993, 482) puts it:

> What we are living through in the final decades of this century is something altogether different. It is nothing less than the collapse of the Euclidean world order of stable entities and commonsense assumptions that have governed our understanding of the world for the past two hundred years.

This change has been variously described as a shift from modernism to postmodernism, from certainty to uncertainty, from objectivity to relativism, from unity to fragmentation. Many of the challenges to contemporary institutional planning and to the planning profession (e.g., from radical feminists, deep ecologists, developmental planners, community activists) could be broadly characterized as "postmodernist." Although the term may be going out of vogue among intellectuals, the challenges and changes continue unabated at the practical level.

Certain assumptions that might be regarded as postmodern are now widely shared by most Western societies. Among these are the rejection of foundationalism, the celebration of difference, the increasing emphasis on rights, the suspicion/rejection of authority, the suspicion of ideology, and the rejection of meta-narratives. In the contemporary context, there are a diversity of positions, goals, and interests, even worldviews; a diversity of deeply held norms and values; a diversity of conceptions of the "good" (life, society, nation, city, and so on), that are often conflicting. There is no single universal "public interest" or "public good." Societies have become increasingly fragmented.

The result of this shift is seen everywhere in the decline in respect for hierarchy and authority in any and all forms. Authority is rejected both at the general level—the accepted moral principle, the justice system, science, the central theory of the discipline, the profession, the university; and at the individual level—the parent, the police officer, the scientist, the teacher, the professional, or the politician. What was once docilely accepted is now routinely challenged, or perhaps even more unsettling, simply ignored.[16]

As we shall see, the postmodernist response is to reject all hope of legitimation and move to various forms of pluralism, to the point of extreme relativism. We want to reject such extreme reactions and point the way to a pragmatic solution to the crises of justification and knowledge. In the pragmatic view (chapter 3), these criticisms need not lead to extreme relativism. Traditional distinctions and justifications can be preserved if they are viewed in context and applied more concretely.

The Role of Theoretical Reflection

The current crisis in planning seems to be an enduring one, perhaps because it is so deeply rooted. Beauregard (1989, 1991) views planning as stuck in the midst of a paradigm shift, suspended over an "abyss" between modernism and postmodernism. Because it is so perennial in nature, the crisis has ceased to engage us. But ignoring a crisis is a particularly ineffective way of addressing it.

We believe that this crisis calls for reflection of a nature usually considered to be "theoretical" or "philosophical." In commenting on our argument for the relevance of normative ethical theory to planning (1992), Hoch (1993) questioned whether there was any practical role for philosophy in planning. He suggested we should study what planners say and do, rather than what philosophers say and do. Our response (1993b) is that the approach we take (which we call "neopragmatism") is nonphilosophical (perhaps even anti-philosophical). It is nonphilosophical in the sense of believing that most of the academic philosophical vocabulary doesn't provide indubitable meta-physical principles from which practical decisions can be deduced.

Neopragmatism is philosophical, however, in the sense of encouraging deep reflection on how things hang together. Philosophical reflection, practical reflection, and meaningful action greatly overlap. When we examine what planners say and do, we find that these cannot be sharply separated from philosophical ideas and that philosophical questions are often raised. This is particularly true in times of crisis, when planners are doing and saying some very different things and when practices are changing in response to new demands.

In periods of normal stable social practice, planning can get along without [second-order] reflection because its deeply embedded normative presuppositions are so widely accepted that they are seldom questioned. Planners often function in an environment of stress and pressure, besieged on all sides, struggling just to keep abreast of daily operations. It is easy to go about the ordinary business of planning activities with these presuppositions remaining in the background.[17] Practices become entrenched and can be learned as a set of skills. Examination and critical evaluation of deeply held presuppositions and theories can play a minor role in education and practice. In stable situations, professionals can get by with what Schön (1983) called "knowing-in-action": the ability to perform the requisite professional tasks without being able to give a reflective explanation for what is being done. Thus, in the 1950s and early 1960s, the dominance of the RCPM went unchallenged.

In times of crisis and change, when the entrenched paradigm (i.e., the RCPM) is no longer seen as serving us, criticism of current practices begins to mount (from progressive planners, feminist planners, environmentalists, community activists, postmodernists, and the like), and citizens begin to actively oppose the work of planners. Then the previously unchallenged presuppositions must be critiqued, challenged, or defended—and confirmed, modified, or rejected. Planning may be challenged as an ideology that claims, for example, that studying

> the problems of circulation, of the conveying of orders and information in the great modern city, leads to real knowledge and to technical applications. To claim that the city is defined as a network of circulation and communication, as a centre of information and decision making, is an absolute ideology; this ideology proceeding from a particularly arbitrary and dangerous reduction-extrapolation and using terrorist means, sees itself as total truth and dogma. It leads to planning of pipes, of roadworks and accounting, that [the planner] impose[s] in the name of science and scientific rigour. (Lefebvre 1996, 98)

This sort of challenge to both the efficacy and the legitimacy of planning became common in the 1970s. This was a reaction, at least in part, to the rather spectacular failure of urban renewal, high-rise public housing, and urban highway construction. Now we also see it as an expression of postmodern challenge to the legitimacy of the profession.

Planning theorists and reflective practitioners began to argue that planning is *political*, in contrast to the earlier modernist view that planning is *technical*.

Krumholz and Forester (1990, 56) observed that "involvement in policy and program formulation inevitably means involvement in politics. This did not *put* politics into planning; it has always been there." It became obvious that various interests were being attended to, and served or not served, by public planning. Normative theories were now recognized, at least by some, as more relevant. But planning was theory dependent all along, even if this may not have been noticed by participants or observers.

When crises disturb the equilibrium, second-order reflection and debate are needed to find new ways to approach problems arising in current practice. The task of reflection on, and critique of, our deeply entrenched normative presuppositions tends to *shift* from the academic (philosopher, planning theorist) to the actor (planner, politician, or citizen). Then, "knowing-in-action" is inadequate; we need what Schön (1983) calls "reflection-in-action"—the ability to deal with unique and novel situations based on an understanding of the reasons for the actions as well as the underlying assumptions. This "reflection-in-action" may well lead to the recognition that planning is not always benevolent; it can also be regressive and oppressive.

Such second-order reflection usually requires some theoretical terms that are different from the vocabulary of current practice. As Walzer (1987, 136) has argued in a related context, the distinction

> between philosophical speculation and actual political debate . . . is an artificial and sometimes misleading line. For philosophy reflects and articulates the political culture of its time, and politics presents and enacts the arguments of philosophy. . . . Philosophy is politics reflected upon in tranquility, and politics is philosophy acted out in confusion.

Similarly, planning theory is planning reflected upon in tranquility away from the tumult of battle, and planning practice is planning theory acted out in the confusion of the trenches.

The two are intimately and inextricably linked. Each changes the other in a dynamic way, as theory (knowledge) is applied to change practice, and practice (action) is reflected upon to modify theoretical understanding.[18] The critique of current planning practices is impossible without questioning the normative precepts and principles (e.g., positivism and utilitarianism) that underlie actions, plans, and policies. The question "Is this a just policy or plan or decision?" cannot be separated from the question "What is justice?" In times of crisis, the practitioner must play a role in reflection on both questions. Meaningful social practices cannot be separated from their justification. An examination of the justification may reveal that deeply entrenched principles and concepts require modification. These principles and concepts are often "philosophical."

What we want to bring into the conversation about planning is not philosophy as an *a priori*, absolutist, meta-narrative, or super-discipline that claims a privileged position above other discourses. However, we believe that neopragmatic philosophy can make an important contribution to planning, particularly by contributing to the justification of meaningful planning practice. In addition, we will argue (chapter 6) that the neopragmatic resolution of contemporary planning issues is tied to the critical procedural method of Wide Reflective Equilibrium(WRE). Underlying this procedural method is both a reasonable epistemological approach and a liberal ethic— that is, it provides a basis for knowledge, truth, and morality.

Can We Have Practice without Theory?

The fact that planners could follow the RCPM without examining their deeply embedded underlying presuppositions may give the false impression that planning practice can be divorced from theory and that the vocabulary of theory is irrelevant to practitioners. This lack of reflection did not arise out of a lack of underlying theory. Rather the theory was undiscussed because it was so widely accepted.

Planning practitioners post–World War II felt ill-equipped to deal with the massive urbanization and the concomitant need for infrastructure and renewal. They decided that planning had to became more scientific and modern. Planning theorists became reflective, and in their second-order reflection they borrowed ideas and specialized vocabulary from other fields. As we shall see in chapter 2, Meyerson and Banfield (1955) adapted the "Rational Decision Model" of Simon (1945) from management and political science. Later, planning also incorporated the ideas and specialized vocabulary of U.S. Defense Secretary Robert McNamara's "Planning Programming and Budgeting Systems" (PPBS), which drew on systems theory and economics (to the point where McNamara allegedly said that he believed it possible to calculate the number of Vietnamese deaths it would require to bring the North Vietnamese to the negotiating table). And economics rests on the philosophical theories of utilitarianism and positivism, so even the technically oriented RCPM is heavily theory laden, although its practitioners may not always be fully aware of this basis.

At one time these borrowed, specialized vocabularies were new and unfamiliar to planners, but they became very familiar. Planners came to talk of benefits and costs, supply and demand, trade-offs, value-free analysis, objective functions, operational measures, decision criteria, weightings, statistically significant differences, correlations, random samples, and so on. This may have given the further false impression that planning theory had no specialized vocabulary, because practice had adopted so much of the vocabulary of theory. The impression that RCPM practice was theory-free was a delusion (and if held today, it is still a delusion). In Habermas's (1984) terms, it is an ideological distortion[19] that avoids challenges to professional expertise and its implicit support of the status quo.

The very intensity of the dissatisfaction with conventional planning that began to be expressed by various advocacy groups in the 1970s led planning theorists to begin to reflect deeply about the very nature of planning and the role of the professional planner. Again, it was natural to borrow ideas and specialized vocabulary from other disciplines, particularly philosophy. This borrowed vocabulary was new and unfamiliar (even alien) to planners. If it has become more familiar to some, it is still alien to others.

Over time, conventional institutionalized planning practice has continued to adopt specialized vocabulary and theory. Borrowing from management, strategic planners talk of scenarios, visioning, SWOT, key factors, and driving forces; borrowing from political science, planners talk of reinventing government and treating citizens as customers.

Like most useful distinctions, stable/unstable and crisis/normal are continua. No social practice is completely static, and planning practice changes (to varying degrees) as a response to dissatisfaction. If the planning profession wants to remain relevant, respected, and legitimate, it cannot continue to pretend that we are in "normal times" and go on ignoring theory. Our political processes are undoubtedly deeply flawed (a few people have too much power), but pretending that planners can be just technicians will not help. In fact, the myth of the value-neutral planning expert greatly enhances and preserves elite power.

AN EMERGING PLANNING APPROACH?

Innes (1995) sees a consensus forming around a new communicative action "paradigm" for public planning. One hallmark of this emerging approach is its focus on practice. Another is that it broadens the conception of rationality to go beyond the narrow instrumental conception of modernism (and the RCPM) to incorporate what Habermas has called *communicative and critical rationality* (table 1-1). Habermas argued that instrumental/scientific/technical rationality serves only one of several important human purposes—i.e., control (originally over the physical world). We also need *communicative* rationality to serve the purpose of understanding within community—interpreting the meaning of actions to the participants and understanding the purposes of institutions. In addition, we need *critical* rationality to serve the purpose of emancipation from (unrecognized) oppression, and to identify where our institutions and organizations fail to actually implement our liberal democratic ideals. The "old" (rational) planning paradigm claimed that planning was a technical, value-free, objective activity. The emerging (communicative action) approach recognizes that planning is inherently political.[20] As Sager characterizes it, the focus has shifted from calculation to communication.

Fischer and Forester (1993) refer to this shift as the "argumentative turn in planning and policy"; Friedmann (1993) calls it "non-Euclidean planning";

Hoch (1994), "deliberative planning"; Chrislip and Larson (1994), "collaborative leadership"; and Healey (1997), "collaborative planning." As Innes (1995) points out, recent changes in approaches to planning do indeed have some of the attributes of a paradigm shift, in that the new normative planning theories have very little in common with the old paradigm (table 1-2).

However, we will argue that this shift is not (or should not be) a paradigm shift in the most radical Kuhnian sense[21] (chapter 12) because (1) it occurred incrementally, and (2) it can be justified by appeal to a broader-level tradition or framework as better fulfilling liberal values and achieving the planning ideal of better living environments. Such incremental shifts can entail new vocabulary and shifts in direction without being radical paradigm shifts.

In advocating a new approach, we are not suggesting that planning jettison all of its past. What is good and useful should be retained. In fact, it could be argued that the "new" approaches seek to restore the original humane vision of planning that was lost in the push to "scientize" the field. Nor are we suggesting a shift to a full-blown postmodernist perspective. Planning should retain its liberal democratic ideals and the ideal of reasoned argument. The recognition of broader forms of rationality is a supplement to, but not a replacement for, the more limited notion of instrumental rationality.

Our dialogical approach seeks to integrate key aspects from the work of a number of contemporary planning theorists whom we identify as contributors to this emerging approach (chapter 8). Our theoretical rationale for this approach draws on, and applies, the contemporary literatures of philosophy and related fields (chapter 6). Although it uses insights from current debates in contemporary philosophical literature, this book requires no prior knowledge of philosophy. Rather, it aims to make the practical implications of contemporary philosophical work accessible and relevant to planning educators, practitioners, and students.

The intent of these theoretical discussions is very practical; the ideas we discuss here have real consequences. Here is an oversimplified example: Planners who are modernists see our social problems as technical and thus solvable by scientific application of universal principles. Planners who are postmodernists tend to see these problems as social and political, unsolvable (at least by science), and they reject the very possibility of universal principles. Planners who are pragmatists see these problems as both social/political and technical, and as amenable to amelioration by applying knowledge in local contexts. Thus, the worldview of the planner will profoundly shape his or her approach to planning.

Our concern is not that planning theory might be flawed by some technical philosophical errors. Rather our concern is that (1) the uncritical retention of modernist assumptions will narrow and paralyze planning into irrelevance, and (2) the uncritical adoption of postmodernist assumptions will push us into an abyss of indeterminacy, with a society so fragmented that it impairs

TABLE 1-2

Changing Approaches to Planning

Aspect of Planning	Old Approach ("Old Paradigm")	Emerging Approaches
Planning theory	Rational Comprehensive	Communicative Action, Social Learning, Progressive, Equity
Planning focus	Calculation	Communicative, Dialogical
Philosophical basis	Positivism	Pragmatism
Implicit normative ethical basis	Utilitarian	Rawlsian
Knowledge sought	Universal, Foundational, Certain	Contextual, Contingent, Fallible
Theoretical focus	Causal	Intentional, Interpretive
Rationality	Instrumental	Instrumental plus Communicative, Critical
Scope of planning	Synoptic, Comprehensive	Incremental, Strategic
Political orientation	Planning is technical	Planning is both technical and political
Ethical orientation	Planning is value-free	Planning is value-laden
Core values	Liberal democratic, Socialist	Liberal democratic, Communitarian
Form of democracy emphasized	Representative	Deliberative, participatory
Ideal of politics	Conflict	Collaboration
Organizational form	Bureaucracy (pyramidal), Vertical, hierarchical	Horizontal (flat), Nonhierarchical
Agent of change	State	Civil society
Tools	Technical, Quantitative Analysis (e.g., Benefit–Cost)	Less technical, plus Consensus building, Dialogical, Communicative, Critical approaches (e.g., Wide Reflective Equilibrium)

our ability to maintain continuity through change, to treat each other in a just and fully human way, and to conduct public planning in a legitimate and justifiable way.

As discussed above, many planning theorists reject the idea of a "new paradigm." Some advocate a plurality of paradigms for a plurality of situations. We will argue that this concedes too much to postmodernism. It leaves us without standards for judging planning actions, and it exacerbates fragmentation by overemphasizing the differences between communities. However, the argument that we need a shared approach with certain key attributes does not mean that we advocate any kind of forced dominance or hegemony of this view, nor does it entail any lack of respect for other approaches to planning. It certainly does not mean that we want to ignore or suppress contextual differences in favor of one dominant culture. Any of these things would be directly contradictory to the liberal democratic values at the heart of our approach.

2

Modernistic ("Rational") Planning

INTRODUCTION

By the middle of the twentieth century, the rising status of science led to an increasing dominance of the scientist aspect of modernism. This status was enhanced by the success of management "science" (operations research) in managing the military logistics of World War II. The social "sciences" promised explanatory models that would allow the kind of "social engineering" of which earlier social reformers (Friedmann 1987) had dreamed. In his classic and influential *Administrative Behavior*, Herbert Simon (1945) proposed a normative model of "rational decision making" based on the "rational maximizer" of economic theory and on positivistic sociology.

Looking to management science for a planning model, Banfield (Meyerson and Banfield 1955) adopted Simon's approach as the basis for a "rational" planning model. Later planners (Branch 1985) broadened the model to incorporate social and economic concerns,[1] culminating in the *Rational Comprehensive Planning Model* (RCPM). As we have seen, the RCPM underlies the dominant "professional protocol" that has guided many practitioners (Hoch 1994). This protocol limits planners to a technical role (removed from the "dirtiness" and messiness of politics), legitimized by claims to objective professional expertise.

This chapter will summarize the RCPM, look at its intellectual roots, and critically examine some of the implications of a scientist and mechanistic planning approach that does not acknowledge the inherently normative aspects of the planning and policy process. We will critique the RCPM on philosophical, ideological, and practical grounds.

THE RATIONAL COMPREHENSIVE PLANNING MODEL

This RCPM proceeds in the following fashion:

STEP 1

   a. Identify the problem or problems to be solved, the needs to be met, the opportunities to be seized upon, and the goals of the community to be pursued, and

   b. Translate the broad goals into measurable operational criteria.

STEP 2

   a. Design a wide range of alternative solutions or courses of action (plans, policies, programs) to solve the problems and/or fulfill the needs, opportunities, or goals, and

   b. Predict the consequences and effectiveness of each alternative.

STEP 3

   Compare and evaluate the alternatives with each other and with the consequences of unplanned development.

STEP 4

   Choose, or help the decision maker or decision-making body to choose, that alternative whose probable consequences would be preferable.

STEP 5

   Develop a plan of action for effectuating or implementing the alternative selected, including budgets, project schedules, regulatory measures, and the like.

STEP 6

   Maintain the plan on a current and up-to-date basis, based on feedback and review of information to adjust steps 1 through 5 above.[2]

Justification

The key advantages claimed by proponents of the RCPM are its [instrumental] rationality, scientific objectivity, basis in value-free social science, and reliance on value-neutral technical expertise. These advantages all "fit" with a modernistic, scientistic worldview. They reflect a strong politics/administration dualism, which in turn rests on the positivists' fact/value distinction discussed in chapters 1 and 3.

Less widely recognized but equally important features of the RCPM are its underlying philosophical pillars of utilitarianism and positivism. As we shall see, the same dualisms also underlie the organizational form of bureaucracy (Weber 1946, 1947).

UNDERLYING PHILOSOPHICAL BASES

Positivism

Positivism asserts that the scientific method is the only path to truth and knowledge—that the only true rationality is scientific rationality. According to positivism, in order to be rational, social *science* (and social practices such as planning that apply it) must follow the scientific method and must be *value-free*. Their knowledge will then be objective and normatively neutral.

The RCPM is a prime example of the pernicious effects of positivism when it is applied to practical human affairs. Simon explicitly based his decision model on the positivistic sociology of Talcott Parsons (1937): "The conclusions reached by a particular school of philosophy—logical positivism—will be accepted as a starting point, and their implications for the theory of decisions will be examined" (Simon 1945, 45).[3] Logical Positivism was based on a search for a universal criterion of meaning. It sought to demonstrate that certain questions—of a philosophical, religious, or ethical nature—were not meaningful questions. In order to do this, it adopted (1) a reductionist view of knowledge: All knowledge is empirical; and (2) an empirical criterion for the meaningfulness of propositions: All propositions must be verified by the methods of empirical science (the verification principle). In practice, this approach leads to a very strong focus on quantification.

Utilitarianism

The second philosophical pillar of the RCPM is utilitarianism. Notwithstanding its claim to be value-neutral, we argue that the RCPM also implicitly presupposes [one interpretation of] the normative ethical theory of utilitarianism. Although it has by no means been completely discredited as a normative ethical theory, utilitarianism no longer commands the near-monopoly position that it once did.

Utilitarianism is a normative ethical theory that holds that the right act (rule, plan, policy, or social system) is the one that maximizes the sum total of whatever is intrinsically good—usually happiness or well-being. It is a consequentialist ethical theory in that it evaluates rightness and wrongness by consequences or outcomes. There are numerous variants of utilitarianism that attempt to measure happiness in different ways and that advocate different political–economic institutions for maximizing well-being (Harper 1987).

Utilitarianism has two compelling attractions for those with a positivistic inclination. The first is that moral issues become resolvable (at least in principle) by the empirical calculation of consequences. The moral analysis of public policy questions then becomes a matter of empirical investigation, applying the techniques of social science. The second attraction is that utilitarianism provides a "common currency of moral thought": The different concerns of different parties . . . "can all be cashed (in principle) in terms of happiness" (Williams 1972, 92). Thus, conflicting moral claims are always potentially reconcilable.[4]

Utilitarians seek a planning process that determines the best means to maximize the "good." Many planners hold to a form of utilitarianism that we call "political utilitarianism." They believe that the determination of what is "good" (the ends or goals) should come from a political process that is outside the scope of the "planner-as-scientist," while the choice of *means* is seen as a technical/social scientific matter (Klosterman 1978). The best choice is the one that seems to command the most political support, i.e., is supported by the most people. Thus, utilitarianism (particularly this version of it) provides a strong rationale for the RCPM. Indeed, the RCPM seems to be the embodiment of utilitarianism applied to public decision making. Unitary utilitarians (who believe in a single definable public interest) most strongly favor this approach to planning and policy, but even pluralistic utilitarians (who acknowledge multiple conflicting interests in society) retain the foundational idea that only the ends are moral, and the means are strictly practical and technical. Thus, despite its claim to be value free, the RCPM would seem an expression of this particular normative ethical theory.

Rationality

One of the most important implications of applying positivism to practical decision making is that there can be no rationality of ends, only of means. The sole test of rationality is whether the means chosen are the most efficient way of achieving the desired ends:

> Action is rational, insofar as it pursues ends possible within the conditions of the situation, and by means that, among those available to the actor, are intrinsically best adapted to the ends for *reasons understandable and verifiable by positive empirical science*. (Meyerson and Banfield 1955, 116) [emphasis added]

The influence of the utilitarian perspective is to severely limit rationality to only one form. The RCPM limits rationality to *instrumental* rationality, i.e. to finding the best means to given *ends* (whatever they are, however they may be chosen). Excluded is any rationality regarding the evaluation and choice of ends. Ends are held to be simply chosen. Public ends emerge from a political process that is separate from the planning process. The planner is the technician whose role is to recommend the technically best means.

CONCEPTUAL CRITIQUE OF THE RCPM

Positivism

The arguments that led to the rejection of positivism in philosophy are many and varied, but three are key for our purposes here:

1. The demonstration that Logical Positivism could not justify its reductionism or its verification principle without begging the question.[5]

2. The verification principle itself could not be verified and would be rejected as meaningless by its own criterion. Positivists responded by suggesting that their criterion was a prescriptive "suggestion" describing what *should* be counted as meaningful. This brings out the *normative* nature of the Positivistic presupposition and leads to our critique here, which emphasizes the normative nature of Positivism.[6]

3. The understanding of a social institution requires an understanding of the normative criteria that are constitutive of that social institution. There is no one-to-one correspondence between the *meaning* of the institution and any set of objective empirical facts (Stein 1973; Winch 1958). The positivistic view that there exists an objective social reality that can be discovered and understood through value-free science is now seen as untenable.

Scientism and Reductionism

The attempt to reduce all knowledge to scientific knowledge, all rationality to scientific rationality, all rational action to instrumental action, Habermas calls the "fallacy of scientism" (Habermas 1971b). The mistake made by scientism is to try to collapse all knowledge into natural scientific knowledge—only one of the many legitimate types of knowledge. Scientism fails to recognize that science itself is a practice that presupposes norms and standards of action and communication that are themselves not empirical. Not only is this failure a logical and conceptual error, but (as we shall see below) Habermas argues that it also plays an ideological function.

The RCPM requires that both means and ends be "operationalized" (in order to be amenable to its scientific, quantitative techniques). This often reduces them to caricatures, since the relationship between means and ends is a causal one, and ends are to be reduced to empirically verifiable phenomena. To a significant extent, scientistic ideology will restrict the range of means to be considered in a way that determines (and distorts) the kinds of ends that are actually being pursued. Taken literally, the RCPM assumes that everything is quantifiable. The epitome of this method is an economist doing a benefit-cost analysis.

The attempt to predict consequences and effectiveness of each alternative assumes not only quantification but also an accurate predictive model (which will involve a further reductionism). In practice, the choice of predictive model will determine what counts as an alternative "solution" (i.e., which alternatives are included in the analysis).

When a reductionistic approach is taken to the planning of our cities, the likely outcome is an environment that is alienating for its residents. Each is in danger of becoming an alienated person whose

> activity is that of a body in the grip of a machine, not of a rational agent acting out of a sense of value. In his own eyes he is what he conceives himself to be in the eyes of the world—a means, not an end, an organism, not a man. (Scruton 1979, 245)

Rather than thinking of themselves as being in control of the physical world, and of buildings and cities expressing their values, the residents are in danger of becoming objects expressing the mechanistic worldview of scientism.

Our urban environments reflect our conceptions of our collective identities (and our conceptions of what is valuable). The physical artifacts found in urban space have meaning beyond their physical functions. Our ordinary language reflects this: We speak of "congenial" town squares, "formal" gardens, "proud and stately" buildings, "cold and sterile" streets. Our public artifacts reflect values that are, at least to some degree, shared. Our freeways reflect the value we place on mobility, speed, and convenience; our parks, the value we place on nature; our jogging paths, the value we place on exercise and fitness. The diversity of an urban environment may tell us something about its culture. The uniformity of a Greek hill town (unless it is externally imposed) may suggest a high degree of shared values; the diversity of London or New York may suggest a great variety of self-conceptions. Ideally, these self-conceptions should be those of autonomous and self-reflective persons in an emancipated society.

A "good city" cannot be described or evaluated solely in terms of empirical observations and generalizations. A "good city" is one in which basic human needs are satisfied, in which rights are not violated, in which people can autonomously pursue their own goals (subject to others' rights)—one that expresses symbolically the shared life conceptions and values of residents. It is generally not created by a grand plan like Houseman's Paris; it is more likely to evolve, like an Italian hill village, or like the oldest parts of London. The recognition that the physical artifacts of society are an externalization of our self-conceptions can lead to an urban planning that is reasonable and rational with regard to *both* its means and its ends.

Urban planners in the 1950s and 1960s were very reductionistic about the social nature of the city. The "urban renewal" approach to "improving" inner-city housing was a physical solution (i.e., new buildings and facilities) to what were seen as physical problems (blight or decay). The social and human consequences of the wholesale destruction of homes, neighborhoods, and communities were apparently unexpected. The "slum" was treated as a physical entity—a set of dilapidated buildings—rather than the manifestation of attitudes, beliefs, ideas, and emotions of residents. How residents feel about their environment is important. It is quite conceivable that some residents viewed their "slum" as a good neighborhood. The public housing projects that replaced these slums were generally failures as communities. They became slums immediately in a social sense, and not too much later in a physical sense. The evidence that this was happening seems to have been ignored until it was undeniable. According to Coleman (1985), British planners continued to advocate massive high-rise public housing construction well past the point where its failure seemed obvious, even to casual observers.

The urban renewal example may seem like flogging a dead horse in that its failures are common knowledge. However, we must point to the close linkage between this failure and the mechanistic and reductionistic approach to planning (epitomized by the RCPM) that produced it. We believe that an understanding of this linkage is crucial to those who seek to assert human values against the growing force of technological "imperatives."

Utilitarianism

What is wrong with utilitarianism? Its most serious flaw is that it ignores moral concerns other than well-being, concerns that are valued in liberal democratic societies and that are reflected in their institutions. These include freedom, autonomy, rights, justice, equity, integrity, and the distribution of well-being in society, as well as utilitarianism's tendency to reduce nonquantifiable conceptions of the good to quantitative conceptions. Writers in normative ethical theory have recognized the importance of the individual and are very critical of utilitarianism, among them Williams (1972), Rawls (1971, 1985, 1987, 1993, 2001), Nozick (1974), Habermas (1971a, 1971b, 1984), and Walzer (1987). Any theory that aspires to provide a normative model for public planning cannot ignore these other ethical values and concerns.

The most relevant critique for the purpose here is that utilitarianism (although it developed out of the Enlightenment) endorses overriding the autonomy of the individual. This is inherent in its focusing on one end-state, property, or attribute (happiness) of all individuals and then seeking to maximize the *total* of that attribute, with no concern about the distribution of costs and benefits. Thus, value is placed on an *attribute* of individuals (or even of other creatures[7]) rather than on the individual person and his or her autonomy (i.e., on the individual's freedom to choose a life worth living). The achievement of some greater good can "justify" overriding the interests or rights of some individuals (even inflicting great suffering on them) "in the Public Interest."[8]

Utilitarians may advocate liberal values (freedom, pluralism, and the like) and institutions but only as a *means* to achieve their goal. For example, John Stuart Mill asserted the "individual's absolute right to liberty with respect to acts which do not harm others" but did so because the "general well-being is always on balance maximized if this right is respected" (Day 1964, 360). Thus, his advocacy of individual rights is contingent on their resulting in the best outcome. In contrast, philosophical liberals believe that these values are inherently good, independent of any positive outcomes (chapter 5).

A good example of a utilitarian perspective being applied is the justification of a new rapid transit line or urban highway as having minimal costs (harm to nearby and displaced residents, who are relatively few in number), which are exceeded by greater benefits (that go to many more people—commuters). It is sometimes acknowledged that this is unjust, but the rights of a few residents simply can't be allowed to impede such huge "social benefits."

In planning theory, we believe the widespread rejection of the RCPM reflects in part a rejection of its underlying utilitarian basis and its violation of liberal values. Anderson (1979), Dalton (1986), and Friedmann (1987) argue that the flaws of the RCPM reflect, and flow from, its basis in utilitarianism.

Rationality and Objectivity

As we have seen, modernism and the RCPM define rationality as being equivalent to instrumental rationality. This is what philosophers call persuasive definition: An arbitrary and stipulative definition is used to get people to accept a controversial conception—in this case, a conception of rationality that is much narrower than our ordinary conception. There is no good reason why we must accept Simon's linear branching decision method as "rational" and our ordinary nonlinear, instantaneous, intuitive, web of decisions as "irrational." Only when this persuasive definition of rationality is accepted does it then follow that "'rational' planning and 'efficient' planning are the same" (Meyerson and Banfield 1955, 314). The result of accepting this narrow definition of rationality is that rationality is reduced to, and equated with, utilitarianism.[9] This is an ideological distortion (see next section).

An increase in efficiency may not always be better; certainly it can claim to *always* be rational *only by stipulative definition!* The historian Collingwood, in discussing the idea of "progress," considers a society of fish eaters whose younger generation invents a more efficient way to catch fish, doubling the average catch from five to ten fish per day. The older generation will

> think that the old method is better than the new; not out of irrational
> prejudice, but because the way of life which it knows and values is built

around the old method, which is therefore certain to have social and religious associations that express the intimacy of its connection with this way of life as a whole. A man of the older generation wants only his five fish a day, and he does not want half a day's leisure; what he wants is to live as he has lived. To him, therefore, the change is no progress. (Collingwood 1963, 325)

There is nothing irrational about this preference for the old, inefficient way.

We are not arguing that public planning should be irrational, nor that there is something wrong with seeking the best means to our ends, nor that exploring alternatives is irrelevant. What is missing from the RCPM is the recognition that neither the articulation of ends nor the choice of means can be value-neutral.

Most goals are chosen for reasons, but for the kind of reasons that cannot be incorporated into a scientistic perspective. Individuals' goals (if they are reflectively chosen at all) reflect their self-conception, their view of the meaning of their own lives. Society's goals should reflect its citizens' views on what constitutes a good society.[10] Reflectively chosen goals are rational; reasons can be given. The choice of goals should not be regarded as irrational.

In addition, the reasons for the choice of means cannot be separated from the reasons for the choice of the goals that are being pursued. The British philosopher Roger Scruton gives the example of roads that are apparently built for a "single dominant purpose": to enable people to move "at their convenience" between points A and B. But he suggests that this purpose is less transparent than it seems. He criticizes the designers of motorways in Coventry for their

> total energetic absorption . . . with the single end of speed, since it proceeds without any true concept of "convenience" lead[ing] to a loss of any knowledge of why speed is important—why it is better that men should live in a world of ceaseless rapid movement rather than in a world where they are satisfied to remain forever where they are. (Scruton 1979, 243)

In contrast, he sees the designers of freeways in Los Angeles as concerned with "the aesthetic of speed, seeking to create . . . roads, tracks, junctions, and flyovers all expressive of an idea of rapid movement . . . the deliberate cultivation of a style of life" (Scruton 1979, 243).

Thus, Scruton argues that a highway should not be seen as merely functional; it is expressive of ideals, of a view of how life should be lived. To reduce the goal to simply "moving between points A and B" commits one not only to a particular account of the goal but also to the kinds of means that will satisfy it.

A Broader Conception of Rationality

Habermas (1971b) argues that knowledge is not value-neutral; he believes that it is tied to human interests. Scientific knowledge is only *one* form of knowledge; it is tied to the human interest in controlling nature. As we saw earlier, Habermas identifies "three irreducible types of rationality related to three distinct types of knowledge" (Nielsen 1983, 121), i.e., scientific, communicative, and critical (see table 1-1 in chapter 1). He argues that none "have cognitive superiority over the others" and that all three "have essential roles in human life and human understanding" (Nielsen 1983, 121). Each corresponds to a human interest—control, communication, and self-emancipation—and each gives rise to a different type of knowledge. While a pragmatist would not want to be quite so categorical in delineating only three kinds of rationality, the key point is that the idea of rationality (or, as we prefer, reasonableness) is much broader than the narrow scientistic conception.

IDEOLOGICAL CRITIQUE

Ideological Distortion

Attempts to reduce all knowledge to the scientific, and all interests to the technical, lead to an inability to even acknowledge, much less satisfy, other human interests. To reduce all knowledge to scientific knowledge begs the question, and functions as, what Habermas calls an "ideological distortion."

"Ideology" is used here[11] in the sense of an idea or belief put forward and accepted as true, that serves the function of maintaining certain relations (e.g., class), when in fact the idea is illegitimate and the belief is not true. Those who are aware of ideological distortions have a moral obligation to unmask them in order to emancipate individuals from the grasp of illegitimate ideas.

Habermas (1971a) contends that our inability to acknowledge an interest in emancipation from oppression means that we are deprived of rational knowledge of what form emancipation could take (i.e., self-reflective knowledge). This distortion "makes impossible the rational criticism of institutions" (Nielsen 1983, 126). It leads us to accept a situation where we are not emancipated, i.e., the status quo. It also makes impossible any rational criticism of the ends that these institutions provide for us. If they were rational and nondistorted, then these social ends would conform to rational human ends. However, in an ideologically distorted situation, people's ends tend to be socially determined to conform to those of the social institution. It is impossible for most people to see that the ends they choose are *not* those they *would* choose if they were both informed and clearly rational.

The distortion of scientism serves an ideological purpose:

> It is Habermas's belief that scientism . . . is the dominant ideology of our time. With it goes the phenomenon of technocratic consciousness, which so deeply affects a large portion of contemporary intelligentsia that they can barely conceive of the possibility of rational argument over the ends of life or any fundamental critique of the social institutions actually in place.

> Such critiquing is viewed as the irrational ideological posturing of irrespon-
> sible and utopian value-oriented intellectuals. Responsible policy-oriented
> intellectuals—the Brezinskis and Kissingers of the world . . . will not engage
> in such posturing. (Nielsen 1983, 125)

Thus, scientism helps to maintain the status quo by preventing social science
and planning from critiquing the social institutions in which they are embedded and the goals that these institutions foist on the members of society.

The urban planners of the 1950s assumed that the problem of poverty
could be solved by the physical solution of urban renewal—replacing old
housing with new housing. Poverty, however, is a very deep social problem
for which there are no mechanistic solutions. The poor are people who are
deprived of what we conceive of as a good life, people who lack access to
wealth, to meaningful work, to an environment that is not alienating. Social
problems like crime, slums, poverty, single teen moms, and so on are symp-
tomatic of a much deeper malaise.

"Urban renewal" arose from a decision process that focused on physical
means and skewed the interpretation of ends in a mechanistic direction. In
so doing, it failed to consider a vast range of alternatives (the very error for
which the "rational comprehensive planners" criticize other planning approaches). Why were changes in political/economic institutions not considered as a possible means to alleviating poverty? Why was income redistribution not an alternative? The planners' attitude of value-neutrality seems to
have precluded such a possibility. Those who benefited from the status quo
did not need to fear that a search for "solutions" to "social problems" like
poverty might include any restructuring of social and political institutions
that could threaten their power and privilege.

Forester (1989) argues that planners have a responsibility to identify
and offset needless (i.e., avoidable) communicative distortions, particularly
those that operate to the detriment of worse-off groups in society. This is a
very different role from that of the neutral technician.

Concealing the Normative

The myth of professional objectivity is an ideological distortion that obscures the political nature of planning. It conceals the fact that planning decisions involve choices between conflicting interests and often redistribute
costs and benefits among different groups in society.

Positivistic approaches like the RCPM tend to allow the "expert" to cloak
his or her normative values in a value-free garb. It gives legitimacy to situations that would not likely be accepted by those who are being "planned for"
if they understood what was really happening. People are duped into accepting plans as the "best scientific solution" when in fact they enhance the status quo and benefit certain elites.

Bureaucrats, who are not accountable to the voters in any way, may be making the real political decisions, ones that further their own careers rather than the interests of their "clients," or that implement their own biases. Thus, planners who at heart are "social reformers" (Friedmann 1987) may present themselves as objective, value-neutral experts and then work surreptitiously behind the scenes to implement their hidden agendas, still disclaiming responsibility for the effects of their actions.[12]

Evasion of Responsibility

That goals are perceived as coming from outside the planning bureaucracy allows the "rational planners" within the organization to disclaim responsibility for the effects of their decisions:

> Bureaucratic behavior is the most nearly perfect example . . . of that mode of conduct which denies responsibility for the consequences of action on the grounds that it lacks full knowledge of the reason for action. All bureaucrats are innocent. (Schaar 1984, 122)

Responsibility is further evaded by the fact that internal bureaucratic decision making is almost always done by committees, so that no one individual can ever be clearly identified as responsible for anything. And of course, reports emanating from bureaucratic organizations are always authorless.

PRACTICAL CRITIQUE

The Real World of Public Decision Making

Forty-five years ago, when the modernist perspective was unchallenged, the RCPM was the dominant paradigm in the fields of planning, policy analysis, management science, and public administration. Charles Lindblom (1959) was one of the first to challenge this paradigm, which he referred to as "synoptic planning" and, implicitly, its underlying perspective. He outlined a number of ways in which the RCPM did not fit the real world of public decision making (1959, 157–65), as follows:

1. There is no agreement on objectives or subobjectives, no way to rank them, and no way to ascertain their marginal values (trade-offs between them).

2. Evaluation and empirical analysis are inherently intertwined—values (ends) and policies (means) are actually chosen simultaneously.

3. There is no test of "good" policy because there is no agreement on values.

4. Democracies change policies almost entirely through incremental adjustment, due to political and legislative/legal constraints.

5. Nonincremental changes entail an unacceptable risk of serious error.

Subsequent critics added others.

6. Goals are often not known in advance—they emerge and change in process.

7. The quantification involved in "operationalizing" goals often severely distorts them.

8. Government decisions are not made by individuals; they involve political struggles among multiple actors (political groups and bureaucratic organizations) with conflicting interests.

Lindblom also advanced an alternate paradigm—disjointed incrementalism—that he claimed was a superior model, not only descriptively but also normatively, to the RCPM. In chapter 7, we will show how incrementalism fits within a neopragmatic planning approach and responds to many of the postmodernist criticisms of planning.

Practical Epistemology

Lindblom alleged that the RCPM is unworkable for complex problems; assumes impossible intellectual capacities, theoretical knowledge, and information sources; and ignores political and legislative/legal constraints (1959, 152–3). Other writers identified further epistemological difficulties:

1. It is impossible to be comprehensive with regard to alternatives or consequences.

2. It is impossible to predict (even probabilistically) consequences of different alternatives with sufficient accuracy that the best one can be chosen.

3. The positivistic assumptions of science are all violated in social contexts. There are multiple variables that cannot be held constant, and social behavior is modified by the research itself.

4. Complex computerized forecasting models have huge, unknown errors—resulting from multiplying the errors for each of numerous parameters (Friedmann 1987).

5. Social situations often have unknown thresholds (or "tipping points") where irreversible change occurs.

6. Nearly all important social problems are [inherently] wicked problems—ones that have no definitive formulation, no agreement on alternatives, and no test of "solution" (because what counts as a solution depends on the choice of explanation of the problem) (Rittel and Webber 1973).

All of the foregoing is just a sampling of the many critiques of the RCPM. Faludi (1973) presents earlier discussions; Mandelbaum (1979), Alexander (1984), Forester (1989), and Innes (1995) represent more recent criticisms.

DEFENSES OF THE RCPM

Those who still advocate the RCPM often acknowledge much of the foregoing critique but claim the RCPM can be (or has been) modified to take care of these problems. Such apparent accommodation is either window dressing (a further ideological distortion) or an alteration so substantial that the resultant model should no longer be called the RCPM.

Inclusion of "Social Concerns"

Rational planners[13] today may claim that they have learned from past mistakes like urban renewal and now recognize social concerns, and that they do incorporate them in their analyses. More recent approaches to urban renewal have focused on the preservation and enhancement of the neighborhood or community as a social entity. But we should be skeptical about such claims. It must be remembered that Meyerson and Banfield (1955, 316) themselves recognized that a public housing authority could have as one of its goals the "preservation of the neighborhood social organization." Unfortunately, this recognition turns out to be a sham, because the goal is operationalized by reducing the social element into a scientistic form.

We are advocating an interpretation of social concerns that cannot be so reduced. For example, a social concern might be "enhancing the potential of persons to become social beings capable of self-reflective knowledge." When the reductionist planner has finished transforming this sort of goal into something that can be operationally defined and measured by "positive empirical science" (e.g., participation rates in adult education, social events, or political activity), it will have lost much (too much) of its content.

Urban "renewers" should have recognized that when they demolished buildings, they also destroyed homes, neighborhoods, and communities. Planners today generally recognize that persons—individually and in groups—want to live the kind of lives they find meaningful and express their self-conceptions in their physical environment. Subject to the rights of other persons, they should be free to do so.

Alternative Goals

The rational planner may respond by claiming that alternative goals *are* considered. But even if this is the case, the scientism of the RCPM again requires that the alternative ends be "reduced" to mechanistic "active elements" (Meyerson and Banfield 1955, 316) that can be "operationalized." Meyerson and Banfield acknowledge that there are numerous public ends, and that "no one course of action will maximize the attainment of all of them" (ibid., 316). They go on to say that

> The planner must make a choice among the relevant ends, either as to those that are to be served at all or as to the relative importance of those that are to be served. Thus a housing authority with the ends "to clear slums" and "to preserve neighborhood social organization" might find the two ends utterly incompatible, and it would certainly find that a gain in terms of one end would necessarily involve some loss in terms of the other. (ibid.)

This is a subterfuge: The RCPM planner winds up reducing nonmechanistic, nonquantifiable goals to mechanistic, quantifiable ones. Then how can the planner choose between these goals?

> In order to make a choice, the planner must know the relative value to be attached to each of the ends. He must know not only that end A is more valuable than end B, but also how much more valuable than A is B, i.e., how much of B should be sacrificed to increase the attainment of A by a certain amount.[14] (ibid.)

But this choice criterion requires commensurable units. Incompatible goals must be reduced to operationalized alternative goals. The reduction skews and distorts the original goal, sometimes beyond recognition. As we have already suggested, the scientistic view that leads to "operationalizing" both ends and means results in an environment that is dehumanizing and alienating. At some point, the planner (claiming to be acting as just a technician) is making the real political decisions—"trading off" and "operationalizing" goals—all the while attributing the choices to the politicians.

"Goal Articulation"

Most rational planners seem to acknowledge a bit of what we are arguing for when they acknowledge that planning is a normative process and add that an important stage in the RCPM is "goal articulation." What is meant by goal articulation? There are a number of possibilities. It could mean

1. A clarification of what people want

2. A reduction of goals to "operational" terms

3. Choosing which goals are most important (i.e., expertise masking the normative)

4. Trying to formulate a consensus regarding goals

5. Fostering a genuine dialogue that attempts to find common interests and to agree on normative grounds for decisions

6. Trying to help people identify their true interests (i.e., eliminating or lessening distortion)

The first three possibilities mean that there has been no real change in the worldview of the "rational planner"; the talk of goal articulation is merely a further ideological distortion, masking the reality that it is "business as usual." The fourth could be a real change, or it could be more reductionism if the goals are reduced to a common quantifiable unit. The latter two possibilities would mean a real change in the planning process. If this is the case, it should not be forgotten that these changes reflect an acceptance of communicative and critical rationality. But acceptance of a broadened conception of rationality leads to a rejection and repudiation of the RCPM's underlying modernist philosophical foundations of positivism and utilitarianism.

BUREAUCRACY

We have seen that the RCPM is the application of positivism to public decision making; bureaucracy is its organizational incarnation. Bureaucracy literally means "rule by office." Most public planning happens within this form of organization. Like the RCPM, bureaucracy claims to be the rational, objective, value-free instrument for achieving public goals. As we shall see in chapter 6, it is really an instrument of control, serving the top-down "societal guidance" planning of the "old paradigm."

The Bureaucratic Claim

Weber (1946, 1947) was the first to formalize a "model" of bureaucracy. Although he presented a justification of it, as a scientist modernist he did not believe that normative justification was possible—because there is no rationality of ends. He was simply describing the arguments that bureaucracy uses to "legitimize" it (i.e., to get people to accept it).[15]

Weber's account clearly relates the emergence of bureaucracy to the shift from the pre-modern to the modern worldview. Whereas the pre-modern basis for the legitimacy of authority was tradition, charisma, or wealth, bureaucracy offers a rational–legal basis. Whereas the pre-modern approach to interpersonal relations was particularism (favoritism to those with traditional personal bonds, status, or prestige), bureaucracy offers universalism (judging persons impartially on merit). Everyone is to be treated equally and justly. Thus, bureaucracy claims to combine efficiency (instrumental rationality) with personal human rights, to embody both the scientific and the liberal humanistic aspects of the enlightenment.

The bureaucratic ideal has four key concepts: (1) *purpose* (the organization has specified goals); *rationality* (actions are directed to achieving these goals); *impersonality* (emphasis on the office rather than the officeholder); and *routine* (written rules and regulations to ensure impartiality and continuity).

The Bureaucratic Organization

The bureaucratic organization (in ideal type) is characterized by the following attributes:

1. Regulations governing official functions are written, as are records of decisions.

2. Each position has a specified sphere of competence: defined obligations, authority to carry out the obligations, and bounded means of compulsion.

3. Positions are given on the basis of competence and performance.

4. The incumbent cannot appropriate or alter the powers of his or her office.

5. There is a hierarchy of offices: Each office is controlled by a "higher" office above it in the organizational "pyramid."

6. Administration is separated from ownership (in the private sector) and from political decision making (in the public sector).

The steps in setting up a bureaucracy can be formalized:

1. Begin with a specified set of objectives (that are taken as given).

2. Specify tasks to achieve these objectives.

3. Cluster these tasks to define offices (positions), with authority commensurate with responsibility.

4. Define the relationships between offices.

5. Find people with appropriate skills to fill each office.

The structuring is governed by several accepted management "principles"; for example, each person should have one and only one "boss," and each boss can supervise only so many workers (i.e., the "span of control" is limited).[16] When the relationship between offices is defined according to these principles, the result is the familiar pyramidal organizational structure. This "chain of command structured on the lines of a pyramid" (Bennis 1966) is often regarded as the defining characteristic of bureaucracy. For a given number of workers in the operating core (i.e., those who produce the actual goods or services), the smaller the span of control, the steeper the pyramid (i.e., the more levels of management).

Underlying Concepts

Bureaucracy shares the underlying concepts of positivism and utilitarianism with the RCPM and thus is open to the same criticisms just outlined above. Rationality is limited to the instrumental (i.e., the scientistic view). Facts and values are sharply separated, as are means and ends. This leads to the strong politics–administration dualism first espoused by James Madison, strongly advocated by Woodrow Wilson (Friedmann 1987), and widely promulgated by the (U.S.-based) International City Managers Association. Today, it finds clear expression in the administrative structure and the nonpartisan political conventions that dominate most Canadian and many American cities.

Function and "Dysfunction"

According to the ideal, this design procedure maximizes rational decision making and administrative efficiency. How does it work in practice?

Strengths

Bureaucracy can be efficient in the sense of not reinventing the wheel: It is stable, reliable, and predictable. However, Mintzberg (1989) points out that these are strengths only under certain conditions: a simple technical process and a stable environment. Bureaucracies do provide some protection for employees (who have come close to having "tenure" if they follow the rules and procedures), and for clients (who are generally treated uniformly and impartially). But the really important advantage of bureaucracy is that it permits *control* of vast numbers of employees. It is difficult to have large-scale organizations, staffed by highly specialized employees, without a significant degree of bureaucracy.[17]

Weaknesses

What mainstream management theorists call "dysfunctions" of bureaucracy are well-known. The mention of bureaucracy invokes the spectre of "red tape" for most of us. Bureaucracies seem to induce petty, self-centered, rigid, and patterned behavior to repress individuality and innovation. They lack incentives for efficiency or risk taking (the cost of failure is high, the rewards of success low). There is very serious goal distortion: The organization's goal is survival, subunits (departments) compete with each other, and individuals strive to conform to the rules rather than contributing to the organization's mission. Perhaps worst of all, public bureaucracies seem to grow inexorably because of virtual tenure, empire building, and rewards to size rather than efficiency or effectiveness.

These "dysfunctions" mean that bureaucracies are weakest in meeting employees' emotional and social needs (their implicit utilitarianism sacrifices the individual for the good of the organization), in coordinating complex technical activities (where work processes cannot be standardized), and in meeting the challenges of a dynamic environment (where unforeseen problems require innovation). In chapter 6 we will present an argument that bureaucratic "dysfunctions" are in fact inherent in the bureacratic organizational form and necessary to its functioning as a tool of social control.

PERSEVERANCE OF THE RCPM

Although it has long been the subject of criticism from both radical and conservative quarters, the RCPM still seems to be widely held by planning practitioners[18] (Alexander 1986, 31, 104; Dalton 1986; Baum 1996), particularly those who adopt what Friedmann (1987) calls the "Policy Analysis" approach to planning, and those whose ethical orientation is "traditional technician" or "technical activist" (Howe 1994).

Several writers have addressed the question of why the RCPM retains so much influence when it is so thoroughly rejected by planning theorists. Baum (1996) believes that planners want to retain the rational ideal of guiding action by knowledge. If this is the case, then such planners should be satisfied with a neopragmatic approach that (as we will argue) does retain this ideal but greatly broadens the notion of "rational." However, they would have to alter their conception of "knowledge" to a less positivistic one.

Conceptually, Dalton (1986) points to a failure to recognize the underlying philosophical bases (utilitarianism and positivism) that we have discussed here. She also recognizes the fit between RCPM and the bureaucratic nature of both the public organizations where planning is practiced and the universities where it is taught, making it very difficult to implement other normative approaches to planning. Most importantly, Dalton links the continued influence of the RCPM to its central role in planning's claim to *professionalism*. As we saw earlier, the idea of profession is closely linked to specialized "scientific" knowledge. Hoch (1994) sees the RCPM as continuing to underlie the dominant "professional protocol" that guides many practitioners despite its notable failure to give them either empirical understanding or normative direction. The notion of giving up this protocol and the "expert" status it conveys provokes a severe identity crisis in the profession. If we planners are not technical experts, do we have anything to offer to the planning process? This may explain some of the strength of the resistance to change.

Finally, Baum argues that the "clockwork model" of the world represented by the RCPM offers psychological safety to students and planners—an escape from the messy and sometimes nasty "snakepit" of the real world of politics and planning. Unfortunately, if and when they are forced to recognize the real nature of their planning contexts, they will get neither sense of direction nor boundaries from this model.

Given the tenacity of the RCPM as the official view of planning's professional protocol, it is fortunate that there has been relatively little *pure* practice of the RCPM. Many practitioners have had more compassion, more common sense, and more commitment to liberal ideals than would be expected within this model. But these planners have lived with very real tension between professional norms and their own practice.

The results of clinging to the modernist view of planning are well documented by Hoch (1994): ineffectiveness, frustration, and disillusionment. It also leads to dishonesty. Howe found that while 27 percent of planners interviewed were "traditional technicians,"[19] 10 percent admitted to a "technical activist" role. These planners adopted the posture of traditional technicians while covertly engaged in political activity to get support for their recommendations. In practice, they were "politically sophisticated activists" (Hoch 1994, 124). The suspicion is that many of the first group may also indulge in some political action at times. Such dishonesty could eventually lead to the discrediting of the profession in the eyes of the public.

CONCLUSIONS

The modernist paradigm that continues to dominate much of contemporary planning practice is fatally flawed. Its theoretical foundations are inadequate and confused, it is practically unworkable, and it is morally bankrupt. The model cannot be salvaged by claiming that it is a useful heuristic because its results are frequently the very opposite of what is intended. This is the great irony. While the democratic ideal is that goals should be set by the political process, reflecting social values, the reality is that the goals are actually set by the supposedly neutral bureaucrats. While all alternatives are supposed to be considered, only a narrow range are actually evaluated (those that fit the theoretical model and the mandate of the evaluating agency). While the best solution is supposed to be selected, the chosen solution will be the one that best fits the predictive model used.

Much of the criticism outlined in this chapter holds within a modernist framework. When postmodernist critiques are factored in, things look even worse for the RCPM and its professional protocol. The postmodernist critique strikes at the very core of "rational" planning. Of more concern to us, it also poses a threat (perhaps a fatal one) to the liberal alternatives to the RCPM.

Part II

PLANNING SHOULD BE PRAGMATIC

Two Responses to Modernism: Postmodernism or Neopragmatism

THE POSTMODERNIST CHALLENGE

In the first chapter, we related the crisis in planning to a more general crisis in society as a result of the shift from modernism toward postmodernism. The assumptions and approach of postmodernism have influenced and fragmented contemporary thought more than is often recognized.

Postmodernists reject modernist ideas of foundations, meta-narratives, reason, efficiency, truth, democracy, and progress. There are no foundations for knowledge and justification; reason is multivocal; truth is relative; epistemologies and moralities are pluralized. Some claim that the ideas of reason, truth, democracy and progress are never anything more than masks for power. They challenge meta-narratives as totalizing oppressive discourses imposed on other cultures or subcultures.

In the postmodernist view, there is no direct experience of reality. Each of us sees the world through the filter of our own paradigm, conceptual frameworks, vocabularies, and language, so each of us lives in a different world, with different rationalities, ways of knowing, and moralities.[1] This view is known as "perspectivalism." The postmodernist world is completely fragmented—the very opposite of the unity of the premodern world.

The way postmodernism challenges science is by considering it to be just one of many paradigms, with no special status or "privilege" over any other perspective. In fact, science is viewed with great suspicion because it privileges white Western male thought and serves the interest of that group, helping it to maintain its cultural and economic dominance. (In Habermas's terms, science plays an ideological role).

43

Ironically, postmodernism rejects the *possibility* of modernist (scientific) foundations for knowledge and justification but still implicitly shares the modernist belief in the *necessity* of foundations. Without foundations, postmodernists believe that everything is arbitrary and relative, that justification is impossible.

While challenges to modernist institutional planning come from many quarters, postmodernism mounts the most radical challenge, one that strikes at the very core of institutional planning. Postmodernists charge planning with ignoring the fact that communities have different (conflicting and incommensurable) kinds of knowing, logic, ethics, and discourse. They want to celebrate plurality and difference, even to the point where this emphasis leads to fragmentation and breakdown of consensus.

They read plans as texts, having a different meaning to each reader, and with hidden "subtexts." For example, Daniel Burnham's *Plan for Chicago* is famous for his slogan, "Make no little plans. . . . They have no magic to stir men's blood. . . ." A postmodern reading sees such master plans as oppressive tools of elite domination, with a subtext of wide-ranging subjugation of society to a single functional and aesthetic perspective[2] (Hoch 1985). A more recent example: world's fairs and expositions can be seen not just as boosters to the local economy but as tools to bypass local planning procedures, speeding the conversion of inner-city industrial land to more profitable residential or commercial uses (Smith 1996).

Our view is that postmodernist assumptions have infiltrated our culture to a greater extent than is often recognized. This poses a serious challenge to the very possibility of justifiable and legitimate public planning. It is a challenge that cannot be met by minor changes in planning, not even by switching to one of the recent normative planning approaches (although they do address some of the postmodernist critique). It must be confronted directly.

POSTMODERNISM

In this chapter, we will give a brief account of the intellectual roots of postmodernism, followed in chapter 4 by a critical account of some key themes of postmodernism that we believe are relevant to planning. This critique comes from a neopragmatic perspective (that will be further elaborated in the second half of this chapter) and a liberal value orientation (see chapters 1, 5, and 6).

Our conclusion will be that the spectre of a postmodern "abyss" (raised in chapter 1) flows from the assumptions of postmodernism, which there is no good reason to accept. If we adopt a different set of assumptions—those of neopragmatism—we will discover that there is no postmodern abyss! This realization will allow us to get on with meeting the practical challenges to contemporary planning.

INTELLECTUAL ROOTS OF POSTMODERNISM

Postmodernism is an amorphous term;[3] it is characterized by a rejection of many of the ideas and themes associated with modernism. Our critique here will focus on what we call full-blown postmodernism: "a way of understanding and conceptualizing that forms a radical break with modernism," one "not commensurable with the Enlightenment values associated with modernism" (Milroy 1991, 183). This is not to deny that, as will emerge in our discussions, there are more moderate versions of postmodernism. For example, Forester views his own work as postmodern in the sense that it critiques instrumental rationality and models of social engineering (1993b).

Postmodernists reject foundationalism, "meta-narratives" (universally true theories that describe or explain reality), [absolute] dualisms (diametric opposites, that allow no middle ground), and scientism or positivism (see glossary).

In addition to rejecting scientism, full-blown postmodernists go on to reject (wholly or in part) the "liberal" aspect of modernism, including the belief that the· autonomous individual person is the appropriate object of moral and political concern, and the core idea that progress comes via rational argument—giving *good reasons* for what we advocate and what we oppose. What postmodernists do celebrate is plurality and difference. As will be shown (chapter 13), tensions arise between the rejection of modernism and the advocacy of respect for difference.

Friedrich Nietzsche

The first significant catalyst to postmodern thinking was probably Nietzsche. Rejection of the Western concern with "truth," "knowledge," and "rationality" reverberates throughout his writings: "For a philosopher to say, 'The good and the beautiful are one,' is infamy; if he goes on to add, 'also the true,' one ought to trash him" (Nietzsche 1968[1901], par. 822). Nietzsche attempts to supplant the concept of truth by that of power, claiming that truth (or knowledge, or rationality) is indistinguishable from (or is a form of) the will to power. Nietzsche also influenced the postmodern climate by emphasizing the view that life itself (and our personal identity) is a social construction, or a narrative.

Michel Foucault

Foucault embraced Nietzsche's challenge. He also examined the relationship between truth and power:

> [T]ruth is no doubt a form of power . . . instead of trying to find out what truth, as opposed to error, is, it might be more interesting to take up the

> problem posed by Nietzsche: How is it that in our society, "the truth" has been given this value, thus placing us absolutely under its thrall? (Foucault 1972, 107)

As we will see (later in this chapter and in chapter 15), Foucault and his followers (often called Foucauldians) share certain criticisms of the modernist tradition with neopragmatists, e.g., the contingency of concepts, vocabulary, language games, and frameworks (except perhaps "power"). He particularly stresses the historical nature of language and its contingent dependence on social relations. He also rejects the absolute dichotomies of traditional philosophy. But unlike the neopragmatists, he uses these criticisms to radically undermine all grounds for productive understanding, cooperation, and social transformation. For Foucault, everything can be reduced to power. We believe that this is a destructive path for planning. For planning to have any meaning, there must be some possibility, some hope, of human betterment.

Foucault's case studies usefully identify, often very insightfully, what we would call unrecognized ideological distortions. He and many Foucauldians extend these insights and claim that *all* relationships and processes should be viewed in terms of power. For Foucault, simply unmasking instances of oppression is not enough, since such unmasking presupposes notions of truth and liberation, notions that (for Foucault) are themselves also masks. Thus, Foucault extends and widens the notion of power to the point where it is all-inclusive. As he says,

> [P]ower is nothing other than a certain modification . . . of a series of clashes which constitute the social body, clashes of the political, economic type, etc. Power, then, is something like the stratification, the institutionalization, the definition of tactics, of implements and arms which are useful in all of these clashes. (Foucault 1989, 189)

In the Foucauldian view, the fact that concepts are contingent and reflect social circumstances is used to support the idea that concepts are often used as a means to maintain certain power relations (i.e., in the original Marxist terms, they are used for ideological purposes.) Although there are different interpretations of Foucault, he seems to go further to say that power *constitutes* concepts and vocabulary—that they can be understood *only* in terms of power.

While Foucault, in his later work,[4] may seem to have favored some of the Enlightenment tradition, his earlier writings are generally interpreted as undermining the traditional notions of rationality and justification.[5] Our interest here is to trace the *effect* of this attack on contemporary thought. Many who have applied Foucault interpret him as viewing *all* claims to truth, rationality, and knowledge as mechanisms for attaining power, as masks for power, and as tools of oppression. For example,

> [T]he self-styled "social constructivists" argue that there is no objectivity in science. Facts, they say, account for little or nothing, and—following the lead of the French philosopher Michel Foucault—the only thing that matters in science, as elsewhere, is power. (Ruse 1994, 40)

This is not to deny the value of Foucault's identification of specific ideological distortions. Our objection is not to these particular identifications but to the universalization that *all* truth and knowledge claims are *nothing but* masks for power and oppression. (Of course, this is a self-defeating claim; if correct, it would also apply to Foucault's own pronouncements.)

Jacques Derrida

The foremost exponent of deconstructionist thought is Derrida. His conception of language and reality has greatly influenced the postmodern movement. His inspiration comes from the structural linguist, Ferdinand de Saussure. Saussure rejected the view—metaphysical realism—that the meaning of a word or sign depends on its relation to an object "in the world," an object that it signifies and to which it refers. Saussure repudiated the notion that language reflects or mirrors "the world." He argued that the meaning of a sign is determined solely by its differential relations to other signs.

Derrida adopts these two themes: (1) the rejection of metaphysical realism, and (2) its replacement by Saussure's semiological difference. However, his poststructuralism profoundly diverges from Saussure's structuralism. Saussure believed that the value of a sign is determinate because the set of differential signs forms a closed, synchronic, ahistorical system. The difficulty with this view is that it leads to incommensurability: No two local synchronic systems will be commensurable. If the meaning of a term is determined (only and completely) by the system of difference within a synchronic language scheme that is necessarily closed, then the meaning of a particular term will not be translatable into any other language since its meaning is given by the closed set of differential relations (of the first synchronic system).

Derrida rejects this assumption of determinacy. He believes that the value of a sign is radically indeterminate and perpetually incomplete:

> Each occasional sign begins by referring back, that is to say, does not begin ... there is not a single reference but from then on, always a multiplicity of references, so many different traces referring back to other traces. . . . (Derrida 1982, 324)

He replaces the notion of "difference" by the idea of *"différance,"* which combines the renunciation of metaphysical realism with a boundless conception of difference. For Derrida the issue is not incommensurability but the indeterminism of meaning. Language and reality become completely undetermined and undefined! This notion of "*différance*" undermines any idea of duality[6] categories in language or in reality, including the contrast between subject and object. It also leaves no conceptual room for the notion of truth. In Derrida's scheme, everything is text, and all text is infinitely ambiguous (Derrida 1989, 148).

Derrida could be interpreted as doing no more than attacking the metaphysical foundationalism of a cultural imperialism that excludes non-elite groups from dialogue. Perhaps he simply wants to see "'hierarchies'—European over non-European, male over female—being disturbed, if not overturned" (Stephens 1994). Bernstein[7] (1992, 182) argues that

> Derrida is always encouraging us to *question* the status of what we take to be our native home, our *arche*. . . . Derrida is not advocating that we abandon all authority, but rather that we never cease questioning it. . . . Those who read him as celebrating formlessness and chaos are missing the bite of his deconstructive exercises.

In this view, Derrida is simply attacking the idea that concepts and beliefs are impervious to change. As Dear (1986, 373) asserts, the purpose of deconstructing modernism should be to examine "the master narratives of prior traditions," to "question their authority," and to reject their "claims of undisputed authority."

But we want to highlight Derrida's influence in bringing us to the brink of the postmodern abyss. Whether he intended this effect is largely irrelevant here. As the important contemporary feminist Martha Nussbaum (1994) writes:

> Why is the assault on reason so attractive to *some* feminist thinkers? . . . First, these feminists, like many other critical social thinkers, have been influenced by French theorists such as Jacques Derrida and Michel Foucault, and by their criticisms of reason . . . they believe that these positions, which try to reduce reasons for a conviction to causes of that conviction and claim that arguments merely reflect the play of social and political forces, have in them something liberating and progressive.

This is the interpretation of Derrida that is so dangerous. While acknowledging that Derrida is "not an extremist," Putnam (1992, 132) expresses this concern:

> [T]he thrust of Derrida's writing is that the notions of "justification," "good reason," "warrant," and the like are primarily repressive gestures. And *that* view is dangerous because it provides aid and comfort for extremists. . . . The twentieth century has witnessed horrible events. . . . Today as we face the twenty-first century, our task is not to repeat [these] mistakes. . . . Thinking of reason as just a repressive notion is not going to help us do that . . . the philosophical irresponsibility of one decade can become the real-world political tragedy of a few decades later. And deconstruction without reconstruction is irresponsibility.

These influences have led to a view of the world very different from that of modernism—a fragmented and indeterminate place where people live in different worlds, with different rationalities, different (incommensurable) language games, different epistemologies, and different moralities; a world that celebrates difference and "otherness"; a world without the notions of truth or progress. It leaves planners with a pressing question: Is there any place for public planning in such a world?

THE PRAGMATIC ALTERNATIVE

Our alternative response to modernism is neopragmatism, which we believe is much more productive. Just as Goldilocks found the first bed too hard, the second too soft, and the third "just right," so we believe planners who find modernism too hard and postmodernism too soft will find neopragmatism "just right." Our critique of postmodernism in chapter 4 will be made from this perspective.

Pragmatists were among the first to challenge some of the ideas of modernism. Classical pragmatism is associated with Charles Sander Peirce, William James, and John Dewey. This original version of pragmatism faded with the rise of logical positivism and linguistic analysis (reflecting the dominance of scientism) in the mid-twentieth century. As these positions were challenged by post-positivism and postmodernism in the 1980s, a number of contemporary philosophers' positions moved toward pragmatism. In philosophy, neopragmatism is associated with the work of Willard van Orman Quine (1969), Donald Davidson (1985), Richard Rorty (1991a; 1991b), Richard Bernstein (1992), Hilary Putnam (1981), and (on some interpretations), Ludwig Wittgenstein (1958). Neopragmatism incorporates new arguments learned from the linguistic turn in philosophy and has altered some aspects of classical pragmatism, particularly those that now seem scientistic.

In the discussions that follow we will see that neopragmatism is similar to postmodernism and very different from modernism in that it:

1. Is naturalistic, nonfoundational, anti-essentialist, and fallibilistic[8]

2. Rejects the idea of absolute dualism

3. Rejects the idea of metaphysical realism

4. Is nonreductive and nonscientistic

5. Deemphasizes the importance of theory

But unlike postmodernism, neopragmatism

6. Is not relativistic; it allows for objective justification within context

7. Retains useful contrasts, viewed as end points of continua

8. Retains a legitimate role for science

9. Does not view differences between communities as incommensurable

10. Can integrate different frames

11. Retains our Enlightenment tradition regarding rationality, truth, and objective (liberal) values[9]

In later chapters, we will see that neopragmatism

12. Is pluralistic and democratic

13. Recognizes the importance of community

14. Provides an (incremental) justification for planning

So, in some senses, neopragmatism is postmodernist (or more precisely, post-analytic and post-positivist) in that it rejects many of the metaphysical presuppositions of positivism and, consequently, of modernism. But it does not, as radical (full-blown) postmodernism does, undermine our liberal Enlightenment values.

Misinterpretations

Pragmatism is frequently interpreted as reducing truth and goodness to nothing more than "what's useful"—of providing a rationale for the status quo, of being inherently conservative, of leading to relativism, of failing to be future-oriented, of supporting a "grab all you can get" mentality unconstrained by morality. Our discussions will attempt to make clear that all of these are misinterpretations.

THE INTELLECTUAL ROOTS OF NEOPRAGMATISM

Our approach to planning draws on the work of contemporary philosophers in the pragmatic tradition who, in turn, draw on the legacy of classical analytic philosophy, logical positivism, and linguistic philosophy.[10] The move away from positivism and analytical philosophy toward pragmatism occurred when these thinkers realized that this analytical approach still held on to the myth of foundationalism and to the idea that there is a unique philosophical method that provides a clear criterion of truth and that the world can be divided according to absolute dichotomies. As Rorty suggests, analytic philosophy:

> is simply one more attempt to put philosophy in the position that Kant wished it to have—that of judging other areas of culture on the basis of its special knowledge of the "foundations" of these areas. (Rorty 1979, 8)

It took Quine, Davidson, Wittgenstein, Putnam, and Rorty to reject this perspective and to lead us onto the pragmatic path.

Willard van Orman Quine

Fact and Value

In his classic "Two Dogmas of Empiricism" (1953), Quine demonstrated that the distinction between fact and value (and the related distinctions between analytic and synthetic, between the necessary and the contingent, between what we mean and what we believe), is not a determinate one. He denied that we can, in principle, sharply separate them (i.e., he showed that there is no general decision procedure or set of rules that can be used to make the fact/value distinction). From this we conclude that it is a mistake to think that the world can be divided according to absolute linguistic categories. The neopragmatic tradition shares this criticism of modernism with some postmodern thinkers. However, this does not mean we have to give up the idea that distinctions are legitimate, important, and useful.

Donald Davidson

Scheme and Content

Donald Davidson (1985) carried the Quinean insight further in rejecting the distinction between (conceptual) scheme and (empirical) content. He demonstrated the incoherence of the idea that we can make a distinction between an uninterpreted world of raw data or experience versus the concepts and language we use to structure (describe and understand) that data or experience. We can make no sense of the metaphor of language mirroring reality or being true to reality. Metaphysical realism—the idea that we can achieve some God's-eye perspective and compare language and the world to see how well it fits, or how true it is—is rejected as empty. (See our discussion of Rorty later in this chapter.) As Putnam says,

> [E]lements of what we call "language" or "mind" penetrate so deeply into what we call "reality" that the very project of representing ourselves as being "mappers" of something "language-independent" is fatally compromised from the start. Like Relativism, Realism is an impossible attempt to view the world from Nowhere. (Putnam 1990, 330)

Thus, Davidson (1985) maintains that we must "erase the boundary between knowing a language and knowing our way around the world generally."

One implication of these insights is that the process of communication presupposes a direct pragmatic dialogue of interpretation without appeal to any intermediate medium such as phenomena, evidence, uninterpreted reality, conceptual schemes, or Platonic forms.

Causal Explanation

Davidson's position could easily be misconstrued. He is not saying that the world is a construction of language.[11] Rather, he is suggesting that the philosophical distinction between language and the world is an untenable one and should be given up. This needs elaboration. Take causal relations, for example. Davidson believes that the causal relations between events are independent of language or, as he puts it, "are not under a description." Causal relations occur whether we describe them or not, whether there is even a language or not. The cause of the separation of the continents was not dependent on the existence of any description of these events or the existence of any language at all. Davidson would not dream of denying this. (In fact, it is a cornerstone of his general account of things—his theory.) Thus, language does not determine what happens in the world.

There is an important distinction between a causal relationship and a causal explanation. However, the essential point emphasized by neopragmatists is that causal *explanations* are one type of description. Providing a causal description does not have any privileged position. The causal account is no closer to reality, no truer, than any other type of description or language game— intentional descriptions, aesthetic descriptions, legal descriptions, moral descriptions. The choice of the type of description depends on one's purposes. Causal explanations are most useful if your interest is technical; the moral account, if your interest is in justice. Some combination may also be useful, because these different types of description are not mutually exclusive and can be used to serve the same interest. For example, determining whether Jones murdered Smith requires a legal or moral description (What is murder?) and a causal description (Is Jones dead?). The only factor besides usefulness that restricts the choice of vocabularies is consistency. This is an issue where language games overlap (e.g., astrology and science), but not where they don't overlap (e.g., morality and science).

What should be rejected is the idea that the causal explanation must take precedence over all others—that once a causal explanation is advanced, all others must be given up—since the causal account is the truest, the most real, the best. Not so! It all depends on our purposes (whatever their cause!). The idea of causal primacy is a positivistic and reductionistic one that plagues society and social practices such as planning.

Ludwig Wittgenstein

Foundations

Another (earlier) philosopher who deeply influenced neopragmatism is Wittgenstein. He taught us to be wary of the search for traditional philosophical foundations for our practices. Our beliefs and their expression in language do not require absolute foundations. Wittgenstein places emphasis on the relationship between language, human action, behavior, and social practice rather than the relationship between language and some transcendental object or some notion of an independent reality that it mirrors or represents. For Wittgenstein, mind and its expression (language) are not conceived as representational, reflecting or mirroring an absolute reality. Rather, language and mind are reflected in practice. Language is a technique that helps us cope with the environment. Bouwsma (1986, 23–4) suggests that:

> [T]he whole point of this emphasis on technique is to help us get rid of the common impression that language is like a mirror, and that whenever a sentence has meaning, there is something . . . corresponding to it.

Theory

Wittgenstein's "theoretical" aim was to purge our ordinary everyday linguistic practices of "theory" (by which he meant abstract metaphysical philosophizing). His view was very antitheoretical: " [W]e may not advance any kind of theory. There must not be anything hypothetical in our considerations. We must do away with all explanations and description alone must take its place" (Wittgenstein 1958, par. 109). For Wittgenstein, as for the pragmatist, we begin and end with practice.

Trust

Understanding our world as nothing but Foucauldian power relations—describing it solely in the vocabulary of power—is inadequate. We need different ways to see the world, other vocabularies, other concepts, in order to create institutions, arenas, forums, and decision processes that express, support, and enhance our normative liberal democratic ideals. We need the vocabulary of truth, knowledge, liberty, and the like, and we need it to be independent of (though related to, in many ways) the vocabulary of power. These other vocabularies can be used to evaluate power, just as the vocabulary of power can be used to evaluate them.

The vocabulary of *trust* has not been given much attention, but it is of equal (or greater) significance, particularly to planners. Power, in its negative thrust, flows in the opposite direction from trust. Whereas unequal power relations can undermine and thwart community, trust will underwrite it. The claim that power is universal stems from the idea that language structures our existence and that concepts generate power over individuals. Language is seen as generating power relations: At the bottom of language is power. In contrast, Wittgenstein saw trust as underlying all of human and social life (Edwards 1982). Here, he recognized the key links of relationship and trust to knowledge.

So we believe that trust is at least as basic as power to understanding human relationships and institutions. In fact, Wittgenstein (1969) argues trust is a necessary condition for community, social, political, familial, and even linguistic relations. It is also necessary for any kind of communication, understanding, knowledge, or learning. If there were literally no trust, then nothing any other party said could be accepted; everything would have to be verified, guaranteed, enforced. Then power would be universal, as Baier suggests in her illuminating discussion of the concept of trust:

> Without trust, what matters to me would be unsafe, unless like the Stoic I attach myself only to what can thrive or be safe from harm, *however* others act. The starry heavens above and the moral law within, had better be the only things that matter to me, if there is no one I can trust in any way. (Baier 1994, 95)

Of course, it would be impossible to live this way. As will be shown in the next chapter, interpretation of what anyone says presupposes a principle of charity: "If we want to understand others, we must count them right in most matters" (Davidson 1985, 142). Thus, contrary to the claims of analytic philosophy and logical positivism, it is not the objective world that is the basis of knowledge and language, but certain important values, like trust. One of the dangers of the postmodern critique is the degree to which it seriously undermines and destroys trust. This is a significant contributor to the crisis in planning.

Essentialism

In addition, Wittgenstein rejects essentialism—the idea that all applications of a term must have something in common that provides its essence. He argues that

> Instead of producing something common in all which we call language, I am saying that these phenomena have no one thing in common that makes us use the same word for all, but that they are related to one another in many different ways. (Wittgenstein 1958, par. 65)

But note that with a pragmatic approach, the essentialism of modernism can be rejected without slipping into the relativism of postmodernism.

Hilary Putnam

Fact and Value

Hilary Putnam argues, as did Dewey and Quine, against a sharp distinction between fact and value, contending that it stems from a faulty moral psychology:

> from the metaphysical picture of the "neutral" facts (apprehended by a totally *uncaring* faculty of reason) and the will which having learned the neutral facts, must "choose values" . . . *arbitrarily.*" [emphasis added] (Putnam 1990, 151)

Putnam believes that even descriptive and scientific language cannot be separated from our interests, interests that are essentially valuative.

The interconnectedness of fact and value blunts the common criticism that pragmatism reduces fact to value and truth to practical interest. The idea of reducing one of these connected ideas to another is meaningless. The concepts we use may be interest relative, but the judgments we make using those concepts can still be objective. He adds:

> My purpose was to break the grip of a certain picture . . . the picture of a dualism, a dichotomous division of our thought into realms, a realm of "facts" that can be established beyond controversy, and a realm of values where we are always in hopeless disagreement. (Putnam 1987, 71)

Scientism

Like postmodernism, neopragmatism rejects scientism and the reductionist idea that it makes sense to give priority to one form of discourse (science) at the expense of others. Putnam argues against the idea that actual scientific practice provides a methodology that, when strictly followed, provides a sure-fire way to arrive at certain truth. Here, Putnam's writing is closely aligned with Thomas Kuhn's (1970) views (but without Kuhn's relativism). Both Putnam and Kuhn show that science can be understood only as a social practice.

Inquiry in general, including scientific inquiry, looks very much like John Rawls's Wide Reflective Equilibrium (WRE), presented in chapter 1 and elaborated in chapter 6. Putnam points out that coherence is a desiderata of scientific knowledge and that disputes about what is coherent and what is not "always cross boundaries; philosophical issues are mixed with 'scientific' ones" (Putnam 1995, 15). He quotes William James:

> [N]ew truth is always a go-between, a smoother-over of transitions. It marries old opinion to new fact so as to show a minimum of jolt, a maximum of continuity. We hold a theory true just in proportion to its success at solving this problem of "maxima" and "minima." (James 2000).

It is an unavoidably cumbersome dialectical interaction between intuition, principle, evidence, background (tradition, theory, and the like) and judgment about individual cases that slowly and incrementally leads to progress. Putnam further expands this process to cover all rational inquiry: "In this way we come to form accounts of what is reasonable in inquiry, and someone might propose a 'theory' that may alter both maxims and singular judgment and so on" (Putnam 1981, 210). The process of inquiry is, of course, continuing and fallibilistic.

Richard Rorty

Conversation

Richard Rorty is perhaps the best known of the contemporary thinkers whom we reference. He is both damned and admired in ways that we believe misconstrue what he is saying, though he is often responsible for these misunderstandings. Many postmodernists take him to be a proponent of their views. We will give an interpretation that leads neither to the savage criticism of some philosophers nor to the praise of postmodern writers. Rorty is the person who actually coined the term "neopragmatism" and brought together under its banner many of the themes we discuss here. He wished to replace foundationalism, transcendentalism, and absolute method by an ongoing and unforced conversation of humanity. The similarity to Habermas's search for consensus is striking. Only in this contextual and messy conversation can we find objective progress. Rorty observes that this

> is far from saying that one person's web [of beliefs] is as good as another. One can still debate the issue on all the old familiar grounds, bringing up again all the hackneyed details, all the varied advantages and disadvantages of . . . [for example] the problem of evil, the dangers of theocracy, the potentiality for anarchy in a secularist culture, the "Brave New World" consequences of a utilitarian secular morality. One will muddle through, hoping that some reweaving will happen on both sides, and that some consensus may thus emerge. (Rorty 1991a, 67)

The incremental process he recommends is also very similar to the WRE process.

"Truth" and "Reality"

We have already alluded to a modernistic view known as "metaphysical realism," which assumes that objects and properties exist independent of the human mind—that linguistic categories, terms, or labels correspond to natural kinds "in the world." Thus, all terms must refer to (or represent) a thing or a fact or a state of affairs that is really "in the world" and should accurately describe (characterize) their nature. Correspondence with "reality" is thus a source of legitimacy for a category or term. The ontological claim is that a term is more legitimate because it refers to (or represents) a thing that is really "in the world." This is a very powerful source of normative justification in a society that is dominated by modernistic scientism.

Rorty completed the neopragmatic turn when he suggested that, given the work discussed in this section, certain perennial debates in the history of thought (i.e., debates about realism versus anti-realism, and theory versus practice) have been completely unproductive: We should give them up and change the subject. Rather than try to refute one side or the other, we should view the entire enterprise as unproductive and turn our attention elsewhere, to more productive activities.

The neopragmatic view is that the notion of "in the world" is a non-starter; it makes no sense. The idea that we can fix what is "real" in this way is, we believe, an illusion. No vocabulary, concepts, language games, or frameworks are universal, absolute, or necessary; they should be seen as contingent rather than absolute. No particular way of talking, no particular vocabulary is necessarily the right one. None can provide an essentially uncontested, universal, outside-Archimedean (God's eye) basis for absolute judgments regarding how things are in themselves. No one vocabulary has an absolute privileged status.

For postmodernists, this view leads to conceptual relativity. However, we argue that it can be maintained without falling into the relativity trap. An interlocutor in Wittgenstein's *Uncertainty* asks, "So truth or falsity depends on agreement?" He responds, "No—We must agree on the language used to put those statements."

Thus, the criteria governing our discussions should not be which ways of talking are the most real, which accounts come closer to "the truth," but rather which accounts are most productive to the human enterprise—which ones are most useful. Rorty states that

> [I]t is no truer that "atoms are what they are, because we use 'atom' as we do" than "we use 'atom' as we do because atoms are what they are." *Both* of these claims . . . are entirely empty. Both are pseudo-explanations. (Rorty 1991a, 5)

Their "correctness" is determined by how well they serve our purposes, rather than how well they conform to "reality." In other words, a neopragmatic planning view suggests that the choice of linguistic form should be determined on the basis of the purpose(s) and goals of the planning process, and not on the basis of what accords better with reality.

In the realist worldview, our forms of representation (categories, terms, labels) are seen as rigidly fixed and given by "the world." A neopragmatic view of decision making in planning rejects this notion of rigid definition. Many of the distinctions that are generally accepted in any historical epoch are not absolute, not ultimate, not "written in stone." Rather than being fixed, categories should be viewed as more flexible and fluid, with properties that are open and changeable. Instead, they are "up for grabs," so to speak; their meaning is set within a larger framework of concepts and is chosen for pragmatic purposes (see chapter 11).

Although certain basic contrasts should be maintained, supposedly absolute contrasts such as "true and false," "reasonable and unreasonable," "subjective and objective," "scientific and political," and so on, should be brought down to earth, contextualized, and related to particular human goals.[12] In so doing, we can neutralize postmodernist attacks on universal meta-narratives (chapter 4).

Rorty could be misconstrued here. He is not maintaining that when we say something is true we are merely saying that it is useful. He believes that the adjective "true" should be used in the ordinary way;[13] for example, the statement "snow is white" is true if and only if snow is white.[14] Nor is he saying that when we justify a particular belief we do so by appeal to its usefulness.

Theory

It is important to be clear about the function of the general account ("theory" if you like) that we pragmatists are providing. It is an example of what John Locke called the "under-laborer" conception of philosophy, and what Wittgenstein called the therapeutic role of philosophy. Under this conception the aim is not to provide a theory at all; rather, it is seen that the sort of discussion we have provided here is necessary in order to clear away a whole host of confusions that we have inherited from a philosophical tradition that prevents us from getting down to business. It is not intended to give a theory of truth; there is no overall meta-narrative, or general account, of what truth is. Its practical importance lies in the fact that many of our practices (including planning practice) are infected by the viruses of philosophical speculation. This is one place where neopragmatists agree with postmodernists and feminists. That is why, as Rorty notes, it is often the goal of the pragmatist to "change the subject."

Justification

For Rorty (following Davidson), we justify a belief in the usual way, by appealing to a web of other beliefs (i.e., beliefs in relation to other beliefs) that provide reasons for this belief. These reasons are not universally valid (as Habermas [1984] believes possible) nor foundational, but ordinary, everyday reasons of the sort we give here and now, even if they are historically contingent. These reasons fit together and are embedded in our social practices, which come and go. As Davidson remarks, "All that counts as evidence or justification for a belief must come from the same totality of belief to which it belongs" (Davidson 1990, 134). What Rorty does argue is that there is no further appeal to anything that allows one to get beyond this web of beliefs and practices, to get "through to reality" or to the "truth."

Language Games, Vocabularies, and Descriptions

Another important aspect of Rorty's view: He believes that our language can be divided up into what he calls "vocabularies" that are more or less related. This notion is closely aligned with Wittgenstein's "language games," Davidson's "descriptions" and "webs of belief," Foucault's "discourses," and is related to Kuhn's "paradigms." Rorty's "vocabularies" are more or less contained segments of linguistic practice that carry with them their own concepts, standards of evaluation, possibilities, and criteria that tell us when particular statements are true or false.

We will use the term "vocabulary" in ways similar to the more familiar "conceptual framework"or "conceptual scheme." It refers to certain related ways of speaking that are connected. A cluster of concepts, terms, and reasons can be identified that evolve organically over time and place. Examples of these different vocabularies include the scientific search for causes, the intentional, the aesthetic, the religious, the moral, and so on. We like the term "vocabulary" because it avoids some implications of "conceptual framework": the insulation, isolation, and independence from other frameworks. It also avoids the idea that language and concepts structure the world; "vocabulary" refers purely to the linguistic.

What counts as a new vocabulary or language game is on a continuum. There is no sharp line between generating hypotheses within an "old paradigm" and generating a "new paradigm" (that can go so far as to question traditional grounds for determining what is true or false). For example, although some fundamentalist theologians will contradict the claims of science with regard to the age of the earth (i.e., working within the same vocabulary or language game as science), other contemporary theologians may not. They may not be making an empirical remark at all when they talk about the creation of the earth (i.e., they may be working within a different vocabulary or language game). This position evolved; it was not a sudden leap.

The Choice of Vocabularies

The criteria for choosing a vocabulary cannot be its truthfulness, because what counts as true or false is *internal* to the vocabulary. Vocabularies come into being, grow, change, and disappear. They carry with them standards in terms of which statements are found to be true and which are false. As vocabularies change, these standards change. But vocabularies as a whole cannot be said to be true or false. In this sense, the criteria for determining truth or falsity are internal to the vocabulary. Scientific vocabulary include ways of determining the truth or falsity of scientific statements, and as scientific vocabulary changes, the ways of determining the truth or falsity of scientific statements also change.

Thus, vocabularies are chosen (or evolve) because they are suited to the purposes of the field, or they serve the purposes of society. Appropriateness is relative to purpose; in this sense, vocabularies are chosen for pragmatic reasons.

The type of descriptions provided by empirical social science does not have any superior role to play. This means that we may reasonably hold on to normative descriptions even after their functional relations are pointed out, just as we need not give up an intentional description even after a causal description is pointed out. When a structural description identifies a relation of power, we may choose to give up a type of description that we formerly accepted. But there is nothing that forces us to do it; we may choose not to. For example, realizing that religion functions to maintain certain economic relations may lead someone to give up religious beliefs, but it is not a compelling reason to reject them.

The likelihood of those who are participants being sensitive to external descriptions (ones provided by other communities), or to new descriptions generated in one's own community, will increase if it is believed that the old ones are losing their purpose—that they are not satisfying needs. This is what occurred when the religious worldview was replaced by scientism, and it is happening again with the current onslaught against scientism. *It seems to us that this openness to change, this dissatisfaction, is what is happening in planning today.* We now face a rising dissatisfaction from postmodernists, feminists, deep ecologists, and the like with a plethora of new vocabularies being thrown at us. What is the poor planner to do? He or she had better get some pragmatic theory in hand.

The upshot of the neopragmatic arguments just outlined is that it no longer makes good sense in general to draw sharp distinctions between theory and practice, between language and the world, between object and thought, between ends and means, unless there are particular contingent reasons to do so. What we "do" cannot be clearly separated from the forms of description, the conception we have of what we are doing.

NEOPRAGMATISM AND CLASSICAL PRAGMATISM

Some differences between neopragmatism and classical pragmatism should also be noted:

1. Unlike classical pragmatism, neopragmatism does not give analysis, theory, or definition of key terms. There is no neopragmatic definition of truth.

2. Pragmatism saw the scientific method as a broad model for all investigation. The earlier pragmatists viewed science as central to knowledge.[15] Neopragmatism does not reify scientific method nor does it place science in a central position in our culture. Science is just one social institution among others.

3. Neopragmatism is not reductionistic. Priority is not given to any one type of inquiry, such as the scientific.[16]

4. Neopragmatism does not place priority on instrumental reason. As Habermas has pointed out, reason comes in many forms depending on context and interest.

The line between classical pragmatism and neopragmatism is loose and somewhat arbitrary.[17] Our broad use of "neopragmatism" includes Quine, Davidson, Wittgenstein, Putnam, Rorty, and Bernstein, although only the last two would be comfortable with the label. We also find pragmatic elements in the work of Kuhn, Rawls, Habermas, and Walzer (see chapter 6).

SUMMARY

Hilary Putnam aptly summarizes the neopragmatic perspective:

> Many thinkers have argued that the traditional dichotomy between the world "in itself" and the concepts we use to think and talk about it must be given up. . . . Davidson has argued that the distinction between "scheme" and "content"cannot be drawn. Wittgenstein and Goodman have argued that the distinction between "world" and "versions" is untenable. . . . Like the great pragmatists, these thinkers have urged us to reject the spectator point of view in metaphysics and epistemology. Quine has urged us to accept the existence of abstract entities on the grounds that these are indispensable in . . . physics, and what better justification is there for accepting an ontology than its indispensability in scientific practice? (Putnam 1987, 21)

To which we would add: its indispensability in social practice. Putnam goes on to argue that we should extend the same pragmatic approach to

> our moral images of ourselves and the World . . . what can giving up the spectator view of philosophy mean if we don't extend the pragmatic approach to the most indispensable "versions" of ourselves? . . . (Putnam 1990, 267).

Neopragmatists value our traditions but reevaluate them pragmatically, examining deeply embedded ideas to pick aspects that are useful to solve real contemporary problems. We can and should generate a coherent perspective to serve our purposes by picking from various perspectives those elements that we find valuable and rejecting those we do not. Thus, a pragmatic view can integrate aspects of theories/frames that may seem to be in conflict: Rawls's Wide Reflective Equilibrium, Walzer's critical interpretation, Habermas's communicative and critical rationality, the liberal notion of the individual,[18] Foucault's identification of power abuses, Rorty's conversation, communitarianism's theory of morality, Nozick's natural rights, and feminism's emphasis on caring and trust. Neopragmatism takes a pragmatic view of philosophy itself.

For example, we will see (in chapter 9) that, for the purposes of public political discussion, we can let go of the essentialistic and metaphysical idea of the transcendent individual ego yet maintain our "political" liberal perspective on the moral and political centrality of the individual. This political and moral idea of the individual can be combined with communitarian elements to serve practical and moral goals. Such an integrated perspective undercuts one communitarian criticism of contemporary liberalism. Neopragmatism does not deny the role of community. As in classical pragmatism, inquiry takes place in the context of a community; however, the community must be open to critique and evolution. Rawls's method of WRE provides a method for achieving this pragmatic ideal.

Neopragmatism thus avoids a lot of "problems" and debates that could hinder us from dealing with *real* problems. Critics (e.g., communitarians) might say we can't avoid these questions. We say they can be avoided with intelligence and a decision not to be intimidated by them. In the next chapter, we will see how this approach helps us resolve, or perhaps dissolve, some of the issues raised by postmodern critiques of public planning.

4

Out of the Postmodern Abyss: Postmodernist Themes

INTRODUCTION

In this chapter, we will give a critical account of some key themes of postmodernism[1] that we believe are relevant to planning. This critique focuses primarily on themes posing a clear threat to the possibility of a normative planning theory that can justify liberal planning practices. Our concern is to highlight those places where full-blown postmodernism goes too far in its rejection of modernism. We particularly want to avoid throwing out the liberal "baby" with the scientistic "bath water." From a pragmatic perspective, this is both possible and reasonable.

FOUNDATIONALISM

Postmodernists reject foundationalism (the belief that absolute foundations for universal truth can established). Where modernism sought to replace religion with science as the foundation of certain knowledge, postmodernism rejects the idea that knowledge can have any foundation. Nothing can be known with certainty. Postmodernism is antifoundationalist in "dispensing with universals as bases for truth" (Milroy 1991, 183), and in rejecting "claims of undisputed authority" (Dear 1986, 373).

Problems arise when some postmodernists go further to deny that we can make *any* judgments about what other people say and believe. This denial presupposes the very transcendental perspective postmodernists want to reject. Any claim that interpretation and judging are not a matter of *our* own understanding requires an implicit appeal to some external perspective that could tell us our understanding is wrong. When postmodernists say that "master narratives violate the complexity and contingency of social reality" (Milroy 1991, 193) or "social reality is a social construction" (ibid., 182), they implicitly assume some other external, "outside" way of knowing and interpreting "reality," a way that is independent of any of our conceptual schemes. But this independent outside perspective is the (modernist) foundationalist assumption that postmodernists want to reject. If there is no such perspective, then the claim makes no sense.[2] So postmodernists at this key point are (unwittingly) retaining the very foundationalism that they claim to reject.

Neopragmatism is also naturalistic and nonfoundational. Our account of how things hang together, our notions of truth, morality, justification, and the like, are naturalistic, not transcendental or *a priori*. There is no metaphysical way of knowing; our knowledge is based on our ongoing practices. Understanding these practices does not involve some absolute perspective. They may be described internally by reflective accounts of our normative practices or externally, for example, by sociological or historical accounts. But these external accounts are not metaphysical—they require no appeal to an absolute foundation or a God's-eye outside perspective.

Practically, we do use liberal democratic notions that can be traced back to the Enlightenment (chapter 1), but we don't agree with Habermas (1984) that they need a *foundation* in that tradition in order to justify them. We don't justify our beliefs—in reasonableness, truth and objective-like values, that all voices should be critically heard, that there should be free and open debate, that we should seek collaborative consensus—by appeal to that tradition. In fact, we don't justify these beliefs at all; we start with them. And they are not immutable; they can be modified. They form the basic intuitions that we believe (here and now) give us decent, reasonable, fair, and just ethical decision making. They seem (to us) to be essential—necessary—for the kind of society we want (Rawls 2001). But they don't have to be grounded in any historical meta-narrative.

Postmodernists' attacks on foundationalism can be taken in different ways. At worst, they are attempting to undermine all validity claims and justifications by arguing that the grounds for judgment are too unstable to sustain any judgment: "[T]here are readers of Derrida . . . who think he is telling us that there is something futile or contaminating about making *any* distinctions or endorsing *any* hierarchical claims" (Bernstein 1992, 182). At best, we could interpret postmodernists pragmatically as merely highlighting the fallibilistic nature of our beliefs. Neopragmatism is fallibilistic; inquiry is viewed as an ongoing process, with no absolute concept of an end to that process. We cannot stand back and conceive of an absolute process of inquiry independently of the context of concrete and practical problem solving.[3] However, fallibilism should not be taken by postmodernists as undermining rationality, objectivity, or the possibility of justification—because we can hold these notions without anchoring them in any metaphysical, absolutism of [empirical or normative] "bedrock truths." Within our institutional and conceptual context, we can still present justifications for planning in general, or for particular plans—giving good reasons for or against them.

META-NARRATIVE AND THEORY

The postmodernist perspective expresses a deep distrust of theory. Indeed, rejection of meta-narratives is often seen as *the* defining characteristic of postmodernism (Lyotard 1987). As we understand and use the term, "meta-narrative" refers to broad theories that claim to be universally true descriptions or explanations of reality. Meta-narratives attempt to derive general social principles that are precisely explanatory/predictive in the same sense as scientific laws. Examples are Marxism, the RCPM, and "stages of development" models.

Postmodernists have a "suspicion of any theory that claims a vantage point of knowledge and truth, a self-assured position of 'scientific' method from which to criticize the various forms of 'ideological' false-seeming or commonsense perception" (Norris 1990, 28). This distrust of theory is related to their political agenda, which emphasizes the failure of modernism to provide a foundation for legitimizing the idea of political progress.[4] On the contrary, postmodernists believe that objective and universal critique is itself a facade, a mask for oppression that marginalizes oppressed groups such as women, the poor, and blacks.

Neopragmatism also deemphasizes the importance of theory and rejects the idea of meta-narrative. Theoretical reflection cannot be sharply separated from practice; they form a continuum. Theory and practice should be seen as a continuous process of reflecting on action and acting on reflection, a process that can be disentangled only in an artificial manner, and only for particular purposes. This view follows from Quine's rejection of a sharp analytic/synthetic distinction and Putnam's rejection of a sharp practical/theoretical distinction (chapter 3). Pragmatists view the contrast between theory and practice as a continuum.

In some senses we cannot escape theory. As soon as we attempt to make any generalizations, we are doing theory. In this sense, we cannot avoid theory. However, pragmatists do try to eschew broad general theorizing in favor of more contextual, contingent, situation-specific intepretation. Grand general theories have done more harm than good in planning. Meta-narratives have no place in a pragmatic incrementalist scheme (chapter 7). However, this does not mean that we cannot have guiding normative principles. These need not (and do not) function as meta-narratives, particularly if they are treated as just one of the elements of a WRE process (chapter 6).

MEANING AND AMBIGUITY

Postmodernists make much of the "ambiguity" (Milroy 1991, 185; Beauregard 1991, 190) that follows from their antifoundationalism. We take ambiguity to mean the inability to fix a universal meaning to a concept. This emphasis on ambiguity reflects one of the foci of structuralist and poststructuralist literary theory. The claim is that words "have multiple meanings . . . they thus possess potential excess meanings. . . . Language always means more than it may be taken to mean in any one context" (Lye 1993, 91). Derrida's emphasis on meaning as determined only in relation to other words and his attempt to eliminate metaphysical notions like representation and absolute meaning create an illusion of instability that can lead to a paralyzing ambiguity (Stephens 1994). The totality of meaning becomes inaccessible. We can never have more than an inadequate and approximate grasp of meaning.

This view presupposes a conception of meaning that is paradoxical. The meaning of a statement in a particular context can never be fully "gotten at" because it is determined by the entire nexus of difference, which is unlimited. Thus, meaning is limitless, and any particular interpretation is unavoidably incomplete. As Borges (quoted by Soja [1989, 2]) says, "How then can I translate into words the limitless Aleph, which my floundering mind can scarcely encompass? . . . Really what I want to do is impossible."

The metaphysical assumption that postmodernists tacitly accept (and we want to reject) is this notion that words have some meaning over and above the interpretation of someone's statements, like fixed exhibits in a museum to which we have no access. Quine rejects this image, since

> [I]t would be forever impossible to know if one of these [meanings] were the right one and the other wrong. . . . there would be a right and wrong of the matter; it is just that we would never know, not having access to the museum. (Quine 1969, 29)

The problem of ambiguity disappears if we view meaning as a pragmatic tool for interpreting linguistic behavior as a whole—for getting at what someone is saying, what he or she believes and means. Neopragmatism does not seek to determine the essential meaning of a word independent of context. Meaning is dependent on the general holistic interpretative account. There is no general rule for deciding whether a disagreement is attributable to a difference in meaning (of a concept), or a difference in belief (about facts). This follows from the rejection of the strict bifurcation of language and world, concept and belief, meaning and truth, fact and value. These contrasts are relative to our interests, and differences are resolved pragmatically subject to those interests.

Furthermore, the line between belief and meaning is not a fixed one (another absolute dichotomy that should be rejected). Instead, we should look holistically at the entire web of interconnected beliefs and meanings.[5] As Putnam (1992, 127) remarks: "The kind of sameness of meaning we seek . . . involves a normative judgment, a judgment as to what is reasonable in the particular case." Shifts of meaning and belief take place (generally gradually) within the web of other meanings and beliefs. Thus, meaning is not an overdetermined property of a word, as Derrida believes, but is connected to interpretation that can be objectively justified.

The upshot of this view is that meanings, beliefs (and the language in which they are embedded) are always tied to interpretation and, consequently, to the ongoing practical, social, and dialogical inquiry that leads to mutual understanding. There are no "private languages."[6] The interpretation process is a matter of mutual partial adjustment. Distinguishing between meaning and belief, between concepts and the world, is relative to a particular pragmatic task of interpreting others. Talk of different concepts makes sense only as part of an interpretation process that makes the people we are interpreting as transparent to us as is feasible.

This approach to interpretation is central to understanding meaning and belief as a pragmatic question. In the process of interpretation, we will of course come across anomalies, cases where people's beliefs and meanings are very different from ours. However, the discovery of such anomalies arises only as part of an ongoing process of interpretation that presupposes a background of common agreement of beliefs and meanings. Only against this common background can anomalies be discovered. This way of looking at differences allows for direct communication because it eliminates any metaphysical intermediary (experience, language, culture, conceptual scheme) between people. Understanding each other becomes a pragmatic question of interpretation. Individuals, communities, and cultures are not incommensurable. We are capable of understanding the concepts, beliefs, and values of others.

DUALISMS

Postmodernists reject dualisms, i.e., "disjunctive pairs in which disjuncts are seen as oppositional (rather than as complementary) and exclusive (rather than as inclusive)" (Warren 1990, 268). They propose that pluralism should replace dualism.

Pragmatists agree with this up to a point. Recall that Quine (1953) demonstrated that there is no sharp line between fact and value. Distinctions are not written in stone or absolutely determined in some essentialist Platonic universe. Contrasts are looked upon as on a continuum serving certain temporary interests. In addition, differences in concepts are not sharply distinguished from differences in beliefs.

What should be given up are *absolute* dualisms, essentialistic dualisms, and the idea that the world is divided into, and is reflected by, absolute linguistic categories. Absolute dualism is the idea that there is an absolute dichotomy between such contrasts as analytic/synthetic, form/content, meaning/belief, fact/value, subject/object, absolute/relative, and appearance/reality. Putnum suggests that we give up thinking of contrasts as absolute dualisms and think of them as continua. He (1987, 27) echoes Noam Chomsky here when he says that we "often take perfectly sensible continua and get in trouble by converting them into dichotomies." The emphasis on the "absoluteness" of dichotomies is important. For example, the assumption is that either rationality has an essence (one property shared by all instances of the use of "rationality") *or* rationality is relative ("multivocal").

The [modernist] essentialist believes this explicitly; the [postmodernist] relativist assumes it implicitly. Both also accept the assumption that we require absolute foundations for our beliefs if they are to be justified. But this presupposes an essential duality on a meta-level, i.e., it presupposes an absolute dichotomy between duality and nonduality. Here again, we find postmodernists unwittingly retaining the very assumption they want to reject.

In contrast, the pragmatist views dualities (contrasts) as continua, as distinctions made for particular (if temporary) purposes, and tied to particular interests. Appeals to different concepts are also relative to our interests. For example, the pragmatist does not have to choose between accepting the narrow modernist conception of rationality (that arbitrarily restricts it to instrumental rationality) and giving up the idea of rationality altogether. Instead, we can widen the modernist conception to include broader notions of communicative and critical rationality. Once we recognize that contrasts need not be absolute, we can continue to use them in a pragmatic way to make useful ordinary distinctions.

Critics of our view have argued that sharp distinctions are sometimes necessary. It may well be that, in some contexts, a clear and sharp distinction is useful and appropriate. Just how sharp or fuzzy the distinction needs to be in a particular context will itself be a pragmatic question.

The rejection of absolute dualism also undermines the notion of a primary and absolute discourse ("meta-narrative"). However, as discussed earlier, a rejection of a narrow scientistic meta-narrative does not mean that "anything goes."

TRUTH AND REASON[7]

Postmodernists believe that "plurality relativizes truth" (Milroy 1991, 186). This relativization of truth leads to a misconception. Milroy (ibid.) and Beauregard speak as if there were different "rationalities," a "plethora of 'supportable' positions" from which anyone can arbitrarily choose, and Dear (1986, 375) speaks of "turning reason against itself." This position derives from the postmodernist rejection of dualisms just discussed.

Pragmatists propose that we widen the modernist conception of rationality to include broader notions, to incorporate our shared views of what is reasonable. This wide conception can be viewed as a continuum allowing for clear instances of rationality, some grey areas (borderline cases), and clear instances of irrationality. The line between rationality and irrationality can change; it is not immutable. Moreover, the various instances of rationality (and irrationality) are not fixed by an essence and will form, as we argue below, an overlapping family of resemblances. But the distinction is real and useful all the same.

"Rationality" is a thin concept, similar to the concepts of justice, truth, and goodness (or planning). It is a highly abstract notion, sensitive to a wide and evolving set of contextual criteria, that evolves (progresses) over time. To say that something is rational is just to say that we can give good reasons for it, that it has been arrived at in an impartial manner, that it is consistent and coheres with other beliefs, that it is sensitive to relevant evidence, within a particular context, and relative to our interests. We will find no single concrete feature common to all applications of the term "rationality." The point of such thin concepts is to sustain conceptual continuity in our beliefs and concepts through time and purpose, in the face of changing theories, methods of verification, values, and beliefs.

For example, at one time our belief that a particular substance was gold was based on facts known about its tangible qualities. These facts provided reasons for believing that a substance was gold. As knowledge progressed, new tests were discovered (e.g., that only gold was soluble in weak nitric acid) that provided additional (or alternative) reasons for believing that a substance was gold. Now, due to scientific advances, we believe that gold is an element with the atomic number 79. Our reason for believing that something is gold has been modified again, and the theories, procedures, and methodology we now use to provide reasons have been significantly altered. However, it would be absurd to conclude from this history that our concept of "gold" has necessarily changed—that King Midas was referring to a different substance. It would be even more absurd to argue that our concept of reason has changed.[8]

Such evolutionary change does not lead us to different incommensurable conceptions of rationality. On the contrary, such change presupposes a continuity of the concept. The idea that, unless we provide an essential nature of rationality present in all applications we cannot have a coherent concept of rationality, is another metaphysical assumption that should be rejected. It springs from the notion that we can apply a term through time only if we can set out, in *advance,* criteria for *all* future applications of that term. *But this is not how language works.* This point is made by Wittgenstein in discussing his notion of language games. He asks:

> What is common to them all? Don't say: "There must be something in common, or they would not be called 'games'". . . For if you look at them

you will not see something that is common to all, but similarities, relationships, and a whole series of them at that. (Wittgenstein 1958, par. 66)

Wittgenstein (1958, par. 67) then adds that we "extend our concept . . . as in
spinning a thread we twist fiber on fiber. And the strength of the thread does
not reside in the fact that some one fiber runs through its whole length, but
in the overlapping of many fibers. . . ." The tendency to deny this arises when
the tired metaphysical assumption of absolute dualism has not really been
given up.

Undeniably, our beliefs, and our reasons for those beliefs, will likely continue to evolve, as they have in the past. Postmodernists put entirely too
much weight on the very metaphysical assumptions they wish to reject. If
the assumptions are rejected, they seem to believe that everything collapses.
As Hilary Putnam eloquently remarks:

> Deconstructionists are right in claiming that a certain metaphysical tradition
> is bankrupt; but to identify that metaphysical tradition with our lives and
> our language is to give metaphysics an altogether exaggerated importance.
> For deconstructionists, metaphysics was the *basis* of our entire culture, the
> basis on which it all rested; if the pedestal has broken, the entire culture
> must have collapsed—indeed, our whole language must lie in ruins.
> (Putnam 1992, 124)

But if we look at the matter pragmatically, we need accept neither absolutism
nor the postmodern abyss.

The key point here is that if postmodernists have *really* given up the
transcendentalism, the absolute dualism, and the foundationalism of modernism, then they can't turn around and deal with differences (between individuals or communities) by saying that the different parties have different
views of reason, logic, reality, or truth. This again presupposes a false picture
of an independent reality, with an absolute (even though inaccessible) conception of reason and truth, that different people or communities view in
different ways.

Perhaps a qualm remains: By emphasizing the contextual nature of concepts, the notion of family resemblance, and the rejection of essentialism,
haven't we tacitly accepted the postmodern view that there are different notions of rationality, relative to different times, places, and communities? No—
quite the opposite. In order to identify these differences (between people
who inhabit distinct times and places and communities) as differences in
rationality, we must first interpret their verbal behavior as "rational"—and
this presupposes continuity of the notion of "rationality" against which we
can judge the behavior. If one acknowledges that "rationality" (like "truth"
and "morality") is neither transient nor transcendent, then difference must
take place against a background of sameness, rejection against acceptance, disagreement against agreement. Difference (and *"différance"*) cannot stand alone!

INCOMMENSURABILITY

While incommensurability is not frequently recognized as one of post-modernism's defining characteristics, we have seen (in the previous chapter) that the approach of Ferdinand de Saussure leads in this very dangerous direction. The danger arises not from acknowledging that there are competing goals or different views of justice and morality but from relativizing these differences to particular communities without the possibility of their coming together. Consensus is ruled out *a priori* since the communities' conceptions of morality are viewed as incommensurable.

The claim is that "there are only multiple narratives, a multiplicity of language games that are locally determined, none of which can be reconciled across speakers" (Milroy 1991, 193); that "the modern world (conceptually and practically) is highly fragmented and awash in incommensurable private languages" (Dear 1986, 369); that "open moral communities engender diverse and often incommensurable narratives" (Mandelbaum 1991, 213). Soja (1989, 222) emphasizes the difficulty of communication in huge multicultural cities like Los Angeles because they have no "shared past."

We believe the idea of different incommensurable conceptual schemes that are not translatable is false. On one level, this seems obvious: If those who make this claim were right, then there is no way that they could come to know this fact because they would be able to understand only their own "language game," and they could know nothing about anyone else's (not even whether it was a language game). In addition, there would be no basis for critique within their own culture, and there would be no way to change anyone's mind about anything. However, the more technical arguments involved (Davidson 1985; Stein 1994; Harper and Stein 1996) are quite complex. Here, space permits only the following brief recapitulation.

While we reject the notion of incommensurability, we do recognize the intimate connection between community and language. Interpretation of what people do (their actions) reflects their intentions, beliefs, and meaning as much as does interpretation of what they say. Language cannot be separated from meaningful action, i.e., from what Wittgenstein (1958, para. 23) calls a "form of life." It has been argued that it is always conceptually possible to understand people of another culture and to interpret their language.[9] Such interpretation must presuppose an overlap of concepts and beliefs, a *shared* worldview that is essentially veridical. While different cultures have different beliefs and (to a limited extent) different concepts, these differences presuppose a vast background of agreement regarding *overlapping* beliefs and concepts. If there were *no* shared background, we couldn't say that people have a language, a conceptual system, or even a culture at all.

Translation or interpretation presupposes a principle of *charity*: "[I]f we want to understand others, we must count them right in most matters" (Davidson 1985, 142). In contrast, deconstructionists seem to have a principle of *malice*; their absolutist concept of meaning dooms all attempts at interpretation to failure. Even the actual speaker or writer doesn't mean what he or she thought was meant. Instead of looking at clear cases to make sure we understand concepts, deconstructionists seize on obscure borderline cases to convince us that interpretation is so difficult, we might as well not even try it.

The incommensurability thesis rests on two mistakes: first, retaining an absolute dichotomy between beliefs and the meaning of concepts; second, assuming that concepts are incommensurable because we can't precisely fix the meaning of individual concepts. We have already seen that meaning is tied to interpretation, as Quine argues, and that the relationship between concepts and beliefs is a pragmatic and fluid one. While translation (and interpretation) must be pragmatic, holistic, and fallibilistic, it is not impossible.

The pragmatist recognizes that none of this need lead us to the alienation of incommensurability. The lack of absolute foundations does not *require* us to accept incommensurability. There are no conceptual barriers between individuals, communities, or cultures. We do not live in different incommensurable worlds. The separation, alienation, and isolation experienced by many in our contemporary society should be seen not as the result of any philosophical thesis (like the liberal conception of the autonomous self) but of certain distortions in our society: the modernist emphasis on technology, overspecialization of labor, reification of market value, and so on. These distortions can be uncovered incrementally by dialogue.

In addition, there are good conceptual and moral reasons not to assume incommensurability unless all attempts at understanding fail. As Dear (1986, 370) says, "[W]e should not comfortably concede the impossibility of connected discourse." We should assume that we *can* communicate[10] and thus attempt to maximize agreement, avoiding unnecessary alienation and the use of power to resolve disagreements.

The implication of commensurability is that dialogue is possible between communities even when beliefs and concepts seem very different. Planners have a responsibility to foster such dialogue and to minimize distortion.[11] Genuine dialogue should be at the heart of any model of planning for the postmodern era. But genuine dialogue must be two-way. One reason why postmodernists may exaggerate the difficulty of interpretation is that their actual experience of "dialogue" is one-way: a dominant culture or community (perhaps represented by a planner) telling others how to live.

RELATIVISM

Postmodernists reject the absolutism of modernism; they often sound very relativistic about both knowledge and morality. For example, some feminists speak of a woman's morality or a woman's way of knowing (Gilligan 1977; Sandercock 1998a). Or critics of development planning often argue that we should not interfere with the moral judgments of indigenous cultures.

Neopragmatism is neither relativist nor absolutist; it rejects the relativism/absolutism dualism as unproductive, and it rejects the idea of different incommensurable languages, conceptual schemes, or private networks of meaning.[12] Talk of differences in meaning makes sense only against a background of interpretation that renders those we are interpreting as transparent as possible. We should give up the idea that meanings are Platonic essences privately apprehended or the Kantian notion of Noumena (external reality), which we can mold like clay into particular realities. Once we give up these ideas, all metaphysical intermediaries between ourselves and others are dissipated. Of course there will be differences, deep differences; but these differences can—at least in principle—be worked out. There is no *conceptual* reason why they cannot.

Note that both the essentialist and the relativist share the idea that, if we cannot now give *eternally* legitimate reasons for our beliefs, then they are completely relativistic. This requirement compels us to remove ourselves from time and place, to step outside our own skins, so to speak, and acquire a Gods-eye perspective in order to compare what we believe to some absolute standard—to "true reality." But, of course, this is neither possible nor desirable; it leads us into absolute dogmatism (another absolute!).

PLURALITY AND DIFFERENT FRAMES

Postmodernists emphasize the recognition and celebration of cultural difference. This raises questions not only of incommensurability but also of justification across different frames. The postmodernist celebration of plurality and difference offers no way to reconcile conflicting accounts or clashing values, no way to proceed when goals are mutually incompatible.

The pragmatic way to deal with differences is not by presupposing incommensurable notions of rationality and truth but by talking about them and attempting to reach consensus.[13] Each party may find (what it believes to be) unreasonable elements in the other's position; they have to attempt to work out these differences. Neopragmatism is closely tied to a pluralistic and democratic model of society, a model that applies not only to morality but to inquiry as a whole. In the pragmatic sense we've outlined here, we can retain objective (even though fallible) truth. That's why *there is no postmodern abyss!* We can provide good reasons for accepting legitimating processes for planning, with confidence, and relative to a continuing critical dialogue that attempts to include all voices.

While the past error was that the wealthy and powerful forced their ideas on other communities, it is equally erroneous to assume that every community is right and should never be challenged or changed. We should respect plurality and difference but not to the point of giving up on communication, or abandoning the search for consensus, and not to the point of relativism (i.e., where what any group or individual believes is right in fact is right; thus all moral positions are equally legitimate). We should encourage all voices to enter public dialogue with their "competing stories," as Mandelbaum (1991, 211) suggests. But these voices should not be received uncritically. We can evaluate, weigh, and judge new voices, thereby enriching tradition and ensuring that social institutions actually work in a way that is consistent with our liberal democratic ideals. True toleration does not require uncritical acceptance of whatever a community (even a marginalized and oppressed one) says. The ideal is not social isolation but unconstrained and undistorted dialogue—a process by which we can learn from each other.

Neopragmatism can integrate different frames. These roughly identifiable webs of beliefs and meaning are not monolithic. We can and should generate a coherent perspective to serve our purposes, by picking from various perspectives those elements that we find valuable and rejecting those that we do not.

JUSTIFICATION

Postmodernists have not come to terms with their own rejection of transcendental absolutism—which means that no outside external justification can be given for plans and policies, for planning, or even for government itself. Their arguments frequently appeal to (or implicitly assume) moral conceptions of justice, equality, and the like as if these conceptions had a universality that their own theories deny.

Wittgenstein recognized that there are limits to justification:

> Giving grounds, however, justifying the evidence, comes to an end—but the end is not certain propositions' striking us as true, i.e., it is not a kind of seeing on our part; it is our acting, which lies at the bottom of the language-game. (Wittgenstein 1969, par. 204)

When justification has been exhausted, Wittgenstein (1958, par. 217) says, "I have reached bedrock, and my spade is turned. Then I am inclined to say: 'This is simply what I do.'"

Although absolute justification is impossible, neopragmatists do believe that objective justification is possible within particular contexts. As we will argue in chapter 7, neopragmatic justification is incremental. We cannot justify or question our worldview as a whole: there is no metaphysical justification. Our practices form a web of beliefs and meaning that is complex and everchanging. Progress involves modifying elements of this web in various ways—eliminating bits here, adding bits there—again, controlled by human interests. There is no systematic method to which we can appeal in this ongoing process. Nor do abstract principles (as opposed to particular concrete judgments or intuitions) have some superior role to play (see chapters 6 and 11). We must view the process holistically.

Summary: A Way Forward

Contrary to some of the false dichotomies implied by postmodernist themes (Milroy 1991), we can recognize that communication is sometimes imprecise without succumbing to the pessimism of incommensurability; and we can accommodate plurality without giving up truth. Planning does not need to remain suspended over the postmodern abyss. The neopragmatic approach offers a way to legitimate planning and change in a nonfoundational world; more radical approaches will wind up resorting to coercion. We also see neopragmatism as the most reasonable response to relativism. It offers a workable way to deal with allegedly incommensurable differences between communities, between paradigms, and between frames.

POSTMODERNISM AND PLANNING

A number of authors have made valuable contributions to planners' understanding of postmodernism. However, no one has clearly articulated the dangers for planning of an uncritical acceptance of postmodernism or proposed a theoretical position from which we can construct a robust contemporary normative planning theory. Much of the work about postmodernism that is best known to planners has focused on its effects on the physical form and the social experience of the city. For example, Harvey (1989) and Soja (1989) both talk about the effect of space–time compression on urban life in its cultural, economic, and political dimensions.[14] While this work is obviously relevant to planning, our focus on normative procedural planning theory and its practical application raises somewhat different issues.

The first discussion of postmodernism and planning theory was written by a geographer. Dear presents an excellent but largely uncritical summary of postmodernism and "deconstructs" the history of (modernist) planning from 1945 to 1985 to reveal the "pastiche of 'postmodern planning'" (Dear 1986, 367). He himself is not a full-blown postmodernist, in that he proposes a "meta-language for discourse on a reconstructed planning theory." Beauregard (1989, 1991) also seeks to deconstruct the history of planning and then to reconstruct planning theory. Beauregard views planning as stuck in the midst of a paradigm shift, suspended over an "abyss" between modernism and postmodernism. He is attracted by postmodernism's critique of institutional planning, but his desire to retain some normative justification for planning leads him (like Dear) to back away from full-blown postmodernism.

The influence of postmodernism can be seen over the past two decades in many of the critiques of rational planning and its modernist pillars of utilitarianism and positivism, along with the rejection of ideals like master planning, monofunctional zoning, and urban renewal. While some of these critiques have had a very positive influence, full-blown postmodernism seems inimical to the very notion of planning as a profession. While Sandercock (1998a) views her planning approach as "postmodern," we would hold that there is no full-blown postmodern planning paradigm.[15]

Allmendinger (2001, 227) has explored the idea of postmodern planning most extensively. He finds that "postmodern social theory at worst precludes planning or at best cannot be easily interpreted as a basis for planning." Postmodern planning will be "eclectic." In fact, there will be many "postmodern plannings." What (if anything) would unite these approaches? The general characteristics sound very much like pragmatic liberalism: "A more postmodern approach to planning requires openness, the opportunity to challenge and expose the status quo and existing power relations, and the need for constant reflection" (ibid., 240). But to Allmendinger, the core value is choice, and "choice means the right to choose a form of planning that is not as liberal" (ibid., 256). Of course, the question we raise is: Who has the right to make this choice to be nonliberal? What about those excluded or harmed by the choice? Do they have rights too? Whose rights prevail? Outside of liberalism, how does a society answer such questions?

Two Dangerous Directions

While we do not see postmodernism as providing a viable new planning approach, we do see it as strongly influencing planning thought. We see the possibility of postmodernism leading in two quite different directions. One disturbing direction in which the full-blown postmodernist alternative leads is aptly expressed by Beauregard. It seemingly

> casts planners as authors of texts, eschews authoritative positions in public debates, succumbs to global forces, and, in a false respect for differences, remains politically silent in the face of objective conditions of inequality, oppression, ignorance, and greed. (Beauregard 1991, 193)

The deconstructionist "emphasis on the 'impossible,' on what we cannot know, threatens to leave us paralyzed, standing mute and solitary . . . before the world's injustices" (Stephens 1994), on the brink of the abyss. If we "become obsessed with deconstructing and delegitimizing every form of argument" and every form of legitimation, we wind up compromising our own "validity claims to the point where nothing remains of any basis for reasoned action" (Harvey 1989, 116). Planning is left in a state of impotence, and planning education is a rudderless ship. After all voices have been heard, what is the planner to do? How can any action be justified? The postmodernist critique leaves us "no way to decide what political actions are better than others" (Hoch 1992, 212). This leads Habermas (1989) to fear that a "celebration of differences may justify a destabilizing anarchy that will pave the way for a repressive political order" (Hoch 1992, 208).

An alternative direction looks even more dangerous. Milroy (1990) suggests that power is what really matters, because the powerful make the rules. The implication of postmodernism's incommensurability thesis is that the only mode of relation between communities is raw power. Truth and morality are determined by the community that holds power. The only way to effect change, then, is to become more powerful and to force your views on others. In fact, many postmodernists seem to want to eliminate the crucial distinction between rational persuasion and the coercive exercise of power. Echoing Nietzsche, Lyotard (1987) argues that, because different communities cannot interact through dialogue in reasonable fashion, the only mode of relation is one of power. He concludes that there is no longer a contrast between force and rational persuasion (Rorty 1991a, 214). This view eliminates the contrast between rational persuasion and coercion. It adopts a new notation—the language of power—that abolishes an existing useful linguistic distinction.

As we have seen, Foucauldians go further to assert that everything can be reduced to power. This increasingly popular view holds grave dangers for planning theory and practice. If planning *theorists* focus too much on power, it could blind them to other realities. All relationships and structures could be reinterpreted within a framework of power, resistance to power, and power structures, seriously distorting our understanding and leading us to miss other important aspects, such as community, solidarity, or trust (chapter 15).

If planning *practitioners* see everything in terms of power relations, and if citizens see themselves as victims, this could induce paralysis and despair. A distorted Foucauldian understanding of planning could make it look hopeless. Both citizen and professional planners need some hope that they can make their world a little bit better. If they come to believe that power is ubiquitous and inescapable, that democratic planning processes are nothing more than powerful elites vying for supremacy, that reasonableness doesn't even enter the picture, then why bother?

No Basis for Planning

We acknowledge the positive implications of postmodernism for planning. The rejection of meta-narrative, the distrust of rigid methodology, the celebration of plurality, the recognition that all voices have a right to be heard, are important if planning is to legitimately express liberal ideals. The rejection of foundationalism vitiates the absolute imperialism of the instrumentally rational technocrat, whose "logical (technically) best solution" (Milroy 1991, 186) has done so much damage, both in the third-world context (Beauregard 1991) and in our own society (Liggett 1991).

However, full-blown postmodernism cannot provide an adequate basis for planning. It is fatally flawed not only by a confused and incoherent analysis but, as we have seen, by an inconsistent retention of many of the metaphysical presuppositions underlying modernism—the very foundationalism and absolute dualism that it purports to reject. Postmodernism gives unnecessary credence to these modernist assumptions in a backhanded manner by presupposing that without them all is lost. Postmodernists go on to flirt with giving up the modernist notions of consistency and rational argument. Of course, this rejection would mean that no reasons could be given for accepting or rejecting postmodernism (or, for that matter, any other view).

This leaves us with the Foucauldian view that we are all in the grips of power in the form of vocabularies, concepts, and social institutions. The only alternative would seem to be complete anarchy: linguistically, politically, and morally. Perhaps this is where Foucault wanted to lead us. But we will argue in chapter 15 that there is no good reason to go there.

CONCLUSION

Our concern is that, taken to its extreme, full-blown postmodernism would inevitably reduce planning to the impotent state feared by Beauregard. It would leave us with no basis for legitimate action. Many planners might not feel any real threat; full-blown postmodernism might seem to be unlikely to dominate planning thought. While this may well be, we see the influence of postmodernism subtly weakening the legitimacy of current arguments made by planners (academics and practitioners), even though they may not recognize its influence.

Postmodernism creates a crisis in planning because it undermines and rejects the modernist bases of planning, yet it fails to provide a substitute rationale. Dear (1986, 379) described planning theory as a "babel of languages" and planning practice as reflecting a "pastiche of free-floating, unsystematized 'theories.'" Beauregard (1991, 193) notes that "the intellectual base of the modern planning project" has been undermined, its "validity decaying and reconfiguring"; yet the full-blown postmodernist alternative seemingly leaves no room for planning. These analyses were made more than a decade ago, but they seem even more true today!

Many planners want to retain a normative basis for their work. They do not want to lapse, "like Derrida, into total political silence" (Harvey 1989, 117). But they do not want to return to the scientism of modernistic rational comprehensive planning. We quoted Hoch (1992, 207) earlier as asking, "Can we take the postmodern insight without giving up the planning enterprise altogether?" We believe this is entirely possible: The neopragmatic approach we have advanced here allows us to adopt a critique of modernism (and modernist theories, practices, and institutions) without the pessimism and relativism of the postmodernist abyss.

Part III

PLANNING SHOULD BE
CRITICALLY LIBERAL

5

Classical Liberalism and Planning

LIBERALISM

The nineteenth century "social reformers" combined the scientific and the liberal aspects of modernism, using scientific knowledge to make urban environments more livable. In the twentieth century, each of the two key aspects of modernism led to a different approach to morality and to planning. The scientistic aspect led to a utilitarian approach to morality and the rational comprehensive approach that dominated North American planning after World War II and still underlies the planning profession's claim to expert status (chapter 2). The liberal aspect led to a negative natural rights approach to morality and the classical liberal (libertarian) approach to planning that characterized North American planning up to World War II. This approach provides a rationale (justification) for several key urban planning interventions (chapter 5). Although their status has waned, both approaches still have a strong influence on North American planning practice. More recently, liberalism has evolved into what we will call *contemporary liberalism*, which advocates a much more interventionist approach to public planning (chapter 6).

As we defined it in chapter 1, *liberal* is a very broad term, one that can encompass a variety of political philosophies (Isaiah Berlin, Richard Bernstein, Ronald Dworkin, Jürgen Habermas, Sidney Hooke, William Kymlicka, Kai Nielsen, Robert Nozick, John Rawls, Richard Rorty, Michael Walzer) and planning theories (John Forester, John Friedmann, Patsy Healey, Judith Innes, Norman Krumholz, Seymour Mandelbaum, Leonie Sandercock,[1] James Throgmorton). Depending on the definition used, the liberal perspective appears to underlie many of the policies of every mainstream political party

(Republican, Conservative, Reform,[2] Democrat, Liberal, New Democrat, Labour). One reason why such a range of different thinkers can be characterized as "liberal" is that, as Rawls (2001) argues, acceptance of what he calls "political liberalism" in the public realm does not require adoption of liberalism as one's private philosophic perspective (chapter 6). In our view, this "political liberalism" is reflected in the work of most contributors to the emerging new communicative planning approach (though many of them would not want to be labeled as liberals).

To a significant degree, liberalism can be seen as the dominant perspective of our North American culture; as such, it has negative overtones to those who are critical of this culture. "Liberal" approaches to feminism, environmentalism, international development, and the like are viewed as uncritically endorsing the status quo. Our moral commitment to the basic liberal political values does not necessarily mean that we endorse the actual functioning of the institutions of any particular liberal democratic society. Reflective critique is essential. This is why we use the term "critical liberalism" to describe the moral political stance that we believe should underlie an appropriate planning approach for a postmodern society.

As we saw in chapter 1, the fundamental common value shared by liberal positions is their focus on the *free, equal, and autonomous individual person* as the basic unit of society, the ultimate object of moral concern, and the ultimate source of value. Views that most clearly contrast with liberalism are those that reject the liberal focus on the autonomous person—statists, Fascists, deep ecologists, radical feminists, Friedmann's radical planners, some Marxists, some postmodernists, some Conservatives, most utilitarians, and many communitarians, among others. Because we view the valuing of the autonomous person as so key to the liberal worldview, we do not include perspectives that reject this basic value within our account of the liberal approach.

CLASSICAL LIBERALISM VERSUS CONTEMPORARY LIBERALISM

Even within liberalism as we have defined it, the focus on the autonomous individual person (as the ultimate object of moral concern) points in different directions for two schools of thought. Classical liberals or libertarians, ironically often referred to today as "conservatives," adhere fairly closely to the ideas of John Locke (1967 [1690]). This is the original "liberalism" of the modernist worldview. In contrast, contemporary liberals or Social Democrats, often referred to today simply as "liberals," have modified the position, giving a much greater role to government and a much greater scope for [public] planning.

For the classical liberal, "equality" refers to equality of opportunity and impartiality of treatment by the state. To the contemporary liberal, "equality" and fairness require some redistribution of wealth to correct inequalities of condition resulting from attributes and capacities seen as "morally arbitrary" (Rawls 1971). *Autonomy* is seen as more important than a formal notion of freedom. In this view, there is some tension between fulfilling the ideals of liberty and of equality.

Classical liberals emphasize negative rights and do not recognize positive rights (unless they can be derived from negative rights). Contemporary liberals do recognize some positive rights; this creates more extensive duties toward other individuals and leads to some restriction of negative rights. Whereas Rawls (1985, 233) defines the duties (as well as rights) of a moral citizen, the only individual duty recognized by classical liberals is respect for the negative rights of others.

The distinction between positive and negative rights is intuitively simple. Positive rights are rights *to* something tangible, often a good or service. In contrast, there is really only one basic negative right—the right to be free. It isn't a right *to* anything. Rather it can be expressed only negatively; it is the right *not* to be interfered with in the pursuit of one's goals.

In practice, the distinction between the two kinds of rights is clearest with regard to the implementation and adjudication process. Negative rights are enshrined in constitutions, charters of rights, and criminal law. In general, these documents specify what can *not* be done to individual persons. Changing any of these provisions usually requires a high degree of consensus (e.g., passing two legislative houses, agreement by two levels of government, adoption by plebiscite). This is because these rights are regarded by liberal democratic societies as very fundamental—not to be changed arbitrarily. The remedy for the violation of negative rights is judicial action by the state, often implemented in planning via quasi-judicial local bodies.

In contrast, positive rights are usually enacted by ordinary legislation and implemented administratively; the remedy for alleged violations of positive rights is usually political or administrative. If someone does go to the courts for a remedy, they must show that they were treated unfairly or partially, that they were denied something that other persons in relatively similar circumstances were given.[3]

Another important difference is that classical liberals are generally modernist. They held (and still do hold) the value of the individual person in an absolute, essentialist, hierarchical, foundational way. This is expressed in the notion of inalienable rights as the foundation of society, from which all other principles can be derived. In contrast, contemporary (political) liberals tend to hold the centrality of the person as a core value, but rights are viewed as less absolute.

Our neopragmatic approach maintains the distinction between positive and negative rights (or between positive and negative liberty) but weakens the absolute dichotomy. We begin with the Lockean emphasis on the autonomous individual but soften it by recognizing that autonomy may require redistribution of economic resources, that different groups in pluralistic societies have very different substantive conceptions of "the good," and that some conceptions and beliefs may be ideologically distorted.

Classical Liberalism and Planning

Elsewhere, we have presented a more lengthy account of the classical liberal perspective and outlined some of its implications for planning (Harper and Stein 1995a). We tried to give a systematic account of this important view, which has many more adherents (and more validity) than generally recognized by planning theory. One reason that this view is important is that it provides the rationale for much of contemporary urban planning practice. However, we do believe classical liberalism has some significant weaknesses. Because of these weaknesses, our critical liberalism draws more on what we call *contemporary liberalism*. Here, we will give a briefer summary of the classical liberal view.

NEGATIVE NATURAL RIGHTS

Classical liberal positions argue that a respect for the equal and ultimate worth of the individual person as a source of value leads to the adoption of a "negative rights" approach to morality. Negative rights are "natural rights" in that all persons have the rights discussed, simply by virtue of being persons.[4]

The most articulate proponent of classical liberal principles is Isaiah Berlin. In his famous lecture, "Two Concepts of Liberty," he distinguished between negative and positive liberty:

> Negative liberty was the core of a properly liberal political creed, leaving individuals to do what they want, provided their actions do not interfere with the liberty of others. Positive liberty was the core of all emancipatory theories of politics. (Berlin, quoted in Ignatieff 1998, 226)

Berlin believed that the idea of positive liberty was very dangerous and could lead to many forms of oppression: "[A]ll such doctrines wish to use political power to free human beings to realize some hidden, blocked or repressed potential." The ultimate example was Soviet communism. He was completely opposed to this collectivist conception of liberalism. Our position is to maintain the distinction but to soften the line between negative and positive liberty.

Berlin did not attempt to directly link the concept of negative liberty to the political and economic institutions of contemporary capitalist societies. This linkage is one that Robert Nozick (1974)[5] has most forcefully argued.

A Nozickian negative-rights approach begins with a basic-rights principle something like the following: "Each individual person has the right to freely act in any way he or she chooses, provided that choice recognizes the same right for every other person."[6] This principle is intended to be an operationalization of Kant's dictum that each person should be treated "never simply as a means, but always at the same time as an end" (Kant 1956). Thus, the only limitation on rights should be the obligation to recognize that every other person has the same rights. This duty places [negative] side constraints on our behavior. These side constraints express the inviolability of each person: "[T]here is no justified sacrifice of some of us for others. There is no moral balancing act. . . ." (Nozick 1974, 33). In other words, no appeal to public good or the public interest can justify violating the rights of any individual. The core idea is that each of us leads separate lives. We want more than just experiences and emotions; we want to do things within the context of a conception of our life that has meaning to us.

Nozick's view[7] is thoroughly modernist. It is both absolutist (the core principle is inviolate: We have no right to interfere with another person's freedom, no matter what) and hierarchical (All other principles are derived from the core principle). However, even Nozick acknowledges the possibility that these side constraints may not be literally absolute; that is, there might conceivably be circumstances in which the abridgement of rights could be justified, where rights are not indefeasible. For example, the prospect of "catastrophic moral horror" might possibly justify the violation of rights (Nozick 1974, 30). He also acknowledges several other circumstances that might justify the abridgement of rights (discussed below), although he believes they will seldom apply. In contrast, our view is that these circumstances may be quite common in contemporary technological urban societies.

Property

The basic rights principle recognizes what Cohen (1986) calls self-ownership: the notion that "each person is the morally rightful owner of himself." Many contemporary liberals would accept the notion of self-ownership. What is more controversial is how it relates to the ownership of objects, particularly in the economic realm.

Suppose we begin with all persons owned by themselves, and all objects unowned. Nozick (1974, 150–53) argues that an acquisition is valid if and only if the object is acquired without violating anyone's negative rights. His rationale is that there is no reason to interfere with any acquisition unless it threatens someone's freedom (i.e., their self-ownership). So if you find gold in an unclaimed area and stake a claim to it, you become its owner; it is yours. From then on, taking it from you would violate your rights. Once owned, objects can be transferred to other persons (i.e., property can be sold), subject to the same proviso.

The difficulty here is that this principle cannot be taken literally; some interpretation is required. Strictly interpreted, any acquisition violates freedom.

Even acquiring a grain of sand violates another's right to acquire that same grain of sand. Many of these "violations" are trivial. But deciding between "significant" and "trivial" violations is not mechanical; it is an interpretative and contextual act.

The clearest case of a property right is an idea (intellectual property). Property rights in land are much less clear because land is a natural resource (which we will discuss later in this chapter).

The Minimal State

A state based on Nozick's principles would be characterized by the free operation of markets—in other words, a *laissez-faire* economic system. The free market is the economic expression of the classical liberal approach; free people freely contract to exchange goods and services in order to achieve their own goals. Under this approach, the only moral grounds for government intervention in such exchanges is the violation of negative rights; indeed, the very *raison d'être* of the state is to protect individual rights. This involves laws to preserve the key institutions of the market system:[8] individual freedom, protection of property rights (e.g., patents and land titles), prevention of fraud, enforcement of contracts, and the like (Harper 1987). This involves a system of laws, a judicial system to adjudicate conflicts, a police force to enforce the laws, and an army to defend against outside intrusion. According to some interpretations of these principles, the sole legitimate role for the state is to provide a set of institutions that protect negative rights. Nozick calls this a "minimal state"; Locke called it a "night watchman" state.[9]

Although a free-market system epitomizes a classical liberal approach, it may be endorsed for other reasons. For example, economic utilitarians often endorse it because it "maximimizes" (their definition) of well-being. If a market system is supported for economic utilitarian reasons, the notion of individual rights will be functional and reductionistic, focused on material measures (e.g., maximizing GNP). Others might support free markets for non-moral reasons—because they believe they will "win" in such a system. So "free-marketeers" are not necessarily classical liberals.

Civil Society

Although its advocates may not always recognize this, arguments for the minimal state presuppose a number of important factors. In order for its political, economic and legal institutions to function, any society needs certain prerequisites:

1. A healthy civil society: a web of voluntary cooperative associations of many types—political organizations, interest groups, churches, families, co-ops, and so on

2. Underlying implicit acceptance of certain moral values (respecting rights, eschewing exploitation)

3. Mutual trust that other members of society will generally follow the moral code, giving some predictability to relationships, and security (of person; of contract)

4. Compassion/care for those who are less well-off (economically, socially, politically)

In addition, Habermas (1984) would point out that there is an implicit assumption that there is no ideological disortion.

The more "minimal" the state, the more crucial are these elements of the "civil society" (a term that refers to the non-government, non-corporate part of the public domain). And normal legal, political, and economic institutions are not enough. The Latin American countries illustrate this very well. Many of them established political constitutions and legal systems based on those of the United States but lacked the supportive cultural background and vital civil society. None experienced the political stability or the economic growth enjoyed by the United States (Fukuyama 1999). The former Union of Soviet Socialist Republics (U.S.S.R.) provides an even more striking example. When there is little or no civil society, the market system alone can neither create nor maintain a functional (workable) society; the result is close to chaos.

Even in societies that have a history of liberal democracy, when the classical liberal position is interpreted (e.g., by "free enterprisers") as legitimizing unconstrained maximization of self-interest (including cheating, fraud, theft, or exploitation), society begins to break down. Some liberals believe that an interventionist state can compensate for this kind of social breakdown. However, many planners no longer share this confidence. Communitarians respond by arguing that society must promulgate certain "civic virtues."

NATURAL RESOURCES

A Lockean Proviso

The real crunch comes on the issue of the ownership of natural resources.[10] If one's acquisition affects other people, they should have a voice. Cohen (1986) identifies two ways of dealing with natural resources: common ownership and joint ownership.

Nozick advocates a form of *common ownership*. He mantains that any individual should be free to appropriate any natural resource (i.e., claim ownership to it) as long as this appropriation does not violate anyone else's right to be free (i.e., to be self-owned). Nozick claims that this condition is fulfilled as long as there is, in Locke's terms, "enough and as good" (Locke 1967 [1690]) left for others. If this "Lockean proviso" (as Nozick dubs it) is not met, then "a process giving rise to a permanent bequeathable property right in a previously unowned thing will not do so if the position of others no longer at liberty to *use* the thing is thereby *worsened*" (Nozick 1974, 178).[11]

Nozick acknowledges that titles to many natural resources do include "the historical shadow of the Lockean proviso" (Nozick 1974, 179) on their appropriation, but he believes that the operation of a free market system "will not actually run afoul of the Lockean proviso," and thus it "will not provide a significant opportunity for future state action" (1974, 182). His claim rests on his belief that the free market produces such an abundance of goods and opportunities that anyone whose Lockean proviso rights have been violated is more than compensated; that is, they are better off because of the existence of the free market system (1974, 177).

This claim seems to us to be the huge flaw in Nozick's argument. In order to justify a free market system, he has to define "better off" in economic utilitarian terms. Other definitions of well-being could lead to a different conclusion. Not everyone who has lost their autonomy would view themselves as adequately compensated simply because they are materially better off. This move takes away from the individual person the decision regarding what counts as "better off." Nozick's claim raises the suspicion that it is the *free market* or perhaps *private property,* rather than individual freedom, that is really paramount for him.

Cohen's (1986) argument against a Nozickian view is to advocate *joint ownership* of natural resources: Each person has an equal interest in each and every molecule of each and every natural resource. This gives each a complete veto over every other individual's economic acts. Cohen postulates that this would result in a system opposite to what Nozick advocates, an egalitarian one in which all wealth is equally distributed, since this is the only system that could command the 100 percent consensus required by joint ownership.[12]

A More Reasonable Proviso

We agree with Cohen that Nozick's Lockean proviso is too weak in that it permits acquisitions of natural resources that destroy options for others, thus (in our view) violating their rights.[13] However, joint ownership seems an unreasonable constraint on individuals—one that would violate their rights by prohibiting actions that really do not seriously infringe on anyone else's rights. We suggested (Harper and Stein 1995a) that an entitlement to a natural resource is contingent on that resource not being scarce (i.e., having a market value).[14] When a resource becomes scarce, ownership of it starts to become "common." The claims of owners of that natural resource become limited, perhaps ultimately extinguished altogether. In other words, property rights are relative to situation—they are contingent on "as good and enough left over," and these rights may change over time with the circumstances. Thus, we argue that they are never absolute or indefeasible. However, classical liberals and libertarians have not generally acknowledged any such limitation on ownership of natural resource property.

If the natural resource has no value added[15] by human endeavor (e.g., uncleared pasture land), the government may simply take some of it away from existing owners and give it to others. If division of the resource among everyone who values it would result in units too small to be useful (e.g., wilderness), the government may legitimately hold enough of it in common that it is no longer scarce. A farsighted government might reserve some of a natural resource in common before it actually becomes scarce (e.g., future urban open space or roads).

However, in many situations, the owner will have added significant value to the natural resource (e.g., cleared and cultivated land). Here, the only fair and feasible approach may be to collect a royalty on the natural resource component and redistribute it to all persons as reimbursement for their common ownership. Other natural resources may have no value without the application of human effort, ingenuity, and risk taking (e.g., petroleum or minerals). This could be recognized by a government auction (as agent for the common owners) of the right to explore for the natural resource, subject to a royalty when the resource is actually extracted.[16]

Limited Positive Rights

The existence of other persons, and of society in general, may also limit the individual's ability to pursue their goals. Nozick's device for applying the "Lockean proviso" to this situation is a hypothetical "state of nature." It is assumed that any person in a "state of nature" (i.e., with no other persons nearby, and thus unconstrained use of natural resources) could obtain adequate food, clothing, and shelter. Thus, if the social, political, and economic institutions of a society, or its technical complexity, render any person unable to obtain adequate food, clothing, and shelter, they should be compensated so that they can obtain same.

So we argue that even a classical liberal (negative-rights) approach should recognize certain limited positive rights. The nature of such positive rights is contingent on the particular society and environment. For example, in a complex technological society, quite a bit of education may be required; in a cold climate, shelter is necessary for survival. Exactly what baseline level is "adequate" will always be controversial. Nozick believes that the baseline would be so low that it would seldom be relevant to society with private appropriation (Nozick 1974, 181). However, we would interpret this proviso as justifying some redistribution of economic resources to provide a minimum living standard in most contemporary societies.

THE REGULATION OF NEGATIVE EXTERNALITIES

Some of the most significant urban planning implications of a classical liberal approach arise from its application to negative externalities. An externality is the unintended side effect of any action on a person (or persons) not directly involved in an original action. These effects may be on the persons themselves, on their holdings, or on unowned things (natural resources).[17]

Although the justification for regulating the effects of externalities is usually couched in utilitarian terms, the concept of externality can be intimately linked to notions of individual rights. As a general principle, a classical liberal position should recognize that each person has a right not to suffer from significant negative externalities. This flows directly from the basic-rights principle. Negative externalities are a direct violation of the right to pursue one's goals without [unjustified] interference—goals such as health, movement, privacy, material comforts, and the like. Negative externalities decrease real, noncreated options for the individual.

The tricky part of implementing a principle like this is that it requires some criterion for eliminating immaterial complaints. A classical liberal might view as "significant" (and potentially subject to regulation) any effects that a reasonable person would regard as important enough to take action to avoid or mitigate.[18]

It should be noted that the right not to suffer from negative externalities, unless it is justifiably overridden, implies the sufferer has a *veto* over the infliction of the externality. In some instances, this could effectively be a veto over the externality-generating activity itself! A homeowner who would suffer significant negative externalities from the construction of a new rapid transit line, a freeway, or an apartment building would be able to veto these activities. Of course, those who favored the activity could compensate (or buy out) the homeowner, but they could not force the person to accept compensation. Here again, not every loss can be compensated by an increase in material well-being.[19]

There are many urban issues to which the notion of negative externality is relevant, including land use; air, water and noise pollution; sunlight access; and transportation. The attempt to apply a negative-rights principle to complex urban problems results in many situations where *prima facie* rights are in conflict. In order to adjudicate, subsidiary principles are required, ones that make explicit some of the notions implicit in a negative-rights approach.

These might involve appeals to a hierarchy of rights, reciprocity of effects, precedence in time, and even comparison of relative harm (Harper and Stein 1995a).

Although there would be a legislative framework, the public decision-making mechanism would also have to involve judicial or quasi-judicial bodies that would evaluate an objection to a proposed action (e.g., a building or a rapid transit line) by applying each principle in turn until one was found that gave clear grounds for either permitting or prohibiting an activity. While classical liberal/negative-rights/libertarian principles are usually put forward in a modernist vein as absolute, in practice the exact nature of each practical principle would have to be the subject of political and legal debate. The priority order in which the principles should be applied would also have to be debated, as this would be key to the outcome in many conflicts. A pragmatic process such as Wide Reflective Equilibrium (chapter 6) would be essential in seeking consensus as to what reasonable persons should be expected to tolerate in an urban environment. So the political decision-making mechanism would be much more important than it might appear.

With regard to the means used to implement these principles, many of the considerations discussed by economic utilitarians will be relevant because a government carrying out justifiable interventions has an obligation to do so in an efficient way. In situations where the transaction costs of private agreements are low (i.e., a small number of inflictors and sufferers), it may be sufficient to clearly define personal and property rights, and then to provide a judicial (or quasi-judicial) process to adjudicate disputes (Bish and Nourse 1975, 111–16).[20] However, in the many urban situations where the number of sufferers (or inflictors) is large, transaction costs become so high that private negotiations and court actions would likely be inadequate. Although the possibility of group (class action) suits (Nozick 1974, 80) would help, direct government regulation seems unavoidable.

URBAN PLANNING

We have already mentioned some planning implications of this approach for resource conservation, wealth redistribution, and pollution control. While these concerns do have local relevance, it is the application of the principles regarding negative externalities to zoning and to transportation that has the most direct consequences for urban planning and urban form.

Historically, the primary urban planning measure advocated by the classical liberal approach has been zoning (or more broadly, controls on built form and development). In the United States, the protection of property rights from adjacent nuisance uses was the rationale for early zoning ordinances.

We would argue that these classical liberal principles, taken seriously and applied to urban planning, would tend to be very conserving of the existing physical form of the city. Once an urban area was developed, it would be very difficult to change land uses (e.g., from residential to commercial, or from low-density residential to higher density), or to construct major transportation "improvements," such as urban highways or rapid transit lines. This is because such changes would seem to require the unlikely event of *unanimous* consent of all affected parties.[21] Alternatively, a rights-based argument might be developed for determining when a holdout was being "unreasonable."

Conversely, these principles could be very permissive with regard to new development: Developers would have a great deal of freedom internally (e.g., with regard to density, layout, circulation, and the like) although they would be limited by negative-externality effects outside their own developments (such as "downstream" transportation and utility impacts) and by requirements to reserve land for future transportation and other public uses (Harper 1987). Of course, the more macro-level impacts of new development (e.g., air pollution in a river valley) could lead to restrictions on population, density, or usage, or even the outright prohibition of development.

Our interpretation of a classical liberal approach to planning bears some obvious resemblances to current North American planning practices. Some aspects of current practice do evidence a great deal of respect for individual rights (for example, preservation of residential areas and attempts to control pollution). In general, the classical liberal stance is most clearly reflected in zoning practices. However, many other aspects of contemporary North American practice, such as transportation improvements and urban redevelopment, seem utilitarian-based. Still other aspects (e.g., inner-city renewal/community economic development efforts) reflect more of a Rawlsian moral perspective (see chapter 6).

If North America had been developed according to strictly classical liberal principles,[22] the difficulties in redeveloping built-up areas would likely have resulted in smaller cities, with employment decentralized to the edges and further development occurring along radial axes formed by major highways out of the city (or any other transportation corridors that had been reserved as the city developed). The shape of the city would then be greatly dependent on how farsighted public authorities had been in reserving land for future anticipated uses.

One interesting divergence is that the classical liberal approach (as we have interpreted it) probably would be less respectful of the "sanctity" of private property rights in land than current North American institutions. It is ironic that the ownership of land is not a clear-cut case of a negative right to private property; in fact (in our view), it may be quite difficult to justify without making an appeal to utilitarian considerations. The Lockean proviso (as we interpret it) is likely to restrict the ownership of agricultural land and to justify the conservation of natural resources, including agricultural land (which could involve limiting urban expansion). The principles outlined are unlikely to limit the ownership of urban land because its scarcity arises primarily from its location relative to other urban activities rather than from any natural attribute. (An economist would say that the value of urban land is a positive externality of urban agglomeration.) However, these principles would not permit the unlimited development that might be expected from a "libertarian" perspective. The right to change land use (or intensity of use) could be quite restricted due to respect for the rights of other persons.

CONCLUSION

The classical liberal emphasis on equality of opportunity, impartiality of treatment, and the negative rights of individuals points to a relatively minimalist role for the state, and thus a somewhat limited role for planning. Zoning is the most obvious urban planning implication. Historically, this has been the influence of classical liberalism, although contemporary advocates (particularly libertarians) are still often "anti-planning."

However, contemporary recognition of certain problems (such as present and potential natural resource scarcity as populations increase, and the problems arising from negative externalities as more of us live in close proximity to each other) could justify a much more substantial regulatory role for public planning. Thus, under contemporary circumstances, we would argue that even a classical liberal approach should be more interventionist, and less "anti-planning," than is often supposed.

6
—

A Critical Liberal Perspective

CONTEMPORARY LIBERALISM

In chapter 1, we outlined the essential elements of the liberal perspective, and in chapter 5, we presented the modernist (classical liberal/libertarian) incarnation of this perspective. We also indicated some of the key differences between the classical approach and the contemporary liberal approaches upon which critical liberalism is based. Several considerations move contemporary liberals to go beyond the classical liberal position toward one advocating additional (more interventionist) roles for government.

Autonomy

The first concern is a substantive one relating to autonomy and equality of condition. Although contemporary liberals share the classical liberals' concern for impartiality and equality, they argue that equality of opportunity is insufficient to guarantee autonomy—that the formal notion of freedom fails to reflect a true valuing of the *autonomous* individual. An individual cannot lead a meaningful life, a life worth living, without access to some level of resources (Nielsen 1981). As Forester argues, "[I]nstitutional pressures work through the medium of power and money, bureaucratization, and commodification to preempt and encroach upon autonomous or even tradition-appropriating social action" (Forester 1993a, 4). To the contemporary liberal, the principle of not interfering with individual freedom changes to not interfering with the individual's ability to live a reasonable, meaningful life, and even to taking positive actions to ensure this ability.

This emphasis on the importance of being able to lead a life worth living moves the critical liberal to advocate significant government intervention to correct oppressive inequalities of income, wealth, risk bearing, or power, and to create a social framework that offsets certain conditions and attributes (seen as arbitrary from a moral point of view) affecting the possibility of autonomy. This intervention may include some redistribution of income or wealth, risk bearing, or power that a classical liberal would oppose as violating rights to freedom but that contemporary liberals believe can greatly enhance the autonomy of the disadvantaged without violating the autonomy of the better-off. In addition to the traditional negative rights (freedom of the person, speech, assembly, movement, religion, and the like), the critical liberal adds some positive rights to education, social services, health care, housing, and some level of minimum income. These positive rights lead to additional planning roles beyond those advocated by classical liberalism.

To the Nozickian critic of such interventions, we pointed out in the last chapter that a literal reading of the negative-rights principle would prohibit *any* appropriation of natural resources, since any appropriation interferes to some degree with someone's freedom. If we cannot interpret the principle literally, then we need to add a *normative* account of when interference with freedom is justified—for example, when no one is worse off, when no one's ability to lead a life worth living is impaired, or when no one's autonomy is impaired.

Institutions and Procedures

The second concern is procedural. For contemporary liberals, many of the values outlined in chapter 1 lead to an emphasis on procedural justice—a focus on the design of legal and political institutions and procedures, in addition to substantive conditions or outcomes. The more pluralistic the society, the more diverse the differing conceptions of the good life and the more important the procedural aspects of its social institutions. This concern leads to a focus on the provision of an institutional framework or structure (political, legal, economic) that satisfies a procedural concern for full, free, noncoerced, undistorted communication and reason in democratic public decision making. It is exemplified in Rawls's (1993) "political liberalism," which attempts to accommodate differences (and avoid conflicts) over both metaphysical issues and differing substantive definitions of the good life.

Ideological Distortion

Another procedural concern is ideological distortion. Classical liberal arguments assume that individuals are capable of informed, rational, noncoerced choice. As we will see, Habermas argues that the distorting ideology[1] of scientism prevents us from reaching self-knowledge because all our communication is systematically distorted. Acceptance of this ideology leads to oppression of the individual because it makes effective critique of oppressive institutions difficult. Acknowledging the possibility of ideological distortions complicates the practice of planning. As planners, we can no longer uncritically accept the goals that individuals express politically. The individual requires a critical awareness of the nature of our social institutions; this may lead to a revision of the individual's goals.

Of course, a belief that someone suffers from ideological distortion gives us no right to impose anything on them. (This is the implication that Isaiah Berlin [Ignatieff 1998] feared.) Rather, those who recognize ideological distortion have a moral obligation to persuade (through reasonable argument) those who suffer from the distortion that they should seek emancipation. This introduces new educative roles for planners.

Intellectual Roots

The normative "liberal" basis for our approach is drawn from the "political liberalism" articulated in the work of contemporary philosopher John Rawls (1971; 1985; 1987; 1993; 2001). His normative ethical theory is an unusually comprehensive one: It offers both a *procedure* for arriving at the ethical principles that should govern a society and the *substantive* principles of justice that (he maintains) would arise out of such a procedure. He argues that his procedure and his principles best embody the moral ideals of liberty and equality for constitutional liberal democracy, giving fair terms of social cooperation between free and equal persons. His "political liberalism" is well-suited to our pragmatic emphasis in that it offers an objective justification for public planning that (1) does not require modernist foundationalism, and (2) fits a liberal democratic context (i.e., it is based on the liberal values we espouse, which are widely shared within Western democracies. In our view, Rawls was probably the most significant political philosopher in the second half of the twentieth century; he is undoubtedly the most relevant to public planning.

Our second source is Walzer, a noted communitarian philosopher who is not generally regarded as a liberal. We view him as a liberal in the sense that his idea of critical interpretation allows for an effective social critique that comes from "inside" society. Our third source is Habermas. Although he has had an enormous influence on planning as the inspiration for "communicative planning" (Forester 1989), he might also seem to be an unlikely source of critical liberalism for two reasons: (1) He is very critical of how liberal institutions function, and (2) he views himself as a modernist, trying to "save the modernist project." We consider him to be a liberal in the sense that he adheres to basic political liberal values. When we interpret him pragmatically, we find that his methods fit within the framework of Wide Reflective Equilibrium (WRE)—he is philosophically conservative in the sense of accepting critical dialogue within our culture. And the "modernism" he defends is the liberal humanistic aspect that we want to retain.

POLITICAL LIBERALISM

Rawls's Ethical Theory

Rawls addresses the contemporary Western liberal democratic society. He recognizes that we can't have a modernistic foundational, hierarchical, deductive basis for our system of social institutions. We need an account that incorporates our moral intuitions (that not only consequences, but also freedom, equality, and justice are important), our existing institutions, our traditions of democracy and pluralism, our differing conceptions of the good life, and an account that can take into consideration our contemporary circumstances (energy, pollution, resource consumption and availability). Rather than develop a universal account, Rawls focuses on pluralistic Western liberal democratic societies with late capitalist economies. He wants to develop the conditions for a decent, legitimate, moral society that works in practice here and now.

Hampton (1989, 795–96) summarizes five conditions assumed by Rawls:

1. There is a pluralism of philosophical and religious beliefs.

2. This pluralism is permanent (the divergence of views is likely to persist).

3. This pluralism can be overcome only by oppressive use of state power.

4. Resources are moderately scarce.

5. Desired gains are achievable only through a well-organized and stable system of fair cooperation between free and equal persons.[2]

These conditions are ones that generally hold in Western liberal democracies.

Rawls recognizes that a pluralistic liberal society (e.g., Canada, the United States, or Great Britain) needs to accommodate very diverse viewpoints and values. He traces our society's ability to accommodate diverse viewpoints to the Western European experience with clashes between different substantive religious and moral conceptions of the "good" (which Rawls calls "thick theories of the good"). A conception of society was developed that tolerated different thick theories of good within a framework of basic democratic political values, many of which are procedural. He refers to this conception of society as a "thin theory of the good." But he argues that even a pluralistic liberal democratic society like ours requires an *overlapping consensus* that supports such democratic political values as tolerance.

Private and Public Realms

To develop a consensus regarding basic social institutions, it is important to put aside or bracket certain controversial (though not unimportant) issues. Among these are differences between various philosophical and religious perspectives. For example, deep ecology (Naess 1973) is a metaphysical philosophical position that differs profoundly from other philosophical and religious positions. The reason why some controversial issues must be put aside is that they are unresolvable—there is no universal forum (with objective criteria that all would accept) where these debates could be resolved. These controversial issues are placed in the private realm. The *private* realm is defined as "that which one does as an individual pursuing what one takes to be the truth, such as theology, moral theorizing, metaphysics" (Hampton 1989, 806). In the *public* realm, we are concerned not with whether an idea is true or false (arriving at the "truth of the matter") but with whether the idea can command consensual support as providing a reasonable basis for public policy in a democratic society.

Another way in which public and private realms can be distinguished pragmatically is their very different aims. In the private realm our aim is to develop a conception that guides our lives, giving us an account (in Rorty's terms) of how things "hang together, in the widest sense," and a framework for structuring and guiding our lives, one that gives meaning to them. For example, Kolb argues that the role of the "Socratic path" in our culture has been to give "unity and coherence to our cognitive struggles. . . . Our cognitive life becomes a whole when the story gives it direction" (Kolb 1992, 14–15). Religious and philosophical perspectives provide such frameworks. These perspectives can play a valuable role in providing life-guiding frameworks, giving meaning and coherence to the lives of those who accept them. In addition, shared private conceptions help members of a subculture make sense of their collective experience (Galloway-Cosijn 1999). As Winch (1964, 105) points out, culture-based beliefs and practices give participants a "sense of the significance of human life."

But many of these private conceptions are both reasonable and irreconcilable. Thus, for Rawls, a democratic society

> is not and can not be a community, where by community I mean a body of persons united in affirming the same comprehensive . . . doctrine. The fact of reasonable pluralism makes this impossible. This is the fact of profound and irreconcilable differences in citizens' reasonable comprehensive religious and philosophical conceptions of the world. (Rawls 2001, 3)

A pluralistic democratic society has to devise public political structures that accommodate this fact.

In contrast, our aim in the public realm is to develop a basis of communal existence. In a pluralistic society, there are many different private conceptions of the good life ("thick" theories of good) and many different private philosophies. What is required is a public conception of society (a "thin" theory of good) that is as wide as possible, one that accommodates as many different (and conflicting) private views of the meaning of life as possible.[3]

In practice, the boundary between public and private realms will be complex and contested. Different thick theories may have very different views as to what is legitimately private (Mandelbaum 2000). Advocates of thick theories will tend to urge that more of their private convictions be addressed in the public realm. For example, some will believe that matters like abortion are private; others, that it should be a public concern. The boundaries will be the subject of ongoing debate. The Rawlsian test for inclusion is that a view command support by an overlapping consensus. But the degree of support that constitutes a "consensus" may also be controversial.

The Importance of the Overlapping Consensus

Each of the constituent cultures/communities of a pluralistic society must be able to accept the values of the political liberal "thin theory of the good"— impartiality, fairness, individual rights, democratic processes, and tolerance for multiple thick theories of the good. People coming from cultures that reject any of these values will have to adapt, accepting these values in the public realm in order to be part of a pluralistic society.

Unless this basic overlapping consensus (with regard to a thin theory of the good) is shared by [nearly] all individuals and groups in society, a pluralist Rawlsian approach won't work. We need substantial common ground in order to debate our differences. A good example of a society that lacks this tradition of shared democratic values is the former U.S.S.R. The danger of a multicultural society is that this common ground will be lost. Liberal democratic societies need to actively promulgate the essential liberal moral values in the educational and political realm.

Rawls's aim is to develop a conception of justice that is *independent* of all the different comprehensive doctrines but that can be seen as *fair* by all of them. He frames the fundamental question as:

> [W]hat is the most acceptable political conception of justice for specifying the fair terms of cooperation between citizens regarded as free and equal, and as both reasonable and rational, and . . . as normal and fully cooperating members of society over a complete life, from one generation to the next? (Rawls 2001, 8)

Citizens as free and equal participants must have two moral powers: (1) the capacity for a sense of justice, and (2) the ability to formulate a conception of the good.

Political, Not Metaphysical

Rawls intends political liberalism to be "freestanding," not in the sense of being universal but in that it is independent of all of the metaphysical positions held as comprehensive doctrines within a pluralistic society. It is not *deduced from* any of the comprehensive doctrines, nor is it a *compromise between* their views, nor between the self-interests of individuals, groups, or associations within the society. Rather, it appeals to all free and equal, reasonable and rational citizens, *whatever* their comprehensive doctrine.

Here is where the distinction between private and public realms is important. While it is possible to adopt a liberal perspective (like Kant's) as one's private philosophical worldview, this is just one of many competing thick theories of the good in a pluralistic society. One does not have to hold "metaphysical liberalism" as his or her own comprehensive doctrine in order (for pragmatic reasons) to accept "political liberalism" as the basis of a public political consensus.

Rationality and Reasonableness

Rawls distinguishes between rationality and reasonableness. He uses "rational" in the way economists do: It refers to choosing the best means to maximize one's own (long-term) self-interest. (In Habermas's terms, this is "instrumental rationality.") Rawls uses "reasonable" to mean an acceptance of fair terms of cooperation and a commitment to abide by them, provided everyone else is also similarly committed. This gives "reasonable" a normative content within a specific context. Thus, Rawls characterizes "reasonable" as "in-between the altruism of impartiality and the narrow self-interest of rationality" (Rawls 1993, 50) assumed by mutual-advantage theory (see chapter 9).

This aspect of Rawls has very important implications for planning. The appeal to reasonableness creates the potential for resolving disputes in ways going beyond a mere *modus vivendi* or compromise of interests, because

> [R]easonable persons are ready to propose certain principles . . . as well as to comply with these principles even at the expense of their own interests as circumstances require when others are moved to do likewise. (Rawls 2001, 191)

Being able to appeal to ideals of fairness rather than just self-interest enormously widens the scope and changes the nature of possible solutions in most situations.

Public Justification

Rawls defines a well-ordered society as one that is "regulated by a *public* conception of justice" (2001, 8). This requires that all citizens mutually accept the *same* public conception of justice (and thus the same principles of justice); that the basic structure of social institutions (and the way they work as a system of cooperation) is publicly known to satisfy these principles; and that citizens understand and are able to apply these principles. Thus, "In a well-ordered society . . . the public conception of justice provides a mutually recognized point of view from which citizens can adjudicate their claims of political right. . . ." (Rawls 2001, 9).

Out of his political conception of justice, Rawls then develops principles, which in turn are used to devise the basic structure of social (political, legal, economic) institutions. These principles "establish a shared basis for citizens to justify to one another their political judgments"(2001, 27). Thus, political debates are conducted within a shared set of premises. In the process of *public justification* citizens attempt to justify their political judgments to other citizens by *public reason*, by "appealing to beliefs, grounds and political values it is reasonable for other citizens to acknowledge" (2001, 27). Here again, we see the key role played by "reasonableness."

Deriving Principles of Justice

Rawls's method for deriving the principles of justice that reflect our overlapping liberal consensus is to devise a kind of thought experiment. The principles should be the ones that would be chosen by free and equal, reasonable and rational persons under a "veil of ignorance."

> The principles of justice are chosen behind a *veil of ignorance*. This ensures that no one is advantaged or disadvantaged in the choice of principles by the outcome of natural chance or the contingency of social circumstances. Since all are similarly situated and no one is able to design principles to favor his particular condition, the principles of justice are the result of a fair agreement or bargain. (Rawls 1971, 12)

The "veil of ignorance" refers to conditions under which hypothetical negotiators of a social contract did not know anything about themselves that would distort their judgments away from fairness:

> In the original position, the parties are not allowed to know the social positions or the particular comprehensive doctrines of the persons they represent [nor their] race and ethnic group, sex, or various native endowments such as strength and intelligence. (Rawls 2001, 15)

They should not know anything about their own attributes (race, gender, disabilities), capacities, or assets, or about their own position in society; they should know only what is relevant to making fair judgments about the principles of justice.

Expressed another way, when we make normative judgments about the suitability of general social institutional arrangements, we should *put aside* what we know about our *own position*. The concept of these "rational contractors" is intended to give us a perspicuous representation of our ordinary moral intuitions about society and governance, as explicated by Rawls and generated by him through a process of Wide Reflective Equilibrium (discussed below).

The Evolution of Rawls's Thought

Since the publication of *A Theory of Justice* (1971), Rawls has been revising or clarifying his ideas in response to a wide variety of criticisms. His work has been criticized on numerous grounds: It is universalistic and foundational; it is rationalistic; it presupposes American values, or metaphysical liberalism, or the Kantian person; its arguments are circular; it allows injustices within families; its principles are too abstract to be applied; it allows the wealthy to gain unequal power; it assumes risk aversion; its "thin theory of the good" is too thin to hold a society together; and so on. Over the years, he has responded to many of his critics in various papers (Rawls 1980; 1985; 1987). Many of these responses were included in a rearticulation of his position in *Political Liberalism* (1993). Finally, all of these responses were brought together in a coherent framework, as a definitive "last word" and restatement of his position in *Justice as Fairness: A Restatement* (2001).[4] We will briefly recapitulate some of these responses later in this chapter and others in chapter 9.

The most significant evolution was the movement in the basis of justification from the metaphysical to the political, from the foundational to the nonfoundational; from the rational to the pragmatic (although Rawls does not use this term). Related to this move, his elaborations move from the abstract to the concrete, from the universal to the particular.

PROCEDURAL APPROACH:
WIDE REFLECTIVE EQUILIBRIUM

With the rejection of the analytical method of the RCPM, do the new dialogical or communicative approaches to planning have any general procedure or method? Since the focus is on communicative understanding and critical awareness rather than analysis, an appropriate method would be one that helps to structure (and stimulate) dialogue and debate.[5] From a pragmatic perspective, we want to start from where we are; take into account the beliefs, intuitions, and principles that we now hold; and move toward an overlapping consensus. We believe that Rawls's reflective process fills this need.

Reflective Equilibrium

A fundamental part of Rawls's procedural ethical theory is the notion of Wide Reflective Equilibrium (WRE). The notion of "Reflective Equilibrium"[6] draws on the work of Goodman (1965) and Daniels (1985; 1996), as well as Rawls (1971; 1993). They have attempted to describe how we might objectively devise the structure or rules for particular types of situations, independent of our own interests or position in society, within a particular set of value commitments. Reflective equilibrium is "a coherentist method of explanation and justification used in ethical theory, social and political philosophy, philosophy of science, philosophy of mind and epistemology" (Nielsen 1996, 13). The idea is to get our knowledge, "beliefs and practices" into the "most coherent pattern we can for the time manage"(ibid., 14). A WRE process is coherentist, contextual, and dialogical. A crucial aspect of the WRE process is its fluidity—its ability to alter positions, to widen the consensual equilibrium by incorporating new ideas, theories, and information. In many respects, it is similar to the consensus-building planning processes advocated by Innes (1996) and Healey (1997).

Internal and External Perspectives

It is useful to distinguish between two kinds of reflective theoretical equilibria—wide and narrow. This distinction is related to another useful contrast between two perspectives that a planner may adopt—external and internal. An *internal* perspective is the standpoint of the participants in a culture, an activity, or language game. It relies on concepts internal to the activity: "[T]he use of the words in a language game cannot be described without using concepts which are related to the concepts employed *in* the game" (Putnam 1994, 269). An internal perspective attempts to give us an appreciation of the meaning of social actions to the participants. To adopt an internal perspective, a planner must participate in the culture and relate to other participants as subjects rather than objects (Winch 1958; Stein 1973).

An *external* perspective is the standpoint of an external observer who is not involved in the culture, activity, or language game. Modernist external approaches generally involve the application of a general explanatory theory and its concepts (perhaps a "meta-narrative") of anthropological function or political or economic structure. To adopt an external perspective, the planner becomes an observer and relates to the participants as objects of observation. Thus, an external perspective allows one to stand apart from society's institutions in order to critically evaluate them. Western societies, which came out of the Enlightenment, place a high value on the critical and analytic and have incorporated them into the culture. For these societies, the internal/external distinction becomes blurred.

Generally, the planner comes with a perspective that is external. This is obvious when dealing with a different culture; it is more subtle when dealing with a community within one's culture. We have argued that a crucial role for the planner is to bring an external perspective into the community, but this perspective will be helpful *only* if the planner also understands the internal perspective of the participants in that community well enough to integrate and apply the external knowledge into the internal framework (Stein and Harper 2000).

Narrow and Wide Reflection

If we seek a reflective equilibrium from an internal perspective, we arrive at a *Narrow* Reflective Equilibrium (NRE), which focuses on the coherence of considered situational judgments and normative principles held within a particular community or culture. This perspective does not bring in [external] background theories and principles. Descriptively, it does not include theoretical accounts of the structure and functioning of society. Normatively, it does not bring in normative ethical theory.

In contrast, a *Wide* Reflective Equilibrium (WRE) widens the NRE by invoking an external perspective that includes background *theories* and principles. These other elements add a critical capacity. Thus, in the moral realm, a WRE has been defined as a coherent set of beliefs that includes the following components:

1. A set of considered moral judgments (that may be intuitive)

2. A set of normative substantive and/or procedural ethical principles

3. A set of background theories that show that the set of normative ethical principles are more acceptable than alternative normative ethical principles. These background *theories* may be both

    a. Normative—incorporating ethical notions (different from those in the normative ethical principles held [e.g., fairness, impartiality]), and

    b. Empirical theories that seek to explain and predict observed behavior

(Daniels 1985)

The crucial difference between wide and narrow equilibria is that a WRE appeals to abstract theoretical notions whereas an NRE does not. Invoking theory brings in a nonlocal, objective, general but still dynamic view. It provides not only a tool for understanding but also a basis for critique. Applied to morality, a primary purpose of WRE is to critique (e.g., to identify ideological distortion).

A WRE process[7] involves seeking *coherence* among the above elements, whether they are internal to a culture or external. It includes reflecting on one's own judgments and intuitions, ethical principles and theories, and background theories, critiquing and justifying intuitions by reference to principles; generating and critiquing principles that reflect intuitions; and using background theories to justify both judgments and principles. All of the interlocking elements fit together as an organic whole. As Goodman eloquently argues when applying reflective equilibrium to the field of logic:

> [R]ules and particular inferences alike are justified by being brought into agreement with each other. *A rule is amended if it yields an inference we are unwilling to accept; an inference is rejected if it violates a rule we are unwilling to amend.* The process of justification is the delicate one of making mutual adjustments between rules and acceptance of inferences, and in the agreement achieved lies the only justification needed for either. (Goodman 1965, 64) [emphasis added]

The goal is a reflective equilibrium wherein all of these factors are coherent and consistent, giving as much sense as possible to our shared life. WRE does not merely reflect/discover existing moral values—it offers a way to interpret them critically. One of the crucial features of this approach lies in the idea that progress and legitimation of judgments depend on fair procedures and do not require an appeal to an absolute outside foundation that is independent of our social framework. It therefore avoids the foundationalist pitfall of modernism.

Notwithstanding our best efforts to dialogue and maximize the scope of our overlapping consensus, major substantive differences will remain in pluralistic societies. Thus, political liberalism stresses *tolerance* with regard to such differences. There is no idea of *imposing* consensus, glossing over disagreements, or muffling bothersome voices. Mandelbaum's strategy of agreeing to disagree comes in at this point (Mandelbaum 1991, 212). Whereas tolerance is a moral *virtue* to philosophical liberalism (i.e., liberalism held as a private philosophy), it is a *necessity* to political liberalism.

While Rawls uses it for developing political principles of justice and basic social institutions, WRE is strikingly similar to the process advocated by Davidson (1985) for dealing with conceptual differences. In addition, Putnam applies WRE to all forms of discourse (not just that of ethics). The pragmatic awareness of fallibility supports a procedural approach that is both incremental and democratic:

> [W]e have no choice but to try to reform and improve the ways of life we already have, as well as to try new ones if we believe them to be better; but these trials must not be at the expense of the right of others to make their trials. (Putnam 1994, 194)

This democratic ideal is linked to a general criterion for knowledge: "A truth worthy of the name has to be world-guided and subject to public discussion" (ibid.).

One note of caution is appropriate here. The general attitude of the [Western liberal] writers we have quoted, an attitude we largely share, is that WRE is progressive—a good thing. However, as we will argue later (chapter 13), there is a downside. Too much critical thinking can undermine tradition, and something of real value can be lost,[8] as communitarians point out.

The Planner's Professional Role

All professionals unavoidably bring some kind of theoretical framework to address any problem. A defining characteristic of a professional is that they have expertise not shared by the general public. A key element of this expertise is a general theoretical framework that they can use to help clients achieve desired futures and solve problems.[9] This is certainly the case with planners—even those who view themselves as social learners (transactive planners) (Friedmann 1987) or postmodernists (chapter 3). Unless they are a purely egalitarian participant (in which case they are not playing a professional role), the planner is invoking some sort of external theory and seeking a WRE.

This raises a general dilemma for any planner (or any other professional) today. Is it their role to offer expertise? If not, then what is their role? Are they professionals at all? If their theory better equips them to deal with problems, then is their external view superior (or more true) than the participants' internal view? We will look at this issue in chapter 13.

Examples of Reflective Equilibria

Some examples may help to understand the dynamics of how a WRE process moves from equilibrium through disequilibrium to new equilibrium.

An example of a position that is not in narrow equilibrium (i.e., there are inconsistencies between judgments) would be someone who is both pro-animal rights and pro-abortion. Here, normative ethical theory would help with an analysis of the nature of rights. In order to establish that an animal has rights and a fetus does not, it would have to be shown that a fetus lacks some property of animals that is morally relevant (to whatever theory of rights is being used); otherwise the two views are inconsistent and cannot be held in equilibrium.

Another example of an appeal to the notion of narrow equilibrium is found in some feminist arguments. Feminists hold that the "persons" for whom we plan are not neutral but are in fact "male." Their arguments appeal to our shared beliefs in the equal rights of *all* persons and maintain that standards have not been consistently applied. They seek to demonstrate to us that we have been unwittingly in disequilibrium and must change to regain equilibrium. Thus, this position[10] does not ask us to change our normative ethical theories but to apply them more consistently and vigorously. They have succeeded in persuading us to change our language; whether the underlying concepts have yet changed is still open to question.

In contrast, our moral views would have to change if we could find properties of animals that give us reason to include them as objects of moral concern, perhaps even as persons. For example, if dolphin language were translated, we would likely begin to treat dolphins as persons. This would be a case of expanding our beliefs on their periphery.

A position requiring a much more profound shift in all components of WRE is "deep ecology," which holds that the environment has inherent moral value (in and of itself) rather than solely instrumental value (due to its value to persons). Such a shift in perspective would involve a conversion, abandoning some of our very deeply held moral notions and their relation to our conception of persons. This would be an extremely radical change with very little link to current moral frameworks[11] (see chapter 12).

A good example of a shift that required changes to all components of a WRE is the shift from urban renewal to urban preservation. It involved not only a change in considered judgments and intuitions (from "Urban renewal is good" to "Preservation is good"), but also a switch from a utilitarian moral perspective to something more like a Rawlsian one, concerned with individual rights and with the well-being of the worst-off (i.e., existing residents of poor, inner-city communities). It also involved the abandonment of supporting normative theories (e.g., a positivistic physical determinism) and empirical (social science) theories, like the "trickle-down" theory of housing (which held that the best way to increase housing for the poor was to build new housing for the more affluent and then let their old housing "trickle down" to the poor), as well as a critical awareness of the unfairness of the actual distribution of costs and benefits of urban renewal. The degree of change required helps us understand why there was so much resistance to this shift.

We will discuss further how a planner can use a WRE process in chapter 8.

SUBSTANTIVE IMPLICATIONS OF
POLITICAL LIBERALISM

Substantive Principles

Substantive ethical theory advocates actual normative ethical principles and judgments. These principles are meant to be applied to judge the rightness or wrongness of specific social institutions, actions, plans, policies, and the like. As we have seen, procedural ethical theory is a level "above" substantive theory. It makes recommendations about the process that should be followed in deriving and justifying substantive ethical principles and arriving at ethical conclusions.

Substantively, we should recognize that both utilitarianism and negative-rights positions articulate important moral intuitions. However, each is incomplete as a moral theory: Neither encompasses all of our intuitions; we need to incorporate both. Rawls's theory is the most promising attempt to do this. We see his two principles of justice as offering an excellent initial starting point for substantive principles of any liberal democratic society.[12]

> 1. *Liberty*: "Each person has the same indefeasible claim to a fully adequate scheme of equal basic rights and liberties, which scheme is compatible with the same scheme of liberties for all." (Rawls 2001, 42)
>
> 2. *Equality*: "Social and economic inequalities are to satisfy two conditions: first, they are to be attached to offices and positions open to all under conditions of fair equality of opportunity, and second, they must be to the greatest benefit of the least-advantaged members of society (the difference principle)." (ibid.)
>
> 3. *Priority*: "The first principle is prior to the second; also, in the second principle, fair equality of opportunity is prior to the difference principle." (Rawls 2001, 43)

The first principle is similar to a Nozickian (1974) negative-natural-rights principle; the second includes consequentialist considerations, reflecting our intuition that outcomes also matter. The priority given to the first principle means that the basic rights and liberties are constitutionally fixed, off the agenda for political debate, beyond any utilitarian or consequentialist calculus. It ensures mutual recognition of perpetual equality for all, regardless of their comprehensive doctrine.

Rawls presents a number of arguments that these principles best satisfy the basic idea of justice as fairness and that they would be adopted by his rational contractors under a veil of ignorance, seeking to specify the fair terms of cooperation between citizens regarded as free and equal, reasonable and rational.

Concretizing the Principles

One of the key factors that moved Rawls from the abstract and theoretical toward the concrete and practical was Hart's (1973) criticism of Rawls's principles as indeterminate when applied. There were no practical procedures to get from principles to institutions to structures to laws, and so on. It was unclear which liberties would be considered *basic* (those essential liberties given priority in the first principle, which should have constitutional protection), and which goods considered *primary* goods (those to which all citizens are equally entitled).

Basic Liberties

In response to Hart's criticism, Rawls spells out the list of liberties that are basic and the way in which they should be determined. The criterion is that basic liberties are those necessary to guarantee equal protection of the full and informed exercise of the two moral powers requisite to citizens regarded as free and equal, reasonable and rational. Rawls's application of this criterion gives five basic liberties:

1. Political liberties and liberty of thought are necessary to the capacity for a sense of justice.

2. Liberty of conscience ensures the opportunity to exercise the capacity for a conception of the good.

3. Freedom of association does the same.

4. Liberty of the person (physical and psychological) is necessary to guarantee the other basic liberties just enumerated.

5. The rights and liberties covered by the rule of law do the same.

(Rawls 2001, 112–13)

All other liberties should be defined by legislation within the institutional structure. Their exercise may be limited by the basic liberties. For example, freedom of speech does not extend to advocating violence against other persons (which violates liberty of the person).

Primary Goods

Rawls also specifies the nature of the "primary goods" to which all are equally entitled. Again, these are developed in a way that is "free-standing"; they are not determined from any of the comprehensive doctrines. These are derived from the requirements of the normative political conception of persons as free and equal citizens (with the requisite moral powers, fully cooperating members of society), as well as the general facts and requirements of social life (Rawls 2001, 57). There are five categories:

1. The basic rights and liberties just discussed

2. Freedom of movement and free choice of occupation

3. Powers of offices and positions of authority and responsibility

4. Income and wealth necessary for personal autonomy

5. Social bases of self-respect

The two principles of justice are then used to assess various possible basic structures according to how they regulate citizens' shares of these primary goods.

Other Substantive Implications

In chapter 5, we discussed some of the substantive planning implications of a classical liberal approach. A contemporary critical liberal approach would share the areas of concern and would use similar tools to address them. However, both the problem definitions and the trial "solutions" would have to come out of a situation-specific WRE process, one that would bring Rawlsian principles into the equilibrium with our intuitions about rights and utility, and with the facts of our societal situation. While we would advocate these two principles as a reasonable starting point,[13] substantive principles should emerge and evolve from the sort of Rawlsian WRE process that we advocate. In chapter 8, we will look at some substantive implications of Rawls's principles for property rights, negative externalities, and natural resources.

CRITICAL INTERPRETATION

Walzer

Most communitarians believe that normative values both (1) arise out of the community and (2) are legitimized by the community's acceptance. In our terms, the result is an NRE. Our concern with this sort of communitarian view would be: Where does critique come in, and how does change happen? In contrast, Walzer allows for effective criticism, while warning that it cannot be too far "outside" the community (i.e., it cannot be too radical philosophically and morally).

Inside Critique

As already noted, a critical element is necessary for WRE. Very traditional societies don't go beyond an NRE; other societies focus more on external critique. However, there is no sharp line between internal and external, or between wide and narrow. Most societies are somewhere along these continua. Thus, most social institutions (and certainly our own) have embedded within them the *potential* for ethical critique. Walzer brilliantly makes this point with regard to Jean-Paul Sartre's opposition to the Algerian War. Though Sartre described himself as an enemy of French ideas, Walzer points out

[T]he principles he applied were well-known in France . . . the idea of self-determination . . . was already there, they had only . . . to extend its application to Algeria. (Walzer 1987, 59)

Thus, Sartre appealed to the ideals of the French revolution—liberty, equality, and fraternity. Effective social criticism must appeal to ethical positions already held (perhaps in an intuitive or nontheoretical form) within that moral culture. Otherwise, the critic can't give good reasons for change to that culture (i.e., the reasons—the arguments—will have no grounds).

Walzer argues that there is a middle ground between uncritical acceptance of the status quo and seeking to radically change (revolutionize) social institutions through what he calls "critical interpretation." The effective social critic must be "inside" the society, standing "a little to the side, but not outside: critical distance is measured in inches." The critic "is not a detached observer . . . not an enemy . . ." because they find a "warrant for critical engagement in the idealism . . . of the actually existing moral world" (Walzer 1987, 61). Few institutions are completely static; there is always disagreement over how they should be interpreted and applied. Learning to apply the concepts of the institution necessarily involves a critical element.

Changes in our social institutions emerge from a critical dialogue, usually in an incremental fashion. This dialogue requires a background of shared values and presuppositions about human nature and society. Walzer draws a parallel between changes in a society's public morality and Kuhn's (1962 [1970]) notion of a scientific revolution or paradigm shift (except that the social changes are generally much more gradual and less dramatic). In many ways this is exemplified by the process of change in law. Thus, most change occurs incrementally within a broader framework of sameness.

Effective Critique

It is important to recognize that even radical planning theories share important assumptions with the established social institutions that they are criticizing, and in this sense they are philosophically and methodologically conservative. (Even when they challenge our basic social institutions, they usually appeal to shared normative ethical theories.) Planning that is too radical (in a philosophical and methodological sense) will be ineffective, unable to communicate with and persuade other planners, politicians, and the public. If there is too radical a break and no (or too little) common ground between the position rejected and the position advocated, the dialogue and debate necessary for the elimination of ideological distortion (see next section) and for persuasion and consensus will be impossible. At best, one might produce something akin to a religious conversion[14] (see chapter 7). There must be some common framework that is shared in order for the planner's arguments to be persuasive. Thus, Krumholz justifies his equity planning as

> serving tradition by affirming what has been advocated consistently through-
> out history: that equity in the social, economic, and political relationships
> among people is a requisite condition for a just and lasting society.
> (Krumholz and Forester 1990, 50–51)

and quotes Plato, Jesus, Thomas Jefferson, and Franklin D. Roosevelt as supportive of "freedom, liberty and justice." This led Hoch to comment that

> [Y]ou advocated for a more politically inclusive system. You . . . pointed to
> the lack of fairness. . . . Your effort was therefore conservative instead of
> radical: restoring a fair balance, rather than inciting a revolution. (Hoch
> 1988)

Thus, the critical liberal planner must combine external and internal perspectives: "outside" the framework of conventional planning practice (in that they
are critiquing it), but remaining "inside" it (in the sense of sharing many of its
basic political liberal values). Both are necessary to effectively critique it and
to communicate this critique to other planners, politicians, and the public.

Of course, we must recognize that those who benefit from the existing
power structures use our institutions for their own ends, but this can be
fought within the liberal democratic paradigm. It is the domination that must
be opposed:

> Criticism does not require us to step back from society as a whole but only
> to step away from certain sorts of power relationships within society. It is
> not connection but authority and domination from which we must dis-
> tance ourselves. (Walzer 1987, 60)

Thus, Marx criticized capitalism using its own notion of equality (Walzer
1987, 43); that is, he argued the hypocrisy of the dominating elite. This is
what he meant by "capitalism carries the seeds of its own destruction." In
order to persuade people to accept domination or oppression, ideology must
appeal to ideas that have genuine moral force. This gives social criticism its
inside starting point (Walzer 1987, 41).

IDEOLOGICAL DISTORTION

Habermas and Critical Theory

Other contemporary liberals focus more on critique of society's institutions and their actual organizational functioning. Some liberal thinkers go
further than Rawls in arguing that another factor that interferes with autonomy is that of ideological distortion. Critical theorists like Habermas have
forcefully argued that individuals in our liberal democratic society suffer from
"ideological distortion"—they fail to recognize that their true interests are

not being served by the existing institutional structure. Thus, the goal of autonomy requires a critique of our contemporary liberal institutional structure. This is a theme popularized by Forester's (1989) "progressive planning."

Ideological Distortion

One of Habermas's contributions was discussed earlier: He greatly broadened the notion of rationality (chapters 1 and 2). In addition to instrumental rationality (which, at least in part, serves the human interest of controlling nature), Habermas postulates two additional forms of rationality. Communicative rationality serves the human interest of understanding within community; critical rationality serves the interest of emancipation from [unrecognized] oppression (Habermas 1984). As we have seen, this broadened conception of rationality is the inspiration for most of the planners who speak of "communicative action" (Forester 1989; Healey 1993; Innes 1995).

"Scientism" (Habermas 1971a) is the notion that all action, thought, and knowledge can be reduced to the "objective" scientific paradigm. It claims that the only valid form of knowledge is the instrumental (scientific/technical) kind; that is, an action is "rational" only if it is an efficient means to whatever ends have been chosen. Habermas views scientism as a reductionistic and distorting ideology. Ideology refers to ideas that function to maintain social relationships. People are led by ideology to believe things that get them to accept social arrangements that are not in their self-interest. The ideology of scientism prevents us from reaching self-knowledge and emancipation because all our communication is systematically distorted.

Acceptance of the scientistic ideology leads to oppression of the individual because it makes effective critique of oppressive institutions difficult (though not impossible). It is a mechanism for a hierarchical, authoritarian, power elite to maintain its control of society behind a veil of technocratic knowledge. As we have seen, this is exemplified by the organizational form of bureaucracy, which is explicitly based on the scientistic fallacy. It serves as a tool for controlling people as if they were objects (Schaar 1984), often by applying the RCPM to planning.

Acceptance of the possibility of ideological distortions has implications for planning. The goals that individuals express politically should not be accepted uncritically. The individual requires a critical awareness of the nature of our social institutions; this may lead to a revision of his or her goals. A crucial part of the planner's role, then, is educative "consciousness-raising": aiding people to critique their own values and goals, and focusing public attention on the implications of planning decisions, particularly injustices that inflict costs on the worst-off groups in society.

Consensus-seeking

Another important aspect of Habermas that qualifies him as a liberal (in our sense) is his commitment to reasoned dialogue for resolving disputes.

Habermas believes that (under certain ideal conditions) we could come to a consensus regarding our moral, political, and social disagreements. In order to achieve the required liberation from ideological distortion, Habermas says we need (1) an ideological critique of present social institutions, (2) a social science that is both explanatory and critical, and (3) an "ideal-speech" situation, allowing for undistorted communication (genuine dialogue and debate), where we can come to a consensus free of constraint, coercion, or manipulation. Thus, Habermas connects the procedural goals of normative ethical philosophy to the requirement for a more adequate social science and to his theory of undistorted linguistic communication. The ideal speech situation is a regulative ideal that requires the first two conditions. Until we achieve undistorted communication, Habermas argues we will not yet be in a position to finally decide whether principles such as Rawls's are the ideal ones. He does believe that (under certain ideal conditions) we could come to a consensus with regard to our moral, political, and social disagreements.

Habermas recommends that we work toward making our political decision-making processes into *dialogues* where we can gain a less-distorted view of ourselves and the functioning of the system we live in. His focus would be on approximating the "ideal speech" situation, in which all participants in dialogue are free from ideological distortions.

In sharp contrast to Habermas's hope that ideological distortion can be uncovered and corrected is Foucault's (1980) view. He believes that *all* beliefs are ideological—that there is no truth or knowledge. This view is self-refuting. If all beliefs were ideological, there would be no way to know (or to demonstrate) this because Foucault's claim itself would *also* be ideological. There is no way for Foucault to "get out of the box" to a god's-eye viewpoint from which he could demonstrate that his claim is true (chapter 15).

Habermas's "ideal speech situation" has been widely criticized as a naive, unrealistic fantasy. We view it as a useful heuristic, a regulative ideal, even though it is practically and conceptually impossible to attain it. (This does not imply that we expect to attain it, nor even that we can conceive of what it would be like to attain it—such a conception would require an outside "god's-eye" view.) All it means, in particular concrete situations, is that we should attempt to identify, draw attention to, and try to eliminate [communicative and ideological] distortions through dialogue and critical reflection.

The "ideal speech" idea has also been criticized as too Kantian and foundationalist. Our interpretation and use of Habermas is not foundationalist; it is entirely consistent with the *coherentist* or nonfoundational approach to procedural ethical theory that does not start from abstract, basic, or universal moral principles (nor does it promise to develop same). Rather it starts pragmatically with our own principles, judgments, and intuitions in a WRE process to move first toward internal consistency and then toward consensus with others.

In advocating consensus-seeking, we are not suggesting that we can agree on everything. Remember that we are seeking a limited consensus on our most basic social, political, and economic institutions—that is, practical mechanisms for deciding on public actions to be taken. This agreement is part of Rawls's (1987) overlapping consensus; it is what Rorty (1990) has in mind when suggesting that "democracy has priority over philosophy." When conceptions of the good vary widely, we have to settle for a "thin theory of the good," consistent with satisfying as many of the disparate goals as possible. The aim is to persuade people with different normative ethical theories, intuitions, political philosophies, and value positions to agree on the same institutional framework. Within this basic framework, we can then seek agreement on more specific practical actions.

We believe that WRE is the most practical way to implement Habermas's recommendations, a way that eliminates the transcendental, universalistic, foundational aspect of his theory.[15] Of course, there is no guarantee that consensus is achievable. Our plea is that we keep trying, because the alternatives seem pretty horrible. A first concern is to counter those current theories that undermine the very *possibility* of consensus. Postmodernist approaches engender fragmentation and distrust that make consensus seem impossible and impede our ability to plan.

A HABERMASSIAN CRITIQUE OF BUREAUCRACY

A pragmatic approach follows Habermas in critically demythologizing bureaucracy and in interpreting its language, to uncover who gains and who loses. Hummel (1977) has developed such an account that is interesting both as an example of the application of Habermas's ideas and because most public planning is done in a bureaucratic context. Hummel is an academic who worked in the administration of a reformist mayor of New York. His analysis came out of his perplexity that clear policy directives arising out of high-quality analysis never seemed to get implemented. They simply disappeared without a trace. Following Habermas, he recognized that understanding this situation required looking beyond individual interactions in specific situations, to focus on systematic distortions at the organizational and structural levels (Forester 1989).

Hummel's first step is to apply communicative rationality to view bureaucracy as a different world with different frameworks from our ordinary social world. Bureaucracy creates its own "world" socially, culturally, psychologically, linguistically, and politically (e.g., bureaucracy replaces people by cases, social norms by operating rules, mastery by specialization, dialogue by command, and politics by administration).

His second step is to apply critical rationality to argue that bureaucracy is morally wrong. It is dehumanizing, destructive of human relations, and destructive of personhood—reducing the bureaucrat to a "cog in the machine . . . a truncated remanent of a human being," an instrument of power, little more than an automaton (Hummel 1977, 5). Bureaucracy is not only "an expression of the drive for rationality and predictability" in modern society, it is at the same time "one of the chief agencies for making the world ever more reliable and predictable," because "the bureaucratic mode of knowing becomes constitutive of things known" (Schaar 1984, 120).

In other words, bureaucracy comes to effectively define what is "reality." And the bureaucracy conception of reality is the same as that of the RCPM: "that which is tangible, discrete, external, quantifiable, and capable of being precisely conveyed to others" (Schaar 1984, 121). People who act from motives embedded in any other reality "are treated as deviant cases." Schaar comments that "bureaucrats still cannot quite believe that the objects of 'urban renewal' see themselves as victims" (Schaar 1984, 122).

Hummel argues that viewing bureaucracy as part of our ordinary world leads to ideological distortion. We must recognize that bureaucrats deal not with people but cases; that they do not care about justice, freedom, oppression, and suffering but about control and operational efficiency; that they are not whole persons but headless and soulless; that they do not communicate in the two-way dialogue of ordinary language but define communication by their own (one-way) language of command; that public bureaucracies are not service institutions but control institutions.

If we suffer from this distortion, we miss the fact that bureaucracy is ultimately completely irrational. Bureaucratic "rationality" is nothing more (or less) than control. Public bureaucracies don't meet the needs of clients or employees. They end in absurdity because their methods for choosing means (i.e., the RCPM) so distort the goals that they are no longer recognizable. Hummel (1977, 201) cites the U.S. general who said of a Vietnamese village shelled out of existence, "We had to destroy the town to save it."

Thus, Hummel's Habermassian analysis gives us a very different picture of bureaucracy as a modernist tool of control and helps us to understand how public goals and means can get so distorted when implemented by bureaucracies. Once we understand this, we are in a better position to resist (from inside or outside) the dehumanizing effects of bureaucracy and the bureaucratic mind-set.

CONCLUSION

Contemporary liberalism's focus on the procedural is particularly important in pluralistic societies where conceptions of the good life vary widely, making consensus on substantive matters more difficult (or even impossible) to achieve. We have drawn on Rawls, Walzer, and Habermas in our outline of the critical liberal ideals that should be expressed in planning procedures. It is crucial that these procedures be structured so that they both (1) are seen to be fair and (2) maximize the chances of reaching informed consensus.

Notwithstanding our best efforts to dialogue and maximize the scope of our overlapping consensus, major substantive differences will remain in pluralistic societies. Thus, political liberalism stresses *tolerance* with regard to differences that do not violate basic political liberal values. There is no idea of *imposing* consensus, glossing over disagreements, or muffling bothersome voices. Mandelbaum's strategy of agreeing to disagree comes in at this point (1991, 212). While tolerance is a moral *virtue* to philosophical liberalism (i.e., liberalism held as a private philosophy), it is a *necessity* to political liberalism.

Critical liberalism provides a pragmatic normative rationale for the sort of planning that even planners who may sound rather postmodernist (Beauregard 1991) often end up advocating, an alternative approach to planning—one that is neither modernist nor postmodernist, one that eliminates the scientistic features of modernism but retains its positive humanistic aspects. This approach preserves the rationale for Friedmann's social learning, for his non-Euclidean planning, for Forester's progressive planning, for Krumholz's equity planning, for Healey's collaborative planning, for Innes's consensus building—providing a firm moral basis for such approaches without appealing to the metaphysical foundationalism of modernism.

Pragmatic Incrementalist Planning

INTRODUCTION

All of the aspects of a new dialogical planning approach that we have outlined thus far—the communicative, critical, liberal, and pragmatic—point in the direction of planning theory and practice that is incremental. Our focus here is a reconstruction and defense of incrementalism as one important aspect of a dialogical planning approach. While we begin with a brief discussion of Lindblom's original disjointed incrementalism, our intent is not to give a complete explication or defense of his thought, fascinating though that would be.[1]

LINDBLOM'S ORIGINAL INCREMENTALISM

In chapter 2, we saw that Lindblom was one of the earliest and most cogent critics of the RCPM (which he called "synoptic" planning). This critique was influential beyond the author's wildest imagination: By 1979 his article, "The Science of 'Muddling Through,'" had been reprinted in forty anthologies.[2] This critique was insightful but (not surprisingly) still very much within the context of the modernist paradigm, its value-free ideal, and its narrow scientistic view of rationality. This led to some tensions in his work. The potential to break out of the modernist mind-set is there, but it was never fully realized.

In addition to his critique, Lindblom also advanced an alternate paradigm—disjointed incrementalism—that he claimed was a superior model not only descriptively but also normatively, to the RCPM. It was characterized by roughly the following elements:[3]

1. Evaluation and selection of ends is intertwined with empirical analysis of means.

2. The focus is on ills to be remedied rather than on positive goals.

3. The test of good policy is agreement.

4. Analysis is limited in terms of neglecting important outcomes, important alternative policies, and important affected values.

5. Analysis is fragmented among many (partisan) participants in policymaking.

6. There is less reliance on predictive social theory and more on past experience.

7. Change is successive and incremental, proceeding by skillfully sequenced trial and error.

(Lindbloom 1979, 517)

Most critics of incrementalism have seemed to accept its validity as a *description* of how planning and policymaking do actually proceed, at least in normal times. Even the original proponents acknowledged that the RCPM is rarely followed, and never perfectly. Simon (1945) recognized that most decision makers "satisficed," that is, adopted the first alternative that satisfied all the constraints or bounds. Meyerson and Banfield (1955) found that the organization that they studied (Chicago Housing Authority) diverged in almost every aspect" from their RCPM ideal. Banfield came to acknowledge that "there are compelling reasons which militate against planning and rationality" (as he defined them) in "all organizations" (Banfield 1959). Thus, Faludi recommended that planning theory incorporate "the behaviourial element" of Lindblom's work (Faludi 1973, 120) as *descriptive* of how organizations function.

What these critics want to reject are incrementalism's normative claims. Whereas Lindblom claims "that for complex problem-solving, [doing better] usually means practicing incrementalism more skilfully and turning away from it only rarely," his critics believe "that doing better means turning away from incrementalism" (Lindblom 1979). Faludi attacks Lindblom for advancing primarily descriptive evidence in support of normative conclusions (Faludi 1973, 120), for committing "the sin of mixing, in an inadmissible manner, factual and normative arguments" (1973, 116). Banfield (1959) asserts that "if the interest is normative" (his norm being increased effectiveness or efficiency), he would advocate the RCPM and would not consider its "lack of realism . . . a defect." Etzioni (1968) worries that we could "incrementalize our way to hell." More recently, Forester (1993a, 77) argues that "as long as questions of illegitimacy and the abuse of power are neglected, [the] satisficer and the incrementalist will be only a deferential and quiescent . . . political actor. In his view, incrementalists will be "ethically dangerous and hardly professional" (ibid.), prone to slipping into opportunism.

Lindblom himself seemed somewhat ambivalent regarding the degree to which incrementalism is an ideal normative process. As his critics note, he often mixed factual and normative arguments. But he did advance at least two normative arguments for incrementalism. The first is that a method that accepts the reality of constraints and works within them is bound to be more effective in achieving goals than one which ignores this reality. Using the RCPM, "the inevitable exclusion of factors is accidental, unsystematic, and not defensible by an argument so far developed," whereas using incrementalism, "the exclusions are deliberate, systematic, and defensible" (Lindblom 1959, 164). The second is that incrementalist politics "helps maintain the vague general consensus on basic values . . . that many people believe is necessary for widespread voluntary acceptance of democratic government" (Lindblom 1979, 520).

Both these arguments are empirical claims that incrementalism achieves certain (implicit) norms. In the first case the norm is efficiency—the primary concern of modernist planning; in the second, the norm is a Rawlsian overlapping consensus on democratic ideals—perhaps a more relevant concern in the postmodern world. Lindblom also hints that incrementalism is fair, impartial, and rational. However (as his critics asserted), these normative elements are not clearly distinguished from his empirical claims, and they are less fully elaborated. Most of Lindblom's defenders focus on the first claim (with regard to efficiency) (Redner 1993). Our interest relates more to the second claim (regarding democracy).

A RECONSTRUCTION OF INCREMENTALISM

Our culture has changed vastly in the forty years since Lindblom put forward his theory (1959), and substantially in the twenty years since his defense of it (1979). As we have seen, postmodernism has challenged and seriously undermined the modernistic foundationalism, scientism, positivism, and utilitarianism that are at the heart of the RCPM.

We have reconstructed incrementalism in a way that responds to the postmodernist critique by incorporating recent ideas from philosophy and ethics. We advance a more systematic normative justification from a neopragmatic perspective. We go beyond arguments that incrementalism is a necessary evil (given the reality of constraints on public decision making) to argue that, from a critical liberal position, incrementalism is the most appropriate form of planning for a pluralistic democratic society with some overlapping consensus with regard to basic liberal values. These liberal democratic ideals (chapter 1) provide the justification for an incrementalist approach to planning.

The most important elements in our reconstituted incrementalism are:

1. In a liberal democratic society, change must take place within a consensually held framework of sameness.

2. The test of good public policy is agreement (consensus).

3. Consensus comes out of debate through the WRE process (chapter 6).

4. Ends and means are not separately chosen; ends emerge and evolve in process.

5. Social "theory" is ad hoc, constantly modified by practice.

6. Change occurs through successive incremental steps, by trial and error.

Although we are not attempting to be definitive interpreters of Lindblom, we do believe that our version is a reasonable interpretation of his original incrementalism, even though it may be different from many interpretations found in the planning literature. Note that Lindblom makes a theoretical distinction between incremental politics, incremental policy analysis, and partisan mutual adjustment (PMA).[4] Pragmatically, we hold that in practice they are inseparable, and we use the term "incrementalism" to embrace all three.

One key difference is that what most interpretations view as "incremental" is the concrete choice or action resulting from the planning process (Forester 1993a). In contrast, our focus is on the nature of the decision process—the way in which the decision is justified—rather than the result of that process. While it may be true that a road or a rail system cannot be designed in incremental segments, the choice to design it (or not) can follow an incremental approach. Another important difference is that we see a dialogical, consensus-seeking process as having *inherent* value in a democratic society, whereas Lindblom seems to have focused more on its instrumental value in arriving at superior decisions (Sager 1998).

The following sections present three sets of arguments for an incrementalist approach to planning: (1) It responds very effectively to postmodern critiques of planning, (2) it fits our political liberal democratic tradition, and (3) it allows for legitimation of change.

INCREMENTALISM AND POSTMODERNIST CRITIQUES

Incrementalism uniquely responds to postmodernist critiques of planning because it does not depend on foundationalism, meta-narrative, dualism, or a narrow (instrumental) view of rationality.

Incrementalism Does Not Require Foundationalism

Incrementalism is unavoidable in a postmodern (post-positivistic, non-foundational) world. As we have seen, positivism attempted to provide a scientific foundation for all knowledge. Postmodernist critiques have pointed to the inadequacy of the positivistic attempt and have undermined the very notion of an absolute foundation for knowledge. In a post-positivistic world, values, beliefs, and knowledge are recognized as dependent on consensus. We have seen that, when we seek to justify a belief or an action (to give reasons for it), we appeal to a "web" of other concepts and beliefs that are shared. If we attempted to change everything at once, there would be nothing left on which to base the justification.

Postmodernists erroneously conclude that this lack of absolute foundations leads to ambiguity. As we argued in chapter 4, the problem of ambiguity disappears if we view meaning in a different way, as a pragmatic tool for interpreting linguistic behavior as a whole, for getting at what someone is saying, what he or she believes and means. We should look holistically at the entire web of interconnected beliefs and meanings. Shifts of meaning and belief take place (generally incrementally) within the web of other meanings and beliefs.

From an incrementalist view, a particular interpretation is similar to an empirical hypothesis: It is tentatively accepted if consistent with the available evidence, to be replaced only when a better one comes along. While interpretation is unavoidably fallible, this doesn't undermine its legitimacy. The notion of progress does not have to be given up (i.e., one interpretation can be better than another), and the quicksand of postmodernist skepticism can be avoided.

As Lindblom (1979, 520) says, incremental steps "do not rock the boat." To switch images to one made famous by Otto Neurath (1973), we view public decision making as analogous to repairing a ship at sea.

> When a beam is taken away a new one must at once be put there, and for this the rest of the ship is used as support. In this way, by using old beams and drift wood, the ship can be shaped anew entirely, but only by gradual reconstruction. (Neurath 1973, 199)

Arguments for change must be made within a context of what is held fast. When circumstances change, it may be appropriate to use new "planks" (new concepts) in our social ship. But these new elements must be fitted to the old. There is no dry dock where we can tear the whole thing apart and rebuild from the ground up. We have to retain enough of the boat to be sure that it stays afloat. Over time, the ship may change a lot. But only incremental change can give us a new overlapping consensus. There is no "outside" foundational perspective that could justify a completely new design for society.

Note that what we hold constant (and base our justification on) cannot be specified beforehand in any mechanistic way; there is no set procedure for change. But change must take place within a context of sameness. The only alternatives to this sort of reasonable argument are unacceptable, and wrong, in a democratic context (see our discussion below).

Incrementalism Does Not Require a Meta-narrative

According to Lyotard (1987), the key defining aspect of postmodernism is its "incredulity towards meta-narratives." Many writers (Wittgenstein, Winch, Stein, Davidson, Habermas) have pointed out the folly of attempting to derive precise predictive social theory having principles that are explanatory/predictive in the same sense as scientific laws. Intentional human behavior cannot be understood without an [internal] investigation of the meaning of actions to the participants.

Predictive theory sufficiently precise to allow the manipulation and control of social behavior is, fortunately, impossible. All of our social theories will inevitably be fallible. As Habermas says:

> The utopia of a preconceived form of life . . . could not be brought to life . . . due not only to a hopeless underestimation of the complexity and changeability of modern lifeworlds but also due to the fact that modernized societies . . . extend beyond the dimensions of a lifeworld that could be measured by a planner's imagination. (Habermas 1992, 15)

Incrementalism requires no meta-narrative; it bases actions primarily on experience. There is no appeal to grand, sweeping, general theories (like Marxism) of how society (or parts of it, like a city) works. As Lindblom (1979, 517) says, "There is less reliance on predictive social theory, and more on past experience."

"Social theory" attempts to give an account of the structure and functioning of society that may lead to (i.e., cause) social conditions, values, and changes in them. Its perspective is external to the society. In contrast, Lindblom emphasizes an internal or participant's perspective (chapter 6). Then the concern is not the cause of change but its justification. This adds a moral dimension: It suggests that policy change depends on normative justification. The obligation is to ensure that it is reasonable by our own standards. For an external (social theory) perspective to be relevant, it must be interpreted into context by those who are situationally located. This is the only way that the application of social theory can be justified.

New ideas are tested (preferably on a small-scale, gradual, or prototype trial basis (Woodhouse and Collingridge 1993) and then modified to correct errors. Incrementalism has often been misinterpreted as being inconsistent with large-scale projects. But incrementalism is an approach to decision making, not a description of the actions that result.[5] However, we should still be wary of the risks of mega-projects—not because incrementalist actions are inherently small-scale but because the consequences of alternative policies/plans in a particular context cannot be determined in advance. We find out by trial and error what works. In addition, long-term projects carry a further risk: We cannot predict how values and goals will change in the future. As Lindblom points out, these uncertainties mean that prudence dictates an incremental approach to change. However, mega-projects are not absolutely ruled out *a priori*; their appropriateness should be assessed in context, following an incrementalist approach.

Progress and Legitimation Are Possible without Absolute Foundations

The consensus-seeking democratic decision making WRE process (chapter 6) fits very well with incrementalism. One crucial feature of this approach is that WRE is not a mechanical algorithm. Nor is it a linear hierarchical process of first establishing absolute universal principles, then deriving subsidiary principles and applying them to specific situations[6] (chapter 12). Thus, change can start anywhere—with considered judgments, general theories, background normative theories, or background empirical theories; provoked by new attitudes, new ideas, new theories, new technology, new empirical evidence; at the level of constitution, federal or provincial statute, implementing regulations, municipal bylaws, or specific projects.

While we have argued that planning theory has no need for absolute universal principles and that principles need to be tested against concrete situations (Harper and Stein 1995c), we still believe that planning theory has a need for reflectively chosen principles. Critical reflection on our principles is important to avoid changes (even incremental ones) that can take us (as Etzioni [1967/1973] warned) in the wrong direction. In our current intellectual climate where change is so readily embraced, constant vigilance is required.

In the terms we used in chapter 6, Lindblom's approach might be characterized as emphasizing a narrow (internal) reflective equilibrium that focuses on the coherence of (1) considered situational judgments, and (2) normative principles (chapter 6). If this is a correct interpretation, then our aim is to widen his notion of equilibrium by bringing in both normative and descriptive background [external] theories (appropriately interpreted in context).

Incrementalism Can Be Legitimated by Neopragmatism

We have seen that neopragmatism is neither modernist nor postmodernist. It shares postmodernism's rejection of the scientistic aspects of modernism but allows us to retain its liberal aspects. The strongest linkage between incrementalism and neopragmatism lies in their shared rejection of universal theory (meta-narrative) in favor of knowledge gained from (and refined by) our practical experiences of attempting to solve real problems.

From this perspective, much of the postmodernist critique of modernism is valid. However, as we have argued (chapter 4), "full-blown" postmodernism cannot provide an adequate basis for planning. Neopragmatism retains the possibility of progress, of planning to make things better.

While Lindblom (1979) might be viewed by some as a modernist in his focus on the efficiency of incrementalism as a strategic approach and by others as a relativist (Dryzek 1993, 225), we agree with Premfors (1993) that he is "in-between." To put it another way, we view Lindblom as a modernist with a strong sense of the modernist flaws that are addressed by neopragmatism. We see congruences between his incrementalism and neopragmatism, and we argue that neopragmatism provides a way to legitimate incrementalism.

Incrementalism Incorporates a
Broader Pragmatic Notion of Rationality

The RCPM demands strict procedural criteria for planning (and for rationality) that are set out in advance and that must function in the same way in all future applications of that model. Otherwise, according to this scientistic view, planning is arbitrary and irrational. Pragmatists believe that this standard is impossible, unnecessary, and undesirable. Of course, in practice, "rational planners" are forced to recognize the impossibility of rigidly applying their methodology; this is explained away with ad hoc elaborations like feedback loops. But these elaborations don't deal with the original faulty premise: that a mechanistic, instrumentally rational decision-making procedure can be prescribed for a social activity like planning.

While postmodernist planners reject the RCPM, they [implicitly] accept its modernist claim: that unless a narrow and impossible standard of "rationality" is met, planning is irrational and arbitrary.[7] If we simply reject this modernist assumption, the postmodern abyss disappears, and we can have planning that truly is rational in a more meaningful sense.

Incrementalism has a pragmatic notion of reasonableness. Rather than give up the notion of rationality, we can widen the narrow modernist conception to include broader notions, to incorporate our shared views of what is reasonable (chapters 6). Then we can accept the postmodernist attack on the RCPM without giving up the possibility of a planning approach that is reasonable or "rational" in the broader pragmatic sense (Harper and Stein 1995c).

Agreement of the Relevant Community Is the
Only Test of Knowledge

Faludi (1973) strongly criticized Lindblom for trying to "replace valid knowledge" by "agreement." Faludi was missing the recognition that knowledge rests on (is determined by) agreement. Implicit in Faludi's view is the idea of an objective outside "god's-eye" view of truth that is independent of any human agency. This reflects a rationalistic "hangover" from positivism and empiricism—the idea that knowledge should have an objective empirical basis.

One of Kuhn's (1970[1962]) main points about science is that its knowledge is based on criteria that are shared by the members of the [scientific] community. The test of legitimacy is acceptance by the relevant community. This community (i.e., scientists) constrains what will be accepted by defining the terms of membership in the community and its normative standards of evaluation and justification. In a nonfoundational world, there is no other basis. There are no "outside" criteria for objectively determining what is true— we can't extricate ourselves from the world to step completely outside it. In an important sense, the only way to test a belief (or change a belief) is by appeal to the relevant community of inquirers. Knowledge is not autonomous; what can legitimately be said to be true has to emerge out of partisan debate.[8] In the case of society, the relevant community is all citizens.

INCREMENTALISM AND THE LIBERAL DEMOCRATIC TRADITION

Incrementalism allows us to retain and enhance the legitimate liberal democratic aspects of modernism.

Incrementalism Is Inherent in a Liberal Democratic Context

We have seen that Rawls (1993; 2001) suggests Western liberal democracy rests on an overlapping consensus with regard to a very limited set of basic values, at the core of which is the ultimate value of free, equal, autonomous individuals. Flowing from these values are a set of *procedural* norms that structure public debate and decision making. These structures allow for widely divergent, even conflicting, reasonable *substantive* values. Very different conceptions (i.e., thick theories) of "the good" held by different philosophical, moral, and religious doctrines can be respected and considered equally (chapter 6). In pluralistic cultures such as in North America, there may be very little agreement on anything beyond these procedural norms. Conversely, in societies where everyone holds the same values and ends, the distinction between procedural and substantive norms would be largely irrelevant.

One justification for incrementalism relates to the fact that we live in a pluralistic society without such a substantive consensus. When we have very different substantive ends,[9] we want procedures that respect these differences, that do not diverge too far from the current consensus, and that limit change to increments that are as small as possible. Of course, it is not possible or feasible to do some things in small increments. Remember, it is the decision process that we argue must be "incremental," not the resultant actions.

We relate incrementalism to liberal democracy because it shares the same pluralistic assumptions. In attempting to find, respect, and work within the underlying consensus, incrementalism very much *fits* liberal democratic values. In contrast, the modernistic RCPM fits with a kind of technological imperialism that sees society as an organic whole, more real than its individual members (Faludi 1973, 113). In practice, it often ignores social consensus in favor of the expert's view of the "public interest." On the other hand, postmodernism fits more with an anarchistic view. It threatens to destroy social consensus in its celebration of difference.

Lindblom's PMA[10] needs a consensually held overlapping Rawlsian framework; it presupposes, and requires agreement on, the basic values and procedural norms of liberalism. This commonality restricts the scope of the political debate. In contrast, postmodernism's emphasis on difference leaves us with nothing but disagreement and no reasonable way to resolve it.

Incrementalism Best Accommodates Consensus-seeking Processes

Lindblom's process of PMA (at its best[11]) could function in a manner very similar to the WRE process, which offers a fair way to take competing interests into account and to attempt to reconcile them. Friedmann (1987, 133) criticizes Lindblom for advocating a "marketplace of ideas."[12] He argues that this "marketplace of ideas" assumes (in common with economics) that each actor seeks to maximize his or her own self-interest. But a "market" of ideas is very different from a market for commodities. The ideal of a marketplace of ideas presupposes that each person has an equal right to participate; it is based on procedural norms of freedom and equality. As already discussed, procedural norms are extremely important in very diverse pluralistic societies because they may be the only elements on which there is an overlapping consensus. Instead of self-interest, we would say that all persons should (and could) begin with a commitment to justice and fairness (i.e., Rawls's [1971] "original position"). All ideas should be given a hearing and their merits debated.

While various popular approaches (e.g., Innes's [1996] "consensus building," Chrislip and Larson's [1994] "collaboration," Fisher and Ury's [1981] "principled negotiation") often seem able to persuade participants that it is in their self-interest to follow a process that is more principled (perhaps even more moral) than positional bargaining, this is not always successful (chapter 10). We endorse Rawls's appeal to reciprocal reasonableness (chapter 6). Still, there is never a guarantee that the participants in any process will behave in a moral way.

Incrementalism Can Incorporate Critique

Lindblom (1979, 523) acknowledges the criticisms that "not all interests are represented" in the process of PMA and that there is "indoctrination" (1979, 520) (and lack of debate) on the "grand issues." His concerns implicitly presuppose (in common with Rawls) some strongly normative notions of justice and fairness. From a liberal perspective, PMA is clearly flawed if only the rich and powerful voices are heard. Incrementalism needs to incorporate a critique to point out injustice and unfairness. In more contemporary terms, we should try to minimize ideological distortion and ensure access for all voices.

We have seen (chapter 6) that Walzer (1987) argues critique is inherent in any social interpretation, and that successful critique must be internal— that is, appeal to values that are already held within a moral culture. In order to persuade people to accept domination or oppression, ideology must have appealed to ideas that have genuine moral force. Of course, as Friedmann (1987) argues forcefully and Lindblom acknowledges, the existing power elites use our institutions for their own ends; but this can be fought by appeal to values already held within our moral culture.

A WRE process helps us to identify, agree on, and incrementally modify shared values. When they are applied to our actual practices, it will often be evident that these values are not being followed. Pointing this out is an effective critique from "inside" our moral culture. "Indoctrination" can be most effectively eliminated by this kind of incremental process.

INCREMENTALISM AND CHANGE

Even though we believe that incrementalism is consistent with much of contemporary planning theory, many planners have expressed fears that it is too conservative, that it will inhibit the kind of changes that are necessary to deal with the current crises in planning, and that it is likely to serve those already in power by failing to challenge the status quo (Etzioni 1967[1973], 1968; Forester 1989, 1993a). While these charges might hold against the original incrementalism, we argue that they are effectively countered by our reconstructed version (i.e., what Sager [1994] calls "dialogically enriched incrementalism").

Incrementalism Accommodates Innovation/"Big Steps"

Critics like Etzioni (1967[1973]) and Friedmann (1987, 133) have argued that incrementalism doesn't allow for "big steps." While Lindblom's defenders have argued that this focus is a misinterpretation (Woodhouse and Collingridge 1993), we argue that dichotomies like "big step versus little step" and "crisis versus normal" should be interpreted pragmatically—as endpoints of continua. Although Lindblom (like Etzioni) is unclear about the definition of "big steps" and "grand issues," he does recognize that the "size of the step in policy making can be arranged on a continuum" (1979, 517). Friedmann would object that if one defines change as a continuum, then just about *everything* is incremental. But this response presupposes an absolute dualism—another "all or nothing" choice between extremes. Incrementalism says that our world is not like that.

Here it is important that what should be incremental is not the resulting actions but rather the justification—the decision process. Thus, our incrementalism would allow for many "big steps" (Lindblom 1979, 521) that deal with "grand issues" (ibid., 523). One way that this can happen is if there is a perception of a *crisis*[13] (Etzioni 1967[1973]). A crisis can take many forms: a new idea, a failure to explain, or a failure to achieve recognized ends. Within our shared frameworks, those who believe there is a crisis seek to persuade the rest of us that this is so. If these crisis advocates are successful, consensus on a particular issue shifts, and a "big step" becomes possible. For example, arguments that there is an "environmental crisis" have resulted in significant changes in public policy. Some "big steps," including many of Etzioni's (1967[1973]) "contextuating" decisions, are justified and can be implemented incrementally—retaining as much as possible. Contrary to more radical interpretations of Kuhn (1970a), even scientific paradigm shifts proceed in this way.

There is another, more obviously incremental, way to achieve "big steps." Neopragmatists offer an alternative account of progress. Kuhn's scenario is that scientists working out the details within the existing paradigm come to a dead end, and cases that are unexplained "pile up" until a revolutionary new paradigm emerges that resolves the problems. An alternative (incrementalist) scenario is that creative thinkers (like Davidson [1985] in philosophy) work out new approaches to detailed problems. Such thinkers are using a WRE process. They may be impelled by new information or new experiences, or by reflecting on the implications of present understandings, to seek a new coherent equilibrium. At the time, they seem to be working within the old paradigm, but when viewed holistically in retrospect, it can be seen that a profound change (which might be called a paradigm shift) has occurred. Only after the fact is it clear that a "big step" has been taken. The Magna Carta was likely not seen as a turning point in history by those who signed it. But this kind of change is not a "big break" (see below); the process and the justification still have been incremental.

We do not want to deny the reality of "shocks"—changes that clearly are not incremental (new technology, new economic conditions, environmental changes)—and that are generally unpredicted and unpredictable. What we do argue is that our attitude in responding to shocks should still be incremental. We should seek to adapt our existing concepts, beliefs, institutions, and practices, modifying as much (but no more) of them as necessary, maximizing consensus by minimizing change, minimizing risk by moving cautiously.

Unfortunately for those who would like a mechanistic formula, there is no specific decision procedure to determine how best to respond incrementally to shocks, how best to integrate the new with the old. While a Habermassian "ideal speech" situation will never be fully achieved, we can move tentatively and pragmatically in the direction of undistorted consensus, adapting to changing situations and values.

What makes a change "incremental" is not its "smallness" but its *contiguity* with our traditions, values, and institutions. In the public sphere, new views must be legitimized and justified by connecting them to our current views in a way that brings them into coherence. Incremental change begins from where we are and reflects our experiences.

Incrementalism Offers the Only Way to Legitimate "Big Breaks"

We can conceive of "big steps" that are clearly outside incrementalism in the sense of rejecting key elements of the underlying consensus: for example, postmodernists (in rejecting rationality), radical feminists (in rejecting the equality of persons), deep ecologists (in substituting ecological principles for the autonomous individual), Kuhn's original account of scientific revolution (in viewing competing paradigms as incommensurable). We would dub this kind of "big step" as a "big break." These "big breaks" *are* outside incrementalism and properly so, since they seek to change too much at once.

We see three possible ways[14] to implement big breaks: coercion, conversion, or consensus. Only the last way is legitimate.

The first way is *coercion*—simply to exercise power. To us, the postmodernist emphasis on difference, plurality, and incommensurability leads inexorably in this direction. If communities are incommensurable, then the only mode of relation between them must be some form of coercion because there is not enough shared background for persuasion or debate (Harper and Stein 1996). This why we have attempted to dissuade planners from a facile adoption of its premises (Harper and Stein 1995b).

The second way is *conversion*—of the entire[15] relevant community to a radical new paradigm outside (unconnected to) the present one. Rorty (1989) has described this kind of clearly nonincremental path to progress as "prophetic"—generating new ways of talking, thinking, and believing.

The difficulty with this radical path is: How can we evaluate such prophetic change? We need a way to distinguish good prophets from bad ones. The new way is self-justifying only to converts. It is possible that the change will later be seen as good. But the change has been caused, not justified. Foundationalism attempts to establish a perspective "outside" either the old or the new paradigm—a god's-eye view from which both ways can be judged. If such an "outside" perspective were possible, then reasons could be given to objectively justify the new way. But without such a perspective, it cannot be justified.

The third route is *consensus*—justification within the old paradigm. Once foundationalism has been rejected, the only way to legitimate or justify is to appeal to "the old way," our shared tradition. As Rorty says, we "Western liberal intellectuals should accept the fact that we have to start from where we are" (1991a, 29). We can not escape our culture, our tradition, our language.

> [We] cannot say what are good or better or worse epistemic conditions in quantum mechanics without using the language of quantum mechanics, . . . in moral discourse without using moral language, . . . in commonsense material object discourse without using commonsense material object language. (Putnam 1981, viii)

This third way is the only reasonable approach to social change.

New ideas may be dreamed up in very bizarre ways, quite unconnected to our normal thought and language. Friedrich August Kekule, the nineteenth-century German architect and chemist, arrived at the idea of the benzine ring while hallucinating about a pair of whirling snakes that grabbed each other's tails. But after he came up with this radical idea, he justified it to the community of scientists via accepted methods of experimentation and observation (Sober 1993, 206). Rorty (1991b, 17) grants that "the great thinkers are the most idiosyncratic . . . like Hegel or Wittgenstein, whose metaphors come out of nowhere, lightning bolts which blaze new trails." But where Kuhn and others see exploration within a new scientific paradigm as a pedestrian activity, Rorty argues that new social thinking is "futile unless it is followed up by a reweaving of the community's web of belief" (ibid.). New ideas must be connected step-by-step back to the old tradition.

What if this reweaving goes too far? For example, how far do we go in extending the notion of moral value to the environment? This is the "slippery slope" problem. At each step, we need to check the coherence of knowledge, intuition, and principle. At some point, we have to just dig in our heels and say, "Enough."

The advantage of incremental over radical change is that each marginal move can be justified and made with reasonable confidence that we are likely making things better, and if not, we can go back. Some radical changes may be progressive, but others may not. As Rorty says, "There is no way of telling geniuses from eccentrics, or creativity from idle paradox-mongering, or poetry from babble, prior to seeing how, over the course of the centuries, . . . [they] are received" (1991a, 172). We can allow eccentrics to write awful poetry or attempt failed radical scientific revolutions because they generally don't hurt other people. But the costs of ill-conceived radical social or political revolutions can be enormous suffering. Even when a revolutionary social change turns out well, we would still question whether the turmoil was necessary. For example, Great Britain and France were both transformed from monarchies into similar liberal democratic societies, but the British evolution inflicted far less suffering than the French revolution.

CONCLUSION

Although his critique was insightful, Lindblom was still very much under the spell of the modernistic worldview reflected by the RCPM. When we examine his ideas critically from a contemporary neopragmatic perspective, we can see aspects that are very rationalistic. Our "reconstructed" incrementalism has tried to retain the strengths of Lindblom's original version while eliminating some of its modernist flaws.

We have argued that incrementalism is distinctly nonmodernist in that it does not require foundationalism, does not require a meta-narrative, can be legitimated by neopragmatism, and incorporates a broader pragmatic notion of rationality (or reasonableness). Yet it is consistent with a liberal democratic context in that it accommodates consensus-seeking processes, allows for progress and legitimation, incorporates critique, and can accommodate innovation/big steps.

Once the absolutism, foundationalism, and mechanism of the modernistic RCPM have been rejected, we see three pathways to change:

1. The postmodernist abyss of relativism in morality and truth and the incommensurability of concepts, where decisions are made by the most powerful;

2. An unjustified leap to a "prophetic" new paradigm unconnected to our tradition, with unpredictable and uncontrollable consequences; or

3. A pragmatic incremental change, disciplined and controlled by its connection to our tradition.

Only the last choice—incrementalism—offers a reasonable alternative in a postmodern world.

This pragmatic, incremental view may seem messy, and (to some) distressingly unscientific, or (to others) alarmingly conservative. But the alternatives are worse—the technological imperialism of the RCPM, the anarchistic babble of postmodernism, or the unsubstantiatable vision of the prophet. We may well wind up with one of these, but planning theory should not encourage any of them. Planning should be critically and pragmatically incremental. This will mean, as Lindblom (1979, 525) said, for an "incrementalist, there is never a last word."

Part IV

PLANNING SHOULD RECOGNIZE AN EMERGING WAY

8

A Dialogical Planning Approach

INTRODUCTION

Our aim in this book is to bring together in a coherent way elements of the best of planning theory and practice from the past three decades. Much of what we advance here has been advocated before. A new approach can be seen as emerging from a number of normative planning theories (approaches) that incorporate communicative and/or critical rationality (or Rawlsian reasonableness) and that are based on values that fit our broad notion of "liberal."[1] In a pragmatic spirit, we propose that compatible elements from these approaches be incorporated by the contemporary planner in developing an emerging dialogical planning approach.[2]

PRECURSORS

While the planning approach we advocate might seem to have originated around 1970, there are a number of precursors. For example, the early pragmatists, particularly Dewey, developed their ideas as a process of "inquiry" for addressing social issues; they saw their task as "developing a philosophy that would make [societal] planning possible" (Blanco 1994, 35). They were very much concerned with how to translate knowledge into action to achieve human ends, to change society. Dewey's planning process had the following steps:

1. Problem recognition

2. Problem formulation

3. Problem solution

4. Reasoning (assessment of solution "fit" and consequences)

5. Experiment (implementation and evaluation)

At first gasp, this approach sounds a lot like the RCPM. However, it differs in several important respects. Dewey recognized that ends and means were inseparable and that problem formulation (now called "framing") suggests and limits problem solutions. Rather than applying absolute/certain knowledge, he stressed learning by doing, through acting to change the world (Blanco 1994). He saw plans as "hypotheses to be worked out in practice, to be rejected, corrected, expanded . . . giving our experience the guidance it requires" (Dewey 1950[1920], 89). So knowledge comes from experience (in a broad sense), it must help to solve a problem, and it is validated by community consensus (warranted assertability) rather than by how well it mirrors reality. In Dewey's ideal political process, multiple publics clustered around common concerns and engaged in discourse (not unlike Lindblom's PMA); technocrats inquired into facts; and the public officials decided. Thus, he did retain some of modernism's fact/value distinction, with a conflict between the need for expertise and the recovery of democratic politics.

Lewis Mumford's regional planning process was another early precursor of communicative or dialogical planning. His ideal of planning was a self-educative process of social transformation, involving everyone in processes of rational persuasion and argument, and demanding *critical* formulation and revision of current values. His process (inspired by Geddes's (1968[1915]) earlier work) included

1. A survey of the historical knowledge of the region

2. An outline of regional needs, expressed in terms of social ideals and critically formulated purposes

3. An imaginative projection of the region's future

4. Intelligent absorption of the plan by the people

5. Translation into action by political and economic agencies

    (Mumford 1938)

He defined community as "people united by common feeling for landscape, literature, language, folkways." He stressed the importance of individual autonomy in that these people, acting "out of self-respect and respect for other regions, contribute to planning." The value of their contribution comes "out of [the] authority of own understanding" (ibid.), in sharp contrast to the RCPM's modernistic stress on the authority of expertise. His ideal of governance involved human scale, autonomous (decentralized) service units, cooperative processes, and avoidance of government compulsion. He was an early advocate of the development of a "learning society" later promulgated by Friedmann (1973, 1987).

CONTEMPORARY LIBERAL PLANNING APPROACHES

Social Learning

Inspired by Dewey, Friedmann (1987) proposed a social learning approach to planning (originally called *transactive planning* [Friedmann 1973]) as an alternative to the scientism and elitism of the RCPM approach. *Social learning* focuses on integrating knowledge and action. As in Dewey's pragmatism, knowledge is derived from experience and validated in practice (Friedmann 1987); it emerges from an ongoing process of mutual learning (a "transactive" process between the professional and the client) in which the emphasis is on application. As in Mumford's regional planning, the "client" is seen as the expert on his or her own life and community—the best interpreter of it.

The most striking feature of this approach is the changed role of the planner—from the exalted position of technical expert to the much humbler one of co-learner. This may be perceived by planners as very threatening to their professional status. Another respect in which social learning is very different from the RCPM is that objectives are not set at the beginning of the planning process; rather they emerge during the process, from ongoing reflection and action.

In Habermas's terms, we would say that social learning recognized that instrumental rationality was an inadequate basis for planning and emphasized communicative rationality. Social learning embodies the *communicative* ideals of our approach.

Progressive/Equity Planning

Forester's progressive planning theory came a step closer to expressing the ideals of critical liberalism. It is explicitly based on Habermas's work, attempting to incorporate both communicative and *critical* rationality. Forester sees planning as "communicative action," the selective organizing or disorganizing of attention to the desirability and feasibility of actions, alternatives, and possibilities (1989, 1993a). At any one time, numerous planning decisions of all kinds are being made, but only a few are noticed by the public or even by the politician. Planners are in a position to influence which items are on the public agenda, and they have a moral obligation to use this influence to democratize the planning process, to promote justice and fairness. Forester also reflects Habermas in his concern with coercion-free democratic discourse. Thus, his emphasis is on listening as practical interpretive activity, seeking to understand decision and communicative processes, and identifying and ameliorating distortions in them.

Progressive planning is also a "refinement of traditional advocacy planning" (Forester 1987, 30). Advocacy planning (Davidoff 1965) sought to

extend traditional institutional planning processes to incorporate the interests of disadvantaged groups in a pluralistic society (thus better fulfilling
liberal ideals and offsetting the powerlessness and lack of resources of the
disadvantaged); the role of the planner was to be an advocate of these groups
in the partisan mutual adjustment of the political process. Forester seeks a
more democratic planning process, assisting these excluded groups by providing them with information, technical resources, and critical analysis.

However, as Hoch comments regarding Norman Krumholz's experiences
in Cleveland, the progressive or equity planner goes beyond the original advocacy role:

> [Y]ou were not really advocate planners, identifying with a client and rep-
> resenting their interests in a partisan manner . . . you advocated for a more
> politically inclusive system. You did not pit the strong against the weak,
> but rather pointed to a lack of fairness in public policies which favoured
> the strong over the weak. (Hoch 1988, cited in Krumholz and Forester
> 1990, 250)

Thus, Forester's ideal planner is an advocate for justice and fairness. His progressive planning includes the attempt to anticipate and correct "systematic
sources of misinformation" (Forester 1987, 46) and the obligation to direct
public attention toward such distortions and injustices. So, for example, in
the Canadian province of Alberta, a progressive planner would help people
to understand that final development decisions are made by a board appointed
by the city council, one that is generally dominated by representatives of the
development industry (who often happen to be the same people funding the
election campaigns of those same councillors).[3] Forester's advocacy aims
would be well served by the WRE method we advocate.

While Forester's procedural approach reflects Habermas, his substantive
positions, particularly his endorsement of Krumholz's equity planning
(Krumholz and Forester 1990) and his concern with inequalities of power
and resources, implicitly reflect Rawls's substantive principles. Our approach
is very similar to Forester's, although we draw on a number of pragmatic and
post-positivist sources, where Forester (at least in his early work) relied more
heavily on Habermas. In addition, we more explicitly incorporate liberal values, Rawls's substantive principles of justice, and his procedural WRE.

Non-Euclidean Planning

Our approach is also quite similar to Friedmann's more recent (1993)
non-Euclidean planning. Friedmann uses "Euclidean" to refer to the engineering model of planning, essentially what we have called the RCPM. He
argues that contemporary planning must respond to four world-historical
conditions:[4]

the collapse of the space-time continuum (into an ever present discontinuous Now), the incipient breakdown of political community, the loss of political control over territorial jurisdictions, and the epistemological crisis engendered by the loss of faith in nomothetic science.[5] (Friedmann 1992, 2).

He believes that the nature and pace of these changes is so dramatic that planning will not survive as a socially meaningful activity unless it responds to them.

Friedmann's non-Euclidean planning has four key attributes:

1. It is *normative*. By this, he means it should have some guiding values that we would describe as "critically liberal": inclusive democracy, voice to the disempowered, integration of the disempowered while preserving cultural identity[6] (chapter 13), sustainable growth, gender equality, and respect for the natural world.

2. Like progressive planning, non-Euclidean planning is *political*, involving implementation strategy and tactics to overcome resistance to change.

3. It addresses the communicative aspect by incorporating *social learning*, bringing together expert and experiential knowledge through a face-to-face communicative *transactive* process involving planners and affected populations.

4. It is also *innovative*: present-oriented (rather than future-oriented), concerned with institutional and procedural changes, focused on resource mobilization (rather than resource allocation), entrepreneurial (rather than bureaucratic), and decentered (focused on the local). It requires lots of negotiation and mediation.

Everything here fits comfortably within our approach.

Communicative Action Planning

Healey (1993, 1997) and Innes (1995) both advocate an approach to planning that (following Forester's progressive planning) is based on Habermas's communicative rationality: reason as intersubjective mutual understanding arrived at by particular people in particular times and places. Public claims are to be judged by Habermas's (1984) criteria of comprehensibility (understanding), truth, integrity (sincerity), and legitimacy.

Healey identifies a number of elements of "planning through debate" or "planning as a communicative enterprise." Planning is an interactive and interpretive process—one involving individuals in diverse, fluid, discourse communities; each community with its own meaning systems, knowledge forms, and values. These discursive communities (like Mumford's regions) engage in respectful discussion (within and between communities). In their discourses they recognize, value, and listen carefully to the positions of others. But they search for translative possibilities between communities, thus avoiding the postmodernist trap of incommensurability (chapter 4). The pluralistic process involves reflexive and critical mutual learning (making it resemble our account of a WRE process).

Healey's ideal planner acts in a facilitative role, attempting to understand diverse viewpoints and mediate competing claims for action, to articulate the interests that underlie positions and to reconstruct them so that they are more convergent (i.e., to build and expand overlapping consensus). Innovation and transformation come from understanding and critique that identify dominatory forces. Another role for planners is to invent new institutions, arenas, and processes within which conflicts are identified and mediated, and mutually agreeable actions and programs are formulated and implemented (Healey 1993).

Innes (echoing Forester's emphasis) stresses communicative planning's basis in practice:

> [T]he long-bemoaned gap between theory and practice in planning is beginning to close as a new type of planning theorist is beginning to dominate the field. These theorists make the gap complaint moot because they take practice as the raw material of their inquiry. (Innes 1995, 183)

However, these theorists go beyond merely documenting practice: "Their purpose is, on the one hand, to document what planners do and, on the other, to reflect critically on that practice" (ibid.). Thus, they aim for both communicative and critical understanding, combining internal and external perspectives, to reach what we would call a WRE.

The key insight from these studies of practice is that planning is an interactive, communicative activity. Innes labeled the new "paradigm" as *communicative action*, reflecting the idea that Habermas's work provides the principal framework because it "confronts directly many of the concerns that emerge from a study of practice" (Innes 1995, 186).

Insurgent Planning—The TAMED Planner

Sandercock's (1998a) approach comes out of a radical reinterpretation of planning history that sees institutionalized planning as an ordering tool, regulating space to control marginalized people who are regarded as threats to the social order. She advocates what she refers to as a "new paradigm" characterized by

1. Communicative rationality

2. Interactive, people-centered, negotiated planning

3. Recognition of new epistemologies (experiential, intuitive, contextual)

4. Community empowerment

5. Sensitivity to the values of multiple publics

Her "insurgent planning" is "dedicated to a social project in which differences can flourish" (1998a, 206). In the multiracial, multiethnic cosmopolis, she argues that social justice requires that "difference is not just to be tolerated, but valorized, given value by the dominant culture" (Sandercock 1998a, 124).

Sandercock proposes five "literacies" as essential to an interdisciplinary planning that aims to serve everyone. These literacies are in the areas of (1) technical skills, (2) analytical or critical thinking, (3) multicultural sensitivity, (4) ecological sustainability, and (5) design. They form the acronym TAMED, suggesting a "frame of mind more humble, open and collaborative than the heroic modernist planner" (Sandercock 1998a, 225).

All of Sandercock's attributes fit within our dialogical approach, subject to the concerns that we have already raised about going too far with different epistemologies and the celebration of difference (which we will discuss further in the next chapter). We would also endorse all of her planner "literacies," provided they are developed in balance (which is her intention).

Strategic Planning

Whether or not "strategic planning" is compatible with a dialogical approach is not immediately obvious. Strategic planning arose in the private sector about 35 to 40 years ago (Ansoff 1965) in response to the realization that "long-range planning" had little or no influence on actual organizational decisions. Management theorists decided that the problem was that it was being done in isolation. Two key groups were not involved in the long-range planning: (1) the actual decision makers, and (2) those affected by the plan. Hence, a process was needed that directly involved these two groups. The apparent success of strategic planning in the private sector[7] eventually led to its widespread popularity in the public sector (Kaufman and Jacobs 1987). One of the most interesting applications involves viewing an entire community or town as the planning unit (Perks and Kawan 1986).

Strategic planning is certainly a significant advance over the RCPM in several respects:

1. It calls for much more inclusive processes, with its emphasis on involving all stakeholders.

2. It broadens the notion of goals and objectives to the generation of a mission statement and a vision of achieving the mission.

3. It removes the focus from analysis of the bare decision to consideration of the context, with the analysis of opportunities and threats in the external environment.

4. It recognizes the realities of the organization in the analysis of its strengths and weaknesses, particularly in relation to the external opportunities and threats.[8]

5. It recognizes the limitations of knowledge and information: Rather than attempting to be comprehensive or synoptic, it focuses on key factors—those that most influence the mission, and those over which we have some control—and considers a very limited number of alternative scenarios.

6. It considers the realities of implementation with future-oriented scenarios.

7. It is incremental in that its scenarios start from the present (internal and external) realities.

Whether strategic planning is a new approach or simply an adaptation of the old paradigm depends on how it is interpreted. If it is applied as a mechanistic, rigid, lockstep algorithm, then it could be seen as an extension of the old paradigm. When the strategic planning process is followed literally and mechanistically, participants frequently exhaust their time and energies on preparation of vision and mission statements that are often too general, too abstract, or too ambiguous to be of much practical value.

On the other hand, if strategic planning is applied as a loose guide to process, then it could be incorporated into a dialogical approach. For example, we have found it is often better to start with problem solving/problem framing, go to a SWOT (strengths, weaknesses, opportunities, threats) analysis, then perhaps back to the vision or mission if necessary. Applied in this loose way, it would more closely resemble Mintzberg's (1994) view of effective strategizing as a very informal, creative, and collaborative process. Although strategic planning doesn't explicitly involve any dialogical or consensus-seeking processes, these can be readily employed by planners who find themselves in an organzational environment where strategic planning is the favored approach, provided it is not too rigidly applied.

ATTRIBUTES OF A DIALOGICAL PLANNING APPROACH

In the preceding chapters, we have outlined what we advocate as the key elements of an appropriate public planning approach. The following is a brief summary.

Liberal

Our approach reflects Rawls's (1993, 2001) political liberalism in holding the core values described in chapter 1: The autonomous individual is central. However, this need not mean denying the importance of community—something we can learn from communitarians. Indeed, the sense in which we use "autonomous individual" presupposes community, in that a person can become an autonomous individual only within the framework of a community.

As we saw in chapter 6, these liberal values lead to a concern for procedural justice in a pluralistic society—to a focus on the design of legal, political, and planning institutions and procedures. This is why we have stressed the importance of a WRE process.

Substantively, our approach is similar to Krumholz and Forester. We advocate Rawls's two principles but as a starting point rather than as fixed, abstract, universal principles.[9] Specific substantive principles should emerge from a WRE dialogue and debate, and they are likely to evolve over time.[10] Any community values that are consensually held should be incorporated.

A place where conflicts arise in practice is between the procedural and the substantive ideals.[11] When we look at Krumholz's experience in Cleveland (Krumholz and Forester 1990), we see situations in which it seems clear to him what is in the best interest of disadvantaged residents. Often under the pressure of time constraints, he does not consult these residents, or seek to mobilize them, or wait for them to organize themselves. He takes action. This may have achieved the desired immediate substantive end but at the expense of the longer-term (procedural) goals of establishing more democratic planning processes and building capacity in the community. The trade-off between substantive and process goals is a pragmatic one, dependent on the situation. There is no magic formula, no right answer, because there is no single overriding abstract principle.

Pragmatic

Our dialogical approach is pragmatic in its "philosophical" approach to knowledge and to justification. As we saw in chapter 3, neopragmatism is postmodernist (or more precisely, postanalytic and post-positivist) in that it rejects many of the metaphysical presuppositions of positivism as well as modernism. But it does not, as radical (full-blown) postmodernism does, undermine our Enlightenment tradition regarding rationality, truth, and objective (liberal) values. Similar to Habermas, neopragmatists hold a broad conception of rationality (including but not restricted to instrumental, communicative, and critical conceptions)[12] or reasonableness. The focus is on giving good reasons, ones that are contextually relevant.

Innes's (1995) account of communicative action planning sounds very pragmatic in the senses we have already described:

1. This approach is practical; it "confronts directly many of the concerns that emerge from a study of practice" (Innes 1995, 186).

2. It is very contextual. Planners are seen as actors in particular contexts: "deeply embedded in the fabric of community, politics, and public decision making."

3. It avoids meta-narratives. Planners do not offer "bottom-line prescriptions or simple models" (ibid.); and they are keenly aware of the "messy part of planning that does not fit into a systematic framework" (Innes 1995, 184).

Communicative

Our approach draws on Forester's, Innes's, and Healey's accounts of communicative action; it involves interactive, interpretive, mutual learning, stakeholder-based, consensus-building dialogic processes. These processes respect differences but seek to build commonalities through a WRE dialogue within and between communities, one that aims to eliminate communicative distortion.

Communication, mediation, and negotiation skills are key to effective planning. Communicative planning involves persuasion but not *all* forms of persuasion or rhetoric. Communicative planning is not just getting everyone to buy your view, not just getting everyone to agree with you, not just getting your plan implemented. It involves giving *good reasons* for acceptance, justifying and legitimating your recommendations and plans.

Of course, like any other "tools," communicative processes can be (and often are) used for manipulation. The planner must be an ethical person capable of establishing and maintaining enduring relationships of respect and trust. Here we are reminded of the importance of Habermas's prerequisites for undistorted communication: comprehensibility, accuracy, sincerity, and legitimacy.

Critical

Our approach requires reflective critical interpretation, essential to eliminating ideological distortion. Following Walzer, critique, legitimation, and justification generally appeal to values already held (chapter 6). Although critique is necessary and important, it cannot be too radical (chapter 9). Difference makes sense only against a background of sameness. The planner has a key educative role in pointing to places where these values are violated or applied inconsistently. As we have already seen, all voices should be encouraged and heard, but they must be heard critically.

Critique also requires an awareness of political and organizational/bureaucratic realities. Planners must be critically aware of flaws in the actual functioning of liberal democratic institutions if they are to avoid being apologists for the status quo. For example, they need to understand the ways urban regimes control planning decisions in their local context (Lauria and Whelan 1995). Otherwise, as Forester argues: "'[N]eutral' action in a world of severe inequality simply reproduces that inequality. . . . Good intentions, when blind to the context of action, can lead directly to bad results" (Krumholz and Forester 1990, 257).

As we saw in chapter 6, our critique may show that autonomy requires more than formal equality of opportunity, more than access to an open process. Active encouragement is often required if the voices of the worst-off are to be heard. We may have to seek out, translate, educate, and inform (i.e., empower) some social, cultural, or ethnic groups.

Incremental

We argued in the last chapter that a dialogical approach must be incremental in both justification and practice. The only possible justification for planning in a postmodern democratic society is an incremental one. The alternative paths to change—coercion and conversion—are not legitimate. Consensus-seeking debate is the only justifiable way. Change must take place within a consensually held framework of sameness. The test of good policy, then, is agreement (consensus) that results from partisan debate through a dialogic process (WRE).

In practice, because we lack precise predictive theories, actual changes should also occur (whenever possible) through successive incremental (experimental) steps, by trial and error. "Incremental" change is contiguous with our traditions, values, and institutions. Incremental planning starts from where we are and learns from experience. Incremental plans are generally non-utopian—the plans are for our world, for ordinary creatures like us.

Political

When we say that the dialogical planner is political, we mean that he or she recognizes the inherently political nature of public planning and policymaking. We do not mean that the planner is a partisan supporter of one political party or an advocate of the interests or positions of one particular community or group. Rather, the planner seeks to democratize the planning process, to open it up to everyone, to make information freely available, to encourage all voices to speak, to raise questions about costs and benefits and their distribution. The planner advocates justice and fairness and educates about political dominance and control by elite groups.

Planner Roles

Within a dialogical planning approach, a contemporary planner can legitimately play a number of roles: reflective critical interpreter, communicator, public educator, mediator, advocate (of justice and fairness), agent of [incremental] change, consensus builder, coalition builder, political strategist, and problem formulator, as well as the traditional technical analyst/advisor. Of course, one planner should not try to combine too many roles at one time or in the same context. Some are clearly incompatible—for example, an advocate for one party should not act simultaneously as a mediator between parties.

We may miss potential roles if we take too narrow a view of planning. When we recognize the ambiguity of mandates and the ill-defined nature of public "problems," we see that planners can play a powerful role as problem formulators—who shape attention and decision-making agendas—rather than focusing solely on case-specific problem solving (Krumholz and Forester 1990, 218). Effective problem formulators must be excellent communicators:

> The single most important requirement for access to power is the ability to write clearly, simply, understandably, giving everything that's necessary, but nothing that's extraneous, in sentences of no more than ten words, in words preferably of no more than two syllables, arranged on the page with a lot of space so that you can see the organization of the argument by the arrangement of space on the page, with indentations and dots and dashes and numbered points. (Ackley, cited by Krumholz and Forester 1990, 218)

Thus, an effective planner must be professionally able (have the analytic skills expected by the modernist mind-set), organizationally astute (understanding and exploiting the political and bureaucratic realities), and politically articulate (able to formulate problems in a way that shapes political agendas) (Krumholz and Forester 1990, 225). Being politically articulate involves knowing how to

> present focused analyses in language others can understand . . . on time, in whatever time is available, whenever they can get a hearing . . . thinking carefully, as Cleveland planners did, about how to teach that audience about important issues at hand. (Krumholz and Forester 1990, 260)

Friedmann (1993) suggests that the "responsible acting professional" take a more "aggressive," "innovative," and "entrepreneurial" role in "seeking value-relevant change within their spheres of competence." However, this entrepreneurial role must be transparent—"radically open to public inquiry." The planner must have a normative commitment; he or she is no longer a value-neutral technician but requires "skills embedded in critical thinking and in a moral commitment to . . . the possibility of a non-oppressive society"[13] (Friedmann 1987, 306).

PROCEDURAL ASPECTS OF THE DIALOGICAL PLANNING "METHOD"

WRE Applied to Planning

We have advanced a WRE process (of seeking coherence between normative planning theories/principles, situational judgments, and background theories both normative and empirical) as the normative method for dialogical planning (chapter 6). Just how would the process of WRE be applied to planning?

A planner might begin by consciously attempting to be objective, that is, putting aside (as much as possible) self-interest and feelings about particular persons. The planner would consider (1) a set of (at least somewhat intuitive) judgments about particular situations (e.g., it is wrong that worst-off groups have no political power; development shouldn't be allowed to destroy inner-city neighborhoods; car commuting should be limited to reduce air pollution, and so on), and select (2) a normative ethical theory or set of normative ethical principles (e.g., Rawls's two principles) that roughly conforms to these judgements, probably modifying certain of these judgments or principles to achieve some level of consistency. Consistency between these two sets would give the planner a Narrow Reflective Equilibrium (NRE) (chapter 6). He or she would then apply (3) normative and descriptive background theories—for example, does my normative ethical theory respect personhood, does it treat all persons impartially, does it protect the innocent, is it realistic in its assumptions about individual and collective behavior, does it take into account how political institutions actually function given the power of the local urban regime?

Equilibrium is sought by working back and forth, revising the judgments, the normative theory, and the background theories until an equilibrium is reached (i.e., these comparisons no longer result in changes to any of the elements). Any of these comparisons can lead to the recognition of ideological distortion. At this point, the planner should have a fairly coherent normative position to apply to planning situations encountered daily. Of course, each new situation has the potential to incrementally change his or her own WRE position.

The same process then also structures debates with others. We start by seeking agreement on an "overlapping consensus" and work from there. There is no fixed entry point or sequence. We may find an initial consensus on shared moral principles, general or specific liberal democratic values, empirical facts, specific judgments, or concrete actions.[14] Rawls's "overlapping consensus" (1993, 2001), including the liberal values listed in chapter 1 (which he believes are shared within Western liberal democracies), may provide an explicit framework for planning debates. As different situations are experienced, judgments or normative ethical theories may change. Even when others hold different normative principles or ethical theories, there will be some institutions, policies, proposals, and principles that can be supported by arguments from more than one normative position. It will usually be the case that determining the right thing to do "is something we have to argue about" (Walzer 1987).

Experience in conducting this sort of ethical argument and analysis can be utilized by planners in many different situations: with individuals, groups, meetings, and public debates. The procedure could be adapted at all levels of planning debate, from a planner interacting with individual citizens to a provincial government devising a new planning act. Of course, there is no guarantee of achieving complete agreement, but it is likely that there will be some agreement on issues that require decision, and it will be a much more solid one than merely a compromise of initial positions.

Thinking about Planning Issues

A more general lesson planners can learn is that WRE provides a different way of thinking about social issues—an alternative to hierarchies and dichotomies. The modernist tradition begins with a hierarchy of abstract theoretical principles and deduces concrete particulars. It also views choices as dichotomies: theory versus practice, abstract versus concrete, principle versus example, utility versus rights, environmental versus economic, process versus outcomes. For example, deep ecology begins with a universal absolute principle ("All organisms and entities in the ecosphere . . . are equal in intrinsic worth" [Devall and Sessions 1985, 67]) and seeks to apply it, regardless of the consequences for people; the RCPM begins with the normative ideal of instrumental rationality; Foucauldians begin with the universal concept of power and then seek to explain everything else using that concept.

In contrast, WRE generally starts "in the middle" with more specific principles, then goes back and forth between these principles and facts on the one hand, and theories on the other. As various elements are brought into coherence, no principle is absolute, and no one "level" has priority over the others. As various contexts are considered, the subtle interplay between principles (e.g., between conflicting interests and rights) is brought out in different ways. Precedent setting is always limited, as the local and contextual factors are never identical.

SUBSTANTIVE ELEMENTS OF DIALOGICAL PLANNING: WEALTH AND PROPERTY

Basic Social Institutions

Rawls argues that two social–economic systems include institutional arrangements that could satisfy his principles of justice, in that they provide the following:

1. A constitutional framework for democratic politics
2. A guarantee of the basic liberties
3. Fair value of political liberties
4. Fair equality of opportunity
5. Regulation of economic and social inequalities by principles of reciprocity (if not the difference principle)

(Rawls 2001, 138)

Both have some collective control over (but dispersed ownership of) the means of production, with market allocation of economic output. He calls these systems *property-owning democracy* and *liberal democratic socialism.* Which one will work in practice may depend on historical and empirical factors.

Rawls eliminates three other possible systems because they violate the principles of justice. *State socialism's* command economy violates the basic liberties. *Laissez-faire capitalism* secures formal equality but rejects fair value of political liberties and fair equality of opportunity. *Welfare state capitalism* rejects the fair value of political liberties, has some concern for fair equality of opportunity (but lacks the policies to achieve it), and has no principle of reciprocity (even though it may have a decent social minimum income) (Rawls 2001, 137–38).

Rawlsian versions of both property-owning democracy and welfare state capitalism involve more redistribution of income and wealth (to the worst-off) than current U.S. or Canadian systems (though not necessarily higher taxation). The two systems might have a similar level of redistribution, but for different reasons. Welfare state capitalism aims to provide a decent minimum standard of life, with protection against accident and misfortune. Property-owning democracy aims to ensure that citizens generally have "sufficient productive means to be fully competing members of society on a footing of equality." These productive means include not only tangible capital but also physical capital: "knowledge, understanding of institutions, educated abilities, and trained skills" (Rawls 2001, 148).

The Distribution of Wealth

Rawls's difference principle would entail a significant amount of redistribution of income and wealth in order to maximize the well-being of the worst-off. This principle has been criticized as assuming a particular risk preference—what economists would call risk aversion, i.e., it is argued that rational social contractors would agree to the difference principle only if they were risk averse.[15] Critics point out that some individuals are risk preferrers: They would opt for a "winner take all" set of rules. They would rather "win big" than "lose small."

Rawls makes clear that the difference principle is chosen because it best fulfills the mandate of his "rational contractors under a veil of ignorance" to ensure that their democratic goals are achieved for those whom they represent as trustees. The priority of the basic liberties (first principle) means that there is *no* potential gain that could justify risking the loss of these liberties. The difference principle does arise from maximin decision rule, but the reason for the rule is that the rational contractors have a responsibility to ensure outcomes consistent with society being a fair system of cooperation between free and equal persons. It has nothing to do with their preferences regarding risk or uncertainty.

The difference principle means that a society governed by the principles of justice will allow unequal wealth and income (perhaps with redistribution via taxation) as long as *everyone* benefits. The society will not go past the point on the average utility curve where *average* material well-being is still increasing but *someone's* material well-being is *decreasing* (i.e., some people's well-being could still increase, but only at someone else's expense)[16] (Rawls 2001, 62). Thus, society stays away from what Rawls calls the *conflict segment* of the average utility curve (2001, 124). This avoids the worst-off (least advantaged) being motivated to violate or renegotiate the terms of cooperation (Rawls 2001, 125).

The Wealthy Could Gain Unequal Power

Many critics argue that the unequal distribution of wealth that arises in a capitalist economy (even one with a high level of guaranteed minimum income) inevitably leads to domination. Those with wealth also gain unequal political power. This concentration of wealth and power tends to lead both the fortunate few and the rest of us to view the wealthy and powerful as "better than" everyone else. This is partly an empirical question. Rawls agrees that this could happen and that it would violate his conception of society composed of free and equal citizens. If it did happen, political liberals would support altering the distribution of wealth (by taxation of income and bequests) arising from the difference principle (which is not held to be absolute). The aim is "to keep property and wealth evenly enough shared over time to preserve the fair value of the political liberties and fair equality of opportunity over generations" (Rawls 2001, 51).

Private Property

One of political liberalism's basic rights is the right to hold, and exclusively use, *personal property*. The rationale is that personal property is required to allow a sufficient material basis for personal independence and a sense of self-respect (which are essential for development and exercise of the moral powers requisite to citizenship). Personal property includes one's dwelling, so a Rawlsian political liberal system would include private residential property (Rawls 2001, 114).

However, Rawls's political liberalism avoids prejudging (at the level of basic rights or constitution) the question of private property in the means of production (including natural resources). The further specification of property rights is left to the legislative stage, subject to the maintenance of basic rights and liberties, where the debate is within the overlapping consensus about the political conception of justice.

Negative Externalities

A society structured by Rawls's principles of justice as fairness, then, will have private residential property and [at least some degree of] market allocation of this property. Residents will be protected against violations of their rights to quiet enjoyment of their homes. A case can then be made for regulating many of the common negative urban externalities (air pollution, noise, and the like) through some form of government control over land use and development. Rawls's first principle would recognize a general right not to suffer from externalities but (unlike the rights approach) would not likely give sufferers a complete veto over the externality-generating activities. Empirical research with regard to the actual nature and extent of urban externalities would be required. Economic utilitarian advice regarding the efficacy of various tools of regulation would still be highly relevant. As is the case with the rights approach, Pareto relevance would not be required for regulation. Subject to constraints protecting liberties, the extent, priority, and allocation of rights in an urban context would be a matter of political debate. Rawlsian WRE processes should be used to conduct these debates. We might expect that particular attention would be paid to eliminating or mitigating those externalities that impact worst-off groups,[17] for example, those affecting poor, inner-city areas.

Urban Planning

A political liberal approach would probably regulate new developments more closely but allow more flexibility in redevelopment of built-up areas than a classical liberal approach (chapter 5). Objectors would not likely be given a veto over change since their property rights would not be regarded as absolute. However, concerns for the worst-off could mean stringent requirements for some land-use changes. The tools of zoning and development control could be justified as serving liberal purposes (though they would not be allowed to play an exclusionary role).

Natural Resources

One area not explicitly addressed by Rawls's two principles is environmental sustainability. Although the extent of the environmental crisis is much debated (often conflating normative and descriptive aspects), there seems to be an emerging consensus that we have gone too far in the exploitation of our planet. A WRE process is well suited to developing an overlapping consensus with regard to some substantive principles relating to the natural environment. If there is no consensus at this level (principles), then it could be used to search for consensus on more concrete local actions (chapter 11).

Sustainability would be an important objective though not an absolute one. In some circumstances, human well-being could override sustainability concerns. A political liberal approach would certainly recognize limitations on private ownership of natural resources, with some form of a Lockean proviso similar to the one we suggested in chapter 5. Natural resource use should always yield benefits to the owners (i.e., all of us) and leave enough for future generations.

THE ORGANIZATIONAL ENVIRONMENT
OF PLANNING

Once we see the close fit between the RCPM, bureaucracy, and the other elements of the modernist worldview, it is easier to understand why individual planners who try to implement emerging planning approaches (see table 1-1) in a bureaucratic context often feel thwarted. As we saw in chapter 6, Hummel (1977, 221) is not optimistic about breaking out of the mind-set: "[M]odernity as a way of life has infinite capacities for closure against any escape from itself." Really effective change in planning would seem to require broader changes in its political, organizational, and institutional contexts.

Alternatives to Bureaucracy

Management theorist Henry Mintzberg points out that bureaucratic control is only one form of organizational coordination. Where bureaucracy coordinates by standardization of work process, it is also possible for a public

TABLE 8-1

Organization Types and Attributes

1. *Design parameters*	Entrepreneurial	Bureaucracy	Professional	Innovative
2. *Environment/ work process*	Simple, dynamic	Simple, stable	Complex, stable	Complex, dynamic
3. *Coordinating mechanism*	Direct supervision	Standardization of work process	Standardization of skills	Mutual adjustment
4. *Specialization*	Little	Vertical and horizontal	Horizontal	Horizontal
5. *Decentralization*	None	Limited horizontal	Vertical	Selective
6. *Decision flow*	Top-down	Top-down	Bottom-up	Everywhere

Source: Adapted from Mintzberg 1989.

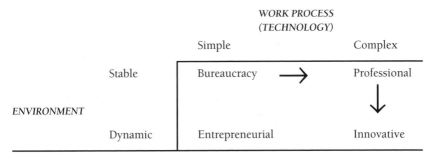

FIGURE 8-1. Conditions for organizational success

Source: Adapted from Mintzberg 1989.

organization to coordinate by standardization of professional skills, or by what he calls "mutual adjustment"—constant lateral communication and interaction (table 8-1, line 3).[18] Each form of coordination corresponds to an organization type (table 8-1, line 1). Professional organizations rely on the standardization of professional skills for coordination; innovative organizations rely on mutual adjustment—that is, continual, ongoing interpersonal interaction.[19] The feasibility of alternative organizational forms depends on two factors: the nature of the environment and the nature of the technical work process (table 8-1, line 2). These factors can be arrayed on two continua. Environments can be characterized as stable or dynamic (i.e., changing rapidly); technical work processes as simple or complex (figure 8-1).

The pressure to move away from bureaucracy to other organizational forms depends on these two factors. As the complexity of the work process increases, coordination by standardization of work process becomes more difficult, and organizations tend to rely more on the standardization of knowledge and skills (i.e., in order to succeed at their mission, they tend to become professional organizations). As the dynamism of the environment increases, solutions from established professions no longer "fit"; creativity and interdisciplinary integration are needed. Organizations are forced to rely on mutual adjustment for coordination (i.e., they tend to become innovative organizations). Innovative organizations are composed of egalitarian project teams drawn from all parts of the organization. Recent advances in information technology have made the required constant sharing of information much more feasible (particularly at larger scales).

Clearly, most planning organizations will experience some pressure away from the pure bureaucratic form. Most have fairly complex technical processes (although development or environmental permitting procedures can often follow a standardized work process). Many planning organizations also function in a dynamic environment, which requires continual adaptation and integration of new knowledge.

Bureaucratic Creep

In contemporary societies, however, there are also strong countervailing forces to the pressure away from bureaucracy. Many public bureaucratic organizations limit restructuring to subunits, often on the grounds that the other forms are more costly but also to minimize loss of control. Thus, professional and innovative organizations often have support staff units that are bureaucratic. Over time, support staffs may come to dominate, because administration is their "thing," whereas the professionals who carry out the organizational mission are much less interested in administration. In addition, the professionals who become line managers often gradually turn into bureaucrats as they become more and more immersed in administration and less and less involved in the actual work of the organization. (Here is a great irony: If you are a really good planner, your reward is that you get to supervise others who do planning, while you yourself no longer do it!)

Exacerbating these tendencies to re-bureaucratize is the increasing external (political) pressure for accountability and output measurement. The demand to quantify usually results in mechanization, returning us to the world of bureaucracy and the RCPM. So even when there are strong pressures away from the bureaucratic organizational form, these countervailing forces may prove to be even stronger. Organizational and institutional reformers need to remain perpetually vigilant against "bureaucratic creep."

Planning in a Bureaucratic Environment

Those who do practice in bureaucratic environments should not slip into a sense of hopelessness, however. Some planners who are fully aware of the forces Hummel articulates are much more optimistic. Forester sees potential for effective actions by articulate, activist, equity-oriented planners who are within public bureaucracies. Drawing on Krumholz's Cleveland experience, he points to three factors that create opportunities for influence (Krumholz and Forester 1990).

1. *The non-monolithic nature of urban politics.* Even though power is economically concentrated, it is politically more fragmented. There are always many bureaucratic and political interests jockeying for position, none of them dominant. Planners can exercise their discretion to develop informal ties across formal bureaucratic boundaries, to share information, to build coalitions, and to influence decisions.

2. *The ambiguities of mandates and problems.* Bureaucratic mandates are usually ambiguous and planning problems are complex, messy, open-ended and ill-defined. There is always the potential to interpret the mandates:

   [T]he Cleveland planners invoked broader traditions of public service, professionalism, and the ideals of a democratic political culture to legitimate their efforts to "expand choices for those who had few." (Krumholz and Forester 1990, 215)

   There is also always the potential to frame the problems in ways that focus public attention and decision-making agendas on the consequences for the poor and vulnerable, to identify "public subsidies for private benefits" (ibid.).

3. *The needs of the powerful.* Because they are in a constant struggle, because they are interdependent, and because they must rely on the cooperation of other actors, the powerful (developers, financial institutions, politicians, and bureaucrats) are all vulnerable at some points: "[T]he power of the 'powerful' is itself contingent and vulnerable" (Krumholz and Forester 1990, 222). For example, the powerful need high-quality information and analysis. These needs can be exploited. Decision makers "need 'information' framed cogently: a succinct and compelling story . . . that will help them interpret the threats and options they face" (Krumholz and Forester 1990, 218). Astute planners can anticipate and exploit the needs of the powerful toward equitable ends.

We must acknowledge the limitations of planning as a profession; it cannot take the place of broader social and political movements. But Krumholz and Forester argue that planners who are "professionally able, organization-ally astute and most of all politically articulate" (1990, 225) can make a dif-ference "in the face of inequality, poverty and human suffering" (1990, 210), even within the context of public planning bureaucracies and modernist mind-sets. And they have a moral responsibility to do this. They also have a moral responsibility to always treat people in a fully human way, to build relation-ships of respect and trust. This is possible in any environment. Regardless of the structure, planners always have some leeway to act. Giddens (1984) calls this exercising "agency" and makes the point that each such act (at least slightly) changes the context and the structure.

CONCLUSION

A new dialogical approach to planning has been emerging incrementally over the past three decades. Even before the era of RCPM dominance, there were significant precursors in Dewey and Mumford. In more recent times, we see elements emerging in the work of Lindblom, Friedmann, Davidoff, Forester, Hoch, Mandelbaum, Innes, Healey, Sandercock, and others. In this chapter we have summarized the features that we believe this approach should ex-hibit. We believe that a planning approach that is critical, liberal, communi-cative, pragmatic, and incremental is essential for effective, legitimate, justi-fiable planning in the fragmented social context of a postmodern society. We also outlined some important procedural, substantive and organizational as-pects of the approach we advocate.

A Dialogical Planning Approach:
Critiques and Questions

INTRODUCTION

N ow that we have presented the elements we believe are essential to an effective new dialogical planning approach, we should pause to address some anticipated critiques and questions. These come from two sources. The first three sections respond to published critiques of "communicative planning" that are relevant because it seems they would also apply to our position. The last two sections respond to questions that we are frequently asked when we present our position in various forums.

There is certainly no unified "anti-communicative" or "post-communicative" or "anti-pragmatic" view. Critiques come from widely divergent, indeed even opposite, perspectives—from postmodern followers of Foucault to top-down instrumentally rational technocrats. And there is no agreed-upon alternative. Some seem to advocate a completely fragmented mélange or "smorgasbord" approach (completely situational, no shared approach, framework, or vocabulary); others advocate a return to the expertise of applied science; still others want to turn to the earlier tradition of the charismatic prophetic designer. The following are some of the more common critiques.

THE COMMUNICATIVE APPROACH IGNORES POWER

These criticisms come primarily from followers of Foucault. In addition to our discussion of Foucault in chapter 3, there is a more detailed analysis of the Foucauldian worldview in chapter 15, where we examine its appropriateness as a basis for contemporary planning theory.

Foucauldian critics of the communicative approach assert that it is naively optimistic and unrealistic about the realities of power. This naivety allows it to be used as a tool of manipulation. Flyvbjerg believes that communicative planning shares "modernity's elevation of rationality as an ideal" that "seems to result in, or at least to coexist with, an ignorance of the real rationalities at work in actual . . . planning processes." While "normative rationality [communicative or instrumental] may provide an ideal to strive for . . . it is a poor guide to the strategies and tactics needed for moving towards the ideal" (Flyvbjerg 1996, 384). As a result, the problem is that "consensus processes . . . are divorced from true centers of power" (Neuman 2000, 345). So there is a "need for greater acknowledgment of relations of power and inequality" (Huxley 2000, 369).

But even if power is recognized, critics are pessimistic; they argue that "it is unlikely that dominant interests will always and everywhere be persuaded by 'the force of better argument' to engage in communicative practices" (Huxley 2000, 372). A "truly successful Communicative Action process is infeasible as power and political action will remain dominant determinants" (Tewdwr-Jones and Allmendinger 1998, p.1981). For example, it is hard to "imagine representatives of a large, powerful property company being prepared to back down in the face of residents' concerns" (Tewdwr-Jones and Allmendinger 1998, p.1986).

Power and Persuasion

Ordinary usage distinguishes between the coercive exercise of power and reasonable persuasion. We should retain this crucial distinction that postmodernists seem to want to eliminate. Forester (1990, 55) recognizes the importance of this distinction: "[I]f power is everywhere, then we need to be much more specific about the kinds of power we find oppressive and the kinds we find 'empowering.'" He is devising a new device to do its work—different "kinds" of power. But there is no reason to give up, and every reason to maintain, the crucial distinction between rational persuasion and power.

We can accept Foucault's insight that rational argument is often used as a form of coercion without jumping to the conclusion that there is no difference between reasonable persuasion and coercion. Maintaining this useful linguistic distinction doesn't presuppose or require a meta-narrative. Of course, language can be used coercively (e.g., Skinnerian conditioning); the point of Habermas's (1971a) critical rationality is to uncover power masquerading as rational justification. But if *all* dialogue were coercive, then we couldn't even identify and critique the *really* coercive instances.

It is also important to note here that maintaining the distinction between rationality (in its broad sense, i.e., *reasonableness*) and power does not depend on a universalistic, monolithic, Platonic conception of rationality. What is "reasonable" depends on circumstance and context.

As we saw earlier, arguments that we should give up the distinction between power and reasonable persuasion are inherently self-refuting. If these arguments are just an exercise of power, then there is no reason to accept them. If they are rational arguments, then they have disproved their own point. The only way we can know that power has been oppressive is through reasoned discourse.

Different Forms of Power

The term "power" is used in many different ways. If it is used in a very broad sense (to encompass any and all forms of social constraints), then it might be claimed that communicative planning does nothing more than replace one form of power by another. But if the term is to be used in such a broad way, then, as Forester points out, we need to distinguish different forms of power. We should assume that all "power" is equally bad. The power generated by a better argument is very different from the power generated by ideological distortion or the power of the gun.

Replacing one institutional structure by another still maintains elements of power; but, as Foucault himself asserts, power may be more or less oppressive. Indeed, as Fischler (2000) argues, replacing one set of power relations by another will always have benefits as well as costs. In certain cases, we would argue that the benefits greatly outweigh the costs. As Charles Taylor remarks: "[I]nstitutions can also free us" (Taylor 1986, 230). The search for better frameworks, better institutions, better ways for going on, is the goal of neopragmatic planning. This is not inconsistent with the way many Foucauldians use Foucault:

> Many people adopt Foucault . . . as a modality of critique of power relations, of domination and inequality, from a basically egalitarian perspective. . . . They are responding to the suggestion that relations of domination and inequality are more subtle and pervasive than we thought. But these goals are indistinguishable from the many generations who preceded them in the "humanist left." (Taylor 1986, 232)

The "egalitarian" goals to which Taylor refers are the same liberal values underlying neopragmatism.

POWER AND ACCESS

Power does give unequal access to planning processes; those with political and economic power can hire expertise, access information, and get their communications through to decision makers and the public. This reality inspired Davidoff's advocacy planning (1965), which was one of Forester's inspirations. To have fair and just processes, it is necessary to do more than open up planning processes. Some disadvantaged groups need education, resources, and mobilization before they are willing or able to enter any planning discourse.

POWER AND CONTROL

Milroy (1990) asserts that "power is what really matters, because the powerful make the rules." As with the concept of rationality, it is a mistake to view power as monolithic. Planning is a very complex and messy process that involves many actors in a variety of roles (politician, planner, other professionals, developer, citizens), with varying degrees of power (Reuter 2002). As Forester points out, all have some vulnerability; none are in complete control of the process (Krumholz and Forester 1990). Certainly, there are situations where some parties have inordinate power; this needs to be unmasked. But it would seem that Habermas and Forester understand this just as well as Foucault, Flyvbjerg, or Yiftachel. After all, Forester's landmark 1989 book was titled *Planning in the Face of Power*. The more fully aware of power relationships planners are, the more effectively they can counter them; but it is not productive to focus solely on power.

POWER AND DISCOURSE

Certainly, power can and does influence discourse, but discourse also alters power. As Reuter (1999) argues, there is a dynamic recursive relationship between discourse and power. While it is true that power can frame, distort, and manipulate discourse, it is equally true that power is generated, legitimized, altered, hindered, and enhanced by discourse. Booher and Innes (2000) found that new forums for discourse can create new sources and forms of power.

The reality of power must be acknowledged. What is required is not the elimination of power but its proper user. Power can be used openly and productively to encourage consensus-seeking forums, or it can be used to coerce, misinform, or distort.

Communicative Planning Lacks Explanatory Macro Theory

Critics believe that communicative planning research is too micro-oriented: It "tends to engage in micro-studies of practice," often glossing over "contextual understandings of power," of "constraints and opportunities," of "wider relations of power" (Huxley and Yiftachel 2000, 337). "Detailed studies of planning practice with reduced emphasis on external constraints . . . fail to provide contexts for critical action" (Huxley 2000, 374). "In its attention to micro-processes," communicative planning is "more closely aligned to the pragmatist philosophical strand of planning theory, with its orientation to knowable social worlds and solvable social problems" (ibid.). This micro focus leads planning theory "back to a substantively vacuous focus on the planning process," one that ignores "institutional politics" and the links between planning and "local, regional and national interests, cultures and coalitions" (Lauria and Whelan 1995, 9).

A related major critique of communicative planning is that its "normative and prescriptive" focus "leaves to one side explanations of why things are as they are" (Huxley and Yiftachel 2000). The stresses on consensus and process "don't serve underlying substance so well" (Neuman 2000), producing a "sclerosis of action" (Tewdwr-Jones and Allmendinger 1998, p.1977).

This criticism may have some truth in that recent empirical work by some communicative planning theorists does have a micro focus, but there is nothing inherent in communicative or dialogical approaches suggesting that substantive, explanatory, or macro theories should be ignored or excluded, except perhaps for its skepticism about meta-narratives. Forester (1989) does focus on the micro and the local because he believes that planners have somewhat limited ability to influence the macro-level structures. And, as institutionalists point out, every act of agency does have some effect on structure (Giddens 1984).

Here it is important to recall that our pragmatic WRE process does aim to incorporate theories of all kinds, including external theories of macro social, political, and economic structure (whether Foucauldian critique of oppression by professional bureaucrats or urban regime theorists' illumination of domination by property interests).

Our approach does not deny that substantive (descriptive, predictive) theories about cities or regions can help planners. When we speak of background theories coming into the WRE, we include this kind of knowledge. Our plans need to be informed by the best predictions available (although we must be careful to understand the underlying assumptions when applying them). For example, theories of sustainability and ecology need to be applied to urban design.

Planning's Relation to the State

Communicative processes are criticized as unconnected to representative government institutions. These processes "typically occur in forums, where issues and policies are discussed . . . not in arenas, where decisions are made and actions are taken"(Neuman 2000, 345). These informal or semi-formal deliberative forums "are not enough to ensure democratic processes of decision making. [Other arenas] capable of linking opinion formation to decision making must have interaction with, and influence over, the state" (Fraser 1990, cited by Huxley 2000, 373). But planning "cannot ignore the state and the public production of space" (Huxley and Yiftachel 2000, 378). Thus, "the failure to problematize the relation between planning and the state raises questions about the extent to which planning can bring about the sorts of social change that the theory suggests are desirable" (Huxley 2000, 370).

Here we agree with the critics—there are serious problems of institutional/arena/forum design to integrate the communicative approach with the structures of representative government, so that it augments and complements it. But governments should not use this as an excuse to reject more collaborative forms of planning, given that the existing participatory structures clearly haven't been able to handle many contemporary problems. Communicative planning and consensus building should have a mandate from government institutions and a link to them.

Conversely, planners' links to the state are also suspect; they may not be able to "act as disinterested mediators exactly by virtue of their roles in relation to the state" (Huxley 2000, 375). Where Forester (1989, 27) suggests that planners often are "legally mandated to make democratic citizen participation in the planning process a reality," Huxley thinks it is "equally possible that planners are members of the 'therapeutocracy' . . . extending their expertise into the management of everyday life" (Huxley 2000, 375). Abram reports that British planners often regard central government priorities (e.g., building housing) as immutable and think that they ought to override local priorities (e.g., preservation of the local environment). "Local-authority planners [are viewed] as state agents whose job is to implement central government policies" (Abram 2000, 355).

This is a valid concern. But here we may be "damned if we do and damned if we don't." Any planning approach can be used manipulatively, either by the state planning agency or by actors within the process. It has long been recognized that rational comprehensive planners or GIS designers can influence outcomes by including, excluding, or varying the weights of their variables. Either planning agencies or participants can also manipulate dialogic processes. For example, they may negotiate ambiguous statements of consensus that are deliberately misleading. However, if this happens, a critical (WRE) process is ideal for uncovering the manipulation.

Power: A Caution

We argue in chapter 4 and again in chapter 15 that planners should be cautious about an increased awareness of power. A fixation on power relations and structures could be dangerous for both planning theory and practice. We also argue that the vocabulary of trust is more useful for legitimate conflict resolution, consensus building, and planning. We do need to be aware of power structures but without letting this awareness dominate and overwhelm our view of planning or inhibiting our ability to develop relationships of mutual respect and trust.

THE COMMUNICATIVE APPROACH FAILS TO PRODUCE MEANINGFUL CONSENSUS

Communicative Approaches Do Not Always Produce Consensus

Critics observe that communicative approaches do not always result in consensus and cannot be expected to do this: "A communicative interchange may require a minimum level of implicit shared meaning and a commitment to understanding, but this does not necessarily entail consensus or even the necessary potential for consensus" (Huxley 2000, 371). Abram found that, in the British context, "increased participation in and knowledge about planning has led to the articulation of conflict rather than any general consensus" (Abram 2000, 352).

A. Hierarchical Contexts

Communicative approaches have never claimed that they will always produce a consensus. If the communicative approach is attempted in situations of top-down hierarchical planning (Friedmann's [1987] "societal guidance"), we would *expect* it to produce critique and dissent. If there is oppression, we should try to stimulate resistance and opposition. This doesn't mean that communicative planning has failed. Here we agree with Huxley: "Conflict of some sort may be inevitable and, indeed, may be positively productive of change under conditions of inequality and repression" (Huxley 2000, 373). Conflict is sometimes necessary and even productive.

B. Conflicting Interests

There may be other situations where no consensus emerges—where we cannot get beyond NIMBYism.[1] Everyone may agree that a light-rail transit line is needed, but no one wants the station next to their house. When there is no consensual way to resolve such opposed interests, we need other structures and rules for decision making, for example, "the majority rules, but there is protection for minority rights." However, these structures and rules need to command consensual support; they need to be seen as fair and just (Rawls 1993).

C. Conflicting Values and Concepts

There may be other, more serious disagreements when various reasonable, disinterested, impartial parties cannot agree on how to proceed:

> [I]t will be unavoidable in our complex modern world that many of our most important judgments will be made under conditions where it is not to be expected that conscientious persons with full powers of reason, even after full discussion, will arrive at the same conclusion. (Rawls 1993, 217)

In such situations, Nielsen holds that "None of the beliefs that various people hold . . . are to be taken as authoritative social norms that require in our public life we must act in a certain way" (Nielsen 1998, 746). We wouldn't go this far; it could produce virtual paralysis. But we should be very wary of any scheme that requires that we choose to apply one, rather than another, of these contested definitions or plans, even if we have the power to do so. Sometimes such choices may be unavoidable; the goal of consensus is not always achievable. Then we still need a just and "reflective solution," arrived at by democratic rules. But all things equal, we should avoid, rather than celebrate, authoritarian planning.

Communicative Planning Produces Superficial Consensus

If the communicative approach does result in consensus, critics predict it will be superficial: "[D]e facto equating of consensus with unanimity . . . builds up an irreversible pressure to reach agreement. . . . They bite off just as much as they can chew, and not a bit more, in order to spit out a yes" (Neuman 2000, 346). The resulting agreements are "thin," "general and vague" (Neuman 2000, 347), papering over fundamental differences in deep values and visions. The focus is often on the peripheral: "Consensus seeking often shuns important issues" (Neuman 2000, 346). At best, the consensus is a "lowest common denominator" (ibid.) of competing interests.

A. A Dynamic Process

Such critiques are quite valid if the consensus-seeking process is viewed as static. If the participants retain their assumptions, their concepts, their beliefs, and their values, then the fundamental differences will remain. The only way to get agreement is to use concepts so thin that they mean very different things to different people. Of course, such agreements fall apart upon implementation.

The whole point of a WRE process is to stimulate and facilitate change: The participants come away understanding some things differently. Reflective equilibrium is "a coherentist method of explanation and justification" (Nielsen 1996, 13) that attempts to bring "our moral beliefs and practices" into the "most coherent pattern we can for the time manage"(Nielsen 1996, 14). A crucial aspect of the WRE process is its fluidity, its ability to alter positions, to widen the consensual equilibrium by incorporating new ideas, new theories, and new information.

Some investigators have found that such transformative changes really do happen in practice. Then the consensus need not be superficial; it can be much more than the lowest common denominator. Cockburn has insightfully chronicled successful attempts by women's peace groups to find common ground among women living in strife-torn areas such as Israel, Northern Ireland, and Bosnia-Herzegovinia. She stresses the difference between "mere dialogue groups and true collaborative projects," observing that the success of such new collectives "hinges on facing up to difference and constantly renegotiating the terms of solidarity" (Cockburn 1998, 211). It is the struggle toward recognizing all citizens, giving up certain dreams, and distinguishing between dangerous fantasies and reasonable hopes that makes these women work toward a different future, one that allows many diverse strands to collaborate. They believe that "apparently deadlocked situations can transform (and be transformed) over time, as needs are differently felt" (ibid.).

Sandercock has documented processes in which "cities of difference" have been managed in ways that were "transformative rather than repressive"— that is, employing dialogical approaches to resolving conflicts that arose from "fear of difference" (Sandercock 2000, 13, 23). She tells of a therapeutic planning process that eventually achieved collaboration between urban Aboriginals and conservative white Australians who were initially too hostile even to meet together. The planning consultant managed to "create the space, in one place, at one point in time, where perceptions might shift, where public learning might occur" (Sandercock 2000, 25), where both concepts and problems could be reframed. Forester has also written about transformative democratic deliberative processes in which "we may change ourselves as well as our strategies and our sense of priorities" (Forester 1999, 218).

B. A Flexible, Nonhierarchical Process

Our studies of decision-making situations have led us to realize that principles and definitions need not come first (chapter 11). Practical decisions on appropriate actions don't require agreement on metaphysical questions (or governing principles, or meta-narratives) regarding the nature of the person, of society, of the city, or of the environment. Instead we should seek agreement on only those practical concepts needed to take concrete action to deal with the particular problems we want to address.

When facing beliefs framed in seemingly incompatible concepts (about the environment, for example), we should try to keep the dialogue in flux. We should strive to set forth these beliefs and concepts, using more neutral terms that are not categorical, value-laden, normative, abstract, or overly general.

In other words, we might reverse the order usually believed to be a necessary precondition to meaningful conflict resolution. We do not attempt to define [what are thought to be] essential terms, nor to provide foundational principles. These processes should be very fluid, flexible, and adaptive; decision makers should not necessarily start by seeking underlying principles or identifying interests. Instead, principles, considered situational judgments, general theories, background normative theories, and background empirical theories should all be explored to find what is shared. Disagreements should then be examined and debated in light of what is shared in an effort to broaden the agreement as much as possible. Thus, change can start with any of these elements.

As soon as it becomes apparent that there is no consensus on an issue, it should be put aside, perhaps in favor of talking about something smaller, narrower, and more concrete. If important central notions such as "the environment" are used, they should be left intentionally vague. If we arrive at successful definition, it will be at the end of the process, not at the beginning.

A successful process will not just paper over difference; it will not just change labels; it will (not even) just change beliefs: The result will be a reconfiguration or reframing of the very terms of the debate. This reframing will generate new concepts and new views of the issues. In the process, anything may change; everything is up for grabs. This is the stuff of great dreams and great plans—unspectacular as it may seem.

THE COMMUNICATIVE APPROACH IS TOO NARROW

Communicative Planning Theory Is Derivative

The communicative approach has been criticized as derivative (i.e., drawn from other disciplines); Neuman argues that planning should have its own unique theory. In his judgment, "[T]he main weakness of communicative planning theory is that it borrows from communicative action theory. This makes communicative planning theory derivative. It helps ensure that planning remains a 'minor profession'" (Neuman 2000).

As we have seen, communicative planning arose out of a recognition that traditional modes of planning (including the entrenched RCPM) had failed. These traditional ways of planning often led to very unfortunate results. The current emphasis on interdisciplinarity arose out of the realization that the traditional professions (architecture, engineering, planning) had not served us well in dealing with urban and environmental problems. Issues like sustainable development forced us to break down disciplinary and professional walls, to relate traditionally separate and isolated disciplines. This led to redrawing the boundaries, making it difficult (perhaps impossible) to speak of knowledge or concepts as "derivative."

Most professions need to be interdisciplinary, integrating knowledge and skills from several disciplines. If any profession should be interdisciplinary, it is planning. For example, a community planner needs to draw on the work of urban designers, planners of urban functions (housing, transportation, parks, recreation, infrastructure), economic and community development planners, social planners (social service delivery, education, health care), heritage and tourism planners, environmental and resource planners, corporate/strategic planners, policy analysts, public administrators, engineers, and architects. Planning cannot hope to deal effectively with contemporary problems if it retains the traditional univocal notion of profession.

Here is a place where critics of communicative planning clearly disagree. In contrast to Neuman's view, Huxley and Yiftachel argue "there is nothing intrinsic to understanding the conduct of planning practice . . . that requires a separate set of theories" (Huxley and Yiftachel 2000), and quote Castells's view "that planning is a profession that applies knowledge from a number of academic disciplines."

We needn't apologize for borrowing from other fields—just as we shouldn't be embarrassed that there is no essentialistic definition of planning (unless it's a paper-thin one). We want to apply WRE to this question. We suggest focusing on the verb ("to plan") and giving up our attachment to the noun ("planning"). Planning is not just one thing with a set of essential attributes. As we have suggested, it is often productive to avoid categories, labels, and searches for grand theories and universal principles. Nouns can cause trouble due to the baggage they carry. Just like the definition of "person" or "environment," the appropriate definition of "planning" will depend on our purposes (Jamal, Stein, and Harper 2002). The idea of planning (like the idea of environment) is in flux. We need a conception of planning that fits the situation, not a universal abstract conception (whether rational or charismatic).

Communicative Planning Ignores the Spatial/Physical

Communicative planning is criticized as ignoring the physical/built form—the spatial aspects—failing to recognize that "planning is a spatial practice" (Neuman 2000), that the "spatial policies of the state . . . give the practice of planning its specificity" (Huxley and Yiftachel 2000).

There are clearly many counter-examples to this criticism. Healey (1997) focuses on spatial planning. Many of the subjects of both Forester's (1999) and Hoch's (1994) research are physical planners. A number of the cases in Innes et al. (1994) also relate to physical planning.

Perhaps the impetus to this criticism is that communicative planning has a strong procedural focus. It seems to us that the same process issues arise with regard to physical planning or urban design as with environmental planning, community economic development, heritage planning, tourism planning, and so on. It is up to the critics to tell us how spatial planning processes need to be different. Finally, there is nothing in communicative or dialogical planning that denies the relevance of substantive spatial theories.

Communicative Planning Ignores the Need for Image

Communicative approaches are taken to task for failing to recognize that "image is king," that "images have been effective in sparking the public's interest and imagination. . . ." They should realize that the "New urbanism attests to the transformative power of images today just as the plans of Burnham and Olmsted, Unwin and Parker, Wagner, Cerda, and others did a century and more ago" (Neuman 2000).

The creation of images by designers is an important part of urban planning. We do live in an age where image is dominant; we are surrounded by images. But when an image is isolated from interpretation and critique, it can and does do a lot of harm. Images can have the power to control. In the absence of critical interpretation, this power can be misused. But particularly in an age of pluralism and of rapid change, the architect and urban designer's image of the city, to be understood, must be interpreted within a framework of critical dialogue. In medieval times, the image of the Gothic cathedral was embedded in a shared framework of knowledge, belief, and tradition, so little interpretation was required. But in contemporary multicultural societies, there are a variety of conceptions and images of the good city. A shared image must come out of, and reflect, a critical and inclusive dialogue. It cannot spring from the mind of a single genius, no matter how creative.

Communicative Planning Lacks a Grand Theory

While Richardson accuses communicative action of "attempting to develop a new unified planning theory" (Richardson 1996 cited in Tewdwr-Jones and Allmendinger 1998), Neuman sees the need for a vision, a grand theory: "[P]lanning needs to develop a theory that is proper to it. When we borrow from the theories of other disciplines, we set back the development and evolution of our own discipline"(Neuman 2000). He would like to see a general theory of planning, modeled after the biomedical "Human Genome Project" or the physicists' "Grand Unified Field Theory" (Neuman 2000).

The failure of technocratic planning is well enough documented that it seems obvious we should not fall back on the search for a new scientistic meta-narrative: planning as applied social science, modeled on the physical sciences. But neither should this technocratic failure lead us in the direction of earlier flawed approaches, toward what Friedmann calls the "Social Reform" tradition: planning that reflects some grand utopian vision of the city or of planning. We want to challenge the view that sees the meglomaniacal visions of Houseman and Moses or the boosterism of Burnham or the totally planned Brasilia as triumphs of great planning. Our own city of Calgary is obviously none the worse for its failure to implement Mawson's 1911 plan— a rather dull, cliched, and pretentious neoclassical "vision."

Communicative Planning Lacks a Vision

In support of the idea that planning needs a grand vision, Neuman (1998, 214) asserts:

> Plans help connect people to places by bringing people together to shape a common destiny for their places and themselves. In so doing, plans link past, present, and future into a willed history. A plan is a history, the story of a place.

This may be possible and reasonable for a monolithic society where tradition and history are shared. But as Mandelbaum (1991) points out, each group in a multicultural society has its own story, its own history, and its own conception of the good city. Thus, there will be very different competing conceptions of the good city in such a society. A grand visionary plan that reflects everyone's history and tradition is much more difficult, probably impossible. So we concur with Neuman's statement, but we draw the opposite conclusion for contemporary large cities in most liberal democratic societies.

There are real problems with the 'grand image' in pluralistic, multicultural societies. Vision doesn't have to come from a super-planner. We do not need a grand theory of planning or an authoritarian vision. A collective vision can, and should, be derived through collective democratic processes.

THE DIALOGICAL APPROACH IS TOO MODERNIST (OR TOO POSTMODERNIST)

As we saw in chapter 3, pragmatism is neither modernist nor postmodernist (at least not in the full-blown sense). This means that to those who are firmly in one camp or the other, pragmatists may appear to be in the opposite camp. Thus, some of these critiques of our dialogical approach reflect a modernistic suspicion that we must be postmodernist, while others reflect a postmodernist view that we must be modernists.

Incrementalism and Neopragmatism Are Also Theories

We claim that incrementalism and neopragmatism both reject theory. Sager (1998) sees a contradiction here in that he regards both of these views themselves as "theory." In some senses, it could be said that we have a theory; it depends what is meant by theory (chapter 14). In the sense of attempting to make generalizations, we cannot completely avoid theory. Pragmatists do try to eschew broad general theorizing in favor of more contextual, contingent, situation-specific theorizing. Pragmatists view the contrast between theory and practice as a continuum.

When we say that pragmatism and incrementalism reject theory, we are thinking of "theory" in the scientistic/positivistic way (see chapter 14) as it is frequently used by social scientists and often by planners. Incrementalism is very skeptical of the practical, pragmatic value of attempting to derive and apply this sort of theory.

Especially in nonscientific contexts (such as politics, planning, morality), the idea of theory does not create problems if the theoretical and the empirical (practical) are seen as mutually reinforcing. One informs and modifies the other, with neither in a superior role. This is the way they are related in the WRE process.

Dialogical Planning Is Another Enlightenment Meta-narrative

Richardson accuses communicative action of "attempting to develop a new unified planning theory" (Richardson 1996 cited in Tewdwr-Jones and Allmendinger 1998). Similarly, Sager (1998) believes that we have a meta-narrative (i.e., our Enlightenment tradition regarding rationality, progress, truth, and liberal values).

Here we disagree. As we have used the term, "meta-narrative" refers to broad theories that claim to be universally true descriptions or explanations of reality. Such grand general theories have done more harm than good in planning. Meta-narratives have no place in an incrementalist scheme. However, this does not mean that we cannot have guiding normative principles. These need not (and do not) function as meta-narratives, particularly if they are treated as just one of the elements of a WRE process.

Dialogical Planning Is Still "Foundational"

Practically, we do use liberal democratic notions that can be traced back to the Enlightenment, but we do not agree with Habermas that they need a *foundation* in that tradition in order to justify them. As we said in chapter 4, we don't justify our beliefs by appeal to that tradition. In fact, we don't justify these beliefs at all; we start with them as essential—necessary—for the kind of society we want. But they do not have to be grounded in any historical meta-narrative.

We advocate using a WRE process for legitimation. But it doesn't appeal to any theoretical background as ultimate. Theories and principles are just elements that are brought into equilibrium. This process gives us a procedure for providing a justification for moral judgments and commitments (e.g., to the rights of individuals) without presupposing an absolute foundation or an absolute transcendent perspective. This position is neither absolutist nor relativist; it avoids the pitfalls of both modernism and postmodernism. It provides all the justification we need for morality. The moral notions central to liberalism—respect for the individual as a moral and political concept— can be derived via this methodology, without the Enlightenment/modernist notion of absolute foundations presupposed by Kant.

Liberalism Requires a Modernist Notion of the Person

Communitarian critics of liberalism argue that the philosophical notion of the autonomous "free floating individual" unrelated to the social context in which one develops is an empty one. The liberal valuing of the person is often related by its critics to a metaphysical (Kantian) notion of the person. It is crucial to recognize that one can accept a critique of scientism and foundationalism without rejecting the basic values of the Enlightenment; and that one can accept a critique of the Enlightenment's metaphysical notion of the person (as a floating atom or a monad of consciousness), without giving up the enlightenment's moral and political view of the individual as the ultimate object of ethical concern (Kymlicka 1987; Rawls 1985; Rorty 1989).[2] The moral and political notion does not require a metaphysical foundation.

It may be that one's initial choice of the goals that one considers worthy is largely socially determined. Liberals can concede such communitarian claims and can reject the *metaphysical* "autonomous person" without in any way weakening the *moral and political* conception of the "autonomous person." It does not follow from the social origin of our initial goals that we should switch from the individual to the community as the proper object of moral concern. To argue that it does presupposes an absolute dualism between person and community, that is, another implicit acceptance of the absolute foundationalism of modernism.[3]

The individual has the right, obligation, and capacity to critically evaluate and modify these community-based goals and values. So when Rawls (1971, 31) speaks of "the priority of the right over the good" and Kymlicka (1987) of the "priority of the person over the person's goals," it is meant in this sense: of persons being able to critically evaluate and modify their ends in the light of moral values. Thus, an appeal to the moral and political idea of the autonomous individual is necessary for critical rationality.

The notion of the person that *is* required for liberalism is someone who is able to play an individualistic and critical "role in social life, and hence exercise and respect its various rights and duties" (Rawls 1985, 233). That is, a creature who has the properties reflected in liberal values: one who is free and autonomous, rational and reasonable, with a capacity for a sense of justice, capable of making choices, of formulating a conception of a good life, and of critically evaluating and modifying this concept. From the point of view of liberalism, all moral concerns, whether of intrinsic or extrinsic (instrumental) value—groups of people (nations, ethnic groups), states, objects, the natural environment—ultimately must depend upon the decisions of free and equal persons (in the above sense) for their legitimacy. Thus, any resolution of disputes regarding moral value must be resolved by reference to the individual person as defined above.

Rawlsian Principles Claim Universal Validity

In Rawls's early work, it sounds as if the argument for his two principles involves nothing more than a transcendent rationality, and that it thus could be argued that his principles can claim to be universally valid.[4] However, his later work makes it clear that this is not the case:

> [J]ustice as fairness is intended . . . to draw solely upon basic intuitive ideas that are embedded in the political institutions of a democratic society and the public traditions of their interpretation. . . . [It] starts within a certain political tradition. (Rawls 1985, 225)

Perhaps this misinterpretation is based on an ambiguity regarding the notion of "universal validity." Rawls does not intend his principles to be universally valid in the sense that they are derived from a transcendent conception of rationality independent of any social or cultural perspective. He does intend his principles to be universally valid in that they apply to all people—that is, "everyone counts and counts equally." This simply reflects the liberal view of fairness.

In this sense, a moral judgment does claim to be universalizable. It is an essential feature of morality that judgments like "One should not torture for fun" are intended to be universal in application. But any judgment is made by a particular person in a particular context (time, place, culture). It is only from within this particular context that it can be considered universally valid. There is no guarantee it won't be refuted in the future; in this sense, no moral judgment is absolute.

Rawls has also been criticized for his apparent rationalism—assuming that moral judgments require a rational foundation based on judgments by some ideal group, rather than being based on our ordinary everyday judgments. This criticism assumes that he is claiming universal validity in the first sense above rather than the second. Again, the point of rational contractors engaged in a WRE process behind a veil of ignorance is to isolate those aspects of our lives that are of moral concern (e.g., concern for fairness). Rawls is trying to get a perspicuous representation of our ordinary beliefs (including the belief that our moral principles should be applied universally—that each person should be treated equally); he is not intending to appeal to some "outside" perspective.

Rawls's later work makes it clear that his two principles rest on normative assumptions that have arisen out of a particular historical context (i.e., the Enlightenment culture), in a society with a tolerance for a plurality of interests and goals, consensually holding liberal democratic values, seeking an "overlapping consensus" of their differing views (Rawls 1985, 1987) and under economic conditions of relative abundance.[5]

Rawlsian Principles Rest Solely on Rational Self-Interest

Mutual advantage theory is often superficially identified with liberalism. Mutual advantage theories attempt to explain or justify[6] liberal democratic institutions on the basis of "mutual advantage" and hold that social institutions can be justified only if they would be supported by any rational person (with full knowledge of their own circumstances) making a *self-interested* choice (Buchanan and Tullock 1962; Gauthier 1978). These persons would accept restrictions on their behavior only if their own self-interest is served. This approach should not be confused with Rawls's political liberalism.

Mutual advantage theory could explain or justify liberal principles only under certain conditions: if all persons had equal power, ability, and resources. But, in fact, these conditions don't hold, so mutual advantage theory cannot explain our liberal moral conceptions. Rawls assumes these conditions of equality not as empirical fact but to argue what position moral persons should accept. Rawls assumes that his rational contractors are consensually committed to a normative ethical notion of fairness; this kind of normative commitment is completely absent from mutual advantage theory.

Dialogical Planning Assumes the "Rational Person"

Critics claim that a communicative approach is impossible because most individuals are not sufficiently rational or self-aware enough to engage in "ideal speech" discourse. Huxley believes that communicative planning assumes "Speakers can achieve a level of self-clarity that allows them to understand themselves and each other with a transparency that denies the fallibility of human life" when, in fact, "the possibility of complete self-knowledge, reflexivity, clarity and transparency to oneself and to others . . . is problematic" (Huxley 2000).

Habermas's "ideal speech situation" has been widely criticized as a naive, unrealistic fantasy. As we discussed earlier, we view it as a useful heuristic, a regulative ideal, even though it is practically and conceptually impossible to attain it. In particular concrete situations, we should attempt to identify, draw attention to, and try to eliminate [communicative and ideological] distortions through dialogue and critical reflection. As long as this attempt leads in the right direction and gives us a better planning process, it does not matter if the ideal is not achievable.

Reasonableness can take concrete form. As already noted, maintaining the distinction between reasonableness and power does not depend on a universalistic, monolithic, Platonic conception of rationality. What is "reasonable" depends on circumstance and context (see our discussion of Rawls's notion of "reasonableness" in chapter 6). However, one can make some generalizations. There are, without doubt, certain features of reasonableness that constitute persuasion as opposed to coercion. Thomas McCarthy suggests the following: open-mindedness; avoidance of dogmatism; willingness to discuss differences, to listen to others, to take their views seriously, and to change our minds; an ability to see things from the perspective of others and to weigh judiciously the pros and cons of issues (McCarthy 1994, 62). This, of course, is an open list, not an exhaustive one. It is neither a hierarchical deductive system nor the instrumental rationality favored by "rational" planners, but it is reasonableness just the same.

The idea of "rationality" should be interpreted practically, as we use it in everyday deliberations. McCarthy gives a good working definition. We do not need an absolute universal conception or an ideal speech situation to have reasonable dialogue. Again, we have to ask: What is the better alternative?

Dialogical Planning Redefines Rationality

Richardson claims that the aim of communicative planning is "redefining rationality in a new communicative way" (Richardson [1996] cited in Tewdwr-Jones and Allmendinger [1998]). Tewdwr-Jones and Allmendinger allege that "instrumental rationality [is] the bogeyman" of communicative planning (Tewdwr-Jones and Allmendinger 1998, pp.1978–79).

As Rawls points out (chapter 6), what we want in our liberal democratic social discourse is "reasonableness." A reasonable notion of "reasonableness" includes all forms of rationality, certainly Habermas's instrumental, communicative, critical, and perhaps others. Instrumental rationality is useful and necessary. We are not suggesting to get rid of it. The problem has been its inappropriate and dominant use (i.e., Habermas's "scientism").

Liberalism Lacks Any Sense of Community

Communitarians criticize Rawls's thin theory of the good as inadequate to sustain a society (Sandel 1996). They believe a healthy society must have substantive shared values. In a society that has a single culture, the shared consensus will likely include substantive values—the sort of "civic virtues" that communitarians value so highly. But in a pluralistic society that includes very diverse cultures and comprehensive doctrines, the shared values will likely be limited to those essential to political liberalism (e.g., tolerance). Rawls distinguishes between a community and a democratic political society:

> The members of a community are united in pursuing certain shared values and ends . . . a democratic political society has no such shared values and ends apart from . . . the political conception of justice itself. The citizens . . . share the end of giving one another justice. (Rawls 2001, 20)

The democratic political society, rather than being a community, is composed of *many different communities* and other kinds of voluntary associations. Its claim to citizens' allegiance rests partly on the fact that it provides a climate that allows and encourages very different comprehensive doctrines to flourish.

However, one of the dangers of any liberal democratic society (not just a Rawlsian one) is that the consensual sharing of liberal values may erode. As Fukuyama (1999, 59) points out:

> [N]othing in the formal institutions themselves guarantees that the society . . . will continue to enjoy the right sort of cultural values and norms under the pressures of technological, economic and social change. Just the opposite: The individualism, pluralism, and tolerance that are built into the formal institutions tend to encourage cultural diversity, and therefore have the potential to undermine moral values inherited from the past.

So we have argued that a liberal democratic society may need to actively promulgate the essential liberal moral values in the educational and political realm. In this [limited] sense, liberal democratic societies do need to "assimilate" immigrants and should actively communicate the elements of their consensus to newcomers (Stein and Harper 2000).

Liberalism Cannot Sustain a Stable Society

Rawls further addresses the communitarian criticisms in his discussion of "stability":

> [I]n order to be stable, a political conception of justice must generate its own support, and the institutions to which it leads must be self-enforcing. . . . [T]hose who grow up in the well-ordered society in which that conception is realized normally develop ways of thought and judgment . . . that lead them to support the political conception for its own sake. (Rawls 2001, 125)

If most citizens accept "the political order as legitimate, or at any rate not seriously illegitimate, and hence willingly abide by it" (ibid.), social cooperation will be stable.

The difference principle means that the worst-off have no incentive to renegotiate (their well-being is maximized). But what about those who could be materially better off at someone else's expense? Their motivation must be offset by other reasons. Rawls suggests three.

First, the public political conception of justice as fairness educates all members of society to view themselves as free and equal, reasonable and rational citizens *engaged in* mutually advantageous *social cooperation*. They agree to the ideal of *reciprocity* or mutuality: "All those who do their part as the recognized rules require are to benefit as specified by a public and agreed-upon standard" (Rawls 2001, 6). They accept the difference principle be-cause it embodies this ideal: "The two principles of justice, including the difference principle with its implicit reference to equal division as a bench-mark, formulate an idea of reciprocity between citizens" (Rawls 2001, 49).

Second, the public political culture fosters *mutual trust* and cooperative virtues, because it is publicly understood that (1) "the three main kinds of contingencies" (i.e., social class, natural endowments, good or bad luck) "tend to be dealt with only in ways that advance the general good," and (2) "the constant shift in relative bargaining positions will not be exploited for self- or group-interested ends" (Rawls 2001, 126).

Third, the more advantaged see themselves as already benefiting by their good fortune in the distribution of native endowments (intelligence, strength, and so on) and by the basic political-economic structure that gives them the opportunity to better their material well-being, provided they also benefit others (ibid.).

In sum, citizens can be persuaded by appeals to *reasonableness* that go beyond narrow self-interests to invoke ideals of justice and fairness.

Pragmatism Is Relativistic

Pragmatism and WRE allow us to establish objective knowledge and stan-dards within relevant frameworks. Compared to foundational modernism, this is relativistic, but not viciously so. We can use WRE to work toward a consensus that can be accepted by all who share the relevant framework (sci-ence, morality, aesthetics, and the like). In morality, we can have standards that are universal in the sense of being applicable to all persons in similar circumstances, but there is no way to compel others to accept our framework or our standards. However, the fact that our WRE has a particular context does not mean that it is relativistic, arbitrary, or subjective, nor does it mean that it cannot be justified.

WRE is Ethnocentric

WRE would be ethnocentric only if communities were incommensurable, that is, if language were culturally determined. We have argued against this claim in chapter 4 and elsewhere (Harper and Stein 1996; Stein 1994). Once we acknowledge that translation, communication, and dialogue within and between communities is possible, then different sorts of questions arise. We might conceive of a continuum with regard to the possibility of agreement between people or communities, where one extreme would be incommen-surability and the other would be complete consensus on principles of justice; on social, political, and economic institutions and policies; and even on specific public actions. The question, then, is "How do we move toward the 'consensus' end?" When different communities or cultures dialogue, the liberal hope is that each will affect the other in reasonable ways, each widening its own perspective and perhaps even changing some of its beliefs.

Dialogical Planning Has a Liberal Values Bias

Tewdwr-Jones and Allmendinger believe that the communicative approach is "a biased process" in that it has a "clear prejudice towards a certain view or set of values" (1998, p.1978) that it seeks to impose. Furthermore, "UK planners do not believe that the planning system could, or indeed should, address these matters"; indeed, they fear that "public consultation and participation ... potentially undermines their professional autonomy" (Tewdwr-Jones and Allmendinger 1998, p.1983). Thus, they conclude that "within the UK, the planner is not under any obligation to facilitate the process of learning, nor is the planner grounded in any ethic of inclusion" (Tewdwr-Jones and Allmendinger 1998, p.1983)

Yes, communicative and dialogical planners do presuppose certain norms: political, liberal, and democratic. This needs no apology. There is no alternative but to start from a normative position. Planning processes need not and should not be value free. On the contrary, there are certain values that any reasonable and legitimate planning process must include. These values are expressed in the very idea of communicative rationality.

Planning is inherently normative. So are notions of rational dialogue and reasonableness; what we use are a set of argumentative virtues or norms for discussion. To accuse the communicative view of bias presupposes the communicative view. Bias means "unfairness," and fairness is one of the liberal norms. What alternative norms should planning employ? Oppression? Charisma? Expertise? Authority? We make no apology for having a liberal-value "bias."

Dialogical Planning Is Too Liberal

Campbell and Marshall (2000) argue that our pragmatic incremental approach to planning is applicable only to North America because it is grounded in American pragmatism and liberalism. Although there are contexts (e.g., totalitarian regimes) where our approach is clearly not applicable, we believe it is very broadly applicable to most democratic countries. Remember that we are using Rawls's notion of "political liberalism," which does not require agreement on the substantive doctrines that might be associated with American liberalism or the metaphysical elements of philosophical liberalism. Political liberalism attempts to accommodate differences (and avoid conflicts) over both metaphysical issues and differing substantive definitions of the good life. One of these "thick theories" of the good that is accommodated may be a more full-bodied substantive liberalism (or several variants thereof).

Each of the constituent cultures and interest groups has to be able to accept the values of the "overlapping consensus" necessary for a workable pluralistic society—impartiality, fairness, individual rights, democratic processes, and tolerance for multiple "thick theories" of the good. Beyond this pragmatic necessity, different politically liberal states may have a variety of political and economic institutions.

A DIALOGICAL APPROACH IS NOT RADICAL ENOUGH

Dialogical Planning Is Too Conservative

"Conservative" can have many different meanings. The WRE process that we advocate is philosophically and methodologically conservative.[7] As we argued in chapter 7, complete break with tradition (what we already accept morally, socially, scientifically) is impossible; even a radical break is incoherent. As we have argued, we must begin within our own context and tradition. If we hope to resolve our differences, they must be publicly debated within a shared context, appealing to an overlapping consensus of shared beliefs and values.

But WRE is *not* inherently conservative in either a moral or political sense. It can tolerate a wide spectrum of views: Nozick, Friedmann, Gauthier, Rawls, Walzer, Habermas, Forester, Nielsen, and Cohen. Which view comes out best in a particular context depends on the way the dialogue goes. The best position will generally be the one that is consistent with the widest reflective equilibrium.[8] The debate continues. For example, Social Democrats interpret Rawls's second principle as justifying inequality of economic condition if it yields sufficient prosperity to make everyone better off; egalitarians argue that such inequality cannot be justified because it leads to a loss of individual autonomy (Nielsen 1985). Either position might call for the overthrow of a government that seriously violates individual autonomy.

Prima facie, it might appear that our incrementalism is a conservative approach and postmodernism a radical one. However, it is postmodernism's view of multiple incommensurable language games that is really conservative in the sense of blocking change. It leaves us with no mechanism for one community or individual to change another's mind. Our approach is *methodologically* conservative (in Walzer's sense) in that it begins by interpreting others in our own terms, but it doesn't end that way. When different cultures, communities and individuals meet, they can communicate, they can learn, critique, and change each other's minds. The solutions to our problems lie in a pragmatic, flexible, holistic, reasonable approach to understanding each other, and in public debates conducted within the traditions of our liberal democratic framework—with an ongoing reflective and critical examination of its tenets.

Dialogical Planning Supports the Status Quo

Several writers have argued that the kind of pragmatic, incremental (chapter 7) approach we advocate here is not enough, that (in Habermas's [1984] terms), it may yield a communicative understanding, but it lacks a critical function. They believe that contemporary problems require more radical change in the social institutions, the liberal values, the self-conceptions, or the ideal of reason in Western liberal democratic societies. Even Hoch (1984, 1992) worried that pragmatism could be a middle-class ideology, one that could distort the planner's view of the world and ignore the reality of power. Earlier, John Friedmann became very pessimistic about the potential (to effect any meaningful change) of the Social Learning[9] planning approach that he formerly advocated. The main reason was that it failed to challenge the existing relationships of power (Friedmann 1987, 216ff).

In reflecting on this challenge, we need to consider the very limited range of options available. In chapter 7, three possible ways to implement change were outlined: coercion, conversion, or consensus. There we argued that consensus is the only legitimate route to change.

Radical Planning

Friedmann set forth "radical planning" in 1987 as a further development of the work of Grabow and Heskin (1973). Friedmann may have well have moderated his position; his [more recent] non-Euclidean (1993) planner sounds less radical. However, his book (1987) is widely used, and the "radical planning" position presented there stills commands a following. More recently, Sandercock (1998b) extended Friedmann's thinking to advocate a new paradigm for "insurgent planning." These authors raise a difficult question: When is planning too radical to fit within a liberal democratic framework?

Radical planning arises from Friedmann's critique of American society, which has marked similarities to both Habermas and communitarian critiques. As we discussed in chapter 1, Friedmann sees planning as being in a crisis that stems from the modernistic worldview/perspective of the Enlightenment. He critiques three key aspects of contemporary (Western capitalist) society:

1. The claim of science to be the only reliable source of knowledge

2. The autonomous individual as the only object of moral concern

3. The dominance of "market rationality"

Because we are in a time of crisis, Friedmann argues, effective planners must be "radical" in order to be transformative of their society. The more fundamental, core, or deeply embedded are the objects of the challenge, the more "radical" will be the planning responses advocated. His call to "challenge the existing structures of domination and dependence" (1987, 223), to "further a new order" (1987, 342), is ambiguous regarding the level of change advocated.

Challenging the Status Quo

Planners can seek to change the status quo at a number of levels:

1. Specific decisions (permits, plans, policies)

2a. Agenda setting (control over information; control over what projects, options, and alternatives are considered)

2b. Organizational structures, arenas, and forums

2c. Informal political–economic regimes and coalitions

2d. Formal political, economic, legal/legislative institutions

3a. Self-conceptions, expectations, perceived needs

3b. Basic "political liberal" values (i.e., the centrality of the autonomous individual as the unit of moral and political concern)

4. Reason as governing communication, social relationships[10]

Changes at any of these levels might be regarded as "radical," but in general each is more radical (closer to changing our "roots") than the one above it.

Different normative approaches tend to focus on different levels. Very roughly, Lindblom, liberal pluralists, and social learners focus on specific decisions (#1); progressive-equity planners focus on agenda-setting (#2a); regime theorists focus on informal regimes and coalitions (#2c); Foucaldian critical planners focus on oppressive structures and practices (#2b, 2c, 2d); Habermassians focus (along with progressive-equity planners, to some degree) on organizational structure (#2b), institutions (#2d), and self-conceptions (#3a); Friedmann's radical planners, as well as feminists, focus on shaping self-conceptions (#3a); communitarians, deep ecologists, and some radical feminists attack basic liberal values (#3b); and postmodernists and some really radical feminists attack our conceptions of reason (#4).

It would be helpful for advocates of "radical change" to be clear about what level they are addressing. In his argument for radical planning, Friedmann sometimes seems to leap from the need to change the *power* structure (level #2) to the need to change the *conceptual* structure of our society (level #3 or even #4). This is where we strongly differ from Friedmann. We argue the opposite view—challenging the power structure requires *acceptance* of the shared conceptual structure. Otherwise, there is no grounds for the critique (chapters 6 and 7).

Our test of whether planning is too radical is "Can it be connected back to our liberal democratic tradition?" (i.e., does it accept #3b and #4?). Planning requires a reasoned justification *within* that tradition. This is why we have argued that a dialogical approach for planning in a postmodern era of fragmentation must be incremental.

Insurgent Planning

As we have seen (chapter 8), Sandercock (1998b) advocates a new paradigm for insurgent planning. Much of what she advocates fits within a critical liberal position. She points to the fact that liberal institutions don't treat everyone equally—that they often marginalize those who are different. She argues that planners should be proactive in redressing the inequalities created by our institutions, in giving voice to the excluded. Much of her argument appeals to our shared political liberal ideals of fairness, justice, equality, and autonomy. For example, she calls for a "more just, equitable and humane society," with a "vision beyond the old class politics and the new politics of group identity" (1998b, 124). However, two aspects of her position concern us.

Our first concern is that Sandercock's celebration of difference could wind up taking us in undesirable directions: "Difference speaks to us with a *collective voice*, in the voice of specific 'social groups.' Thus, it is beyond liberalism" (ibid.). This is ambiguous. In what sense is it beyond liberalism? Does it mean valuing the group or an attribute of the group ("difference") above the individual? If so, then she could be heading us down a very dangerous road.

Our second concern is with Sandercock's epistemology of multiplicity. Elaborating on Gilligan's (1977) ideas, she identifies six different ways of knowing: (1) dialogue, (2) experience, (3) local (specific and concrete), (4) symbolic and visual, (5) contemplation, and (6) action. While we would not dispute that knowledge can be gained in all these (and other) ways, the key issue for public planning and policy is: How do we deal with competing public claims emanating from these different ways of knowing? Are they commensurable with each other? We need some shared values, some overlapping consensus, some common framework for debate and reconciliation of our different claims.

We agree that marginalized groups should be "allowed to be different within an inclusive society, . . . to be acknowledged and valued as different, . . . with the right to make claims on the political community and to participate in it" (Sandercock 1998b, 124–25). However, too much emphasis on difference can cause us to lose sight of the tremendous amount that we hold in common.

Summary

A practical crisis (such as an environmental crisis, or the disintegration of urban society) may suggest the need for radical political change, but it does not necessarily imply the need for a radical methodological and philosophical break with tradition, nor for a different conceptual framework or radical paradigm shift (chapter 12).

If radical approaches to planning require a rejection of our fundamental moral notions and much of our underlying liberal democratic consensus, they will not be able to engage in a dialogue with other views that still accept the basic liberal democratic consensus. This leads in the direction of coercive intervention, as Walzer (1987) points out. Only *within* a commitment to liberal democratic social institutions and basic values do critiques such as Friedmann's and Sandercock's have meaning and the power to effect genuine change.

CONCLUSION

Some of these critiques suggest areas in which we believe that communicative or dialogical planning could be improved:

1. We could more explicitly recognize macro structures, better integrating theories of political and economic power (but should not become fixated on power and power structures).

2. We could pay more attention to the problems of designing links to the political institutions of representative democracy.

3. We could make it clearer that unanimity is not always attainable and pay more attention to devising ways of dealing with this.

4. We could design flexible processes designed to reframe concepts, beliefs, and debates.

5. We could concentrate more on the physical–spatial aspects of planning.

Contrary to what some critics imply, none of these suggestions relates to any kind of fatal flaw in communicative approaches to planning.

The Purpose of Criticism

The communicative and pragmatic approaches have been subjected to a growing critical scrutiny. Valid or useful criticism of public social practices like communicative planning should have one of two aims: (1) to improve the approach to planning (the theory or the practice/implementation), or (2) to argue that communicative planning is fatally flawed in theory or in practice. Other possible (but in our view, not very worthwhile) aims might be to dispute the claim that communicative action planning is a new paradigm or that it is the dominant paradigm.

Critics of communicative planning seem mixed as to which aim they intend. We would strongly argue that it is incumbent on anyone who has the second aim (to discredit communicative planning) to provide a better alternative and that we take the normative values of political liberalism (chapters 1 and 6) as the criteria for "better." There is no point to attacking communicative planning as unworkable unless there is a better replacement.

This returns us to the question: If the communicative approach is flawed, what is the alternative approach to planning? What approach best equips planners to deal with the realities of power in a contemporary liberal democratic society? In chapter 7, we identified three possible alternatives for public decision making:

1. Top-down coercion (power rules)

2. Charisma ("the prophet")

3. An inclusive democratic process of "reasoning together" that attempts to move toward consensus

To try to imagine an exhaustive list, we might add:

4. Top-down manipulation

5. Expertise/authority

6. Anarchy/chaos

The fourth alternative (manipulation) is always undemocratic and wrong in our view (Stein and Harper 1996); so is the first (coercion), at least beyond the minimum degree necessary for having a society. The second and fifth alternatives (charisma and expertise) are both wrong as the primary means and also are unstable (although they might play a secondary role). One thing we hope is clear by now: If the intention is to replace communicative planning with something that works better, the proposed replacement should not have the negative attributes of the RCPM discussed earlier. The technocratic applied science of the RCPM—the myth of the apolitical expert planner—cannot be expected to address the critiques and issues outlined in this chapter. As we have seen, they simply serve as a very effective mask for power and oppression (chapter 2). Finally, the sixth alternative (chaos) leaves us without a society for which to decide anything.

Our Best Hope

The remaining possibility is an inclusive democratic process of "reasoning together" that attempts to move toward consensus (which doesn't imply unanimous agreement). Persuasion through reasonable argument is the only alternative to power. Such an inclusive democratic process will look a lot like a WRE process. In a broad sense, it will be dialogical or communicative planning. Thus, our position is that in the contemporary context, a dialogical approach is the only way. No matter how flawed these approaches to planning may be in application, we need to focus on improving them (both in theory and practice); certainly we must incorporate their insights into whatever approach we adopt.

We believe that our dialogical position can be consistent with many interpretations of Foucault (though not the most extreme and radical). As Fischler (2000, 359) argues: "[B]etween Foucault and the 'new' planning theorists, there is agreement as well as disagreement. . . . Foucault would find much to his liking in the writings of communicative planning theorists." We can recognize the validity of Foucault's specific unmaskings of power and oppression without generalizing to conclude that all governments and all of their institutions are inherently oppressive.

Whatever kind of planning we are doing, one thing we really should avoid is divisive absolute dichotomies—between communicative and instrumental rationality, modern and postmodern, theory and practice, process and outcome, normative and descriptive theory, form and substance, images and words, representative democracy and participatory democracy, agency and structure, internal and external, global and local, Foucault and Habermas, communicative planning and critical planning. Planning needs to pay attention to all of the above, to recognize when they are in conflict, to bring them together pragmatically in a creative WRE dialogue, with sensitivity to specific contexts.

We believe that the best hope lies in a broadened interpretation of communicative planning, one that is liberal, critical, communicative, pragmatic, and incremental (i.e., "dialogical planning"). Such an approach can take seriously, and can incorporate, the legitimate criticisms of communicative theory and practice.

10

Dialogical Planning in Practice

INTRODUCTION

In recent years, various approaches to public decision making have emerged that incorporate some significant elements of what we are advocating here. Among them are a focus on communicative rationality, a critique of the status quo,[1] an aim of including all stakeholders, an attempt to build consensus, a non-modernist approach to knowledge and to justification, a recognition of the importance of normative values, a respect for differing values, and an attempt to build relationships of respect and trust. None of these approaches should be seen as the full application of dialogical or communicative planning theory, nor should they be hailed as universal panaceas. However, most have achieved some degree of success in particular circumstances.

Many of these approaches come from fields outside planning; some relate to civil society rather than to government. They include various forms of alternative dispute resolution, such as principled or interest-based negotiation (Fisher and Ury 1981), collaborative leadership (Chrislip and Larson 1994), consensus building (Innes et al. 1994), collaborative planning (Healey 1997), and peacemaking (Cockburn 1998).

PRINCIPLED OR INTEREST-BASED NEGOTIATION

Fisher and Ury (1981) were pioneers in the field of what is now called alternative dispute resolution (ADR). They initially developed principled negotiation for two-party negotiations. The idea was to get away from positional bargaining (where party A wants $X, party B offers $Y, and the

185

outcome is somewhere in-between), by establishing principles that both parties agree are fair, and then applying them to the dispute at hand. Later, they and others associated with the Harvard Negotiation Project developed the idea of parties stepping back from their positions to identify their underlying goals or interests, then seeking common ground among them. When this is done, it is often possible to come up with new ways of framing the "problem" and thus find solutions that satisfy the interests of both parties better than a positional bargain would have done. This works particularly well where there are unrecognized opportunities for mutual gains.[2] These ideas have been successfully applied, most notably in labor disputes, and in the Strategic Arms Limitation Talks (ibid.).

While the processes of ADR can inform the design of planning processes, and the techniques of ADR can be usefully employed, Margerum (2002a) points out some very significant differences between ADR and collaborative planning. In ADR, there is usually a defined conflict, the key stakeholders are readily identified, the time frame is relatively brief, and the focus is on outcomes. In contrast, collaborative planning forums usually involve multiple conflicts and more diverse interests and issues; they are more broad-based, more long-term, and ongoing relationships are often as important as the outcome. In addition, WRE planning processes seek to go deeper than finding a confluence of interests, to stimulate participants to identify shared values, and to develop new shared concepts and frameworks; ideally, they may even transform worldviews (chapter 11).

COLLABORATIVE LEADERSHIP

Chrislip and Larson (1994) draw on Robert Putman (1993), who argues that the success of democratic government depends on "'social capital': the network and norms of trust and reciprocity that facilitate coordination and cooperation for mutual benefit" (Chrislip and Larson 1994, xii). Putnam promotes the idea of "civic community": the social networks and norms of civic engagement, marked by "active participation in public affairs and a steady focus on the public good rather than on narrower parochial interests" (ibid., 12).

Putnam calls for a new democracy and citizenship: "a deeper, more intimate and more inclusive kind of democracy—one that is more consensual than majoritarian. It is a shift in the practice of democracy from hostility to civility, from advocacy to engagement, from confrontation to conversation, from debate to dialogue, from separation to community" (ibid., 4). Chrislip and Larson define collaboration as "a mutually beneficial relationship" whose partners work together "toward common goals by sharing responsibility, authority, and accountability for results." Its purpose is "to create a shared vision and joint strategies to address concerns that go beyond the purview of any particular party" (ibid., 5). The collaborative premise (and the hope) is that "if you bring the appropriate people together in constructive ways with good information, they will create authentic visions and strategies for addressing the shared concerns of the organization or community" (ibid., 14). Chrislip and Larson document a number of multiparty situations where this hope seems to have been realized.

CONSENSUS BUILDING

Innes describes consensus building as "a method of deliberation" that addresses "complex controversial public issues where multiple interests are at stake" (Innes 1996, 461). It employs "face-to-face group processes" involving "representatives of public agencies, interest groups and local governments, in a search for common ground" (Innes et al. 1994, vii). This planning approach is "built on the tools of alternative dispute resolution, such as mediated negotiation and the insights of . . . [Fisher and Ury's] *Getting to Yes* . . . " (Innes 1996, 461).

Consensus building fits well with what we have outlined in this book in that it draws on Dewey's pragmatism and Habermas's critical/communicative rationality. It is pragmatic in "emphasizing the importance of learning communities and empowerment" (ibid., 461). It also aims to "resemble the theorists' account of critical rationality," i.e., it seeks consensus through critical deliberation that attempts to include all stakeholders, to empower and inform them equally, and to approximate the conditions of ideal speech.[3]

Consensus building is done in groups created by "citizens, public agencies, or even legislatures . . . to supplement traditional procedures for policy development and plan preparation." They have used "consensus building for planning and policy tasks on geographic scales ranging from neighbourhood to nation" (ibid., 461). Groups have worked on affordable housing, land-use planning, city budgeting, waste-treatment plant siting, a state development and redevelopment plan, managing water resources and fisheries, growth management, and environmental planning.

Innes, Gruber, Neuman, and Thompson (1994) documented and evaluated fourteen cases in which consensus building was applied to growth and environmental management issues in California. Eight of these fully matched their criteria for consensus building and are briefly described in Innes's 1996 article, "Planning through Consensus Building: A New View of the Comprehensive Planning Ideal." One of these cases is summarized later in this chapter. Some of Innes's findings are described below.

Representation

In most of the cases, Innes found that all active interests were represented; three of the groups incorporated additional stakeholders. Participants generally chose inclusiveness to achieve political support and legitimacy.

Outcomes

Most stakeholders developed a better understanding of the situation, developed new networks, and used these networks to coordinate and collaborate. Significant agreements were reported on draft legislation, indicators, problem descriptions, issues, monitoring standards, practice guidelines, policies, and plans. Substantial elements of their work were often formally adopted.

Social Capital

Stakeholders came to appreciate the possibilities for shared benefits through joint action. The consensus-building process created social, political, and intellectual capital.

Public Interest

Consensus building seeks to find and broaden what is shared, what is held in common—including the interests of the weakest—and what is good for the resource or region. As Friedmann (1973) postulates, "[T]he good that is shared creates a moral community whose members agree to be jointly responsible for that which is precious." Participants learned that they all depended on common economic, fiscal, transportation, or ecological systems. Political will often followed from discovery of shared interests.

Planners' Roles

Innes found that paid staff in these processes attempted to practice what she would call communicative planning, more or less as Forester (1989) would define it:

> They warned, framed problems, called attention, organized, negotiated, explained contexts, tried to prevent players from manipulating or lying. They tried to create many of the conditions of ideal speech and communicative rationality. They also tried to build new practices and institutions for anticipating the analyzing alternatives, and deliberating. The result is a collective vision that was facilitated by the planners rather than synthesized by them. (Innes 1996)

And broadly speaking, Innes judged that consensus building seemed to work.

PEACEMAKING

Cockburn studied successful peacemaking efforts by women's groups in three contemporary war-torn areas: Northern Ireland, Bosnia-Herzegovina, and Israel-Palestine. She found several common factors that enabled them to "sustain a critique in an environment deformed by essentialisms" (Cockburn 1998, 14),[4] including their emphases on inclusivity, shared values, and democratic processes, as well as challenging gender stereotypes.

Gender

Uniquely among the approaches we have discussed, participation in these peacemaking groups is restricted to women. This is justified by a belief that the violence in their war-torn countries is gendered—that it is based not only on rigid ethnic/cultural identities ("us" versus "them") (chapter 11) but also on gender stereotypes.

Inclusivity

These groups deliberately include a wide variety of ethnic, religious, and national groups. They focus not only on bringing these groups together but also on building bridges to an even wider and more diverse circle of women. In our terms, they continue to widen their WRE.

Shared Values

"Identity" (who you are) is deemphasized in favor of emphasizing what individuals think, say, and do. They find shared political values and goals but recognize and accept differences on "significant political issues." In this sense, their "negotiation is never complete, and is not expected to be so" (ibid.). In our terms, they focus on finding and constructing an overlapping public consensus.

Democratic Processes

A central concern is democratic processes that seek to give equal voice and equal influence to each member and each "side." They attempt to build "social spaces" where each individual feels safe to participate—spaces that allow and respect differences without collapsing them into a spurious unity. In our terms, they seek communicative understanding and an ongoing undistorted dialogue.

All four of the women's groups that Cockburn studied achieved remarkable successes in transforming situations that were widely regarded as hopelessly deadlocked, and in achieving dialogue between groups seen by others as incommensurable.

CASES

In order to explore the potential usefulness of a dialogical planning approach, some of the issues that arise from attempts to implement communicative and pragmatic approaches, as well as the factors generally supportive of success, we will briefly examine a number of cases. These cases represent a variety of contexts, ranging in scale from an inner-city community center to a national park policy task force. Some seem quite successful; others, obviously flawed. The successes give us hope that the kind of planning we advocate can work in practice. The flaws suggest areas for caution and correction.

Most of the cases we have summarized have not been published in readily accessible form. In addition to the sources cited in this chapter, the interested reader can find other narratives about new approaches to planning that have been published—for example, those by Hoch (1992); Sandercock (1998a, b); Susskind, McKearnen, and Thomas-Larmer (1999); Forester (1999); and Margerum (2002a).

In examining cases, it quickly becomes evident that "success" is not easy to define. Whose perspective counts? No real-world planning process will be seen as a success by everyone. What a dialogical planner sees as a success probably would not be seen positively from a modernist RCPM perspective. So we should not expect to be able to establish universal criteria and provide empirical "proof" that our way is superior. Different readers may have quite different evaluations of "success" in these cases.

The approach we have advocated would define success in terms of both process and substance.[5] Ideally, we would want to meet both procedural criteria (e.g., inclusiveness, equality, undistorted communication) and substantive goals (e.g., fairness, justice, production of a justifiable and practical plan or policy). As we discussed in chapter 6, the priority concern for a critical liberal democratic approach will be the perspective of the citizen/clients, particularly those who are worst off. And finally, we would like to meet these criteria both in the short term and in the medium to long term.

An important caveat: The reader should note that, unless otherwise stated, the sections of each case headed "evaluation" and "issues" express the authors' opinions, rather than those of the person who documented the case (who may well disagree with our judgments).

STEEN COMMUNITY CENTRE

Source:	Mulgrew (1995)
Location:	Winnipeg, Canada
Date:	1982–92
Scale:	Inner-city community (Wolseley)
Scope:	Project
Theoretical "model":	Grassroots communicative approach (no formal theory)
"Product":	New multiuse community center, playground
By-product:	Improved planning process for community facilities

Background

This case takes place in an inner-city community (Wolseley) with numerous infrastructure needs, limited land and financial resources, some funding available through fairly narrow provincial and city programs, and a valuable resource of committed and active residents. The community adopted a grassroots communicative approach, first to forge an alliance between two diverse community groups, and then to negotiate with public-sector bureaucracies that largely followed the RCPM.

The two organizations were a sports and recreation association and a community child-care center. Both operated in a small building on leased space on the local school grounds. When agreement could not be reached with the [inflexible and uncooperative] school board to allow expansion and upgrading of their center, the two groups began to look for other ways to accommodate their needs. However, tensions arose due to an imbalance in funding available: Child-care programs could draw on well-funded provincial programs; recreational centers could not.

Events

The two groups (sports and child care) formed a committee, chaired by a local community activist (Angela Mulgrew, who authored a study of this case[6]), charged with "bringing opposing forces together into a united focus to find a community solution" (Mulgrew 1995, 102).

This committee drew on an already established network of residents and their contacts (including land use, heritage, and social planners; architects; landscape architects; lawyers; environmentalists; civil servants; and politicians) to conduct a [government-funded] needs survey and to draw up a physical plan, which achieved a high degree of consensual support. Their "communicative actions were based on a personal and professional ethic of achieving equity for the community. Information was flowing and the process open" (ibid., 104). They obtained the support of both their provincial MLA [member of the Legislative Assembly] and their local city councillor.

With this political support, they were able to obtain funding and the necessary planning approvals to acquire a vacated church across the street from the school, to remodel it for child-care and recreational use, and to close the street between it and the school.

While the school board maintained a narrow interpretation of its responsibilities throughout the process, the [city] parks and recreation held a broad interpretation, accepting responsibility for community development. Its view of planning broadened through this process, until by the end it had issued a pamphlet advising community groups on how to develop the kind of cooperative, communicative partnership that the Wolseley group had pioneered (City of Winnipeg 1989).

Evaluation

The open communicative planning style, with a commitment to liberal equity concerns, enabled this inner-city community to obtain a high-quality child-care and recreational facility, to increase open space, and to begin to change the way planning was done in their city.

As a result of her experiences, the chair of the committee discussed above decided to pursue a degree in planning. She struggled to develop a reflective understanding of her practice, which had been largely intuitively based. Eventually, she encountered some of our work and discovered that it helped her to make sense of her experience (Mulgrew 1995). She came to characterize her approach to planning as critical, liberal, pragmatic, and incremental.

Issues

Planner Roles

It is noteworthy that professional planners seem to have played no formal role in this process, although a number played informal roles in aiding the community group. Planning innovation came largely from the civil society, not from institutionalized planning in the government sector. It came (in the words of one participant) from "the hard work and sacrifices of time and energy that ordinary citizens have to expend, to get fairness in a system that is secretive, rigid and adversarial" (Mulgrew 1995, 138). Should it be that difficult, and should it require that much community volunteer energy and talent, to get fairness from our political system?

VICTORIA PARK

Source:	Stockland (1998); *Calgary Herald* (1998)
Location:	Calgary, Canada
Date:	1998
Scale:	Inner-city community
Scope:	Land use (redevelopment from residential to commercial/recreational)
Theoretical "model":	Principled negotiation
"Product":	Plan for area redevelopment

Background

Victoria Park is one of Calgary's oldest and poorest neighborhoods, with some of the city's lowest-priced rental housing and a population mixing long-time residents and transients. It is bounded on the north by downtown and on the south by the grounds of the Calgary Exhibition and Stampede. The "Stampede," touted as "The Greatest Outdoor Show on Earth," is a major tourist draw. Its facilities include rodeo and grandstand, large convention/exhibition areas, and the Saddledome (home of the NHL Flames). It is one of the most powerful organizations in the city; its board includes many corporate-sector "movers and shakers."

Events

In the early 1970s, the Stampede Board quietly purchased about five blocks of Victoria Park (roughly 20 percent of the total community) and announced plans for expansion. The community was not organized and essentially powerless, and the expansion went ahead. The Stampede continued to purchase property adjacent to its expanded boundaries. However, the Victoria Park Community Association became more organized and received some support from other community organizations and (to varying degrees) from the city planning department. Amazingly, it successfully resisted expansion plans for the next twenty-five years. The downside was that no one believed that you could beat the Stampede Board, so little investment (or even maintenance) occurred, leading to a very decaying environment.

None of the stakeholders were happy with this "lose–lose" outcome. Residents and business owners watched in despair as the part of their neighborhood under threat became more and more derelict. The Stampede Board was stalemated, unable to muster enough political support to expand its boundaries.

These three groups of stakeholders were brought together by planning consultant Glen Lyons. He was able to persuade them all that they "had to find the solution themselves, that no magic government or institutional wand would be waved to settle the problem" (Stockland 1998). He followed a principled-negotiation approach. After six months of negotiations, the group reached agreement in principle on a development plan that all could live with.

The plan incorporated expansion of the Stampede grounds, a retail/entertainment complex, commercial zones, and residential uses (including some permanent affordable housing). It included a commitment to upgrade infrastructure, parks, and transportation, and to tackle prostitution, panhandling, and crime. This plan was eventually accepted by property owners, residents, and the Stampede, and was finally adopted by the city council.

Evaluation

The *Calgary Herald* characterized the outcome as "a sweet victory for consultation, cooperation and community planning that provides new hope for the continued prosperity of the city's biggest tourist draw and a neighbourhood too long neglected. . . . It illustrates a deep-felt commitment to preserving the inner core" (*Calgary Herald* 1998). Bringing these warring groups to a consensus was clearly a major achievement.

Issues

INCLUSION

Lyons was not hired by the city government, so inclusion was not part of his mandate. While the deal struck was probably as good as the community could ever expect, the concern was for those who were not at the negotiating table—the tenants, the street people, and the homeless. The fear was that these least-powerful groups would bear a disproportionate share of the costs.

COMMITTEE ON RESOURCES AND THE ENVIRONMENT (CORE)

Source:	Andersen (1997)
Location:	British Columbia, Canada
Date:	1992–96
Scale:	Regional (4 regions)
Scope:	Land use, resource exploitation, environment
Theoretical "model":	Shared decision making (interest-based negotiation)
Intended "product":	A set of consensual regional land-use recommendations for each region that would be used to develop regional land-use plans

Background

CORE was created in 1992 as a provincial government response to political conflict regarding [non-urban] land use throughout the province:

> Incidents concerning the appropriateness of tree harvesting in Clayoquot Sound, South Moresby . . . the Cariboo and elsewhere received world-wide media coverage. The Clayoquot Sound Sustainable Development Task Force, created in 1989 in hopes that a consensual process would resolve the controversy, had failed in 1990. Pressure from environmental and Aboriginal groups to protect old growth forests was escalating in the form of road blocks and peace camps. First Nations all over the province were pressuring the government to address unresolved land claims, and forestry companies were demanding an end to the confrontations so that they could log their timber leases. (Andersen 1997)

CORE's mandate was to develop a provincewide strategy for land use, natural resource, and environmental management that was in the public interest. Public input was sought to address various concerns regarding land-use issues of regional scope through roundtable shared decision-making processes aimed at developing "an outcome which accommodates rather than compromises the interest of all concerned" (CORE 1993, 19). The hope was to avoid "positional bargaining," where each participant begins with a position and then compromises toward some "middle ground."

Convening the roundtable involved identifying groups that represented various stakeholders and clustering them into "sectors." Each seat at the table was occupied by a spokesperson representing a coalition of groups with similar interests, backed by a steering committee. Each of these "sectors" was labeled, for example, as tourism, outdoor recreation, agriculture, wilderness conservation, forest industry, fisheries, labor, community economic development, community residents, local government. Each sector coalition was to define its interests, which had to be satisfied in order to achieve consensus.

"Product"

The persons at the table had to define their own process and rules governing participation, defining "consensus," and ways to handle disagreements. (Most adopted CORE's suggested process with minor variations.) The provincial government's intent was for stakeholder representatives to reach a set of consensual regional land-use recommendations that CORE would present to the Cabinet. The consensual recommendations were to include land-use allocations (including protected, special management, integrated, or intensive resource management areas); transition and mitigation strategies (for adversely affected communities); and issues requiring community-based planning, implementation, and monitoring. If no consensus could be reached, CORE would take the information generated and create a recommended land-use plan. In any event, the actual decision-making power remained with the government. However, the government did make a commitment to attempt to legislate consensual land-use plans produced by the roundtables.

Events

The process was applied to four regions that had serious land-use controversies.

CARIBOO-CHILCOTIN

This process bogged down in a dispute over the boundaries of their area: whether or not to include some existing protected areas. Inclusion would significantly affect the proportion of the land base that was protected, which in turn would alter the *prima facie* case for more protected areas. Subsequently, the roundtable was unable to reach a consensus on a land-use plan, and discussions collapsed. Six sectors submitted separate plans to CORE, which conducted a workshop to obtain feedback on land-use alternatives and then prepared a land-use plan.

VANCOUVER ISLAND

This roundtable was able to develop a vision statement for 2020, sector interest statements, a land-use designation system, and policy recommendations regarding socioeconomic transition and resource management. However, it concluded that there could be no consensus on land-use allocation without a [provincial government] strategy to assist communities adversely affected. Three sectors developed their own land-use scenarios. CORE then developed a land-use plan based on the roundtable's outputs, which added twenty-three protected areas (a 30 percent increase in area) and decreased annual timber harvest by 4.5 percent.

WEST KOOTENAY-BOUNDARY

This roundtable produced a vision statement, sector interest statements, a land-use designation system, management guidelines, an impacts-analysis system, a socioeconomic transition strategy, land-use policies, and land-use allocations for 80 percent of its area. CORE negotiated the remaining 20 percent with individual sectors and devised a plan recommending eight new parks, management areas for sensitive resource development, and initiatives to offset unemployment caused by the plan.

EAST KOOTENAY

This roundtable produced land-use policies, a socioeconomic transition strategy, recommendations for implementation, and land-use allocations for 90 percent of its area. The CORE plan included the roundtable's recommended policies, six new parks, rehabilitation measures for one area, and wetlands management guidelines for another.

Evaluation

Andersen (1997) argues that evaluation of this kind of process can be done only by the participants. She sent surveys to all participants in the four roundtables; thirty-two (36 percent) were returned. They rated 65 percent of the forty outcome goals as at least "partially achieved" (25 percent as "achieved"); more than 75 percent of the thirty-five process goals as at least "partially achieved" (25 percent as "achieved"); and 50 percent of the twenty-two goals relating to "building relationships" as at least "partially achieved" (but only 5 percent as "achieved"). Fifty-six percent (56 percent) of business–government respondents rated the process as at least "somewhat successful" (only 12 percent as "successful"); 75 percent of other respondents rated it as at least "somewhat successful" (but only 6 percent thought it "successful").

Overall, Andersen judged the CORE process as a success relative to previous planning efforts. Particularly given the highly confrontational nature of the situations in these regions, Andersen concludes that CORE does demonstrate the "power of consensus processes in general, and shared decision-making processes in particular" (Andersen 1997, 149). As a land-use planning process, she found it "workable but cumbersome" (ibid., 147). It is also noteworthy that the more successful facilitators were those with land-use planning experience. As an exercise in interest-based negotiation, she judged it a success. The "commitment of all involved [in] the process" over three years was "phenomenal" (ibid., 148). As a new public decision-making forum (which the British Columbia government claimed it to be), Andersen found it an improvement over previous approaches, definitely increasing public involvement in policy-making.

Issues

PLANNING PROCESS

Andersen thought that the provincial government should have defined a clearer policy framework (including targets for the percentage of each area to be protected), defined planning area boundaries, devised some socioeconomic transition policies, and given clearer guidance with regard to expected outcomes. In other words, the process needed a clearer and more focused mandate.

NEGOTIATION

Negotiations were largely interest-based, with the exception of the Cariboo conflict over area boundaries and some of the specific land-use allocations, which became very positional. However, there was much room for improvement. The mediators were seen as neutral but not effective. Information needs were not met. And Anderson detected apparent government "bias favouring of certain sectors and interests" (ibid., 149).

PUBLIC FORUM

Participants were not really partners—the attempt at "shared decision making" degenerated into more conventional consultation. Success would require better government support with regard to information, resources, provincewide policy frameworks, and a communication strategy. A serious problem was the lack of communication with interests who were *not* at the table.

GROWTH MANAGEMENT CONSENSUS PROJECT

Source:	Innes, Gruber, Neuman, and Thompson (1994)
Location:	California
Date:	1990-91
Scale:	State
Scope:	Growth management legislation
Sponsors:	State legislature, private foundations
Stakeholders	
involved:	Environmental, housing, business, ethnic, social equity groups, local governments, government councils
Facilitation:	One professional
"Product":	85-90 percent agreement on principles for legislation

Background

A large number of fragmented and conflicting growth management proposals were on the legislative agenda in the late 1980s. Developers, builders, and local governments requested a moratorium and a consensus-building process, supported by legislators wanting to break the gridlock. California State University in Sacramento agreed to manage the process, which was formally outside of government. The university group drew up a broad list of thirty-two statewide interest groups that picked their own representatives.

Events

Participants were grouped into "caucuses" to represent "interests" and to develop positions on issues. They then met in cross-caucus discussions (e.g., environmentalists with developers) to try to resolve differences. Finally, conclusions were reported to the larger group.

By-products

1. Participants gained a better understanding of social equity implications of growth management.
2. Some social and political capital was developed.
3. Some participants joined a subsequent process to design legislation (which, unfortunately, was never passed).

Evaluation

Most believed that the process was valuable; they better understood other views, developed relationships, and learned to work together. Opinions differed widely with regard to how much was substantively accomplished.

Limitations

1. The importance of this process was undermined by parallel formation of a new state Interagency Council on Growth Management.
2. Success depended heavily on the high degree of personal commitment and the skills of the facilitator; momentum was lost with her departure and the dissolution of the group.
3. A shared information base would have enhanced the process.
4. The process failed to engage or satisfy key stakeholders (local governments, some development and business interests) who were crucial to passing or implementing legislation.
5. Unfortunately, at the insistence of several stakeholders, consensus was defined as 100 percent agreement,[7] virtually guaranteeing there would not be consensus on many points.

CANMORE GROWTH MANAGEMENT STRATEGY

Source:	Jamal (1997)
Location:	Canmore, Alberta, Canada
Date:	1995–96
Scale:	Town (population 7,000)
Scope:	Physical, economic, social
Representation:	About 19 interest groups
Public input:	Public meetings
Theoretical "model":	Interest-based, collaborative, multiparty consensus
"Product":	Growth Management Strategy for town of Canmore
By-product:	Collaborative learning

Background

The mountain town of Canmore is located in the Bow Valley on the Trans-Canada Highway, 100 kilometers from Calgary, just outside Banff National Park. Originally a mining center, it now plays several roles in addition to being a resident community of old-timers and newcomers:

1. A residence for about 1,000 Banff workers

2. A community of cottagers (second-home owners) from Calgary

3. A provider of spillover accommodation when Banff is full

4. The service center for a tourist and recreation corridor that attracts a large number of visitors in its own right

Recent population growth had averaged more than 7 percent a year. For over a decade, the community had experienced controversy concerning the scale, type, and pace of development. The town council had historically been split between "green" and pro-development factions, with the balance of power shifting from election to election. External pressures for growth included federal government limits on expansion of the Banff townsite (see next case) and provincial government promotion of Canmore and the adjacent Kananaskis country provincial recreation area as tourism destinations.

Much of the recent controversy had focused on two major large-scale resort proposals. Some resident groups had expended time and energy as intervenors into a quasi-judicial hearing about one of these developments (the Three Sisters site). The political environment was described as "ugly," with multiple conflicting interests (seen by many residents as incompatible) and with a loss of confidence in the local government developing over time.

Events

The Growth Management Strategy (GMS) process was triggered by a 400-signature petition gathered by a local resident, calling on the council not to approve any development on the Three Sisters site unless approved by a referendum. Instead, the [then newly elected] mayor chose a consensus-based community process to develop a growth management strategy for the town. The process would involve both local and external stakeholders in the hope of avoiding a polarizing referendum vote on the issue of growth and development, one that might further divide the community.

The facilitators who were hired proposed a multi-stakeholder, community-based, and interest-based consensus-seeking process. Mayor, council, and local government officials opted not to participate directly in decision making (wishing the process to appear "arm's length"). They left the convening up to the two facilitators, though they assisted in calling the public's attention to this community-based effort. Hence, representatives from the local government, such as the planners, attended the process only as a liaison to the mayor and council and/or to provide technical assistance where required.

Participants in the Growth Management Committee (GMC) were selected to represent a broad spectrum of interest groups. The facilitators selected people with a stake in the community, but some key players who held "no-growth" positions believed they were left out or thought they had to stay out of the process because they were informed that "no-growth" could not be on the agenda (since this was a consensus process).

The committee developed its own ground rules over the first eight months. The most controversial was [what they called] the "shotgun" rule: If any group X withdrew from the process, that would end it, i.e., the Committee would report to the council that they were "unable to develop a GMS because group X had withdrawn." This led to a focus on making recommendations that everyone could "live with," i.e., that were not so offensive to any group that they would risk withdrawal from the process.

The group split for two initial exercises. A vision statement (Canmore In 2015) was developed to guide policy and decision making. A land base map exercise (showing built-up land uses, future zoned uses, wildlife uses, and natural features) highlighted physical limitations of the valley and clarified choices, interconnections, and conflicts between uses and resource protection. Later, they divided into four subcommittees to deal with the key issue areas identified in the vision exercise: social, environmental, cultural, and economic.

The committee was eventually able to produce a GMS that everyone could "live with." One of the most contentious issues was whether to specify limits to residential growth. This issue was deemed too "hot" to deal with initially but was brought back on the table later. The outcome was a 6 percent annual limit recommended for five years, followed with a shaky agreement on 6 percent for the next five years.

By-products

1. The GMC process and the GMS were used as an election banner during the local election that took place a few months after the GMC had produced its report. The mayor was reelected, and three GMS committee members were elected to the council.

2. A threshold and monitoring committee was set up by the council.

3. A town cultural officer position was created.

4. Submissions were made to the Banff-Bow Valley Study (see next case) regarding the impacts of Banff Park policies on the town of Canmore.

Evaluation

In many ways, the process was very successful. The map was a particularly valuable tool for organizing information and helping to understand choices (although potentially it could have been used to "shape" reality, as more than one participant expressed to the researcher). Intensive negotiation and dialogue helped some participants to overcome hostility and distrust, to discover interest and values in common with their "opponents." Communication did occur, developing trust and respect-based relationships. Commitment grew through dialogue and action. However, not all the participants or all the community fared so well in the process.

Issues

Inclusion

Not all participants had the positive experience discussed above. Some thought they were not being heard or accepted in the committee. They wanted to leave but were deterred by the "shotgun" rule: They feared the collapse of the process would bring community opprobrium on them and their group. In addition, a number of resident segments were left out of the process. For instance, there was little participation by lower-income, less "well-connected" residents, such as those who lived in the trailer park. Yet, subsidized housing was a major concern identified by GMC participants.

Process Design

There were also some difficulties with the process design. Rules were invoked selectively at times, and several were seen by some participants as oppressive. The rules were also held rigidly (i.e., there was no mechanism for change, even when they were seen to be counterproductive by some participants at various stages in the process).

Selection of participants as representatives of perceived interest groups meant that they came with "labels," which made stereotyping almost inevitable. The attempt to incorporate values and guiding principles in the vision statement gave an aura of spurious agreement, uncovered when more specific issues were addressed. (We will discuss these last two issues in the next chapter.)

BANFF-BOW VALLEY STUDY[8]

Source: Jamal (1997)
Location: Banff, Alberta, Canada
Date: 1994–96

Scale:	National park and community
Scope:	Environmental, economic, development
Representation:	14 "sectors"
Public input:	Public forum, public meetings, vision statement survey
Theoretical "model":	Consensus decision making; roundtable
"Products":	• Vision statement for Banff-Bow Valley
	• *State of the Valley* report
	• Summary report of the roundtable (including goals and strategies for long-term management)
	• Final report of the task force

Background

The town of Banff is a world-famous historical tourist destination located within Banff National Park (Canada's oldest and a World Heritage Site). Growth projections showed that the town's population could grow from the current 7,700 to 20,000 in the next twenty years, with annual visitors increasing from five million to at least ten million (possibly as high as twenty million). Environmentalists were concerned that development would destroy the ecological integrity of the park. Business interests were fearful that development would be frozen.

The Banff-Bow Valley Study (BBVS) was initiated by the then Minister of Canadian Heritage, Michel Dupuy, in March 1994, as a two-year study commencing in June 1994 and resulting in a final report to the Minister in June 1996. The study, focused on the Bow River watershed within Banff National Park, was to be a comprehensive analysis of the environmental, economic, and social issues within the watershed. It was expected to culminate in a set of strategies for the long-term management of the Banff-Bow Valley so as "to protect the environmental integrity, as well as the social and economic vitality, of the Banff-Bow Valley for future generations" (BBVS 1995, 2). The BBVS task force was announced by the Minister on July 5, 1994. Supported by a Secretariat that provided administrative and professional support, the Task Force developed a four-phase study process. The first phase included the development of a public participation process in the study and initiation of an ongoing process of developing a knowledge base to provide a baseline for decision making.

Events

A multiparty roundtable was selected by the task force as the mechanism to be used for enabling public input into the task force's report, based on a process of dialogue and consensus decision making. Key stakeholder groups were identified and convened by the task force under sector headings (e.g., Park Users, Commercial Outdoor Recreation, Local Environment, National Environment, Social/Health/Education, Tourism, Federal Government, Local Government, Culture). Each of these sectors, in turn, represented a number of organizations. The chairs of a number of sectors that had a large membership were assisted by steering committees. Process and procedure rules were established, and interest statements were developed by each sector. Of the fourteen sectors at the table, the two First Nations sectors dropped out early in the process. The provincial government of Alberta attended in observer capacity only.

One of the early tasks of the roundtable was to approve a mediator, brought in to assist them. The participants spent a large amount of time constructing a vision for the valley. The final product included an introduction, a core vision, key themes, principles, and values. In addition, the participants assisted with a number of tasks including compiling a compendium of information on the state of the valley and negotiating on a few of the issues they identified as important to address. Through discussion in the July, August, and September meetings, the table identified four key negotiation issues: (1) ecological integrity, (2) appropriate use, (3) community health, and (4) visitor and resident requirements for capital infrastructure. Due to time constraints, they agreed to work on only the first two issues. The table's work was compiled into a summary report that was ratified by the sector members and used by the task force as guidance in developing its report to the Minister. Aspects of the final report were incorporated into the 1997 Banff Park Management Plan. Subsequently, the new Minister of Canadian Heritage imposed a commercial development freeze on the Banff townsite.

Evaluation

From the viewpoint of the federal initiators, this exercise was probably viewed as a success in that it produced and legitimated a set of recommendations that seemed to fit with their objectives. However, as a planning process, the case illustrates some of the problems that can arise in participatory processes. A government-initiated process, it was seen by some participants as controlled and focused on substantive outcomes rather than on a fair, inclusive process.

While a number of positive benefits occurred through the Banff-Bow Valley Round Table (BBVRT) process, such "consensus" processes need to be examined and managed very carefully to ensure that meaningful participation takes place. Even the visioning process was not simply one of warm, fuzzy hand-holding; it resulted in a joint vision that was interpreted differently by different groups. The label of a "consensus" process in this case meant that parties were cautious about including certain statements into the vision. As one participant noted, the BBVRT vision was better characterized as a "negotiated settlement" than a consensus-based vision. He thought that it was interest-based: a "compromise of his position versus my position" (Jamal 1997, 106).

Issues

ECOLOGICAL DOMINANCE AND THE ROLE OF SCIENCE

Since much of the table time was spent on ecological issues, social issues were marginalized during the issues-negotiation phase. Not surprisingly, a business participant thought that the process was skewed and was "window dressing" on a predefined problem. From his point of view, the process did not allow participants to deliberate and frame the problems themselves. He saw the situation as the following:

> We've got a national transportation corridor. We've got Canada's premier tourist destination, that's the reality; how do you deal with it? And instead the Bow Valley Study addressed it from ecological integrity [which] means this, this place doesn't have, or is unlikely to have, ecological integrity and therefore we have to shut the doors. (Jamal 1997, 97)

This participant was also disconcerted by the fact that the final report of the task force was formulated based on the "precautionary" principle, among others.

The BBVRT process can be characterized as an instrumentally driven process that relied on appealing to science to legitimize the growing threats to "ecological integrity" of Banff National Park. For instance, the term "ecological integrity" was rhetorically applied to frame this concept as something uniform and unambiguous. As one environmental group participant stated:

> We believe that the ecological integrity of the Banff Bow Valley is really on shaky grounds right now and there's some serious problems. Our frustration has been on the scientific community not coming forward and saying that unequivocally. The cumulative effects assessment we believe will illustrate that clearly. (Jamal 1997, 92)

Yet, as a public-sector participant noted, such scientific terms are misleading in the way they are used: "Our use of terms like 'cumulative impacts' has exceeded science's ability to reasonably describe and predict that. I think in some cases our words are ahead of our knowledge" (Jamal 1997, 96).

REPRESENTATION ISSUES

Public information of the process was enabled through various means, including a few meetings locally and nationally, BBVS newsletters (three issues), public access to the roundtable meetings, and some media coverage, as well as through sectors meeting with their constituents. How well did dissemination of information and decision making occur at the group-member level of each sector? A number of participants at the steering committee, subcommittee, and sector-chair level thought that learning and participation were strongest at these levels but that the influence of activities and actions from the circles closest to the roundtable did not extend out to the public, or even to the various groups represented by steering committee members.

As in most of these cases, a major concern is with who was *not* at the table. Upper-middle-class, well-educated, articulate, professional, and business interests were very well represented at the table. Most other voices seemed to have been left out.

Another concern was expressed about the lack of presence of some of the larger business interests in the park (e.g., Canadian Pacific Hotels and some of the ski resort owners), especially considering the continued development activities in the park while the process was taking place. As one participant wondered, were these bigger business interests accessing the Minister directly while others were being kept busy at the roundtable?

The Three-Table Problem

The "two-table" problem is much-discussed in the labor negotiation literature. It refers to the fact that the parties at the negotiating table have to go back and "sell" any agreement they have made to *another* table (their organization), to people who were not party to any transformed understanding, any new respect and trust that may have been generated at the first table. When there is a history of hostility between parties, this may be an extremely difficult selling job.

The Banff-Bow Valley task force had a "three-table" problem in that each participant was a sector chair representing a number of different *groups*. Thus, the second table comprised representatives of these groups, who, in turn, had to sell any resulting agreement to their organizations, whose members were very distant from the original table.

CONCLUSION

For the pragmatist, the key question is "Does a dialogical/communicative approach help to improve planning practice?" Given our understanding of the importance of context, we would not expect the answer to be an unequivocal "Yes" or "No." We are not surprised to find that it works better under certain conditions than others.

Table 10-1 summarizes factors that we have found contribute to the success or failure of planning processes. Consensual planning processes that

TABLE 10-1

**Factors Contributing to Success of
Dialogical/Communicative Planning Processes**

Positive	*Negative*
Selection and Composition	
Legitimate selection process	Biased selection process
Inclusionary	Exclusionary
Stakeholders directly involved	Stakeholders' representatives involved
Small group involved	Large group
Individual members selected for representativeness, attributes	Members formally represent interest groups (or sectors)
Context	
Grassroots origin	Government-initiated
Small scale	Large scale
Specific, concrete issues	General, abstract issues
Simple problems/issues	Multiple, complex/"wicked" problems/issues
Agreement on problem framing	Strong disagreement on problem framing
Strong external incentives to succeed (delay costly, litigation difficult, government intervention feared)	Weak external incentives (alternative arenas, litigation feasible, government intervention unlikely)
Historical antagonisms	Strong sense of community
Wide ideological differences	Ideological consensus
Operation	
Legitimate/credible process	Lack of legitimacy
Autonomous	Government controlled
Clear links to political decision makers	No links to political decision makers
Well-defined mandate	Ill-defined mandate
Well funded	Poorly funded
Trained facilitator	No or untrained facilitator

TABLE 10-1 (continued)

Factors Contributing to Success of Dialogical/Communicative Planning Processes

Positive	Negative
Operation *(continued)*	
Some planning expertise	No planning expertise
Good background information and technical advice	Lack of background information and technical advice
Subcommittees (if group is large)	No subcommittees
Relations of respect and trust developed	Disrespect, distrust
Ongoing public engagement (during process)	Inadequate public engagement
Flexible decision rules (e.g., definition of "consensus")	Rigid decision rules
Organizations and Interest	
Well-prepared stakeholders or groups (agenda, information, comprehension)	Unprepared stakeholders or groups
Good-faith negotiation (sincerity)	Bad faith, manipulation
Strong member commitment	Weak member commitment
Power and Capacity	
Genuine political support/commitment	No (or fake) political support
Equal power of participants	Power disparities
Recommendations implementable	Strong barriers to implementation

Source: The categories in this table are based on Margerum 2002b, but the list of factors was developed without reference to Margerum. We modified our presentation by grouping factors according to his categories and added about six factors from his analysis.

meet more of these conditions are more likely to work. Some of these factors suggest ways to improve almost any process (e.g., by inclusionary, legitimate selection processes; well-defined mandates; adequate resources; assistance to unorganized stakeholders; ongoing public engagement; good information and technical assistance; a focus on developing relationships of respect and trust;

trained facilitators with planning expertise; and flexible definitions of consensus). Others suggest that some contexts will be inherently difficult (e.g., large scale, numerous stakeholders, large groups, weak external incentives, historical animosities, multiple and complex issues, power inequalities, availability of alternative arenas, bad faith, manipulation). These are the areas that challenge us to be creative and innovative, where further experimentation and research could be most productive. For example, Margerum (2002b) examined twenty cases to develop recommendations for overcoming some of these obstacles to consensus building.

Most of these cases achieved at least some substantive success in terms of their sponsors' objectives. Procedurally, many still had much room for improvement, but they seemed to work better than the old approach, supporting the contention that some of the directions we have suggested for planning show promise. Overall, it seems fair to conclude that the emergence of a dialogical planning approach has a lot of potential. But our approach needs to be tried out and modified to fit each particular planning context.

We do not claim to have found any magical or mechanical success formula, nor do any of the other dialogical or communicative approaches we have discussed here and in chapter 8. The exercise of professional judgment in context will always be a key element. And, it must be remembered that any approach or process is vulnerable to manipulation and abuse at any stage. No amount of process design or facilitation skill can compensate, if relationships of respect and trust are not developed (i.e., if Habermas's ideal speech conditions have not been reasonably approximated.)

Implicitly, some of the planning processes we examined bear some resemblance to a WRE process. However, none of them fully implemented this process. We want to be clear that consensus is not the ultimate goal of dialogical planning processes. A legitimate consensus must be meaningful, reasonable, and fair in its context. As we discussed in chapter 9, a forced consensus that is thin and superficial is likely to fall apart in concrete application. A transformative WRE process attempts to go beyond thin consensus to incorporate critiques, reframe problems, and create new possibilities, formulating deeper and more durable agreements.

Thus, most of the cases described could have benefitted from a more explicit use of a transformative WRE process. Understanding how to use a WRE process could help in expanding the overlapping consensus among disparate communities, groups, and cultures at many different scales. In addition to the general account of how a planner might use a WRE process in chapter 8, we will present some more specific ideas in chapter 11 concerning negotiating, dialogic, and decision processes in the kind of highly contested and controversial situations—the "wicked problems" of Rittel and Webber (1973)—where planning is most difficult.

Part V

PLANNING SHOULD AVOID MODERNIST AND POSTMODERNIST TRAPS

11

The Search for Clear Categories and Universal Principles

INTRODUCTION

In this section, we look at some traps that commonly beset contemporary planners. The first is a modernist trap; the second, third, and fifth are postmodernist; the fourth could be either.

PROBLEMS WITH CONSENSUS-SEEKING PROCESSES

Several of the cases in chapter 10 illustrate common practices often recommended by popular approaches to participatory planning, as described below.

Identification of "Interest" Representatives

"Stakeholders" or "interests" (i.e., interest groups) are identified, and representatives are appointed to serve on roundtables, steering committees, or other collaborative bodies that are aimed at finding common ground and a consensual endorsement of plans, policies, or actions. These stakeholders are usually described in general categories, with which they often closely identify (Cormick et al. 1996; Freeman 1984; Hoberg 1993; Huxham 1996).

In the Banff case, the labeling of sector representatives tended to pit "environmentalists" against "commercial developers" and, similarly, juxtaposed social and cultural sectors against environment or business. As one "environmentalist" expressed, given the views attributed to categories like preservationist or conservationist, he preferred not to be typed with a such a label.

213

Jamal's study of this process suggests that "segregating groups by 'interests' may tend to exacerbate divisiveness and differences among stakeholders" (Jamal 1997, 293). As one participant observed, "Any time you label, you exclude" (ibid., 129).

Seeking Agreement on Shared Categories and Principles

As a starting point, agreement is often sought on shared definitions of key terms and general categories, as well as on general principles that will guide debate over more specific issues (Weisbord et al. 1992). Early in the Banff process, participants spent considerable time developing a shared vision statement, including certain broad principles, such as the need to put "limits" on development.[1] Several of the groups jockeyed (generally successfully) to get "their" words into the statement. As one environmentalist respondent explained:

> [T]he word "limits" is in there . . . there may be differing interpretations . . . but at least it's part of the vocabulary . . . we've said restraining ourselves for future generations is important to us. We value the intrinsic, [we] intrinsically value other forms of life. (Jamal 1997, 105)[2]

This participant did recognize that certain terms and concepts may hold different meanings for different participants, making agreement difficult. Although the vision exercise was a long, tedious process of piecing together a statement that all the participants could live with, there was little debate on what such terms or concepts meant. This meant that the apparent agreement on abstract principles fell apart whenever concrete decisions had to be made. As we shall see below, this may not always be a reasonable way of proceeding. In this case the exercise was not necessarily positive since the categories were viewed in an essentialistic way and were deeply contested.

Similarly, the park's mandate was expressed in broad and abstract concepts that participants thought required clarification. A senior government official was invited to speak to the roundtable on this matter. But again, the "meaning" of the mandate was not debated or discussed at the table, at least not in any way that could provide for a better understanding of sector concerns. For an environmental participant, fears were evoked by the word "dual" [mandate], which presented the danger of implying a balancing of use and preservation.

Several business- and government-related sectors were also uncomfortable with ecological strategic goals developed jointly by the roundtable members. While the environmental sectors called forth the science to legitimate the "ecological crisis" in the park, business participants feared the practical implications of this information for economic considerations:

> I have a great fear of adopting these [ecological] strategic goals because I
> don't know where I am and where I'm going. . . . I don't want to be hemmed
> in. (ibid., 94)

When broadly expressed goals mask real differences, there is a valid concern
that they may be used manipulatively to claim that all participants supported
something that they had no intention of supporting.

In situations characterized by a history of controversy, these initial moves
often generate barriers to the consensus sought—barriers that are nearly in-
surmountable. What we wish to suggest is that in such situations, this process be reversed—that such identification occur at the end rather than at the
beginning of the process. Dealing with these problems raises some theoretical questions that have general application to planning. This theory helps us
in understanding how these problems arise.

WHY DOES LABELING CREATE PROBLEMS?

Naming

Naming, labeling, or categorizing that places people in a politically loaded
category can often kill the dialogue that communicative planners want to
encourage. If we avoid labeling individuals as "environmentalists" or "developers," they are more likely to enter a dialogue with each other. We are better
off just describing our beliefs to each other! We may discover that many of
them overlap, which can provide a basis for dialogue. If we avoid labeling a
set of beliefs as "environmentalist," more people can subscribe to them; certainly fewer will reject them outright; and more will be willing to debate them.

In addition to avoiding labels, we should seek neutral language—for
example, staying away from "environment," "intrinsic value," and the like.
In these contexts, neutral language is more helpful than normative, value-
laden language. Normative language works when dealing with a single shared
culture; but in a context with disparate values, it is often exclusionary.

Names often cause trouble because of the baggage associated with them.
People become committed to the categories they use and often develop a close
identification with these categories, both in their own minds and in the perceptions of others. Sometimes this identification (indeed, the very conception
of what a category is) leads to difficulties. Categories also have a strong influence on human relations, in particular power relations between individuals,
which often distorts and unbalances discourse and decision making. The
power of traditional categories is something we should try to overcome, as
Foucault (1972) and Flyvbjerg (1998) have pointed out. For example, those
who appeal to the notion of ecological integrity (in our Banff case) are invoking the power of science to support their cause.

Essentialism

The inclination to commit to categories (and this conception of their nature) is strongly influenced by a particular philosophical tradition, one with a view of language that, in our view, is deeply flawed. This tradition presupposes that categories, or general terms that pick out natural kinds "in the world," have precise definitions that reflect the essence of that category. Consequently, they seek definitions that determine this essence, leading them to search for the essential element common to all uses of terms, such as "the environment." But, to return to the practical issue, when and if the term or its use is contested, this search for essence can stall a planning process at the very beginning.

To vastly oversimplify, these difficulties date back to John Stuart Mill's theory of meaning; he argued that words have a denotation (roughly, reference) and connotation (roughly, meaning or sense). The denotation of a term is the class of items to which it refers; the connotation is the properties shared by all members of that class. The connotation is roughly associated with the meaning of the term and provides its [essential] characteristics or attributes. In this essentialist view, all terms must have these features,[3] and all items "in the real world" must be referred to by these terms. Thus, the existence of a term confers "reality" on that to which it refers by virtue of certain properties that determine what it is (its essence). Those properties or characteristics are seen as rigidly fixed.

The effect of this view on the dynamics of communicative action are profound. People become committed to categories because (1) they confer reality, and hence legitimacy, and (2) they confer this legitimacy on a class of people (or group as a subclass) by virtue of the essential properties that determine the denotation of that category. With this legitimacy often comes power. One's very identity is determined by those identifications.

In contexts of extreme and deeply embedded conflicts, Cockburn (1998, 13) found that

> Essentialism is not merely an interesting theoretical concept. It is a dangerous political force, designed to shore up differences and inequalities, to sustain dominations. It operates through stereotypes that fix identity in eternal dualisms: woman victim, male warrior; trusty compatriot, degenerate foreigner.

A key skill for conflict resolution is learning to "avoid the labeling and limiting of others" (ibid., 15).

A NEOPRAGMATIC ALTERNATIVE

A neopragmatic alternative views categories more flexibly. On this pragmatic view, categories are fluid; they are not fixed, not set in stone. The neopragmatist rejects the notion of essence and rigid definition. We accept the arguments of Wittgenstein (1958, para. 65) when he discusses the idea of family resemblances:

> Instead of producing something common in all that we call language, I am saying that these phenomena have no one thing common which makes us use the same word for all, but that they are related to one another in many different ways.

Rather than a set of essential properties, items that share the same term have a family of characteristics. All of them have some of these attributes, but no one attribute is common to every member. The properties that fix terms are open, ever changing.

Names versus Descriptions

We may find that, in certain cases, there are good reasons to avoid categories and general terms and to replace them by descriptions. This may apply even in sciences like biology that focus on definition and nomenclature. As the eighteenth-century biologist Georges de Buffon argued,

> A good description without definitions . . . a particular to exceptions and almost imperceptible gradations are . . . the only means of estimating nature. If the time lost in forming definitions had been employed in making good descriptions, we would not in this day have found Natural History in its infancy; we should have had less trouble to take her baubles ... for we should have written more for science and less for error. (Leroi 1997, 30).

So even in science, essentialism can be seen as counterproductive.

Once we accept the idea that categories are not fixed and do not require an essence—that they involve characteristics, properties, and descriptions that are loosely connected and open—then those categories lose their psychological power. For certain purposes, they can be replaced by a set of overlapping descriptions. Instead of names, we can "look for beliefs which are relatively central" (Putnam 1990, 291), recognizing that these beliefs are relative to interest and context.

Thus, the neopragmatic view is that there is no sharp line between essence (naming) and attribute (describing). Names and their meanings come and go, evolving over time, and it is not helpful to write the definition in stone. Our ontological commitments can be softer, more flexible, and open. Yet they are not radically decentered, as Jacques Derrida would have them. Rather, neopragmatism blurs the line between central and peripheral elements, between central and peripheral issues. This allows for fluidity of discussion. For example, in negotiations between Israel and Syria, there was agreement on more than sixty issues, but none of them were seen as "central." It might have been fruitful here to give up the distinction; then some "peripheral" issues could have become "central."

New Names

We want to clarify what we are saying here so that there is no misunderstanding. What we are suggesting is that the choice of linguistic form, names, categories, and labels should be in the service of our goals rather than being their master. Once one gives up the essentialist and metaphysical realist[4] conception of general terms, they can be used in a productive (and creative) manner. But the choice of these referring expressions is a creative process, and it is tied to our purposes.

Even in physics, there are linguistic choices to be made, e.g., whether or not we speak of properties or objects. As Putnam (1990, 27) notes:

> [E]ven a space–time region is a matter of convention . . . some philosophers think of points as location predicates, not objects. So a space–time region is just a set of properties . . . and not an object (in the sense of concrete object) at all, if this view is right.

Which choice we make depends on our purposes. This is true in physics and in planning contexts—for example, conflict resolution.

In planning contexts, we choose new linguistic groupings that will encourage consensus between conflicting positions. But this is more likely to be useful toward the end of the process rather than at the beginning, when entrenched categories will tend to divide rather then encourage agreement.

After agreement has been reached—after we have reconfigured some of our beliefs—then a new name, label, or definition provides a useful shorthand for the new shared description, one that summarizes a redescription of the world[5]—hopefully a better world. And that is our [neopragmatic] ontology. This is most likely to occur under conditions of maximum fluidity, conditions that encourage new possibilities—a new "world," if you like.

This fluidity provides an alternative to the traditional confrontational and hierarchical conception of the planning process that seems to flow from the RCPM process of choosing an option from a fixed set. As one participant in the Banff-Bow Valley task force put it:

> [I]f we're looking at choosing options, which is what decision making is about, and if we're looking at choosing between preservation and development. . . .

When she looked at these options as the fixed categories of either preservation or development, then she saw the process as leading to a winner and a loser and thought, "We're not going to win. We're never going to win." The space of accommodating other perspectives diminishes when beliefs and values are perceived to be so diametrically opposed that a "win/lose" frame is adopted instead of openness to dialogue and debate.

WHY DO ABSTRACT UNIVERSAL PRINCIPLES CREATE PROBLEMS?

Another aspect of the traditional philosophical position that we, as pragmatists, want to critique is the search for abstract principles. The idea underlying this search is that there is a hierarchy, with abstract principles at the top, from which are deduced more specific principles, and then concrete actions. This idea underlies the common planning/roundtable practice of beginning by seeking agreement on governing principles, which we observed in chapter 10.

Deep ecologists often feel the need to provide a new abstract universal metaphysical principle for their new environmental ethic. Armstrong-Buck (1986, 241) maintains

> [that] the natural world has intrinsic value . . . is intuitively . . . acknowledged by many people. . . . [T]he growth of this [view] into a widely shared ethos capable of guiding human activity . . . requires . . . an adequate metaphysical theory, since a metaphysical theory can give penetration to, and a wider and consistent application of, our intuition.

Behind this urge is a foundational idea: that moral judgment flows from indubitable first principles. But there are no such first principles! This should be clear from the vast variety (and unending nature) of disagreement about purported first principles available.

One thing we have learned from the postmodernist and pragmatic attacks on modernism is that there is no god's-eye perspective, no Archimedean point that can give us an absolute perspective for grounding our beliefs—not god, nor science, nor some universal conception of rationality. Very often, what had been thought of as indubitable truths turned out, on closer inspection, to be temporal prejudices or ideological distortions. If there are fixed points, they are relative to a larger framework. As Wittgenstein (1958, para. 144, 142) suggests:

> What stands fast does so, not because it is intrinsically obvious or convincing; it is rather held fast by what lies around it . . . it is not single axioms that strike me as obvious, it is a system in which consequence and premise give one another mutual support.

Furthermore, many of these proposed first principles are consistent with a variety of inconsistent concrete judgments. The problem is that these principles are so abstract, and so open to multiple interpretations, and so remote from ordinary life, that they are useless as a basis for the justification of practical concrete action.

We are not denying that principles (non-metaphysical ones) do have a role to play in the process of justification, but it is not a hierarchical one—abstract principles do not have any privileged position. Rather, they are part of an interactive process of holistic mutual adjustment. As Richard Rorty (1990, 298) remarks, there is a "give-and-take between intuitions about the desirability of particular consequences and intuitions about general principles, with neither having the determining force."

On this view, principles are only one factor in justification, important but not superior to a host of other factors, including considered judgments (i.e., intuitions) and background theories and information. We weigh one against the other, sometimes modifying principles and other times modifying intuitions, in a search for a coherent reflective equilibrium. It is an incremental and nonhierarchical affair: incremental as our beliefs and concepts evolve over time and nonhierarchical in blurring the lines between theory and practice, between abstract principle and concrete intuition, and between judgment and action (chapter 7). As a constitutional theorist has remarked,

> [T]he skill of making and maintaining a constitutional commonwealth is not a matter of a solitary, clever person deducing general rules from essential definitions. Rather, it is a practical skill that "must be gained by . . . exercising of that Faculty [of reasoning] by reading, study and observation," as well as by "Conversation between man and man." The reason why it is a practical skill acquired by "use and exercise" is that "actions and the application of remedies to them" are "so various," "different," and "diversified from one another" that abstract rules are a hindrance rather than a help "when it comes to particulars."[6] (Tully 1995, 114)

Summary

Combining the points made above (naming and absolute principles) leads us to some pragmatic conclusions regarding the sort of process that should be applied to contestable debates. It gives us the flexibility required to enhance the probability of success, of consensus. We can reverse the sequence often taken to be necessary. We need not begin by "getting to the heart of the matter"; we need not identify opposing forces in terms of essentially contested categories. As we try to develop standards, we often find that "the very activity of trying to formulate principles leads us to change our view about particular cases" (Putnam 1992, 130). We suggest the RCPM idea that planning involves deciding between predetermined and mutually exclusive options be replaced by a planning process that seeks to synthesize and integrate the initial options.

This does not in any way affect the legitimacy or credibility of particular points of view. What it does do is loosen categories or points of view, freeing and opening them up to possibilities that would be eliminated by a slavish attachment to predetermined categories or labels. Out of this process, new and more fruitful categories will arise. And finally, it frees us from seeking hard-and-fast principles that will do more to kill process than enhance it.

RECOMMENDATIONS FOR PLANNING PROCESSES

From the above discussion, we derive five practical ideas concerning public negotiating, debating, and decision processes in the kind of highly contested and controversial situation where planners often find themselves.

Flexibility Is Key

These processes should be very fluid, flexible, and adaptive; we don't necessarily start by seeking underlying principles or identifying interests. Change can start anywhere—with considered judgments, general theories, background normative theories, or background empirical theories; provoked by new attitudes, new ideas, new theories, new technology, new empirical evidence.

When facing a seemingly impossible dialogue (about the environment, for example), we should try to keep it in flux. Our consensus seeking should strive to develop shared goals and beliefs about the environment. We should aim to set forth these beliefs in neutral terms that are not categorical, value-laden, normative, abstract, or overly general.

The Process Should Not Be Hierarchical

The process cannot follow a mechanical algorithm. It should not follow a linear hierarchical sequence of first establishing absolute universal principles, then deriving subsidiary principles, and applying them to specific situations. Abstract principles do not have a privileged hierarchical position in this process. Rather, they are rules of thumb that form one element in an interactive process of holistic mutual adjustment. For example, we do not need (as some deep ecologists claim) a new absolute universal principle to justify preserving our natural environment (chapter 12). This is an important implication of the rejection (by both postmodernists and pragmatists) of foundationalism.

Principles and Definitions Need Not Come First

Practical decisions on appropriate actions don't require agreement on metaphysical questions (or governing principles, or meta-narratives) re the nature of the person, of society, of the city, or of the environment. For example, we do not need to agree on whether the environment or species or individual have inherent or instrumental value. Instead, we should seek agreement on only those practical concepts needed to deal with the problems we want to address.

In other words, we may need to reverse the order usually believed to be a necessary precondition to meaningful conflict resolution. We do not attempt to define [what are thought to be] essential terms or to provide foundational principles. As soon as it becomes apparent that there is no consensus on a issue, it should be put aside, perhaps in favor of something smaller, narrower, more concrete. If the use of important central notions such as "the environment" is unavoidable, their initial definitions should be left intentionally vague. If we do arrive at agreement on definition, it will more likely be at the end of the process, not at the beginning.

Stress the Shared Framework

Consensus seeking requires debate, conflict, argument. In the midst of disagreement, it is easy to forget that debate is not even possible unless there is a broader framework of agreement. In seeking consensus, it is important to find, emphasize, and build on whatever is shared (even if it seems trivial).

Trust Is Key

As we saw in chapter 3, a significant degree of trust is a necessary condition for any kind of communication. If there were literally no trust, then nothing the other party said could be accepted; everything would have to be verified. Interpretation of what anyone says presupposes a principle of charity (assuming what the other person says is generally true). Disagreement and debate make sense only within a larger framework of agreement on concepts and beliefs. Thus, trust is an intellectual necessity for both communication and agreement, but it also has an emotional component. Establishing and building trust is an important tool for the planner. The need for trust makes it important to begin decision processes by finding, and focusing on, areas of agreement (chapter 15). Without trust, we really do have the postmodern abyss!

A Brief Example

There is no better example of two groups with divergent positions than Israelis and Palestinians. A 1998 description of the Oslo peace process shows it as a good illustration of some of our recommendations: Traditional categories were avoided; the discussion was decentered; consensus began with small, concrete matters; central issues were not defined; peripheral and central issues were not distinguished. According to a reviewer's account:

> As the (Oslo) process unfolds, the Israeli negotiators increasingly come to appreciate that their occupation was also corrupting the Palestinians through humiliation and economic degradation. Gradually the Palestinians came into focus as people, as humans, and not as the impersonal "Arab." (Schmermann 1998, 10)

Eventually, relationships of trust and respect were developed, and an "impossible" agreement was reached. Unfortunately, its subsequent implementation was tragically lacking in trust, respect, or honesty, and the process reversed itself to the present dismal situation.[7] This illustrates how fragile trust can be and how important it is to maintain. If planners can play a role in facilitating processes that create and maintain mutual respect and trust, this is an essential role indeed!

The Radical Paradigm Shift

THE CHALLENGE OF SUSTAINABILITY

One of the most pressing challenges to contemporary planning comes from the growing recognition that our public decisions have serious environmental implications. In order to respond to the challenge of environmental sustainability, Beatley (1994) persuasively argues that planning criteria must be broadened to include a wide variety of ethical factors in land-use decision making.

Many environmentalists argue that because the modernist approach has so clearly failed to deal with the current environmental crisis, we need a complete break with the moral foundation of Western civilization. They believe that the very notion of sustainability is misconceived, as there is nothing worth sustaining in our moral culture. They urge us to move away from what they call the anthropocentric value system to a new perspective where human beings no longer have priority in the scheme of things and have no special privilege (Leopold 1949, 220). We will refer to this view as "deep ecology" (Naess 1973) or "biocentric egalitarianism" (Taylor 1986).

We focus on two aspects of this position that have significant implications for planning. The first aspect is that those who hold it want to construct a new moral paradigm that would be appropriate to a new environmental culture. They often appeal to Kuhn's (1970) notion of a paradigm shift. For example, Livingston (1985, 12) asserts that "deep environmentalism is concerned with accomplishing a fundamental 'paradigm shift,' an appropriate way of culturally perceiving the relationship between man and nature." The second aspect is that the new paradigm is often reduced to a single ultimate absolute moral principle, such as Leopold's (1949, 224–25): "A thing is right when it tends to preserve the integrity, stability and beauty of the biotic community. It is wrong when it tends otherwise." We have already discussed the second aspect in chapter 11; we will consider the first aspect here. Planning theory is still struggling to respond to these claims and to incorporate environmental concerns. The traditional technocratic RCPM approach exacerbates the problem. Recent significant contributions in the area of planning ethics (Hendler 1995) have attempted to integrate ethics, environmental concerns, and planning (Beatley 1994, 1995; Jacobs 1995). While it is of great practical value, much of this work seems to accept the claims of deep ecology. We believe these claims must be viewed more critically.

A RADICAL PARADIGM SHIFT?

The Nature of Paradigm Shifts

Kuhn's (1970) notion of "paradigm shift" is notoriously ambiguous and has been used in a variety of different and conflicting ways. These uses vary from incremental modifications in our thinking, beliefs, and ways of behaving, through to very radical shifts in conceptual schemes that lead to a complete chasm of incommensurability between old and new paradigms.

An example of an incremental (but very significant) shift occurs when one realizes that dwindling resources and environmental desecration may require shifts in the use of productive resources as well as changes in economic and political institutions (e.g., limitations on property rights, on human freedom, on population growth, and so on).[1] While such changes are often referred to as paradigm shifts (Rees 1995), we view them as incremental. It is only because so much is held constant that they can be debated and evaluated (chapter 7). No radical shift in our basic moral perspective is needed. Instead of a radical paradigm shift, we have the continued reweaving of our moral beliefs (along with other beliefs) that constitutes moral change (progress). We would describe the current shift in planning (to a communicative or dialogical approach) as incremental in this sense. While radical environmentalists may claim that this is too conservative to deal with the current crisis, we reply that even minor modifications in thought and beliefs can lead to major shifts in practice.

What we want to critique here is the more radical use of "paradigm," a use consistent with Kuhn's original intent[2] and still employed by some interpreters (Feyerabend 1993; Livingston 1985; Naess 1973; Taylor 1986). In its most extreme form, a radical paradigm shift is where different paradigms are seen as entire conceptual schemes that are incommensurable; each paradigm is completely opaque from the point of view of the other with respect to both meaning and reference.[3] In this extreme view, different paradigms become unintelligible to those who have not *converted* to them, "such that those within different paradigms literally live in 'different worlds'" (Rosa 1995, 24). Thus, even if the same words are used in the new paradigm they will mean something quite different.

Radical Paradigm Shifts and Justification

Essentially, the difficulty with this approach is that it leaves no room for a critical and interpretive perspective from which to determine the meaning, reference, and justification of elements within different paradigms. Unless there is some overriding Archimedean point outside either paradigm (an assumption both we and Kuhn reject), there is no way to evaluate and interpret two different competing paradigms. Thus, a radical paradigm shift precludes any possibility of legitimation and justification of views to those who inhabit the established paradigm.

In fact, a radical paradigm shift in ethical perspective would be a shift to a paradigm that is not an ethical perspective at all. If our disagreement is so fundamental about what you call moral and what I call moral, then we must ask: Is it really "morality" that we are both talking about?

In contrast to this Kuhnian view, the pragmatist sees the entire process of interpretation of a conceptual scheme, language, or paradigm as one of grafting that scheme onto one's own. It requires significant overlap between perspectives (paradigms). Any talk of differences in concepts and beliefs also requires this overlap.

Radical Paradigm Shifts and Language

The Kuhnian view of radical paradigm shifts presupposes a segmented, rather than a holistic, view of language. It assumes that language can be segmented bit by bit and finds maximum coherence on the level of paradigm, so that segments of language (paradigms) can be severed from other segments of language. This means that a radical paradigm shift carries with it the possibility of drastic alteration of key concepts.

Thus, deep ecology requires a shift from an anthropocentric ethic to an ecocentric ethic. It holds that "all things in the biosphere have an equal right to live and blossom . . . all organisms and entities in the ecosphere . . . are equal in intrinsic worth" (Devall and Sessions 1985, 67). But this is a false view of language. Language should be viewed as holistic. As Wittgenstein (1969, para. 141) observes: "When we first begin to believe anything, what we believe is not a single proposition; it is a whole system of propositions (light dawns gradually over the whole). . . ." From our pragmatic perspective, one can speak of segments of language such as morality and science, but these language games cannot be sharply severed from each other or from the language as a whole. The meaning and reference of terms and the justification of beliefs cannot be isolated and segmented as Kuhn suggests.

Here we can see how justification and the determination of meaning cannot be sharply separated. When the shift becomes as radical as the deep ecologists propose, not only do we find it impossible to justify the shift, but the terms we use start to lose their meaning and reference. At some point, it is no longer clear that we know what apparently ordinary terms mean. Perhaps this is why some interpreters view deep ecology principles as metaphorical rather than literal.

Whenever we utter a sentence, there is a whole lot more that is presupposed. In an important sense the entire language is presupposed. Changes in the system can occur in many ways, but only if the system as a whole maintains stability. The model of holism can be captured in Otto Neurath's (1973) image of the ship at sea: It can be altered and improved fragment by fragment, but not completely and not all at once. There must be significant overlap of concepts and beliefs between paradigms as well as commonality within paradigms: "[A] change which is a veritable improvement from both perspectives is not a ["revolutionary"] transition between two incommensurable paradigms, but a piece of ["evolutionary"] progress *within* a prefixed horizon" (Rosa 1995, 24). It is this commonality of concepts and beliefs that makes it possible for change to be both intelligible and justified.

A PRAGMATIC, INCREMENTAL APPROACH

Instead of attempting to find a radical new paradigm or an acceptable universal metaphysical principle, we recommend a society that is pragmatic. As Richard Rorty (1990, 286) observes:

> [W]hen such a [pragmatic] society deliberates, when it collects the principles and intuitions to be brought into equilibrium, it will tend to disregard those drawn from philosophical . . . accounts of the self or rationality.

The foundational view has things the wrong way around. The search for ultimate first principles, more often than not, stems from a commitment to action rather than a source of its justification. Environmentalists are often looking for an ex poste rationale for doing what they intuitively believe is right.

As we saw in chapters 6 and 11, principles are just one element in a WRE process of holistic mutual adjustment, important but not superior to a host of other factors, including considered judgments (i.e., intuitions) and background theories and information.

In some ways, Arnie Naess's (1992, 53) position sounds similar.

> What is more pressing then debating norms is to work out ... priorities of certain kinds of action. ... environmental ethical views make up only part of a total and can only be understood internally related to a *total view*.

Naess had come to recognize that first principles are of little use for arriving at a general, intersubjective legitimation of concrete action. But he is too sanguine regarding this situation because he believes that ". . . people with seemingly deeply different religious or metaphysical ultimate views may work together in practical efforts to improve the ethical standard of human environment interaction" (Naess 1992, 57). At this point we part company with Naess because he seems to be saying, "Base your action on whatever metaphysical first principle you like so long as the action is right." Beatley's (1994, 17) position seems similar; he describes his approach as "moral pluralism, which suggests no single paradigm is applicable in all circumstances," i.e., which moral approach applies will be determined by the "specifics of each land-use case." This gives the impression that we should look at each moral theory independently, deduce the consequences for particular situations, and then choose one we like for that situation. But what do we do when several different moral approaches are applicable, and they give conflicting answers? As Naess or Beatley present it, the choice then appears arbitrary. Of course they and other environmentally friendly individuals may agree on what are the right views, but how do they persuade others? How can they justify their views? Their positions are incomplete.

But we have seen that one can't deduce, justify, or legitimize right action and belief from absolute and *universal* metaphysical principles. So how *can* one justify or legitimize right belief? Our answer to the question of justification involves bringing the deep ecology view into Wide Reflective Equilibrium. The problem with Naess's position is that his reflective equilibrium is not wide enough. While WRE *is* coherentist, it is not viciously circular. Any circularity involved is perfectly benign. Coherence is sufficient to provide justification when the equilibrium is wide enough—when the vocabulary, the language game, the form of life, are rich enough to provide interlacing legitimation. There is nothing further to which we can appeal!

Neopragmatism gives no privileged status to deep ecological (or any other) principles. When looked at this way, the deep/shallow distinction disappears, and our moral concerns with regard to the environment can no longer be sharply separated from other moral concerns. Our concern for the tree must be weighed against our concern for the livelihood of the logger. Once these moves are made, the apparent need for a moral paradigm shift disappears!

The Necessity of Incremental Change[4]

Ironically, those who reject foundationalism

> often see themselves as revolutionaries . . . saying that our language and our culture need radical change before our utopian hopes can be realized. . . . This insistence on radicality is foundationalism turned on its head. . . . (Rorty 1995, 201)

But this "urge to make all things new, to insist that nothing can change unless everything changes" (ibid.) is inconsistent with antifoundationalism.

As we argued in chapter 7, incrementalism is unavoidable in a postmodern (post-positivistic, nonfoundational) world. Positivism attempted to provide a scientific foundation for all knowledge. Postmodernist critiques have pointed to the inadequacy of the positivistic attempt and have undermined the very notion of an absolute foundation for knowledge. In a post-positivistic world, values, beliefs, and knowledge are recognized as dependent on consensus.

We do not mean this to be conservative in the sense of disallowing unconventional points of view, radical utopian alternatives, or ingenious unorthodox proposals for change. As we have said, all voices must be heard and evaluated. What we do mean by incrementalism is that in the public sphere, new views must be legitimized and justified by connecting them to our current views in a way that brings them into coherence.

What this does preclude is the very possibility of the violent break with our tradition that the proponents of a radical paradigm shift suggest. That is why deep ecologists who seek such radical change all search for indubitable metaphysical principles to legitimize their view. No such search is necessary, nor can their principles provide sufficient legitimation for concrete action. In fact, the statements made by deep ecologists that seem to imply the need for a paradigm shift must be interpreted incrementally if they are to function in a way that is productive.

REFLECTIVELY CHOSEN PRINCIPLES[5]

While we have argued that planning theory has no need for absolute universal principles (chapter 11) and that principles need to be tested against concrete situations, we do believe that planning theory has a need for reflectively chosen principles. As we saw in chapter 1, the extent to which philosophical reflection is relevant to a practical social activity like planning practice depends on the social context. If society had a high degree of consensus and solidarity, and if planners and planning theorists shared this consensus (or even agreed about what is wrong and how to fix it), then there would be little practical need for deep reflection on the principles that legitimize planning. But here and now, there is no such consensus. This is very evident in the area of environmental planning. Even the most deeply entrenched principles are "up for grabs."

Every conceptual move has benefits and costs. In contemplating any change, we should be aware of what is *lost*. For example, it has been argued that we should change the nature of responsibility to shift the stress from the individual to society, or that we should broaden the definition of rape to include verbal harassment. What we should carefully consider is: Do we want the social and legal consequences of these shifts? Various deep ecologists argue that we should expand the circle of moral concern to include all sentient beings, all living beings, or even all of the environment. Do we really want the consequences of giving trees or even rocks the same rights as people?

Other deep ecologists advocate expanding the notion of teleos (end purpose) to non-persons: "All organisms are teleological centres of life in the sense that each is a unique individual pursuing its own good in its own way" (Beatley 1994, 123). From this it is then argued that we have a moral obligation to preserve that good (of ecosystems, for example). What this does is extend the notion of moral goodness to areas that have never been objects of moral goodness. If we do this in a consistent way, however, we will include "goodness" that we might not want to consider as moral goodness. For example, the state, the multinational corporation, or the capitalist system each have their own teleos (ends). Does this make them "good"? We should consider the costs of giving up this distinction between goodness in the purely teleological sense and goodness in the moral sense. In each case, we need to be very aware of what we are giving up, as well as what we expect to gain.

We should modify concepts and develop principles that best reflect our current experience and our intuitions, using a WRE process. Critical reflection on our principles is important to avoid changes (even incremental ones) that take us in the wrong direction. In our current intellectual climate where change is so readily embraced, constant vigilance is required.

JUSTIFICATION AND CAUSE

We have argued that it is essential that shifts in (moral) thought be justified. But, as a matter of fact, they may not be justified at all. Even though the question of justification is so crucial, it does not necessarily arise. The paradigm shift may occur whether or not it is justified; it may be *caused* by factors that leave out justification (e.g., propaganda, Skinnerian conditioning, habit, brain surgery). Thus, we may come to exclude "women," "blacks," "Jews," or "Muslims" from the class of moral objects as easily as we may include classes of animals. We may come to regard people as no better than trees or corporations or nations. The shift may occur even if we never address the question of whether it *should* occur. But we have a moral obligation to address this question.

One might ask: Why bother with justification; isn't it part of one more dualism found in the Enlightenment tradition that has been rejected by deep ecologists and postmodernists? Could we not, and should we not, give up the practice of justifying our beliefs and actions to others? The answer is, again, a pragmatic one. We would submit that maintaining this practice is essential for our [moral] purposes. Some postmodernist thinkers, as well as scientific reductionists, are in favor of eliminating the distinction between justification and cause, between rational persuasion and coercion (physical and non-physical). A famous example is B. F. Skinner (1971), who argues that rational persuasion is just a form of behaviorial modification. But there is no good reason (except a mistaken desire to reduce everything to science) why we should destroy this crucial contrast.

The distinction between justification and cause is important. Justification requires giving reasons that are good and sufficient within the context; and it is always propositional. Particularly in the public realm of liberal democratic societies, justification requires an ethical basis. The only possible basis for our decisions is what we know, and have good reason to believe, here and now.

The distinction between justification and cause should be seen as a continuum. At one end we have rational persuasion; on the other, behaviorial conditioning and physical coercion. Toward the center of the continuum we find examples of tacit, non-physical coercion, e.g., advertising, propaganda, ideological distortion, and so on. If we gave up the distinction between justification and cause we would no longer have a reason to treat any of these differently. For example, we could no longer talk about eliminating ideological distortion or false consciousness. If we gave up the contrast between justification and cause, then everything would be manipulative, and thus nothing would be manipulative.

But do we want to view all argument in this way? We don't think so. Neither do most environmentalists. They seek to change minds in a reasonable fashion. They want to *persuade* us of the justice and *legitimacy* of their cause; that is what all the articles and books are about. For our practical purposes, justification is important (even though it cannot be given an absolute foundation).

IS RADICAL CONCEPTUAL CHANGE SUPPORTABLE?

We have suggested that incremental conceptual change, through reweaving and modification of concepts and beliefs, can lead to very significant change. Could such change still be radical enough to support the extreme alteration in paradigm and ethical principle suggested by the deep ecologists?

Postmodernists might think they could appeal to Richard Rorty for support here. He argues that radical conceptual change is possible and perhaps desirable. He suggests we could adopt a new language game that

> does not pretend to have a better candidate to do the same old things which we did when we spoke the old way. Rather, it suggests that we might want to stop doing those things and do something else. But it does not argue for this suggestion on the basis of antecedent criteria common to the old and new language games. For just insofar as the new language game is really new, there will be no such criteria. (Rorty 1989, 9)

In other words, perhaps we had best just change the subject! Rorty essentially is accepting the idea that a radical paradigm shift brings with it the opacity we noted above; thus, a radical paradigm shift within a specific area of inquiry is impossible to justify upon grounds internal to the area. Rorty accepts the radical nature of Kuhn's thought: "It seems to me that Kuhn and his fellows have shown that there never was some thing called 'the method of the natural sciences'" (Rorty 1980, 43). There are no methodological canons that could be used to justify a shift. However, perhaps it could be justified on other grounds (e.g., moral grounds) even though there is no shared meaning or reference. Or perhaps it does not need to be justified at all.

In considering Rorty's suggestion, it is important to understand the context. He is speaking about the modern philosophical tradition, which he believes has exhausted itself. He argues that this tradition has not served us in the ways we had hoped it would. It has failed to provide an absolute foundation for our thought (moral or scientific). In other words, philosophy has not served our interests—practical, scientific, or moral. For example, Rorty asserts that discussing the nature of truth is no aid in determining whether or not Jones missed the bus, and discussing the nature of the metaphysical self does nothing to answer whether or not we should redistribute wealth in order to aid those individuals who are worse off than ourselves. And he believes that the proper "method" in contemporary philosophy is not to attempt to refute philosophical positions, since that would involve the very philosophical vocabulary he believes we should abandon. Rorty suggests that

> Interesting philosophy is rarely an examination of the pros and the cons of a thesis. Usually it is, implicitly or explicitly, a contest between an entrenched vocabulary which has become a nuisance and a half-formed new vocabulary which vaguely promises great things. (Rorty 1989, 9)

His method is "to redescribe lots and lots of things in new ways, until you have created a pattern of linguistic behavior that tempts the rising generation to accept it" (ibid.).

Is this the sort of thing the deep ecologists want to do when they speak of a paradigm shift? We think perhaps it is. This is a view held explicitly by some deep ecologists, and others seem close to it. In an important statement of his deep ecological perspective, Naess argues for

> rejection of the man-environment image in favour of *the relational, total field-image*. Organisms as knots in the biospherical net or field of intrinsic relations. An intrinsic relation between two things A and B is such that the relation belongs to the definitions or basic constitutions of A and B, so that without the relation A and B are no longer the same things. The total-field model dissolves not only the man-in-environment concept, but every compact thing-in-milieu concept—except when talking at a superficial or preliminary level of communication. [emphasis added] (Naess 1973, 95)

What Naess hopes to achieve through the use of this semantic stipulation is a moral perspective that removes all reference to the individual person. This position would require a radical shift away from traditional morality to a new way of speaking. Our traditional concerns for human rights, for example, would have no role to play once the new language is accepted. But is this a situation where we really want to change the subject? Is our concern for the environment something other than a *moral* concern? We think not.

How do we judge a suggestion like Naess's? We cannot do so from some commonly held, shared moral position since the proposal is that we make a radical break with that tradition. To use Rorty's rhetoric, we cannot (and need not) argue for the new vision by using some common vocabulary. That would be futile since the whole point of the radical paradigm shift is to replace that old vocabulary with a new one. We have, in an important sense, changed the subject. But then how do we accept the recommendation? What is the point of the change? Rorty suggests that the test for accepting the new vocabulary is whether it "vaguely promises great things." Great for what? How is it more fruitful? Here is where the analogy between Rorty and deep ecology ends.

When Rorty proposes a new philosophical vocabulary that "tempt[s] the rising generation to accept it," he does not want a new vocabulary for its own sake. He does not want the new vocabulary of Goebels and Rosenberg, tempting as it may have been to a new generation of Germans, to replace the old liberal bourgeois vocabulary. Something *remains* standing for Rorty. It is *morality*. Rorty (like Rawls) does not want to give up the liberal democratic concern for the individual. In fact, when Rorty speaks of "great" or "better" things, he intends to preserve our moral vocabulary. It is our moral and practical interests as we know them that tell us what is "great," what is "better." It is interesting to note Kuhn himself argues that what bridges different paradigms are the values of the scientific community, which are held constant. Even in science, it is not the values that shift.

This is the crucial difference between Rorty and the deep ecologist. Rorty wants to give up our conception of philosophy for a moral reason: He argues that it will help to achieve a more humane, moral, and creative society. Perhaps this makes sense. The deep ecologist wants to give up our conception of morality for a moral reason. This makes no sense at all.

HOW DO DEEP ECOLOGISTS "JUSTIFY" THEIR POSITION?

Why does the deep ecologist want to give up conventional morality? What goals do they have? What reasons can be given for the change? What justification can be offered? We can conceive of several possibilities. Except for the first one, all tacitly acknowledge our inability to completely break free from our conventional morality (to completely abandon our societal "ship").

Reductionism

Deep ecologists may attempt to reduce the moral perspective to one based on science or ecology, e.g., bio-egalitarianism (Odum 1974). Thus, Aldo Leopold (1933) suggests that the shift to what he calls "ecological conscious-ness" is a stage in biological or ecological evolution. He argues that the

> extension of ethics is actually a process of ecological evolution. Its sequence may be described in biological as well as philosophical terms. . . . These are two definitions of one thing.

We would reply that this reductionistic and scientistic approach misconstrues the type of justification required to solve our environmental (and social) cri-sis. Why is this shift "better" than our current morality? It is not *morally* better. His claim is a nonstarter; it always begs the question. Such a claim can be made only after the new vocabulary has been accepted. But we have not (so far) accepted the shift; we are still within the old paradigm, asking why we should accept the new one. From this perspective, the change is both unintelligible and unjustifiable.

Enhancing Existing Values

Deep ecologists may argue that by following the preferred new morality (pantheism, eco-feminism, bio-egalitarianism, and so on), we will also encourage—in fact, enhance—our other deeply embedded values (fraternity, sorority, and freedom, for example). Whether this claim is correct will be a matter of empirical investigation; we doubt that it is correct. But the point to be made here is that the test of justification is those deeply embedded values and not the proposed new morality.

Conformity to Existing Values

Deep ecologists may modify their new principle to conform to our present values. This is an old philosophical gambit; as Austin (1961) might say: "Here's the part where you say it, and here's the part where you take it back." Thus, the biocentric egalitarian puts forward a principle like "Humans are not in-herently superior to other living things" (Beatley 1994, 123) but then ac-knowledges the need for a hierarchy, where some impacts on the natural environment are permissible for "important social purposes" (ibid.), which may include cultural and recreational values.[6] This modification makes it conform to our moral intuitions. It is done to avoid obvious counter ex-amples that are morally repugnant. The basic bio-egalitarian principle would value a child no more than a tree. A hierarchy brings it back into conformity with our ordinary morality. Then we are no longer dealing with a radical view. But is there now any point to the new principle?[7]

Borrowing Words

Deep ecologists may borrow the words of the old view—concepts that are taken to be morally relevant such as consciousness, rights, personhood—and either change their meaning (another way to "just change the subject") or else extend their application in a way that eliminates all significant contrast from their application. For example, Livingston (1986) attempts to extend the concept of consciousness to refer to just about every natural phenomenon. This extension severs the conceptual relationship between consciousness and morality, which is based on the idea that we should be concerned about objects to which a course of action *matters*—objects who are subjects, who experience pain and pleasure, who care about what happens. When consciousness is extended to all objects, the concept then becomes empty.

Environmental Crisis

Deep ecologists may argue that our old way of thinking and talking will inevitably lead to a deterioration of the natural environment and (at best) severely diminished opportunities or (at worst) a destruction of everything, including future generations. And this (according to our conventional sense of morality) is morally wrong. What if we believe that an environmental crisis is imminent, and rational persuasion will not get the behavior changes necessary to avert the crisis? Could we then be morally justified in advocating a radical paradigm shift to get people to accept "new speak," if this would *cause* people (rather than persuade them) to modify their behavior?

An example of this last position can be found in an article on environmental ethics and education which suggests that

> We believe that the seriousness of our environmental predicament suggests the need to develop much more harmonious and respectful relationships within the earth community. Some of the newer concepts in environmental ethics in many ways represent more appropriate ethical models far better suited to the problems at hand. (Martin and Beatley 1993, 125)

In other words, we should inculcate an ethic of respect for the intrinsic value of the environment; if we do not, the world will come to an end. There is great irony in this view since it attempts to justify a biocentric egalitarian ethic (based on respect for the intrinsic value of nature) on *instrumental* grounds, i.e., on the grounds that our *human* interests will not be served unless such an ethic is adopted. This sounds as if we pick and choose an ethic in each situation in order to solve the "problems at hand," making the choice of ethic instrumental—merely a means to some other end. But the whole point of deep ecology is to reject both instrumental and "anthropocentric" arguments!

A further sense in which this position is unethical (probably uninten-
tionally) is that it appears to advocate manipulation rather than education or
persuasion. Assume that the supporting claims are true (even though we
don't believe they are). The problem, then, is that we would have two classes
of people: the elite, for whom the shift is justified on moral grounds ("It will
save our world"), and the masses (including our students), who are unable
to grasp the urgency of the crisis (the rationale for change) and who are
being manipulated into doing the "right thing." This paternalistic elitism
would be profoundly undemocratic. History should make us very suspicious
of those who want to dominate the world in order to save it; they are often
more interested in the domination than the salvation.[8]

AN AUTHENTIC MORAL VISION

A Moral Vision

We believe that, contrary to the arguments of deep ecologists, we do
have the normative resources from our moral tradition that can provide the
moral basis of *meaningful* sustainable development. The scientistic views that
we outlined are distortions of a moral perspective that we have in our grasp.
The scientistic account of morality is a truncated notion of morality, one that
is impoverishing rather than enriching. And (as we discuss below) the deep
ecology view, if taken literally, leads to actions that are clearly immoral.

This does not mean that our moral views should be frozen. Of course our
moral views can, do, and often should, change. But given what we have said
regarding the holistic nature of our thought, such change should be incremental, modeled on a WRE process. Rather than model moral change on a
radical Kuhnian view of science, perhaps a better model is one patterned on
the change that occurs in legal institutions or, perhaps, in literary criticism.

Nor does this mean that we are closed to other points of view. Other
perspectives, either self-generated or the accumulated wisdom of others (other
cultures), may well be invaluable in a critical evaluation of our views. But in
the final analysis, it is we who must make that judgment, applying our ethical tradition, our intuitions, and our scientific knowledge to the current situation, as best we can, in a process of WRE. The alternative is (overt or covert)
totalitarian manipulation (Rorty 1991a).

The Authentic Individual

Unless an authentic moral vision (of the person and of society) is recov-
ered by critical reflection, even incremental change can lead us in very wrong
directions. The amalgamation of the [economic] utilitarian conception of

morality, the instrumental notion of rationality, the atomistic notion of the individual as an isolated satisfaction maximizer, and the materialistic view of progress as economic progress are caricatures of an authentic moral vision.

The authentic individual—the truly autonomous individual assumed by political liberalism (Rawls 1993)—far from being an alienated utility maximizer, is an individual situated in a community, a community that is itself situated in a meaningful environment. Only under these circumstances can a person have a basis for validating his or her actions. Rawls (1980, 544) suggests:

> As free persons, citizens recognize one another as having moral power to have a conception of the good. This means that they do not view themselves as inevitably tied to the pursuit of the particular conception of the good and its final ends which they espouse at any given time. Instead, as citizens, they are regarded as, in general, capable of revising and changing this conception on reasonable and rational grounds.

The choice of the ends of life can—indeed must—involve rational reflection. And the reflection required goes beyond the limits of maximizing quantifiable utility. Authentic values such as friendship, love, solidarity, integrity, creativity, and harmony reflect our true interests and our true needs. These values give meaning to the world we live in and thus give meaning to our lives.

As David Papineau (1992) suggests in his review of E. O. Wilson's book, *The Diversity of Life*:

> Killing a species is not just economically unwise . . . it is wrong. The diversity of nature is as much a part of our heritage as paintings and buildings. It may not be our own creation, but it is an essential part of the world that nurtures and makes us human. We quite rightly go to great lengths to preserve the Parthenon and the Mona Lisa. But our descendants will not thank us if at the same time we allow the elephant, the chimpanzee, and hundreds of other species to perish.

These are ends worth having, ends higher (to borrow a term from Charles Taylor [1989]) than those presented to us by a materialistic and distorting ideology. Good arguments can be made for these ends, but certainly not in terms of instrumental rationality.

CONCLUSION

Our concern here is not with correcting some esoteric theoretical error. The worry lies in the practical application of these ultimate principles, which could lead to severely harmful consequences. If we take the bio-egalitarian position seriously, then people are of no more moral concern than any other life forms. Leopold (1933) believes that a civilized man's "sense of right and wrong may be aroused quite as strongly by desecration of a nearby woodlot as by a famine in China." And Spitler (1982, 260) argues that if animals and plants had the same inherent worth as humans, then killing a human would be considered "no more morally reprehensible than swatting a fly or stepping on a wildflower"—a position he considers totally unacceptable, as should we all. Do we really want children to be treated the same way as trees and mosquitoes? When a principle violates our moral intuition so clearly, there is something very wrong with it.

In one way, deep ecology could be interpreted as bearing a disturbing similarity to communism, fascism, and nazism, which advocate that the interests of some collectivity should override those of the individual person. For communism, the collectivity is the proletariat; for fascism, the state; for nazism, the master race. For deep ecology, is it the ecosystem? Regardless of the nature of the collectivity, in the end, the consequence is real suffering by real individuals—you, us, and our children. Perhaps such principles are meant only to be metaphors, although they are seldom presented in this way. If the metaphor becomes literal, it will require (or at least tend to cause) us to denigrate human rights and interests. And this is a real danger.

Our primary purpose here is not to provide an argument against deep ecology or any other particular view. Rather, it is to make a plea for a pragmatic and incremental approach to the solution of environmental and other problems, an important although not exclusive concern in the twenty-first century.[9] We believe that the notion of sustainable development captures this incremental approach. Depending on the point of view adopted, the idea of a radical "paradigm shift" is either dangerous or it is consistent with this gradual approach (i.e., it is not really radical).

We have argued that providing a sustainable environmental basis for planning requires no paradigm shift and no jettisoning of traditional morality. What we do require is a reaffirmation of our deeply entrenched moral values, values that may have been temporarily lost by many in today's alienated and impoverished society. These values include respect for individuals in the context of community, respect for dialogue and for reason (while acknowledging the power of intuition and emotion), more equitable distribution of both political and economic power, and the virtues of moderation, humility, and the willingness to change one's mind. These "old" values also include a concern for the environment, not merely as instrumental to our well-being and survival, but also for its intrinsic value, as something worth preserving for its own sake. We need to recapture a perspective that is truly worth sustaining.

Significant changes are needed in the way we make decisions if planning is to become environmentally sustainable. We plead for a view that is inclusive, a dialogical view that strives for an overlapping consensus of all those who seek solution of the environmental crises. We believe that eloquent advocates of sustainability like Beatley can justify their [generally very reasonable] practical positions without adopting a radical view. The most unproductive thing we could do is to advocate radical paradigm shifts or new absolute metaphysical principles, or to argue about the differences between deep and shallow ecology. This simply causes divisions among those who should be allies. Deep ecologists and bio-egalitarians and other "radical environmentalists" are in grave danger of fiddling while Rome (our planet) burns.

13

The Multicultural Trap (Relativism)

INTRODUCTION

This chapter is concerned with certain tensions generated in the idea of a pluralistic liberal multicultural society. It shows how postmodernistic critiques of modernistic approaches to multicultural planning can be reconstructed from a pragmatic point of view. Different ways of viewing multicultural planning (including a reconstructed Enlightenment position) have value in enhancing our understanding of a multicultural society and in seeking more just solutions to some of its problems. Thus, pragmatism (1) presents a different way of seeing the tensions (one that avoids the contradiction of the postmodernistic approach) and (2) suggests a theoretical strategy for dealing with them.

North American society has always been composed of people with numerous different cultures of origin (including aboriginal peoples), and it has been enriched by a constant influx (at varying rates) of immigrants from many different cultures. In spite of this, North American society (at least until quite recently) has been characterized by a single dominant culture. This culture emphasizes a critical/analytical perspective coming out of the Enlightenment, often referred to as "modernism" (chapter 1).

The modernist worldview and its associated universalist planning approaches (e.g., social reform, pre–World War II and rational comprehensive planning, post–World War II) tended to be assimilationist, pressuring all comers into conformity with the dominant culture (Burayidi 2000, ch. 2). This approach has become more obviously problematic as immigrants increasingly come from cultures that are very different from the dominant culture—that is, they are "traditional" (non-modern—they lack the critical/ analytical perspective of modernism). The more different from the dominant culture is the culture of origin, the more wrenching the process of assimilation.

POSTMODERN CRITIQUES

Postmodernists have critiqued the dominant culture and its vocabulary as hierarchical, reductionistic, scientistic, universalizing, anthropomorphic, and patriarchal. They have attacked the assimilationist tendency and advocated a multicultural approach to public planning and policy, one that celebrates difference, one that encourages and facilitates maintenance of the identity of the originating cultures. Many of these critiques of planning in a multicultural society have a similar structure: (1) attack the dominant approach; (2) provide a replacement approach; and (3) plead for respect for other narratives.

Attack the Dominant Approach

The dominant planning approach (Western, modernist, patriarchal) is attacked on grounds both theoretical (reliance on rejected notions) and practical (oppressive consequences).

Postmodern feminism critiques what it calls logocentric (or phalocentric) thought; that is, they argue that the way of thinking that has come down to us through the Enlightenment is paternalistic, hierarchical, and leads to social structures that are oppressive of women and minority groups. In presenting this view, postmodernists attack the vocabulary, ideas, and concepts that they believe are constitutive of logocentric thinking. These include dualism, universalism, reality, objective truth, rationality, theory, meta-narrative, absolute goodness, knowledge, and scientific objectivity (chapter 4).

Developmentalism as an approach to non-dominant cultures (whether in our society or in the "third world") is critiqued as a distorting ideology, one that masks the dominant culture's attempt to assimilate non-dominant cultures. Marxist and other modernist views are seen as presupposing a notion of "development" that should be deconstructed:

> The "stages of development" model espoused by modernization theorists revolves around the dichotomies underdeveloped/developed and traditional/ modern. Many Marxists also maintain the belief in evolutionary progress from pre-capitalism to capitalism and finally to socialism. (Connelly et al. 1995, 23)

Postmodernists further critique the dominant culture's practice of imposing labels—like "backward" and "underdeveloped"—on non-dominant cultures:

> Through the process of labelling and normalization, individuals, classes, genders, ethnic groups and even nations become redefined according to one-dimensional labels which simplify and therefore belie their complex histories and motivations. They become portrayed as passive "clients," "victims," "target group members," "cases" in programs apparently intended for their benefit. (Connelly et al. 1995, 25)

The labels of the dominant vocabulary are seen as insidious ideological distortions: "It is as if the label itself provides the diagnosis of the problem and proposes a particular solution" (ibid., 25). Planning agencies and experts are guilty of the imposition of the dominant culture's "categories and technical knowledge" (ibid., 26).

"Modernism's universalizing claims" are attacked by "unpacking or deconstructing the power relations, assumptions and hidden agendas implicit in a body of language or discourse." Such deconstruction unmasks "political agendas embedded in key terms . . . environment, equality, helping, market, needs, participation, planning, population, poverty, progress, production, resources, science, standards of living, state and technology" (ibid., 27).

In sum, what these critics reject is the idea that there is (1) some universal account that predetermines the way things are to be and (2) some ahistorical standard that prescribes what should be. These ideas are viewed as myths or subterfuges that act to suppress and control non-dominant cultures in favor of the dominant culture. Habermas (1984)[1] would say that the dominant culture's planning approach is an ideology, and we should replace it with something more legitimate. So then, what do we replace it with?

Provide a Replacement Approach

Postmodernists wish to replace the modernistic vocabulary and ideas with their own notions. A radical paradigm shift, a new language game, a new vocabulary is advocated:

> Within anthropology, a major paradigm shift has occurred since the 1970s. The challenge to evolutionary (or stages) models of historical change has led to a re-examination of the world system, and a critique of earlier studies . . . which portrayed certain societies as "primitive." (Connelly et al. 1995, 24)

The replacement usually appeals to thinkers like Foucault or Derrida. Theory still enters, but as a critical account of power relations and "normalization" (Foucault 1980). Normalization is

> the process through which a citizenry becomes re-organized and labelled according to bureaucratically imposed categories which privilege or punish according to certain standards and rationales. The arbitrary nature of

these standards is disguised, so that they come to appear rational and self-evident. (Connelly et al. 1995, 25)

Thus, the proposed (replacement) approach recognizes the significance of power relations and celebrates difference and the significance of the "other." They talk of envisioning "alternative possibilities for human association generated by a range of new social movements (indigenous, peasant, feminist, environmentalist)" that are not "mere technical or managerial improvements on the existing developmental paradigm" (ibid., 26).

An alternative vocabulary is proposed. This creates an "either–or" situation. In providing a new vocabulary, they ask us to give up the old vocabulary of the dominant culture. No longer is there talk of progress or development. The "alternative" theories focus on people as the agents, or creators, of their own histories. Local histories are the focus of research: Mini-narratives replace meta-narratives.

Plead for Respect for "Other" Narratives

The idea that there is only one legitimate perspective is seen as an idea that serves the patriarchal interests of the dominant culture. Postmodern feminists speak of different realities, different "voices and knowledge" (ibid., 26), different moralities, different ways of knowing (Gilligan 1977). They urge planners to respect the narratives of the "other" (e.g., aboriginals, ethnic groups, women)—to expand the worldview of the dominant culture to recognize and validate other cultural values and other ways of knowing.

Postmodernists seek the "recognition of the importance of identity," the "recovery and strengthening of difference," a "focus on identity, difference and culture," to "give rise to the complex diverse and multi-layered realities of the third world women's lives" (ibid., 25). They want to go beyond the [liberal pluralist] recognition of the need for public institutions to encourage respect and understanding of non-dominant cultures; they advocate [what Nussbaum (1997) calls] the politics of identity, which is the view that public institutions should provide the individual with self-legitimation through identification with a particular minority culture. In this view, recognizing that different cultures, traditions, and genders have different views on these matters is not enough; they want us to accept the
legitimacy of all these different views.

A corollary of this approach is that public institutions (both planning and educational ones) should deemphasize the values of the dominant culture. This advocacy has had some influence in the United States and a great deal more in Canada, where we have a federal ministry of multiculturalism that subsidizes a wide range of activities designed to encourage and legitimate non-dominant cultures.

THE CORE TENSION

We believe that there is merit in this perspective, but it also presents difficulties. There is a conflict between the second and the third steps. Whereas the third step ("plead for respect for all narratives") presupposes that all accounts are equally good, the second step ("provide a replacement meta-narrative") presupposes that some accounts are better or *truer* than others. What these critics really want to do is to distinguish between stories that are good, true, and liberating versus those that are not. They would like to reject the latter.

Herein lies the core tension. Rejection and replacement of the dominant approach presupposes criteria for evaluating some accounts as *better* than others. Then we no longer have a postmodernist proposal to eliminate meta-narratives but a proposal for a *new* meta-narrative. What is being proposed by the postmodernists is just as much a universal, general, abstract description as the modernist account. But, by their own account, they aren't entitled to look upon their views as "better" or as closer to "the truth" or "reality" or "rationality" than any other. Another way to put it: They want to claim their view is "right" while arguing there is no such thing as "right." While the postmodernists want to reject the privileging of the dominant account, they really have not broken away from the (modernist) worldview associated with the dominant culture.

TWO USEFUL DISTINCTIONS

External and Internal Perspectives

In trying to resolve the conflict just described, we find it useful to distinguish between external and internal perspectives. As we saw in chapter 6, an internal perspective is the standpoint of the *participants* in a culture, an activity, or language game. It relies on concepts internal to the activity. An external perspective is the standpoint of an external observer who is not involved in the culture, activity, or language game. External approaches usually involve the application of a general explanatory theory (and its concepts) of anthropological function or economic structure.

The relevance of external accounts to internal ones (and the closeness of the two) varies across cultures. The internal view is usually associated with accepted standards, beliefs, and practices. Thus, cultures that take a strictly internal perspective tend to be more static and conservative. These "traditional" cultures have little use for background theory and resist external views. The critical, analytical, external view is not valued. An external observer attempting to gain an *interpretive* (internal) understanding usually does so by *participating* in the culture. In contrast, the external view tends to be associated with a critical attitude toward accepted standards, beliefs, and practices. Cultures that incorporate an external view are usually more dynamic.

However, the internal/external distinction should not be interpreted as necessarily coextensive with the distinction between members of a culture and non-members. It relates more to the distinction between cultures that are traditional, noncritical, and conservative versus those that are nontraditional, critical, and dynamic. So it is entirely possible for members of a culture (particularly a nontraditional one) to take an external view of that culture. Thus, as discussed in chapter 6, Walzer (1987, 61) can argue that the effective social critic must be "inside" the society, standing "a little to the side, but not outside."

This is possible in our dominant culture because the critical, analytical view is highly valued and the external view is almost part of internal practice. Here, internal and external are much closer. In Marxian terms, our cultural superstructure includes a critical account of the relationship between superstructure and structure (economic relations). Such cultures are analytic, scientific, critical, in flux. A very clear example of this second type of culture is the culture of liberal planning academics.

Wide and Narrow Reflective Equilibria

For understanding the problems of accommodating non-dominant cultures in a multicultural society, we have found that another related contrast is more useful—between wide and narrow reflective equilibria. We saw in chapter 6 that an internal perspective might seek a *Narrow* Reflective Equilibrium (NRE), which focuses on the coherence of (1) considered situational judgments and (2) normative principles. This perspective gives expression to the mini-narrative—the local story of the culture. It does not give an explanatory or critical account of moral or other practices by bringing in [external] background theories and principles (normative or descriptive). In contrast, a *Wide* Reflective Equilibrium (WRE) widens the NRE by invoking an external perspective that includes background theories and principles. These other elements add a *critical* capacity.

As we have seen, a WRE process involves seeking *coherence* among the above elements, whether they are internal to a culture or external. When the WRE process is followed, progress and justification of judgments do not require an appeal to any absolute outside foundation that is independent of our social framework. Beauregard (2000) regards the values of liberal democracy as "absolutes or at least universal political principles." It may be that these values can be deduced from particular philosophical conceptions, but for the pragmatist they need not be. These values arise out of a WRE process; they are practical and situationally contingent, not universal and not absolute. In no way do they presuppose or require an absolute, universal or Archimedian point. They are merely accepted as necessary conditions for a pluralistic democratic society. A commitment to these values does not assume people are disembodied rationalists, nor does it require any denial of tradi-tional culture as a source of their beliefs. Rather, justification depends on legiti-mate procedures. By legitimate, we mean open, uncoerced, fair, and fallible.

As discussed above, many critics of modernist planning and develop-ment approaches want to eliminate the use of [external] dominant vocabu-laries (either Marxist or capitalist) that they describe as *a priori*, arbitrary, universalizing discourses. Instead, they want to use a postmodernist, Fou-cauldian (1980) analysis of power. But aren't the proposed alternative vo-cabularies also based in the dominant culture? Does not the idea of recover-ing voices or traditions also reflect the dominant culture? They are simply substituting one external vocabulary for another; and they are still appealing to a wider equilibrium. Their analysis is just as *a priori*, arbitrary, and univer-salizing as any other external one. In Western Enlightenment cultures, exter-nal perspectives—whether modern or postmodern—usually come from the dominant culture. The key distinction is not whether the views are from the dominant culture but whether they look at a society from an internal view or an external view, whether they are satisfied with a narrow or a wider reflec-tive equilibrium.

THE PARADOX OF MULTICULTURALISM

Non-dominant cultures within a multicultural liberal society experience a conflict between NRE and WRE, between tradition and critique. NRE tends to be static—to conserve both what is good and what is bad in the culture. WRE allows for dynamics and change; ideological distortions are more likely to be identified and corrected.

The Need for an Overlapping Consensus

The multicultural approach (which encourages a continuation of NRE in the non-dominant cultures) creates its own problems, particularly if taken too far—the most extreme form being Beauregard's (2000) "strict" multi-culturalism. As we have seen (chapter 6), even a pluralistic liberal demo-cratic society like ours requires an *overlapping consensus* with regard to cer-tain basic values like tolerance.

Each of the constituent cultures of a pluralistic society must be able to accept the values of this overlapping consensus—impartiality, fairness, indi-vidual rights, democratic processes, and tolerance for multiple "thick" theo-ries of the good. This is one reason why pluralistic liberalism emphasizes process and dialogue in the political realm. We try to leave as much as pos-sible of the substantive ("thick theories") to the private realm. It is not that these beliefs are unacknowledged or denigrated or seen as unimportant.

Rather, we have to learn to live with our differences concerning them. A procedural focus aims to accommodate significant, substantive, private differences. The aim in the *political* realm is not to discover truth but to devise institutions and practices that have political legitimacy.

People from originating cultures that do not accept these values will have to adapt, changing some values to become part of a pluralistic society. For example, if a culture believes in a theocratic state that enforces its particular thick theory of the good and imposes it on everyone, then people from that culture must give up that aspect to become part of a pluralistic culture. To this degree, they have to accept the values of the dominant culture. This doesn't mean that they must give up the rest of their internal thick theory of the good. It doesn't mean that they must give up their identity to participate in the political realm. Nor does it require (as Beauregard [2000] claims) that they give up claims to "special competence" in interpreting their own "local knowledge."

However, a "strict" multicultural approach to planning that seeks to preserve *all* aspects of the originating cultures will be in a paradoxical position if members of these cultures refuse to accept the very values that cause the pluralist society to be willing to try to accommodate them.

Arguments for a Widest Equilibrium

Many theorists (Nielsen, Rawls, and Daniels) believe that moral theory should be seeking the *widest* possible reflective equilibrium. Rawls "remarks that it is clearly [WRE] that we should be concerned with in moral philosophy," because in WRE, "we are presented with all the possible sets of moral principles, 'together with the relevant philosophical arguments for them'" (Nielsen 1985, 27, 28). Whereas an NRE (because it is not critical) is likely to "leave our sense of justice pretty much intact," a wide process entails the "realistic possibility that our sense of justice may 'undergo a radical shift' . . . There are no judgements on any level of generality that are in principle immune to revision" (ibid.). In other words, the argument for seeking the widest possible equilibrium is that it allows for critique and change, which are highly valued in our Enlightenment-based culture.

Arguments against a Widest Equilibrium

The difficulty with the claim that we should always seek the widest possible equilibrium is that it underestimates the negative effects of the critique involved—a problem to which planners need to be sensitive. There are arguments that wide reflection and critique are not always salutary. Williams (1985) argues that scientistic cultures (in which science and analysis are important values) tend to undermine the very possibility of moral knowledge. As Putnam (1992, 90) puts it:

> If we become reflective to too great a degree, if we absorb too much of the absolute [i.e., scientistic][2] conception of the world, we will no longer be able to employ our ethical concepts. . . . [W]e cannot stop being reflective, but we can be *too* reflective. We are in an unstable equilibrium.

Thus, he believes that too much reflection and external criticism undermine cultural practices, leading to the destruction of valuable social practices including moral values.

In a "true common culture," Scruton (1990, 119-20) argues that change will not be valued; it may be seen as a threat to the continuity of tradition:

> There is only limited scope . . . for change and innovation. Indeed, innovation is never a value in itself, but at best a necessary accommodation to changes arising from outside. Too much innovation—especially in those customs and ceremonies which provide the core experience of membership—is inherently threatening to the culture. Tradition, on the other hand, is of the essence. . . . Through membership, I see the world as it was seen by those who went before me, and as it will be seen by those who are yet to be.

Accepting an external account can be destructive of these valued social practices. As Scruton (1990, 109) warns:

> To the observing anthropologist steeped in functionalist and utilitarian thought, the dance is a means to raise the spirits, to increase the cohesion of the tribe, in time of danger. Thus, description explains and justifies. But it does not tell us what the dance means to the dancer. If the tribesman thinks of the dance in that way he is alienated from it. He loses his motive to dance, once he borrows the language of the anthropologist.

So, the external account of the functionalist anthropologist can rob the social activity of its meaning and lead to its demise.

A problem for highly reflective cultures is that those who take a critical external perspective and are sympathetic to change seem to be prone to alienation, and this alienation can damage the social fabric. This is one of the key criticisms of Rawls's political liberalism leveled by communitarians. They believe that a Rawlsian overlapping consensus (regarding a thin, good theory of the good) does not provide the necessary social and institutional bonding necessary to cement members of culture into a unified whole. They advocate the revival of civic virtue, character formation, and substantive moral discourse (Sandel 1982; Etzioni 1993). Too much critique will tend to dissolve the social glue.

The Dilemma

When we contrast these two views (i.e., Nielsen and others versus Williams and others), we understand why certain traditions (e.g., circumcision) are criticized by some observers external to the culture and defended not only by their participants but also by other observers who are external.

How would postmodern critics respond to the following? When all is said and done, fully informed, sophisticated, and educated Muslim women may decide to maintain a traditional (internal) position with regard to certain social relationships which, from an external perspective, are patriarchal and subservient. Are they wrong? Yes, wrong if they accept an external functional, structural account. But why *should* they? There is no *a priori* answer; there is no compelling reason why they should. There are very obvious tensions concerning whether (and to what extent) feminist analysis should be accepted by other cultures, and at what cost.

A postmodernist observer of a traditional custom (e.g., wife burning or circumcision) may disapprove—find it morally wrong—yet refuse to intervene on the grounds that we should respect the other culture and its [internal] standard, holding that we have no right to judge it. This is a completely inadequate response; we must attempt to engage a culture when its practice is so clearly oppressive. Here we have a choice. Either we remain silent (say nothing normative/evaluative at all), or we speak from a particular perspective—not a universal, ahistorical one, but our own.

The conflict for postmodernists is: Are they willing to take an external perspective, to adopt a form of meta-narrative? The postmodernists should recognize that saying we should never intervene is a meta-narrative that requires an external perspective just as much as does saying the practice is wrong. Even to claim that each culture is right internally, they must take at least a minimally external perspective.

The dilemma faced by observers of other cultural practices is that the participant's internal understanding gets them (at best) to an NRE. The external critic points out how these conceptions work from an outside view. Someone like Habermas (1984) might say that the internal NRE is ideologically distorted. How do we decide?

A PRAGMATIC INTERPRETATION OF CULTURAL DIFFERENCES

What is required is a replacement for the modernist approach—one that acknowledges the postmodernistic critique of dominant cultural practices yet gives us some grounds, something to hang on to, that can still be a means of human betterment. The problem is that the postmodernist's step number 2 (the replacement meta-narrative) and step number 3 (respect for other narratives) don't do the job. Why? They leave us no basis for judgment or for action. Because there are different realities, different voices, different ways of knowing, different truths, different meta-narratives (all claiming legitimacy), there is no way for us to evaluate any of them (to decide whether they are a better replacement). This is the dilemma of relativism.

Our response to this situation comes from a neopragmatic perspective. This interpretation of different accounts of planning is that each narrative is a language game. Differing views are seen as different vocabularies—no one nearer to the truth than the others.[3] Such an approach allows us to recognize alternative accounts. Then we try to bring them into a noncoercive dialogic planning process.

From a pragmatic perspective, a strong moral critique appealing to both normative and empirical theories, using science as the servant of one's moral position, will be part of this dialogue. Yet a moral critique is internal; it does not provide an absolute position. Its success depends on whether or not it convinces in a noncoercive way.[4]

Both internal and external perspectives are relevant, important, and legitimate. However, neither perspective is superior to the other. A neopragmatic view sees this distinction as a continuum; a balance is possible. For most purposes, we need both kinds of understanding. Ignoring either the internal or the external perspective is dangerous.

A danger arises from the functionalist anthropologist's positivistic idea that an [external] understanding of the mechanism underlying a social practice/institution *replaces* the internal understanding. This is a reductionistic myth. The external understanding may be relevant, it may even replace the internal, but it does not necessarily do so. Certainly a critical WRE does not *require* giving up the internal account. For example, suppose that morality can be explained genetically or functionally. This doesn't undermine or replace the moral practice. Understanding the mechanism doesn't replace moral motivation—why should it? If postmodernists argue that the external view should supersede the internal one, they are being reductionistic—that is, retaining the modernistic assumptions that they claim to reject.

When dealing with practices (moral or otherwise) that are not part of the dominant culture in a multicultural society, planners may be more inclined to take an external perspective. (This is most likely if the planners are from the dominant culture, as they often are.) Then they are in danger of missing the significance or meaning of the institutions or traditions to those who participate in them. To the external observer, the legitimacy of the internal view can be hidden; the observer may be too quick to condemn without understanding the meaning to the participant. He or she may assume that there is oppression and ideological distortion (which gets the participant to accept practices that are not in his or her own best interest). Here, it may be more important to be reminded of the internal meaning rather than the external view of structure.

The participant may disagree: From an internal perspective, the practice is believed to be justified. The danger here is that he or she may not see the belief as ideologically distorted, to understand the way his or her own culture works. This may be because the participant is not part of a highly reflective culture (i.e., unfamiliar with issues of how cultures work). Such a case is more likely in a non-dominant ("traditional") culture. Thus, a purely internal account is likely to lack a critique of the status quo. When dealing with their own culture, the external (structural) relations are more often hidden, and many people are likely to settle for an internal view. Here, pointing out these relationships may lead us to liberation.

The key question is: Lacking a god's-eye perspective, how do we determine the extent to which the internal NRE is ideologically distorted? Is there really ideological distortion? The problem is that there is no objective "fact of the matter" outside of the process. What are legitimate true interests can be ascertained only *within* a context. There is no absolute answer. This is where the neopragmatist differs from Habermas (1984), who believes that ideological distortion can be objectively identified.

Is the situational choice about how wide the equilibrium should be (i.e., how much reflection is appropriate) "objective"? For the pragmatist, this question is not a concern. The notion of objectivity drops out because it serves no useful purpose.

A PRAGMATIC PROCESS OF RECONCILIATION

The neopragmatic reconciliation is to engage in a noncoercive open dialogue in which the external critic seeks first to understand the internal participant's view and then to convince them that their understanding is distorted and their practice oppressive and wrong. The neopragmatic hope is to engage participants in a consensus-seeking dialogue using all available means, involving reason, passion, intuition, and experience. This needs to be done in a sensitive, noncoercive way. As Nielsen (1996, 448) says

> I am not trying to set reason and passion in opposition to each other. And I am not trying to collapse the distinction either, or to give one precedence or authority over the other. Wide reflective equilibrium appeals to both. Within the holistic, largely coherentist method that is reflective equilibrium, both what it is reasonable to believe and to do and our sympathies . . . play an important role.

We try to help participants see the structural, power, class, gender, and other relations that we believe are oppressive. What many planning theorists have argued—that planning needs to stress the dialogical, communicative, deliberative, consensus-building aspects, and to design new institutions for fostering dialogue—is particularly true for a multicultural society.

From this perspective, evaluation is pragmatic, guided by this interactive, noncoercive dialogue. Does each approach to planning help us to understand and solve social problems? What is the pragmatic value of these different perspectives? Different purposes will be better served by different vocabularies. The choice of perspective, then, is made on pragmatic grounds. The distinctions we have made here (internal and external, wide and narrow) should be seen as pragmatic ones that are end points of continua. The ultimate goal of a dialogic process is to reach a consensus, ideally one where the distinctions disappear.

The degree to which a reflective equilibrium is "wide" (that is, invokes a critical external perspective) is a continuum. We should not assume as an absolute *a priori* meta-narrative principle that WRE has a privileged position[5] (i.e., that wider is always better). Both modernism and postmodernism tend to assume that their external accounts are privileged. They may be underestimating the impact of a WRE's external critique. As we have seen, too much reflection and criticism can destabilize social values and institutions—particularly moral ones. We should recognize that a WRE undermines cultural practices and beliefs that are inconsistent with the pluralistic liberal democratic state. Of course, as critical liberals, in general we do believe WRE to be the best approach. In this regard, the communitarians have a point; our social institutions (particularly planning and educational ones) need to uphold and promote essential liberal democratic social values if we want to have a functioning pluralistic liberal state. And this may not be consistent with the politics of identity.

This is the dilemma of a multicultural society. How much of the non-dominant cultures is to be protected and how much is to be changed? Going too far in either direction can lead to disasters. A pragmatic perspective looks for a situational balance. The trick is to restrict the extent of reflection in order to preserve as much as possible of those parts of a tradition that are critical to personal identities. This is particularly true for marginalized groups, who may require such identity to rectify past injustices and to gain self-respect. This delicate balance acknowledges differences while retaining a basis for cooperative action in a pluralistic society. It recognizes both the need to preserve identity and the requirements of a decent pluralistic society.

The pragmatist claims no absolute answer—only the hope that a dialogical (WRE) planning and political process (with participants sharing at least some liberal democratic values, seeking to understand each other and to build a wider consensus) will lead to a workable resolution of these tensions. But it may not. There are no guarantees. Some traditions may have values that are simply unacceptable to, and cannot be accommodated within, a pluralistic liberal society.

The pragmatist sees the dominant culture as having both good and bad sides. The bad side may be more obvious—domination, exploitation and oppression. But there are some things for which the dominant culture need not apologize—insisting on tolerance is one of them. Some aspects of the dominant vocabulary can be liberating. We want to retain and promote these aspects.

The only sense of "better than" that is consistent with post-positivistic critiques is this pragmatic one. It is not absolute! What will count as improvement will emerge from the dialogue. The only meta-narrative we need for this purpose is one that connects human practices (linguistic and other) to the possibility of human flourishing, as it is defined by this process. All of the different accounts (including a reconstructed Enlightenment position[6] without metaphysical aspects) can be looked at pragmatically, in terms of their contribution to improving the situation of non-dominant cultural groups in our society.

CONCLUSION

From a neopragmatic perspective, we should acknowledge and respect the identities and the stories of all cultural groups, but these stories should be heard critically and evaluated carefully. A neopragmatic approach does not seek a meta-narrative; it does not provide any universal solutions. Judgments must be made about particular situations in context.

For observers from the dominant culture, the difficult question is determining when there is oppression and distortion in a more traditional culture. The pragmatic reconciliation is an open and noncoercive dialogue that will give us a more internal understanding of the other culture and give them a wider, more reflective and critical view of their own practices. Ultimately, the liberal goal is for each person to have autonomous choice.

But there are limits to what can be accommodated. A WRE process is *necessary* at some level if we want to have a pluralist society. Beauregard's "strict" multiculturalism is a non-starter; it *guarantees* that a pluralist society will not work.[7] The idea that we should accept everything in every tradition is itself a universal principal, one that would destroy pluralism. It leaves us few options: at best separation; at worst, violence. There is no reason why we should accept it. We argue that not only are political liberal ideals consistent with accommodation of other cultures, but consensual acceptance of these [largely procedural] ideals is *required* for a pluralistic society.

For too long, we have seen the powerful elites of the dominant culture impose their views on non-dominant cultures, often as a tool of economic and social exploitation. We believe neopragmatism (even though it originally came out of modernism) can bring some of the advantages of the dominant culture without its exploitive features. Avoiding the relativism of postmodernism and the universalism of modernism, neopragmatism can acknowledge the legitimacy and identity of non-dominant cultures while reflectively critiquing their oppressive aspects. This is the promise of pragmatism in a pluralistic, liberal, multicultural society.

14

The Rejection of Theory

WHY DO MANY PLANNERS REJECT THEORY?

The Problem with Theory

We argued in chapter 1 that planners need theory because the current crisis has strongly theoretical roots. Why, then, do many practitioners reject theory as irrelevant? Before trying to address this question, we need a working definition of the term "theory." We rather hesitantly provide this rough definition for provisional purposes, and there are reasons for our hesitancy. One of the postmodern criticisms of the notion of theory is that one cannot draw a sharp line between theory and practice. Or, to put it another way: All practice (or observation) is "theory-laden." This renders the definition of theory problematic. As neopragmatists, we believe that a theory/practice distinction can be usefully made, but only in context, for particular purposes, and viewing the two terms as end points on a continuum. This allows us to retain such useful distinctions without having to defend either their universality or their absoluteness. But it leads to our caution concerning general definitions.

Our provisional definition of "theory": the attempt to provide abstract, general, or universal principles that are generalizations from particular cases.[1] The purpose of these principles is to explain, predict, or (in the case of normative theory) justify the particulars to which they apply. In science, these particulars involve observations; in normative areas, they involve particular normative judgments. So far there is nothing in this account of theory to render it irrelevant to practice—especially if the line between the particular and the general, the abstract and the concrete, the theoretical and the observational is not seen as a sharp one. It is also important that the relationship

254

between the theoretical and the practical (empirical) be seen as mutually reinforcing; that is, each one informs and modifies the other.[2]

What does create problems is a [modernist] view of theory and practice that presupposes a hypothetical-deductive conception whereby observations or judgments about particulars are deduced from the theory or principles and then tested against empirical "reality." In normative matters (e.g., public planning), this latter conception leads to the idea that decisions can be deduced from universal principles in a linear, almost algorithmic manner.

The hypothetical-deductive view of theory is often accompanied by another conception of theory that causes even more trouble. This conception of theory, and in particular a conception of "theoretical terms," has become a deeply embedded part of our Western tradition (and a major source of confusion). That is the idea that theory and the terms found therein (hypothetical constructs) have a different ontological status than the "facts" they seek to explain, predict, and justify. This creates an absolute bifurcation (as opposed to a continuum[3]) between theoretical (abstract) entities on the one hand and nontheoretical (concrete) entities on the other.

This bifurcation has engendered a historical debate regarding the status of theory and practice in our Western tradition. We believe that this debate has had a profound effect on our society (including an important effect on planning). On the one hand, rationalists claim that abstract theoretical entities are the entities that truly exist. Plato, the archetypical rationalist, gave primary existential legitimacy to [what we would now call] highly abstract theoretical terms. Everything else is illusion, particularly our ordinary everyday world. In opposition, empiricists have argued that it is the experiential phenomena—the facts—that have the greater claim to existence. It is the facts that are *real*. With the rise of science in the twentieth century, the empirical view became dominant. This dominance is what Habermas (1971a) calls "scientism."

The Positivistic Approach to Theory

This issue has greatly influenced planning practice whether practitioners know it (or like it) or not. In fact, the idea of an absolute dualism between theory and practice is itself very much an expression of a theory (RCPM) and a worldview (modernism). It is a mask for a key positivistic assumption discussed earlier—that there is a sharp line between fact and value, between action and talk. We believe that the perceived irrelevance of planning theory is to some degree a delusion fostered by the modernistic worldview; it shows that this view retains a significant influence on contemporary thought.

This theory/practice dualism is the contemporary version of the old debate between rationalism and empiricism. Contemporary empiricists (i.e., positivists) reserve the higher status for the facts, often reduced to experiential phenomena. For them, theoretical entities are convenient myths used to pre-dict experiences. In its application to human action, positivism separates talk from action. Talk is theoretical; action is in the "real world" of concrete facts. This presupposition classes behavior (and action as a subclass of behavior) as more objective than thought and language. The more remote the talk is from its observable empirical base, the less legitimate it is held to be. Theory is most removed from the class of observable empirical phenomena and therefore least legitimate. Philosophical theory is seen as worst of all.

This positivistic attitude is at least partially responsible for practitioners' suspicion of theory. One source of their discomfort with theory may stem from a positivistic bias. This is ironic when we note that planning *practice* is quite far down toward the "wrong end" of the scale (i.e., away from action). As Forester (and many others) have pointed out, most of what planners do is "talk." They don't build things—they talk, and their talk (to varying degrees) influences the talk and decisions of others (e.g., politicians) whose talk and decisions influence still others (e.g., developers) whose talk and decisions cause others (e.g., contractors) to "act" to build a house or a road or some-thing else that is "real" (i.e., concrete). The fact that planning theorists high-light the importance of what planners do by calling it "communicative *ac-tion*" (Forester 1989) shows how deep-seated this assumption is, even among those who so strongly reject the worldview of modernism and the theory of RCPM.

The positivistic dualism was itself a reaction to the traditional rational-ists' idea that there is *a priori*[4] knowledge, based on reason or thought or God's will. This was a salutary move, but positivism held on to the idea that there is a hierarchy in language, with a preferred class referring to observa-tional or experiential characteristics "in the world." Although it rejected the idea that we can gain knowledge about "reality" through pure speculative (armchair) thinking, it retained the idea that there is something called con-ceptual analysis, based on the distinction between analytic and synthetic state-ments.[5]

Within "theory," the highest status was accorded to universally appli-cable general theories that produced propositions that could be confirmed (or disconfirmed) by empirical investigation. This conception of theory is captured nicely by Mandelbaum (1996, xiii–iv):

> "[T]heory" was a prestigious and restrictive term. . . . not to be confused with empirical generalization or statistical patterns nor with a normative catechism or a policy proposal. In its full rhetorical splendor, theory was composed of a set of propositions brought together in a symbolic world that generated accurate forecasts and postdictions, that disciplined the chaos of our sensory observations so that the rhetorical form revealed and mir-rored what we assumed was the hidden order of Nature, Man, and Society.

And in the normative realm:

> Theory forced our jumbled expressions of value, virtue, and preference into a coherent hierarchy so that immediate choices followed ineluctably from a small set of principles and decision rules. (Ibid.)

It is this kind of theory—perhaps better called a "meta-narrative"—that both postmodernists and neopragmatists emphatically reject.

A Pragmatic Approach to Theory

One of the most significant contributions of pragmatic thought is to deny the [general and absolute] legitimacy of bifurcations like theory and practice while still acknowledging their usefulness for certain contingent and practical purposes.

As we saw in chapter 3, Quine demonstrated that the distinction between fact and value (and the related distinctions between analytic and synthetic, between the necessary and the contingent, between what we mean and what we believe), is not a determinate one. In principle, we cannot sharply separate them.

Quine also rejected the idea that there is a class of purely empirical concrete statements that are free of all theoretical elements—that is, he demonstrated that a clear general distinction cannot be made between the theoretical and the nontheoretical. He still uses the notion of observation statements, but he "frees the definition of observation sentence from any dependence on the distinction between the theory free and the theory laden" (Quine 1990, 8). Terms are no longer divided into two classes, one theoretical and the other not.

If the distinction between the theoretical and the empirical is to be made, it will be for practical purposes. This applies even to science:

> The "great achievements" of science, its great "theories" are not . . . to be thought of as isolated hypotheses but rather as fruitful research programmes. And once such a "theory" is lit upon, it is quite irrational . . . to abandon a programme which is generating "dramatic, unexpected, stunning" predictions merely because there are "known facts" which seem to be incompatible with the principles on which the program rests, its core doctrines. . . . What destroys [the] programme is not an anomalous observation but the emergence of a better, more fruitful programme. (Passmore 1985, 111)

We conclude from these insights that theory and practice are ends of a useful continuum but not dichotomous opposites.

Theoretical reflection cannot be separated from practice. The idea that there is a sharp distinction between theory and practice originates with Kant's distinction between pure reason (theory) and practical reason (practice, including instrumental and moral value).[6] As Stout argues:

> Kant was not wrong to distinguish cognitive (theoretical) and practical dimensions of human life. He was wrong, however, to distinguish them sharply—in effect, handing over to each an essentially separate domain of culture with its own conceptual framework and constitutive rules. (Stout 1988, 262)

What we need to do is stress integration:

> to display the cognitive, practical . . . dimensions of human life diffused throughout the culture, inseparably interrelated and not parcelled out as the special responsibilities of the scientist, the moralist, and the strong poet. (Ibid.)

Theory and practice should be seen as a continuous process of reflecting on action and acting on reflection, a process that can be disentangled only in an artificial manner. A distinction between the two may be useful in certain contexts, for particular purposes. The line will be drawn at different points, depending on context and purpose.

The dualism between theory and practice arose from theoretical, philosophical talk. The fact that those who reject theory seem unaware of this is a kind of ideological distortion. Even though pragmatists reject theory as the positivists conceived of it, the pragmatic goal of providing different types of descriptions that reunite theory and practice will also require a bit of philosophical talk. This is the kind of theory we do believe is very relevant to planning today.

PLANNING THEORY AND PLANNING PRACTICE

The practitioner is not *always* wrong to dismiss what planning theorists are talking about: Certain *kinds* of theory (e.g., mechanistic, scientistic social theories) are not useful. But without some practical theory, planning is in danger of combining the worst of both postmodernism and modernism—paralyzed by relativism, jumping on every trendy bandwagon, still serving entrenched bureaucratic and development industry interests, yet attempting (with ever-diminishing credibility) to cloak it all in claims of objective professional expertise. Ironically, those who are most critical of theory talk seem to be those who are most affected by past theory, that is, those who implicitly or explicitly follow the RCPM. Perhaps what they want to reject is not theory but theory that challenges their own practices.

We see three major ways in which planners need to "do theory" (in the pragmatic sense) if the profession is to remain relevant by responding to the pressures for change:

1. Reflect critically on current theories, vocabularies, or language games (descriptions, behaviors, practices)

2. Generate alternative theories, vocabularies, or language games; or at least become familiar with those proposed by others

3. Evaluate these new theories, vocabularies, or language games

Critical Reflection on Practice

Deeply entrenched practices may involve actors who are unaware of the presuppositions, concepts, and descriptions underlying their practice. The RCPM and its professional protocol epitomize this kind of "unreflectiveness." The planner as pure technician who "just follows a method" to "find the means to given ends" is doing so under a set of descriptions that (as discussed in chapter 2) involve utilitarianism and positivism, a sharp separation of ends from means, and of politics from administration.

Consider a transportation planner who had done elaborate evaluations of [a rather narrow range of] alternative designs for a roadway expansion. The evaluation weighted each criterion (e.g., 5 percent for aesthetics, 20 percent for cost, 15 percent for number of houses displaced, 10 percent for effect on access to a nearby hospital, and so on). But when asked to legitimize the criteria or the weighting, he was literally speechless. Perhaps if the planner was aware of the relation of rational planning to positivism and to utilitarianism, he would have at least understood the question. As discussed in chapter 2, the reductionism of the RCPM reflects both. Moral issues become resolvable (at least in principle) by the empirical calculation of consequences, applying the techniques of social science. But the emphasis on quantification is very dangerous: Moral concerns that are unquantifiable are either ignored or distorted by spurious quantification. If the planner had some understanding of the weaknesses of utilitarianism, he might have had some response.

When one is engaged in an entrenched, habitual practice, it is difficult to stand back and see it in a holistic way. We have presented (chapters 6, 13) the holistic critical process of WRE. We saw that a reflective internal perspective (that of the participant, the practitioner), which focuses on the coherence of considered situational judgments and normative principles, gives a "narrow reflective equilibrium." A reflective external approach (the "theoretical" critic) seeks a "wide reflective equilibrium," which also brings in background theories and principles (both normative and descriptive), including critical accounts of the structure and functioning of society. When dealing with our own culture/practice, these external (structural) relations are often hidden, and we are most likely to settle for an internal view. Pointing out these relationships may lead us to challenge the structures. Awareness of the critiques of our social, political, and economic institutions is necessary for the reflective practitioner.

Hoch's 1994 book, *What Do Planners Do?*, is a good starting point—he supplements the (more or less) reflective accounts of practitioners with his own insightful critical comments.

Generation of New Practices

Theories (types of descriptions) create practices. *New* theories (new types of descriptions) create new practices, new behaviors, and with them, new standards to evaluate these behaviors. If the practitioner is not aware of or able to utilize the language and skills involved in the legitimation of these vocabularies, language games, or redescriptions, he or she is doomed to obsolescence.

When Hoch examined research on planning effectiveness, he discovered that the "measure and meaning of effective planning has changed over time" (Hoch 1994, 264). He found that

> Research that confidently started out as a test of how well and to what extent politicians and citizens follow the plans made by professional planners has ended up questioning whether rational planning is even a useful and reasonable approach to resolving urban problems.

We would say that this is because the description (practical and "theoretical") of planning itself has changed; the criteria for "effective planning" have been redefined because the conception of planning has changed.

As new type of descriptions are formulated, new practices are created. For example, we saw in chapter 13 that postmodern feminist accounts of development planning see the modernist approach as an ideology, one presupposing a notion of "development" that they deconstruct: a new vocabulary, a new type of description has been generated, which in turn is creating a different kind of development planning practice. This change in type of description may be seen as reflecting a paradigm shift (Connelly et al. 1995). Planners need to be aware of, and to understand, such new practices. Innes (1995a), Healey (1997), and Chrislip and Larson (1994) give informative accounts of new forms of practice and new institutions for collaboration (see chapter 10).

Evaluation of New Practices

Not every new theory (type of description) should be accepted. In determining whether or not we should accept the new type of description, the new vocabulary, or the new language game, there are three pragmatic criteria: intelligibility, legitimation, and applicability to practice.

Intelligibility

To make a new vocabulary intelligible, it must be grafted on to our existing vocabulary; otherwise, the two vocabularies will be incommensurable (chapter 4). This is why we have warned against the advocacy of "radical paradigm shifts"[7] (chapter 12), where different paradigms are seen as entire conceptual schemes that are incommensurable.[8] In this extreme view, different paradigms become literally unintelligible to those who have not *converted* to them, precluding any possibility of justification of the new paradigm to those who inhabit the established paradigm. As we argued (chapter 7), implementation must then rely on coercion or conversion.

In contrast to this Kuhnian view, the pragmatist sees the entire process of interpretation of a conceptual scheme, language, or paradigm as one of grafting that scheme onto one's own. It requires significant overlap between perspectives. Any talk of differences in concepts and beliefs also requires this overlap. Our shifts in the vocabulary or language game need to be pragmatic and incremental, disciplined, and controlled by connection to our tradition.

As we argued in chapter 7, proposals for change must build bridges back to where we are right now. Rorty (1991b) argues that an important role does remain for philosophical theory: to test and connect old and new vocabularies in a reasonable and practical manner, reweaving the community's web of belief. New ideas must be legitimated by connecting them step-by-step back to the old tradition. This reweaving inevitably involves a lot of "theoretical" talk.

Legitimation

The important question regarding new vocabularies and new practices is their legitimation. One primary goal or role of planning theory is to deal with the question of the legitimation of new theories, vocabularies, or language games. If you give up the notion that some types of descriptions are privileged (i.e., they are "more real"), then new descriptions require legitimation. Why choose one over the other?

The question of legitimacy in planning relates to what planners do—create new futures that satisfy human needs, in a political environment. This places us in the realm of values. How useful a theory is depends on how well it fits with our moral culture, our basic liberal democratic values.

Pragmatic planning theory provides a way to justify or legitimate planning in a post-positivistic era. We have argued that the only sense of "better than" that is consistent with post-positivistic critiques is a pragmatic one. For a new planning vocabulary to be justified, it must appeal to accepted normative standards in our moral culture. While these standards are not immutable, they cannot all change at once.

Why bother to legitimate new theory or practice? The current crisis requires new theories and new practices. There are a variety of possible ways[9] to implement social change. We have argued that only consensus-seeking dialogue is consistent with a democratic society (chapters 7, 9). This is the only way to legitimate the change in a post-positivistic world. If change is not legitimated, we can't know whether it will make things better, whether it will address the concerns that have led to pressures on government (and on planning) to change.

With an increasingly shaky institutional base (decreasing support from senior governments, marginal functional status within local governments), planning needs to be able to make persuasive arguments that appeal to the moral culture in which we are situated. In attempting to legitimize or justify the choice of new planning vocabularies (theories and practices), we must relate them as best we can to the old, saving what is best in the old and replacing what is worst. For example, planners must be able to demonstrate both that a development decision will adversely affect a community (e.g., decrease low-cost housing or drive out employment) *and* that this is unfair and unjust.

Application to Practice

To be worthy of adopting, a new vocabulary must work in practice better than the old one. It must meet some of the concerns that led to the current dissatisfaction. If citizens are concerned that they have no voice, then a deliberative, dialogical planning approach is more likely to meet this need than the RCPM. But we have to try it in practice to see how it really works. If our approach doesn't work in practice, then we have to modify it until it does. This kind of interaction is how we should develop new theory. These are important and perhaps difficult "theoretical" tasks for planners whether their primary role is theorist or practitioner. But they are not optional ones!

A Two-Way Street

We agree with Hoch (1996) that theory and practice "must be joint partners." But partnership is a two-way street. Certainly, planning theory should study the "skillful planners" whom Forester (1996) admires, and theory must be communicated as clearly and practically as possible. Still, the current context demands that practicing planners pay some attention to theory (in the pragmatic sense discussed above), that they engage in critical reflection about current practice, and that they participate in the generation, legitimation, and "reweaving" of new planning practices. The survival of the profession depends on it. A profession that chooses to remain ignorant of its own "theory" will inevitably be in a reactive posture, particularly in the present dynamic social and intellectual context. This would be a deeply ironic position for a profession that claims expertise in helping society envision and realize a better future!

15

Power, Trust, and Planning

CONTRASTING APPROACHES

Planning is supposed to be a positive exercise. It is intended to be a fair and democratic process, aiming to produce environments that are better places to live decent and healthy lives. However, we have seen that sometimes planning is not what it seems. An apparently open and democratic process may turn out, on critical examination, to have undercurrents that serve certain [elite] interests other than those it purports to serve. Such insights have been extended and generalized by some followers of Foucault (Foucauldians) to claim that *all* supposedly legitimate planning processes are a sham in the sense that they can be understood only in terms of those who have the most power to advance their own interests. In light of the increasing influence of the Foucauldian school, we decided to end this book with a more extended critical evaluation of the Foucauldian perspective and its implications for planning than was presented in chapter 4.

While we generally agree with Fischler's (2000) stress on the agreements between the Habermassian and the Foucauldian schools, several important issues arise from the significant differences between them. In this chapter, we want to draw attention to one very significant contrast regarding the role of power in public planning processes. We will contrast our neopragmatic approach to power (that is similar to Habermas's) with the Foucauldian approach.

Without in any way denigrating the importance of the Foucauldian critique of social institutions or Foucault's methodological contributions, we see some serious flaws in his approach. These flaws can lead to grave dangers in any attempt to develop a *planning theory* based on Foucault.

We want to be clear that we are not presenting a complete analysis of Foucault's thought. Nor are we advancing a comprehensive theory of power.

Rather, we are concerned with the implications of certain ideas. In this chapter, we will consider how an anti-foundational assumption that Foucauldians share with pragmatists can lead in very different directions when power is considered. These directions have important implications for planning theory and practice. This assumption is the *contingency of concepts*.

In chapter 3, we discussed the neopragmatic approach to concepts. We saw that neopragmatism rejects the idea of metaphysical realism—the view that linguistic categories, terms, or labels correspond to natural kinds "in the world," and that all terms must refer to (or represent) a thing or a fact or a state of affairs that is really "in the world." Correspondence with "reality" is thus a source of legitimacy for a category or term; it is a very powerful source of normative justification in a society dominated by modernistic scientism.

We have discussed the neopragmatic view that no vocabulary, concepts, language games, or frameworks are universal, absolute, or necessary—that they should be seen as contingent rather than absolute. No particular vocabulary is necessarily the right one. None can provide an essentially uncontested, universal, outside Archimedean (god's-eye) basis for absolute judgments regarding how things are in themselves. There is no reason to give any vocabulary an absolute privileged status.

In other words, a neopragmatic planning view suggests that the choice of linguistic form should be determined on the basis of the purpose(s) and goals of the planning process and not on the basis of what accords better with reality.

For postmodernists, this view leads to conceptual relativity. However, we have argued that it can be maintained without falling into the relativity trap. An interlocutor in Wittgenstein's *Uncertainty* asks, "So truth or falsity depends on agreement?" He responds, "No—We must agree on the language used to put those statements" (Wittgenstein 1969).

This means that the useful distinctions that we make are contingent on social contexts—particular sets of social circumstances. Pragmatists take this insight in certain directions. For example, this approach allows the social sciences to bridge the divide between such supposed opposites as objective/subjective, scientific/political, or theoretical/practical. The idea that social sciences must follow rigid rules of objectivity modeled on the methods of science is just one of the orthodoxies that neopragmatists reject. Social science is interpretive; understanding cannot be separated from objective description. Nor should it be separated from social critique—as both pragmatists and critical theorists such as Habermas (1984) have shown.

As we saw in chapter 11, this perspective is particularly helpful in dealing with debates characterized by essentially contested concepts such as "natural" or "environmental integrity." We argued for a neopragmatic approach to planning that puts aside debates framed by traditional absolute categories, such as metaphysical debates about the nature of the environment. Thus, recognizing the contingency of concepts could assist planners in consensus-building efforts. This is an example of the interpretive and critical aspect of social science implicit in the pragmatic approach.

Foucault and Foucauldians share this same insight (the contingency of vocabulary, concepts, language games, and frameworks). Foucault acknowledges the contingency of all concepts (except perhaps power) and also, in company with the neopragmatists (particularly Rorty), rejects the absolute dichotomies of traditional philosophy. As Rorty notes, Foucault and the "arch-pragmatist" Dewey "make exactly the same criticisms of the tradition" (Rorty 1982, 204). But where the neopragmatist uses this insight to promote human ends and provide "social hope" (Rorty 1982)—a primary goal, we think most planners would agree, of contemporary planning—Foucault takes the insight in the opposite direction. We believe this direction is misguided and unproductive for planning.

THE FOUCAULDIAN VIEW

In chapter 3, we saw that many Foucauldians extend these insights about contingency to claim that *all* relationships and processes should be viewed in terms of power. They extend and widen the notion of power to the point where it is all-inclusive. They seem to go further to say that power *constitutes* concepts and vocabulary; that is, they can be understood *only* in terms of power.

Three things are happening in Foucault's arguments:

1. The vocabulary of power is elevated to *a privileged* status

2. The meaning of "power" is *extended* to cover all human social behavior

3. The argument equivocates between two *different meanings* of "power": the new extended and privileged meaning of "power" and its ordinary use, which applies only to a subset of human behavior

The Vocabulary of Power Is Privileged

For Foucault, power becomes the most significant operating notion that governs discourse and hence social reality (since Foucault, along with other postmodern thinkers, eliminates the language/reality contrast). Power consequently becomes the one *exception* to the contingency thesis discussed above. Thus, the contingency of truth, knowledge, reality, reason, and freedom must be expressed in terms of the "universalist" presence and operation of power:

> Truth isn't outside power, or lacking in power . . . or the reward of free spirits. Truth is a thing of this world: it is produced only by virtue of multiple forms of constraints. And it induces regular effects of power. Each society has its regime of truth, its "general politics" of truth/power/knowledge. (Foucault 1984, 131)

It is important to notice that Foucault is not suggesting merely that those with privileged access to the truth (as a result of greater knowledge or expertise in power-sensitive areas such as health care) can use that access rhetorically[1] in order to attain and maintain power, thus distorting fair and equal access to power. Rather, he is saying that power *replaces* knowledge and truth as the only distinction.[2] All truth statements are *purely* (nothing more than) rhetorical: "[P]ower defines what counts as rationality and knowledge, and thereby what counts as reality" (Yiftachel et al. 2001, 11). This is the idea we reject! Of course, truth and knowledge *can* be used for rhetorical purposes. But this does not mean that truth is *nothing but* rhetoric.

Throughout much of Foucault's work, he seems to agree with pragmatists and with other postmodern thinkers that vocabularies are contingent (in the sense discussed earlier). However, he wants to confer a privileged status on one vocabulary—his vocabulary of power. For Foucault, power (and resistance to power) permeates all relations! Thus our concepts do not, as the pragmatists believe, serve our human needs, aspirations, and hopes, nor as the critical theorists suggest, our emancipation; rather, they serve only to perpetuate networks of power. Power is everything!

This is rather ironic because one of the key postmodernist criticisms of modernism is that it privileges one vocabulary—the vocabulary of science. This privileging of the vocabulary of science leads to scientism. We contend that giving the vocabulary of power such a privileged status is equally pernicious and should be considered as another form of reductionism.

Foucauldians cannot have it both ways. Either power becomes an "objective," universal, absolutely true concept (in which case Foucault must give up his contingency thesis) *or* power is a contingent concept—its meaning is "up for grabs," as are all other concepts. Then one must ask whether Foucault's notion of power is one worth maintaining. In his view, everything (all institutions and relationships) becomes an expression of power and resistance to power. In fact, power becomes the only functioning "legitimate" concept allowed by Foucault. All other notions (truth, freedom, self, reason) are nothing but masks for power: "[T]ruth is no doubt a form of power . . . " (Foucault 1972, 107). What are the consequences of this extension? We will return to this question later.

The Meaning of "Power" Is Broadened

Foucault provides often brilliant and illuminating accounts of the power relationships we find ourselves enmeshed within, without our realizing that we are so enmeshed. However, he extends his insights to the point where the notion of power becomes vacuous. In other words, he eliminates the traditional notion of power: "Setting aside the old model, where power is a matter of one person (group) exercising sovereign control over another; where some give orders and others obey, where some impose their will on others" (Taylor 1986, 84). Thus, Foucault replaces the conventional interpretation of power with a quite different one. In this interpretation, power (and resistance to power) is manifested in, indeed constitutive of and intrinsic to, *all* social relations: linguistic, institutional, economic, religious, and so on. Since these social relations are omnipresent and indeed, as some argue, constitutive of what we are, we are everywhere (at least in any organized society) enmeshed in relations of power from which we cannot extricate ourselves:

> When one speaks of "power," people immediately think of a political struc-
> ture, a government, a dominant social class. . . . This is not at all what I
> think when I speak of "relations of power." I mean that in human relations,
> whatever they are—whether it be a question of communicating verbally . . .
> or a question of love relations, institutional or economic relations—power
> is always present. (Foucault 1985, 11–12)

These relations govern, define, structure and constitute our actions, thoughts, and beliefs.

In Foucault's terms, anything that restricts (governs) behavior is an exercise in power. Since all vocabularies, concepts, and social institutions (because they are normative) restrict what we say or do, they all represent power. As McCarthy (1991, 64) observes, Foucault:

> defines power relations in terms not unlike those that the sociological tra-
> dition uses to define social relations. . . . In Foucault's definition only ac-
> tions that had no possible effects on the actions of others, that is, that were
> not social, would be free of the exercise of power.

So, *all* social interactions are seen as power relations.

For Foucault, all truth, knowledge, and rationality are merely reflections of power relations, an observation that follows from his definition of power as any set of relations that restrict: "The exercise of power . . . is a total structure of actions brought to bear upon possible actions; it incites, it induces, it seduces, it makes easier or more difficult; in the extreme it constrains or forbids absolutely" (Foucault 1983, 220). Even rationality, because it restricts behavior, will be seen as a form of power. For example, if you don't want to be hit by lightning and there is a severe lightning storm outside, you cannot go outside and be thought rational. Rationality restricts one's behavior; therefore, it is a form of power. In the same way, truth and knowledge are also seen as restrictive.

Certainly, it can be useful to look at various social relations, as Foucault does, and to demonstrate how certain forms of knowledge or certain disciplines (sciences, sociology, psychology, management sciences) supposedly dedicated to the determination of truth turn out to function as oppressive regimes that govern and control through the creation of normalized behavior. But to put everything in terms of power is to make a stipulative and persuasive definition of power. It is surely a far cry from its ordinary use, and very misleading, as we argue below. Interpreted not as reference or accurate representation of reality but (purely) in terms of its restricting effect, this use of "power" is itself "government" (i.e., restriction) of what is to be said and not said, done or not done: Everything must be understood and expressed in terms of the web of power relationships in which we are enmeshed.

Of course, if power is ubiquitous, then this would seem to raise the possibility of positive power. For Foucault, power can also be productive (i.e., positive or beneficial or good); he expresses the belief that relations of power are "above all, productive" (Foucault 1988, 118). As Baynes et al. (1987) express it: "Power, Foucault insists, is also and essentially positive, productive, and 'capillary'—it circulates throughout . . . the social body; it is an aspect of every social practice, social relation and social institution." Thus, the negative sense of power is widened by Foucault to include [what others might call] positive power. Therefore, we should "Cease once and for all to describe the effects of power in negative terms: it excludes, it represses, it censors, it abstracts, it masks, it conceals" (Foucault 1979, 194). So Foucauldians may argue that he has been unjustifiably criticized for perceiving all relationships as oppressive in that they are reflective of relations of power. Power can be regarded as productive in the sense that it creates new forms of knowledge and action, new ways of speaking, new ways of determining what is to count as true and false—that is, new conceptual frameworks, new vocabularies. It is no longer an inherently negative notion. Of course, it must be recognized that any new knowledge will also restrict and thus is also a new form of power in a Foucauldian world. Thus, for Foucault, power is no longer necessarily associated with oppression.

What Foucault is doing here is again describing *all* relations in terms of power. The question is: Why do this? Why use "power" to describe things we already have other words for—for example, reasonable persuasion, new knowledge, new vocabularies? Why abandon useful distinctions—true/false, legitimate/illegitimate, justified/unjustified? There is no good reason why we should accept this claim.

Now, any term can be extended to cover all of a particular kind of behavior. For example, some socio-biologists claim that "everyone is selfish." If one points to obvious counter-examples (e.g., Mother Theresa was not selfish), the term is then stretched to cover this case (helping the poor made Mother Theresa feel good). Eventually, the term is used to describe *all* human behavior (or at least all voluntary behavior). But then the term "selfish" has become meaningless and useless; now, we need a new distinction to separate "good selfish" from "bad selfish," where "good selfish" means what "unselfish" used to mean. Similarly, we can use "power" in an all-encompassing way to describe all relationships as the exercise of power. But then (as Forester [1990] and

Fischler [2000] point out), we will need (for moral purposes) to distinguish legitimate power from illegitimate power.

Here, the Foucault position gets us in a bind. We need an account that distinguishes good power from bad power. But if the only vocabulary is power itself, then there is no basis for such distinctions. All we can do is replace one set of normatively neutral vocabulary by another. The vocabularies created, and the actions or realities they constitute, also become the working of power relationships and, it would seem, we are its victims.

The old use of "power" serves important purposes, particularly in a democratic society—for example, we still want to distinguish uncoerced actions from actions that result from coercive power; we still want to distinguish persuasion by reasonable argument from the exercise of force. Revisions to definitions need not eliminate our ability to make such distinctions, nor should they.[3]

The problem is that the valuable insights Foucault provides about the bureaucratic nature of science (exemplified by the "rational comprehensive" planning model) make sense only if they turn out *not* to be what they are purported to be—if they turn out to be masks for power in the guise of applied scientific knowledge and truth, or in the guise of serving human ends. This is *not* what we thought it to be; this is power masked as science. But as Taylor has pointed out, if Foucauldians want to make this kind of observation, they must hold on to the *non-distorted* (non-vacuous) notions of truth, knowledge, liberty, and the like that are *independent* of the concept of power, and of the vocabulary of power.

The first step is that the vocabulary of power is given a privileged position: All descriptions are to be couched in terms of power. The second step is a linguistic trick. Power becomes universal by casting the net so widely that it captures everything. Once the concept of power becomes universal, it excludes nothing. Then the term "power" no longer has any meaning; using it says nothing. Hence, we call this broadened use of the term "power" vacuous. But this is too much! What is the point of so widening the meaning of power that it covers everything?

Two Different Senses of "Power" Are Conflated

The analysis of power has a justified and important place in contemporary thought (including planning thought). It is often the case that reasonable decision-making processes are distorted by the ideological use of contingent concepts in a way that maintains power relations. If we hope to have reasonable and fair decision-making processes it is important to be aware of, to anticipate, and to counteract such distortions (Forester 1989). Thus, the critical use of the term "power" (which Rorty terms "pejorative") by both critical theorists and Foucauldians has an important constructive point that revolves around the coercive, insidious, and repressive role that power often plays in our lives as social beings.

This use of "power" arises from Marx: Ideological distortion is used by those with economic wealth (those who have control of the means of production) to dupe ordinary people into accepting institutions that do not operate in their interest (i.e., institutions that support existing power relations). It stems from the Marxist notions of ideology and false consciousness. As critical theorists point out, power is often masked within social institutions, whether they be religious, political, or economic, or within contemporary conceptions of rationality and bureaucracy. And no one does a better job of unmasking than Foucault.

But Foucauldians really don't stick to the new broad definition of "power"; they equivocate between it and the traditional (more negative) notion of power. At best, this equivocation is confusing; at worst, it is dishonest. The two different senses of "power" become conflated.[4] First, there is the special broadened or vacuous use discussed in the previous section. Second, there is the (more ordinary) pejorative or negative use of "power" discussed above.

The sleight of hand comes here. Having widened the meaning of power to apply to all behavior, the *pejorative* meaning then gets applied to *all* power. What Foucauldians seem to do is to shift from the vacuous to the pejorative use; that is, all relationships are expressions of power *and* this is *bad*. Thus, we should view all institutions and relationships with suspicion (and presumably resist them) because they are inherently oppressive and manipulative.

The use of power in this pejorative sense is an implicit critique (though Foucault claims critiques are just another reflection of power—which is, of course, true given his broad definition of power). But critique requires normative *justification*, and it requires shifting back to the *old* (narrower) meaning of power. We need a normative basis (even if provisional and contingent) to judge power as good or bad, to distinguish the legitimate exercise of power from the illegitimate.

The Result: The External Theory of Power Overwhelms Internal Understanding

As Forester (2001, 264) points out in his insightful critique of Flyvberg's 1998 *Rationality and Power*, Foucauldians present

> two kinds of analysis without integrating them: (1) a critical-hermeneutic "inside" analysis which tells a story in the actors' own languages of projects and projections, and costs and benefits, and pros and cons; and (2) a presumably "explanatory" theoretical analysis about "rationality and *realrationalitat*" and "power" and their influences from the "outside."

We made a similar contrast between internal and external perspectives in our discussion of pragmatic multicultural planning (chapter 13). We saw that when dealing with a community within his or her own culture, the planner cannot take a purely external perspective. What the planner can do is use an external perspective to critique particular elements or aspects of the culture while holding the rest of its "web" of concepts, knowledge, and beliefs constant[5] as a reference point for incremental change (chapter 7).

What Foucauldians want to do is use their external perspective to reject the entire internal view at once. In a Foucauldian world, the outside theory— that everything is a consequence of power relations—dominates, overwhelms, and comes to replace the particular understanding of the local situation. The very same cases that are alleged to substantiate the theory no longer have any significance. As discussed in the next section, this could have disastrous results for planning.

WHERE DOES THE FOUCAULDIAN VIEW LEAD US?

Planning Theory Could Be Distorted

We would not dispute the assertion that "the powers that shape the urban environment can be, and often are, regressive and exploitive" (Yiftachel et al. 2001, 10). But as we argued in chapter 4, if planning theorists focus too much on power, it could blind them to other realities. Everything could be reinterpreted within a framework of power and power structures. There may be a parallel here with utilitarianism. When utilitarianism held sway in moral theory, there was a pernicious tendency to reinterpret all moral intuitions, and all behavior, in utilitarian terms. When economic utilitarianism dominates public decision making, there is an equally pernicious tendency to operationalize everything in distorted commensurable (monetary) units.

Similarly, if we focus on planning as a "set of institutions enmeshed within 'grids of power' that shape cities and regions" (ibid.), this could seriously distort our understanding, leading us to miss other important aspects of the relationships or structures: aspects like community, solidarity, or trust. And distorted understanding could lead to framing problems in ways that are "solved" by very inappropriate "solutions."

Anarchy or Worse

By Foucault's definition, we are all in the grips of power in the form of vocabularies, concepts, and social institutions. The only alternative, then (as we argued in chapter 4), would seem to be complete anarchy—linguistically, politically, and morally. Foucault (1984, 57) wants to "question the social and moral distinctions between innocent and guilty." There is no [even provisional] point of view for judgment.

Furthermore, even anarchy won't work in Foucault's world, because he denies the requisite natural free human subject necessary for anarchy. In Walzer's (1986, 61) analysis:

> Foucault's radical abolitionism, if it is serious, is not anarchist so much as nihilist. For on his own arguments, either there will be nothing left at all, nothing visibly human; or new codes and disciplines will be produced, and Foucault gives us no reason to expect that these will be any better than the ones we now live with. Nor, for that matter, does he give us any way of knowing what "better" might mean.

We cannot make any distinctions, any judgments, any plans. In fact, we cannot say or do anything at at all. Perhaps this is where Foucault wants to lead us. But it seems totally inconsistent with the idea of planning (regardless of how planning is defined)!

Victimhood

It seems to us that, despite Foucault's gestures toward positive power, and regardless of his stated desire to eliminate moral categories, and although Foucauldians may deny it—what they really want to argue is that we are the *victims* of our institutions, and thus their power over us is *negative*. For example, Allen speaks of citizens "subjecting themselves to the routines of state power" (Allen 1996, 328), being "defined as 'other' within some power relations" (329), suffering "oppression" (329), being in "unequal" power relations between "landlord and tenant" (333)—all negatives suffered by victims.

Of course, we as planners are inclined to urge such victims to resist, to take liberating action, and to applaud them when they do so. So Allen admires those (unfortunately rare) citizens who "contest the definitions of themselves inherent in state administration" (328), those who sense "the necessity of speaking out collectively against oppression" (329), those who reflect the "radical root image of democracy" (329), those who "refuse the forms of subjection inherent . . . in the modern democratic state" (331), those who share a "deep concern for the misfortunes any individual might face" (333), those who seek a "common basis for action" (333). But to advocate or to commend such actions, we need a normative basis—for example, liberal democratic values. And there seems to be no place for such normative bases in a Foucauldian world.

Planning Practice Could Be Paralyzed

If planning practitioners see everything in terms of power relations, and if citizens see themselves as victims, this could induce paralysis. An acute awareness of power and power structures could also create feelings of disempowerment, of inability to exercise any agency, of fatalism, quietism, and despair.

> [T]he more powerful the vision of some increasingly total system or logic . . . the more powerless the reader comes to feel. Insofar as the theorist wins, therefore by constructing an increasingly closed and terrifying machine, to that very degree he loses, since the critical capacity of his work is thereby paralyzed, and the impulses of negation and revolt, not to speak of those of social transformation, are increasingly perceived as vain and trivial in the face of the model itself. (Jameson 1984, 11)

As we argued in chapter 4, if citizens and professional planners lose hope and come to believe that power is ubiquitous and inescapable, that democratic planning processes are nothing more than elites vying for power, that reasonable arguments are irrelevant and useless, then why bother?

In addition, we need some grounds for judging when particular processes have gone wrong, when corrective action is needed. When Flyvbjerg judges that the answer to his "value rational question ("Where are we going with planning and democracy in Aalborg?") was clearly "Astray" (2002, 357), we want to have strong grounds for supporting him. The idea of going astray makes sense only if we can say that what happened isn't what *should* have happened, that the process was somehow distorted. We must be able to conceive of a *legitimate* process as a norm for evaluating actual processes. But if the external theory explains everything as a consequence of power relations, then "going astray" makes no sense. In Giddens's terms (Healey 1997), structure is completely dominant, and there is no room left for agency.

Consensus Becomes Theoretically Impossible (Relativism and Incommensurability)

In Foucault's hands, the contingency of concepts seems to lead to relativism. There are two moves here. The first relates to the production of truth. When he uses the word "truth," Foucault does not mean "the ensemble of truths which are to be discovered and accepted, but rather the ensemble of rules according to which the true and false are separated and specific effects of power attached to the true" (Foucault 1984, 131). Thus Foucault (1979, 114), asserts that "Power . . . produces reality, it produces domains of objects and rituals of truth."

The second move leads to the relativism. As Foucault (1980, 131) says: "[E]ach society has its regime of truth, its 'general politics' of truth . . . the mechanisms and instances which enable one to distinguish true and false statements. . . ." His notion of "regime" is very much like the notion of a conceptual scheme, where statements, judgments, beliefs, and the reality they construct are relative to that scheme. What follows from this idea is the conclusion that these schemes or regimes are incommensurable (chapter 4); therefore, they cannot be criticized or understood from any external point of view, from any other conceptual scheme, or any other regime. (Although, it seems for Foucault, there is one regime-independent point of description— the description presented in terms of power relations, in his archaeologies and genealogies).

This relativism leads to the view that there are incommensurable institutions, societies, worldviews. Each regime becomes a windowless monad. Such a view leads to a factionalization of society into interest groups and subcultures, a very undesirable outcome for planners. Communities become isolated from each other, and communication becomes impossible. Then there is no way to resolve difficulties except through the use of force or coercion (chapter 4).

Thus, for planners, an extremely important (and highly undesirable) consequence of the Foucauldian view is that consensus is no longer even theoretically an option. This is particularly disturbing for communicative planners who wish to reach consensus and enlarge the conception of "we." To us this has a tragic irony: The great advantage of a pragmatic approach to planning, and the value of recognizing the contingency of concepts, is that it allows for the possibility of consensus between previously isolated groups or cultures. The regimes or the relativist conceptual schemes, and the realities and languages they constitute, are not isolated from each other. We can understand and evaluate regimes—our own and others—using vocabularies other than power (chapter 4).

Critique Is Groundless and Resistance Is Futile

Taylor points out that the relativistic view (just discussed) leads to the extremely conservative conclusion that regimes cannot be criticized at all because there are no normative grounds for criticism or change. Foucauldians would deny that their view is conservative, pointing out that Foucault advocates resistance to grids of power at every point. But this resistance seems like an act of pure desperation—the only reaction left, if power is seen as all-encompassing and overwhelming. It seems more sad than noble.

Further, resistance in a Foucauldian framework is meaningless. It may turn out not to be resistance at all; it may simply be an expression of false consciousness. For example, civil rights protesters, or G8 demonstrators, or voters who support a green party, may believe they are resisting when really they are not. If so, Habermas would say that they are ideologically distorted. How can we tell? We need criteria to distinguish true resistance from false resistance. But Foucault doesn't allow for any such contrasts; everything is reduced to a web of power relations.

In fact, Foucault's conception of resistance is empty, unless he steps outside his own worldview. In his worldview, we can't resist X in order to replace it by Y, which is "better"—because there is *no such thing* as "better." Habermas could say that Y is less distorted or truer than X; Rawls could say Y better conforms to political liberal principles of justice as fairness; but Foucault can't say anything like that. Suppose we were to accept the Foucauldian view of "knowledge" and "truth" as a grid of power and resistance to power. Is there any reason to believe that the Foucauldian vocabulary itself is not just a grid of power relations? Then why not resist the Foucauldian vocabulary, leave "knowledge" and "truth" intact, and retain the ability to make useful Habermassian and Rawlsian judgments?

We would argue Foucault's last work recognized this emptiness because he stopped using the term "resistance" and talked instead of "transgression"—that is, simply violating a boundary, a norm, or a standard. Transgression is resistance without purpose. It is clearly devoid of positive connotations or normative content. This is utter and complete nihilism! So Foucauldian resistance (or transgression) is blind, devoid of meaning, a futile gesture, a nihilistic scream. It might feel good, but it offers *no basis* for planning.

Consensus Becomes Difficult in Practice

If participants in planning processes see everything in terms of power, this could breed suspicion and mistrust, making it ever more difficult to develop the relationships of mutual respect and trust so essential to collaborative planning. On a broader scale, social solidarity will be further eroded. (See our discussion of trust in the next section.)

Even if people don't fall into Foucauldian despair, there could be a tendency to focus on identities and labels and to freeze everyone into fixed roles, interests, and positions. As we saw in chapter 11, general terms, names, and labels have often impeded rather than enhanced dialogue. Individuals often get categorized in ways that are politically loaded and that can kill the very dialogue that planners want to encourage. Such labeling and categorizing make it difficult to reframe concepts and frameworks and to come up with new solutions.

AN ALTERNATIVE VIEW

A Contrast with Habermas

At this point, it is useful to contrast Habermas and Foucault. Habermas is interested in power that distorts relations, particularly communicative relations. He wants to replace distorted relations with undistorted ones (i.e., his ideal speech situation). To Habermas, communication that is undistorted is liberating and it is freer: It is free from the influence of power.

For Foucault, however, even an ideal speech situation is an application of power, because all discourses are structured by power: "[P]ower is co-extensive with every social relationship" (Foucault 1982, 224). In particular, all communicative relations "produce effects of power" by "modifying the field of information between parties" (Foucault 1982, 218).

Planners must ask: Which description better serves the purposes of planning? Which contributes more to useful planning theory? It seems obvious to us that views like Habermas's hold much more promise for planners in a liberal democratic society.

A Pragmatic View

The idea of the contingency of concepts does not necessarily lead to any form of vicious relativism. On the contrary, the openness it allows, the connection to human needs, or, to use Rorty's (1982, 203) words, the "social hope" it provides, allows us to put planning on a sound basis, using social science and the philosophy of language as its servants. This is an optimistic view, one that can be used effectively in the planning process. As Rorty has argued, critiquing certain concepts and distinctions as divisive, outmoded, or masks for oppression, and suggesting others to replace them, can have a liberating effect on both process and product.

Ironically, Flyvbjerg's well-known Aalborg case is an excellent example of this. He uncovers a situation where power is at play under the guise of rationality. An urban preservation project aimed to reduce auto traffic in the historic core by one-third, but this goal was subverted by the fact that the only parties who were consulted before proposals were submitted to the city council were a council committee, the police, and the Chamber of Industry and Commerce. Thus, the chamber's special elite position enabled it to secretly negotiate changes in policy that conformed to what Flyvbjerg calls its "rationality": What was good for Aalborg was the view that "the car is king" (Flyvbjerg 2002, 357), in contrast to the planners' "rationality," that is, the core would remain viable only if auto traffic there were significantly reduced. In his account,

> The fate of the Aalborg Project would be decided by these two rationalities fighting it out, and the group who could place the most power behind their interpretation of what was rational and what was not would win. (Ibid.)

However, he writes that he was able to "change things for the better, if only modestly by calling attention to my results," where "better" means "more democratic, and "more effective in fulfilling the objectives of the Aalborg Project" (ibid., 361).

What did he do? Flyvbjerg pointed out that the positions of those with power might have been *rational,* but they were not *reasonable* (particularly in Rawls's (2001) sense of these two terms, discussed in chapter 6). This had force *only* because the citizens *expected* reasonableness and were able to recognize that the actions he critiqued were *not reasonable.* Contrary to his claim that the decisive aspect was "which party can put the greatest power behind its interpretation" (ibid., 360), the elites' power did *not* define or determine rationality or truth. Flyvbjerg is right that his "studies altered the power relations" in Aalborg, but he seems to misunderstand the reason. It was the recognition by citizens that the arguments and interpretations of the council committee, the chamber of commerce, and the police were *unreasonable* (in Rawls's sense) that gave his argument force and ultimately won out. The only power Flyvbjerg had was the power of the *more reasonable argument* in a dialogue set within a liberal democratic framework.

Flyvbjerg might argue that his reasonable argument is just another form of power. This is exactly what we have been critiquing. There is no reason why he can't do this; he *can choose* the vocabulary of power as the ultimate framework of analysis. But there is no reason why he *should* make this choice. We believe it is much more *useful* for democratic planning to employ the vocabulary of reasonableness and to retain the ordinary *distinction* between outcomes of reasonable open argument and outcomes resulting from the exercise of power. What Flyvbjerg did was *good* (according to liberal democratic values) because it changed the reason for the Aalborg outcome from power to reasonable argument.

An increased awareness of power imbalances is important to help us to design processes that address the inequalities (Galloway-Cosijn 1999). External theories of structure are useful in identifying and addressing local distortions. But we need not, and must not, give up the internal local, inside perspective. The external theory must serve as a tool to the internal understanding, not overtake or replace it. So we do need to be aware of power structures, but without letting this awareness dominate and overwhelm our view of planning.

To pragmatists, the Foucauldian moves are something that *can* be done but *should not* be done. There is no reason why we should accept them. We should be cautious that an increased awareness of power does not turn into a fixation. As we have seen, an obsession with power relations and structures could be dangerous for both planning theory and practice.

The idea that understanding our world as nothing but power relations— describing it solely in the vocabulary of power—is inadequate. We need different ways to see the world, other vocabularies, other concepts, in order to create institutions, arenas, forums, and decision processes that express, support, and enhance our normative liberal democratic ideals. We need the vocabularies of truth, knowledge, liberty, and so on, and we need them to be independent of (though related to) the vocabulary of power. These other vocabularies can be used to evaluate power, just as the vocabulary of power can be used to evaluate them.

The Importance of Trust

There is another vocabulary that has not been given much attention but that is of equal significance, particularly to planners: the vocabulary of *trust*. We saw in chapter 3 that trust underlies all of human and social life as a necessary condition for community, social, political, familial, and even linguistic relations (Wittgenstein 1969). The Foucauldian claim that power is universal stems from the idea that language structures our existence and that concepts generate power over individuals. Language is seen as generating power relations: At the bottom of language is power. In contrast, Wittgenstein viewed trust as underlying all of human and social life: "[A]t the bottom of human life is not thought understood as intellection, as the justified literal representation of reality . . . at the bottom of human life is trust, a particular mode of action" (Edwards 1982, 182). Here, he recognized the key links of relationship and trust to knowledge.

Perhaps it is conceivable that there could be a world without any trust. In that world, power could generate and maintain human relations. But, as Baier (1994, 95) suggests in her illuminating discussion of the concept of trust:

> Without trust, what matters to me would be unsafe, unless like the Stoic I attach myself only to what can thrive or be safe from harm, *however* others act. The starry heavens above and the moral law within had better be the only things that matter to me, if there is no one I can trust in any way.

Of course it would be impossible to live this way.

So we believe that trust is basic, rather than power. Trust is also a necessary condition for any kind of communication, understanding, knowledge or learning. If there were literally no trust, then nothing any other party says could be accepted; everything would have to be verified, guaranteed, enforced. Relations based solely on power could not generate any kind of communication. Each person would be a "windowless monad." The very possibility of truth, understanding, knowledge, or learning would be ruled out.

This same point underlines our earlier criticism of Foucault's idea that "each society has its regime of truth." We must approach others, their languages, institutions, and regimes with Davidson's (1985) principle of charity. To interpret what anyone says, we must assume that most of what they say and believe is true and coheres, on the whole, with most of what we say and believe. In other words, we must trust! That some of these relations are distorted by relations of power is certainly true (and can be unmasked), but distortion cannot be the norm. Thus, underlying our regimes is not just power but the assumption of truth, charity, and the trust it requires.

It is this assumption, and the powerful arguments for it (Davidson 1985; Stein 1994), that allow for the social hope of which Rorty speaks:

> What Foucault doesn't give us is what Dewey wanted to give us—a kind of hope which doesn't need reinforcement from the idea of a transcendental or enduring subject . . . what Dewey suggested was that we keep the will to truth and the optimism. (Rorty 1982, 206)

A pluralistic society requires trust in order to incorporate new cultures in creating a multicultural society: "We cannot integrate 'them' so long as 'we' remain 'we'; 'we' must be loosened up to create a new common space in which 'they' can be accommodated and become part of a newly reconstituted 'we'" (Parekh 2000). How different this is from Foucault's perspective. He (Foucault 1984, 335) says in direct opposition to the above:

> I do not appeal to any "we"—to any of those "we's" whose consensus, whose values, whose traditions constitute the framework for a thought and define the conditions in which it can be validated. But the problem is, precisely, to decide if it is actually suitable to place oneself within a "we" in order to assert the principles one recognizes and the values one accepts or if it is not, rather to make the future formation of a "we" possible, by elaborating the question.

The previous two quotations bring our differences with Foucault into sharp focus. Foucault seems to advocate a radical paradigm shift here. For us, planning for change is an incremental affair. We start from where we are, start from the current conception of "we" and expand it. We do not form a radical break from the here and now; we do not seek a radical paradigm shift.

This, in a nutshell, is where we strongly differ from the Foucauldians. We side with Rorty (1989, 64) here: "I disagree with Foucault about whether in fact it is necessary to form a new 'we.' My principal disagreement with him is precisely over whether 'we liberals' is or is not good enough." It is our pragmatic position that a radically new "we" (in the sense that Foucault seems to suggest) is neither practically nor morally possible. What we as planners should do is not *give up* the current "we" but *expand* it incrementally to make it more inclusive. At least this is the position of those who hold liberal values and see in them the potential for liberation through reform of our institutions and practices (Rawls 2001), rather than suppression through an all-encompassing interpretation of power.

Perhaps some of the institutions of modernity (e.g., the health sciences, psychology, the legal system, bureaucracy) do serve to "normalize" our behavior, but they are not all that modernity and its liberal institutions have given us. Besides, these institutions can also be reformed, as critics of rational planning and bureaucracies have suggested.

At the societal level, trust is required to create institutions, arenas, forums, and decision processes, to demonstrate and recommend shifts in them. At a more micro scale, trust is a necessary condition for dispute resolution. Viewing power as basic overlooks and obscures the underlying trust.

The building of community, the formation of solidarity, the inclusion of the disenfranchised, the move toward consensus—these all require trust. In fact, trust is central to both our individual and our collective lives: "[W]hatever matters to human beings, trust is the atmosphere in which it survives" (Bok 1978, 31). We earlier mentioned a therapeutic planning process documented by Sandercock (2000, 13, 23) as an example of a transformative process that changed the perceptions of Aboriginals and conservative white Australians who were initially too hostile to even meet together. The same case also demonstrates the importance of trust. The facilitator met separately many times with each group to gradually build relationships of respect and trust. It was because of their trust in her that they were eventually willing to come together and find new ways of framing the problem and a creative solution. What enabled this shift, and the ensuing collaboration, was an environment where *trust* had been created. The very *worst* thing in this situation would have been to make them more aware of power relations!

As Baier (1994, 96) suggests, "It seems fairly obvious that any form of cooperative activity, including the division of labor, requires the cooperators to trust one another to do their bit." Thus, trust is essential to the work of planners. Without trust, all will collapse.

Our brief discussion of trust here raises interesting questions for further research. What is the relationship between trust and power? What are the effects of betrayal of trust? Are there different kinds of trust? If so, how are the different kinds of trust related? These are issues we plan to investigate in subsequent research.

CONCLUSION

We believe that making power the central concept of description and analysis has very negative consequences. Given that all concepts are contingent, it is clearly possible to view all relationships in terms of power, but there is certainly no reason why we must do so. The key question, then, is: Why should we see the world this way? We have argued that viewing all relationships in terms of power is a very bad idea, one that itself distorts both theory and practice, with very negative effects on planning and decision-making processes.

We have accepted the idea of contingency of vocabularies but have taken it in a very different direction than Foucault did. While Foucault's critiques and his methodologies have much to contribute to planning (Fischler 2000), a Foucauldian view is not an adequate *basis* for planning theory. It seems to us that Foucauldians are still seeking an objective and universal category, an external perspective from which to judge. In this respect, they are in the tradition of modernist utilitarians (justifying all behavior in terms of its goodness) or Freudians (describing all behavior in terms of sexual impulses) or socio-biologists (describing all behavior in terms of selfishness) or Marxists (describing all behavior in terms of relations of economic production).

As pragmatists, we don't accept any of these categories as universal or privileged. All may be useful in particular circumstances, in the pursuit of particular goals. So we are not advancing trust as a new universal or privileged vocabulary or concept. Rather, we are recommending it as an extremely useful concept for planning in a liberal democratic society.

In a liberal democratic society, the *more useful*[6] pragmatic question is: Do we view power as basic or view trust as basic? Both perspectives may be necessary and useful, but the kind of democratic dialogue needed cannot be based on Foucault. To put democratic dialogue at the center, we need a different approach. While we certainly do need to be critically aware of power relations, we believe that trust is the more basic and the more useful concept for our purposes.

In contrast to the Foucauldian approach, our arguments follow Rawls in appealing neither to power nor to [narrowly rational] self-interest, but rather to an idea of *reasonableness*, which embodies both rationality and morality (chapter 6). This allows us to imagine democratic planning processes that go beyond desperate maneuvering for power, that go beyond *modus vivendi* solutions, that go beyond the bleak Foucauldian picture of planning. It suggests that people see themselves not as helpless victims of power but as free and equal, rational and reasonable citizens of a democratic society that is based on ideals and principles of justice as fairness. This gives hope and purpose to the public planning enterprise.

16

Conclusion: Key Strengths of Dialogical Planning

Our dialogical planning approach is a pragmatic synthesis of valuable insights from contemporary philosophy and planning theory. From political philosopher John Rawls, we have incorporated wide reflective equilibrium, the difference principle, and the concept of reasonableness; from philosophers Donald Davidson and Richard Rorty, the fluid nature of language and concepts; from critical social theorist Jürgen Habermas, critiques of scientism, the concept of communicative and critical rationality, and the importance of power. We also drew on, and were inspired by, the innovative interdisciplinary work of planning theorists John Forester, Charles Hoch, Judith Innes, Patsy Healey, John Friedmann, Leonie Sandercock, James Throgmorton, and (last but not least and never invisible) Seymour Mandelbaum. We have attempted to integrate many of their insights into our approach.

For various reasons, this book has been in process for an unusually long time; much of the manuscript was completed in 2001. Since then we have encountered a number of new issues, critiques, or misinterpretations of our position. In conclusion, we will briefly address some of these in reiterating the key strengths of our dialogical planning approach.

A RESPONSE TO BOTH MODERNISM AND POSTMODERNISM

A key theme of this book has been that neither modernism nor postmodernism can provide an adequate theoretical or practical basis for planning: There are dangerous pitfalls inherent in each of them. We have drawn on philosophers Richard Bernstein, Richard Rorty, Donald Davidson, and Ludwig Wittgenstein to present neopragmatism as clearly distinct from either extreme.

Our dialogical approach avoid the pitfalls of modernist and postmodernist perspectives while incorporating useful and valid elements from both. As we argued in chapters 3 and 4, it avoids the foundationalism, essentialism, absolute dualism, metaphysical realism, scientism, and utilitarianism of modernism while retaining the Enlightenment tradition regarding rationality, truth, and objective (liberal) values, a legitimate role for science, and the possibility of legitimation for planning. It allows us to adopt a critique of modernism (and modernist theories, practices, and institutions) without the pessimism and relativism of postmodernism, and to retain postmodernism's tolerance, pluralism, and respect for diversity. For contemporary planning, we remain convinced that neopragmatism is Goldilocks's bed, which is "just right."

A PRAGMATIC, NORMATIVE RATIONALE FOR PUBLIC PLANNING

Rawls's political liberalism provides a pragmatic *normative rationale* for public planning—the sort of planning that even planners who sound rather post-modernist (e.g., Beauregard 1991) often seem to wind up advocating. By retaining the positive liberal (humanistic) aspects of modernism, our approach provides a normative rationale for many of the communicative and critical approaches we have discussed—Friedmann's non-Euclidean planning, Forester's progressive planning, Krumholz's equity planning, Healey's collaborative planning, Innes's consensus building—establishing a solid moral basis for such approaches without appealing to any modernist metaphysical foundations.

REASONABLE ARGUMENT

As might be expected, our claim to have found a middle ground from where we can preserve liberal democratic values has been disputed, most vigorously by Allmendinger (2001). While modernists see our approach as dangerously postmodernist, he attacks us as modernists. According to Allmendinger (2001, 149) our approach is "not some middle way, but a highly conservative and modernist approach parading as 'post-modern lite.'"

Because we argue for the need to maintain the distinction between rationality and power, and hold that "persuasion through rational argument is the only alternative to power" (Harper and Stein 1995c, 241), Allmendinger assumes that we are "wedded to the binary notions of modernism" (ibid.), i.e., that we accept the modernist's absolute dichotomy between them. The point we made in the article he quotes (much of which is incorporated in chapters 3 and 4) is that most useful distinctions are continua, which include "grey" areas that are generally disputed. We certainly do want to retain the useful and legitimate distinction between rational argument and power, between reason and coercion. But (as we pointed out) what counts as a "reasonable" argument depends on the context. Ethics, art, law, science, religion, and planning all have their own concepts and criteria (shared within their communities) for reasonable argument. Further, what counts as reasonable (or rational) shifts, usually incrementally, over time.[1] None of the postmodern critiques should stop us from making the distinction between reason (or rationality) and coercion (or power).

It may be that Allmendinger (and others) have misinterpreted our use of rationality and rational argument as advocating retention of the modernist's focus on instrumental rationality. To avoid such a misunderstanding, we have emphasized *"reasonableness"* (following Rawls's [2001] use of the term) rather than "rationality." What we advocate is the practice of giving good reasons, within specific contexts, for beliefs and actions. A conception of reason that is *context-based* still works (i.e., it is legitimate and useful for our purposes). It can be used to establish provisionally fixed points within given contexts from which reasonable arguments can be advanced and objective judgments made, without accepting the universalist assumptions that modernists make and postmodernists attack.

There is no *good reason* why we must let the modernist push us toward accepting any overarching absolutist universal conception of rationality or truth; nor is there any *good reason* to let postmodernist critics force us to give up our ordinary everyday conception of reason and truth. The same can be said of other concepts that, we argue, should be maintained: justification, legitimacy, validity, justice, democracy. We need these concepts if we want to move toward a society of free and equal, reasonable and rational persons that can practically implement liberal democratic ideals.

A BASIS FOR PRACTICAL CRITIQUE

Critique is a core element of Habermas's thought; it was also a key part of communicative action planning as Innes (1995) defined it. It is equally important to dialogical planning. Unfortunately, as communicative planning becomes more mainstream, this aspect has been severely diluted. Some practitioners seem to believe that if they are talking to people, then they are doing communicative planning. Communicative rationality is not just about talking to people; it is about understanding the meaning of their environments, social institutions, social conventions, and so on, and their reasons for actions. Critique, evaluation, and assessment—comparing how things *are* to how things *ought* to be—are inherent in a dialogical process. Planners should be providing people with a critical understanding of planning as it works in *their* local context. Critique is also a key aspect of Davidson's view of the fluidity of language. So is innovation (see next section).

Our approach gives planning *a basis for practical critique*—some grounds for judging when particular processes have gone wrong, when corrective action is needed. The idea of "going wrong" makes sense only if we can say that what happened isn't what *should* have happened, that the process was somehow distorted. This requires that we be able to conceive of a *legitimate* process as a norm as part of (internal to) our planning processes. But if we were to accept any external theory as explaining everything as a consequence of *external* forces (e.g., power relations), then "going wrong" would make no sense. In Healey's (1997) use of Giddens's (1984) terms, structure would be completely dominant, and there would be no room for any individual agency.

INNOVATION AND CREATIVITY

We call our theory incremental because we believe that change must always begin from where we are, and justification must appeal to our current web of belief. Nonetheless, there is significant room for innovation. To incorporate creative new ideas into our overlapping consensus, we have suggested (Stein and Harper 2005) Quine's concept of a "radical interpreter" (Quine 1960). When the radical interpreter attempts to translate a language with no affinity to our own, he or she fits each new concept into our web of belief as best they can. In the process, our own concepts or beliefs may change. The task of a radical interpreter trying to incorporate new ideas within the same culture is no different in kind. The more alien or radical the concept, the more our web must be reconfigured. Some new ideas will be fairly easy to incorporate; others will require a major reconfiguration of our web of belief.

The reason why there is room for radical interpretation lies in Davidson and Rorty's recognition that language is fluid, always in a process of change, and that concepts are contingent on culture, place, and time. We should not view language as a set of rigid rules. Our rejection of the idea that rigid rules govern language stems from the rejection of the idea that there is a sharp line between analytic and synthetic, between meaning and belief (chapter 4). Meaning is always in flux. Every time we use a word in context, there is some movement, some change in meaning. There is a continuum between radical change and adherence to strict rules.

Our willingness to engage in radical interpretation should be governed by our pragmatic interests. It depends upon weighing what can be gained (What can we now do to further our ideals that we couldn't before?) against the cost (What have we lost by altering our concept?).

A WAY TO ADDRESS WICKED PROBLEMS

A practical skeptic might say, "Your theory of language may fit with and support your dialogical theory of planning, but so what? What difference does it make to a practical planner?" Well, it does in fact make a great deal of difference. One's view of language structures one's thinking, talking, and doing. For example, in chapter 11 we saw that the tyranny of labels can lock us into positions and lessen our ability to resolve conflict. More generally, a flexible approach to language enables dialogical planning to deal with what Rittel and Webber (1973), in their damning critique of the RCPM, called "wicked problems." They argued that the rational decision model (contrary to its promise of clear and quick solutions) was unable to deal with most significant *real-world* planning problems, because they (like most social problems) are "wicked problems." This critique, along with Lindblom's (1959) earlier one, paved the way for the innovative approaches we have discussed. However, many of these new approaches fail to directly address the question of what kind of model would best deal with wicked problems.

Although we want to avoid the mechanistic implications of the term "model," our pragmatic dialogical planning approach does offer a working model that is well-suited to dealing with wicked problems. Our WRE process deals effectively with the attributes of wicked problems that Rittel and Webber identified:

1. There is no definitive formulation of the problem.

2. There is no ultimate test of a solution.

3. The set of potential solutions is open (not enumerable).

4. The nature of problem resolution is determined by the choice of explanation.

5. The problem is never really solved but only displaced by a new problem.

Our approach deals with wicked problems most effectively because it combines the non-hierarchical flexibility of the WRE process with the fluidity of language and interpretation discussed in the previous section. It expects problem definitions and solutions to arise gradually from dialogue, and it encourages the reframing of problems. Our process facilitates the interaction of different perspectives, explanations, and assumptions as it examines particular cases by moving back and forth among normative and descriptive theories, principles, intuitions, and judgments (chapter 6). The transformative character of WRE processes (chapter 9) facilitates the creation of innovative solutions. This approach never presumes to have found the ultimate solution: It implements as incrementally as possible, and it remains open to new problem formulations and solutions whenever possible.

When engaging in dialogical processes to solve wicked problems, we must remember that "consensus" is *not* the ultimate goal. The goal is a *reflective agreement* that is (1) as wide as possible, and (2) respects our liberal democratic ideals. At the conclusion of a WRE process that seems to have achieved its transformative ideal, we need to be as clear as we can about the values and definitions we assume to be shared. Otherwise, we are in danger of a thin and superficial consensus, which is likely to fall apart in concrete application (chapter 9).

A REASON FOR HOPE AND FOR VISION

Our approach offers contemporary planning, here and now, a reason for Rorty's (1982) *social hope* that we can make things better. This is in marked contrast to the ideas of postmodernists in general and Foucauldians in particular; we have argued that, taken seriously, these ideas lead to nihilism and despair (chapters 4, 15). Acceptance of the claim that power determines everything is likely to make it a self-fulfilling prophecy. As we have argued, if both citizens and professional planners were to believe that power is ubiquitous and inescapable, there would seem to be no basis for hope that things could be better (chapter 15). In contrast, we have seen that the Rawlsian conception of *reasonableness* embodies both rationality and morality (chapter 6). This gives hope and purpose to the public planning enterprise.

Finally, we also draw from Rawls a *vision* of free and equal, rational and reasonable citizens of a democratic society based on principles of justice as fairness, engaging in democratic dialogue. Public planning can enhance this vision by following fair and reasonable processes. This kind of vision does not arise from narrow rationalism (chapters 1 and 2), nor from pure self-interest (chapter 9), nor from confused normative moral relativism (chapter 13), nor from a Foucauldian perspective (chapter 15). To put democratic dialogue at the center, planning needs the Rawlsian political liberalism of Dialogical Planning.

Endnotes

Introduction

1. These views include include those of Forester, Innes, Healey, Hoch, Mandelbaum, Throgmorton, and ourselves.

2. These approaches include communicative planning, dialogical planning, progressive planning, equity planning, pragmatic planning, collaborative planning, consensus building, and the argumentative turn in planning.

3. Earlier critics include Lauria (1995), Richardson (1996), Tewdwr-Jones and Allmendinger (1998), and Flyvbjerg (1998). More recently, there was a symposium in the *Journal of Planning Education and Research* (2000), and most recently another article (Flyvbjerg 2002).

4. Held at Oxford Brookes University in 1998.

5. These labels are potentially very confusing because "communicative" planners draw on the critical theory of Habermas (1984). In contrast, Yaftachel's (1999) use of "critical" refers to postmodernist critiques like Foucault's (1980).

6. It is difficult to attribute this view to any one individual, but it seemed to command a fairly wide following at the Oxford Planning Theory Conference.

7. See our discussion in chapter 12.

8. A political philosopher might say "contemporary pluralistic liberal democratic, late capitalist societies under conditions of moderate scarcity."

9. These philosophers include Wittgenstein, Quine, Davidson, Putnam, Rawls, Rorty, Nielsen, and Bernstein.

10. Friedmann (1987) defines the public domain as including (1) the government sector, (2) the corporate (business) sector, and (3) civil society.

11. Unlike corporate plans that are made for the planner's own organization.

12. Yiftachel's definition combines those of Lefebvre (1991) and Friedmann (1998).

13. Although we do use a *process* that is modeled on that of philosopher John Rawls (1993; 2001).

14. Specific liberal values are enumerated in chapter 1 and discussed in chapter 6.

15. Our neopragmatism differs from that of Blanco and Verma, who advocate a more (instrumentally) "rational" planning process closer to that of the classical pragmatists; our approach is more similar to that of Forester and Hoch.

16. A Wide Reflective Equilibrium (WRE) will be defined in more detail in chapter 6.

17. A "WRE" is a state where all the elements outlined are in coherence; a "WRE process" is a process of seeking to move toward such a state.

18. Although this understanding may be more limited than some proponents of such theories believe.

19. This is not to downplay the importance of the product—the plan or design or policy or decision (Neuman 1998). But the product is much more context specific.

20. Philosophers call these normatively laden concepts "thick concepts."

21. Normative and descriptive elements are never neatly separable but are always intertwined. Whether or not it is true that all knowledge is evaluative, planning knowledge certainly is evaluative.

Chapter 1

1. On the enlightenment influence, see Friedmann 1987. Friedmann views the dominance of "market rationality" as another key aspect.

2. See Groat (1992) on the effect of this conflict in architecture.

3. This view is known as "realism" or "metaphysical realism" (see glossary).

4. This view is known as "logical positivism" (see glossary).

5. Of course, the planner still has some degree of agency and responsibility, regardless of context or structure.

6. Rational planning was adapted by Meyerson and Banfield (1955) from Herbert Simon's normative model of rational decision making, which was explicitly based on the positivistic sociology of Parsons (Simon 1945, 45).

7. It is difficult to come up with a label for this aspect that does not have negative connotations. Liberalism and its notion of the individual have been widely criticized. For an extended defense of liberal ideals, see Rawls (1993; 2001).

8. Our outline of these values is adapted from Rawls (1985).

9. Institutions are "accepted ways of doing things."

10. Of course, the planner should be aware that the local culture of those communities being consulted may interpret his or her actions from the perspective of their own stories, values, and beliefs. However, these stories should not be viewed as incommensurable (Harper and Stein 1996).

11. See glossary.

12. As will be discussed in chapter 13, we believe planning is in a crisis, but we do not believe it needs a radical paradigm shift to rescue it.

13. SWOT is the strategic planning acronym for "strengths, weaknesses, opportunities, and threats."

14. As we will see in chapter 6, what communitarians are attacking is Rawls's (1993; 2001) "political liberalism."

15. Friedmann views the crisis in planning as having dimensions both practical (inability to deal with the nature and pace of change) and intellectual (1987, 312).

16. Many authors see these changes as resulting from the technological shift from an industrial to a postindustrial or information economy. This is seen as causing what Fukuyama (1999) calls the great disruption: changes in the nature of work, a decline in kinship as a social institution, looser ties with much smaller social groups, and a loss of trust and confidence in government.

17. If they *are* examined, it is usually by philosophers doing philosophical ethics, reflecting on our current practices, institutions, and entrenched principles.

18. Friedmann refers to this interactive process as the hermeneutic circle (1987).

19. See chapter 6 for an explication of the idea of ideological distortion.

20. See glossary.

21. See glossary and chapter 12.

Chapter 2

1. This approach has had a number of other labels, e.g., "policy analysis" (Friedmann 1987), "instrumental planning" (Klosterman 1978), "rational planning" (Harper and Stein 1988), "synoptic planning" (Sager 1994), "Euclidean planning" (Friedmann 1993).

2. After (Robinson 1972, 27–8). For other versions, see Meyerson and Banfield (1955, 314–20), Friedmann (1987, 78), and Alexander (1986, 20). Hodge (1986, ch.6) uses Robinson's definition. Black (1990) presents a more elaborate schema.

3. Simon's assertion is a clear counter-example to Friedmann's claim that "Policy Analysis has, strictly speaking, no distinctive philosophical position" (1987, 79). Perhaps what Friedmann meant is that it has no distinctive *political* stance—it can serve almost any political master.

4. Thus, utilitarianism eliminates the possiblity of moral dilemmas (situations where one must choose between conflicting moral claims that are both valid).

5. See glossary.

6. This critique parallels in many ways that of critical theorists such as Habermas (1971a; 1971b).

7. Hedonistic utilitarianism, which values pleasure, should encompass non-persons; other versions of utilitarianism, which place value on the achievement of reflectively selected goals, include only the happiness of persons.

8. The term "public interest" has many different definitions. When used by utilitarians, it denotes the choice that maximizes total happiness or well-being.

9. Planners (Klosterman 1978; Alexander 1986) who do speak of a rationality of goals are basing their position on some other normative ethical theory. For example, following John Rawls (1971), goals are said to be rational if an impartial, rational self-interested person would choose them under ideal conditions (i.e., using a Wide Reflective Equilibrium procedure, which we outline in chapter 6). However, as Rawls (1985) and others have pointed out, this is not a value-neutral decision in the sense that the RCPM requires.

10. For critical theorists, the process of articulating reflective social goals is a complicated one, involving the elimination of ideological distortion, an adequate critical social theory, and an adequate moral perspective (Habermas 1971a) (see chapter 6).

11. "Ideology" is sometimes used in a broader sense to denote the legitimation of a political position, whether or not it is justified or rests on true beliefs.

12. Howe (1994) calls such planners "technician activists" because they pose as technicians while actually acting as political activists.

13. Our "rational planner" may be a bit of a caricature in his slavish defense of the RCPM.

14. This statement makes very clear the linkage between the RCPM and utilitarianism, particularly what we have called "economic utilitarianism" (Harper 1987).

15. Weber distinguishes between *de facto* legitimacy (getting people to accept something) and *de jure* legitimacy (giving genuine normative arguments for it). It seems that he did not believe that *de jure* legitimacy is possible.

16. These accepted principles are violated by some contemporary (non-bureaucratic) organizational forms, e.g., Mintzberg's (1989) "innovative" or "adhocratic" structure.

17. As discussed in chapter 8, there are other organizational forms that can permit large scale, at least under certain conditions.

18. It appears that the RCPM is still taught by a surprising number of planning educators (Klosterman 1992).

19. "Traditional technicians" are those who hold to the RCPM professional protocol in theory and do not admit to violating it in practice (Howe 1994).

Chapter 3

1. This view is known as perspectivalism.

2. Hoch is not a postmodernist, but his reading of Burnham reflects a postmodernistic approach.

3. See Dear (1986), Milroy (1991), and Harvey (1989) for a discussion of definitions of postmodernism. Milroy sets out "a continuum of positions" of "nonpositivist approaches to social life" (1991, 183). Our "full-blown postmodernism" is the most radical of her three definitions.

4. We should note here that Foucault himself underwent significant transformation of his thought, especially in later life. But there is still a dominant Foucauldian perspective, particularly his archeological account of power, that is influential among many of his followers. It is this account that we criticize as having unfortunate consequences for planning.

5. Like all relativists, Foucault ends up holding on to at least one absolute: his own genealogy.

6. Dualities divide things into distinct opposites, generally with no possible in-between.

7. Norris (1990) has a similar interpretation.

8. Fallibilistic means being open to the possibility that our understanding of anything could be wrong.

9. However, these liberal notions are no longer viewed as foundational absolutes.

10. The contemporary versions of empiricism.

11. Davidson is not proposing a form of "linguistic idealism."

12. If pragmatists wish to eschew anything (and this is the closest they come to positivism) they eschew the tendency toward nominalization and reification of abstract nouns like *truth* and *reality*. They are quite satisfied with the adjectives (*true* and *real*) and believe that anything worth saying can be said with the adjectives. They are perfectly happy to distinguish between true statements and false ones, real ducks and decoys. But the quest for TRUTH and REALITY as abstract nouns just gets you into trouble.

13. Although Rorty is less sanguine about the abstract noun "truth."

14. This is as close to "correspondence" as Rorty gets.

15. Although pragmatism might be seen as a precursor to postmodernism, in this particular aspect it was modernistic. However, the classical pragmatists were not narrowly scientific.

16. Quine is an exception to this point.

17. In fact, some neopragmatists are closer to some classical pragmatists than to other neopragmatists.

18. Our article on normative ethical theory (Harper and Stein 1993a) attempts to integrate the first four of these aspects.

Chapter 4

1. Our themes are similar to Milroy's (1991).

2. Conceivably, the postmodernist could revert to scientistic reductionism, i.e., appeal to an empirical anthropological claim.

3. Here, neopragmatists are more like Dewey than Pierce (Stout 1988).

4. Habermas (1984) attempts to establish such a foundation when he engages in ideological critique.

5. The notion of a web of concepts and beliefs comes from a philosophical position known as "holism." The idea is that we cannot justify a concept in isolation; the unit of justification is the whole language.

6. Descartes presupposed the idea of private languages.

7. We are assuming ordinary intuitive notions of truth and rationality.

8. An actual paradigm shift cannot involve a complete break in the continuity of our concepts, as Feyerabend (1965) seems to argue. Kuhn has apparently acknowledged this (1970b).

9. We might encounter a community whose "language" resists our most imaginative attempts at translation. The view that still attributes a language to their vocal utterances after all attempts at translation have failed is an empty one. It has no more substance than attributing an incommensurable language to animals, plants, or stones. If a people have a language (what we call a language), it has to be one that we could, in principle, understand and therefore interpret.

10. We may come across segments of a community's language that we find difficult to translate, but the conclusion we should draw is that we have not been imaginative enough to create an appropriate account of their language.

11. See Forester (1989) regarding avoidable and unavoidable distortions.

12. Neopragmatism also rejects the appearance/reality distinction as an absolute metaphysical dualism (as opposed to its practical use in distinguishing, for example, a real duck from a decoy, a real oasis from a mirage).

13. Although consensus is conceptually possible, it is never guaranteed.

14. Both Harvey and Soja are limited by their adoption of a Marxist framework, which we see as essentially modernist.

15. We see strong liberal elements implicit in Sandercock, even though she may seem to reject liberalism (chapter 9).

Chapter 5

1. Friedmann and Sandercock are difficult to categorize. Friedmann sometimes adopts stances that don't seem "liberal" to us, e.g., his "radical planning"

(1987) approach; but his "non-Euclidean" planner (1993) seems within the liberal tradition. Sandercock (1998) styles herself as "radical," but we think that her "TAMED" planner also fits within the liberal tradition.

2. Reform refers to the now-defunct Reform Party of Canada.

3. Note that this is essentially a negative rights argument in that it appeals to the notion of impartiality. If there are to be positive rights, they must be allocated fairly.

4. In more technical terms, this normative ethical theory is deontological (involving rules or norms that should be obeyed because of their *inherent* rightness), and monistic (all of its principles are derived from a single basic underlying principle).

5. This position is also advocated by David Gauthier (1978). His "mutual advantage" theory is superficially similar to Nozick in that both begin with individuals in a state of nature and attempt to derive a society. The difference is that Nozick begins with a moral principle based on the liberal valuing of the inherent worth of the person; Gauthier assumes only self-interest (see chapter 9).

6. This statement is adapted from Nozick (1974, 28-35).

7. We use "Nozick" here to represent his 1974 views, which he apparently eventually rejected.

8. These institutions enjoy something like an overlapping consensus (see chapter 6) of support by other moral perspectives (and different interpretations of these perspectives) for different reasons.

9. Even this "minimal state" appears to violate the rights of those individuals who don't wish to be protected. However, Nozick's (1974, chapters 4, 5) justification of this apparent violation is that those who reject the minimal state (desiring to protect their own rights and arbitrate their own disputes) pose a substantial threat to the rights of others.

10. Nozick actually speaks of "unowned objects" in the quote below (1974, 178). We are applying his analysis to "natural resources," i.e., objects that are part of the natural environment, rather than the result of any human endeavor. Economists refer to "natural resources" in contrast to [human-created] capital, [human] labor, and [human] management or entrepreneurship.

11. Emphasis added. Nozick notes that this provision would not preclude acquisitions that worsen others' situations in *other* ways—for example, worsening due to a more limited opportunity to appropriate, or worsening a seller's position by acquiring some of the materials to make whatever he or she is selling, and then competing with the seller.

12. Cohen also argues that Nozick's Lockean proviso would allow someone to acquire all of a natural resource under certain conditions (specifically, if the acquisition makes no one worse off and it makes some people better off than they would have been if it had not been acquired).

13. The persons denied the options may be better off than if the natural resources had not been acquired (thus satisfying Nozick's Lockean proviso), but still be worse off than if they had been able to acquire some of the natural resource.

14. This test is crude because it assumes the existing distribution of wealth.

15. When we speak of value being added in this discussion, we mean value to persons. Value to persons may be approximated by economic value as measured in the marketplace, but it is not identical. As we discussed above, "better off" should not be viewed solely in economic terms.

16. The process we have described is followed by many governments, e.g., the province of Alberta, with regard to petroleum exploration.

17. Some activities intrinsically involve side effects. It is in the nature of any competition that the entry (or exit) of any one contestant unavoidably affects other contestants. For example, the entry of an applicant for a job or an educational program alters the prospects of other applicants; the entry of a buyer or seller in the housing market affects all other buyers and sellers of housing. Economists refer to such intrinsic (price) effects as "pecuniary externalities" (Bish and Nourse 1975, 111). Negative rights approaches are not concerned with regulating pecuniary externalities because no rights are violated. Individuals should have the right to pursue their goals, not necessarily the right to *achieve* them; the new entrant does not normally alter the ability of other competitors to pursue their goals. The outcome may be altered, but there is no general right to outcomes. Thus, our discussion will refer to "non-pecuniary externalities."

18. In contrast, the economic utilitarian would regulate only those negative externalities that are "Pareto-relevant," i.e., those that sufferers are willing to pay enough to cover the cost of elimination (or amelioration) of it (Bish and Nourse 1975, 112). A negative externality is "relevant" if there is anyone willing to pay *anything* to eliminate it. Thus, the classical liberal position (as we interpret it) would have a criterion closer to the economist's "relevant" definition and would regulate many externalities that are not Pareto-relevant (i.e., the sufferers are willing to take action to prevent it but are not willing to pay enough to cover the cost of elimination). Even though Nozick (1974, 79) appears to accept the utilitarian (Pareto) criterion, we do not see a negative rights-based argument for it.

19. This position assumes informed, rational, non-coerced choice. In Habermas's terms (chapter 6), there is no ideological distortion.

20. Of course, a rights-based approach will be concerned with the correctness of the assignment of rights (an issue to which utilitarians would be indifferent).

21. Again, those who favored the activity could compensate (or buy out) the homeowner, but they could not force the person to accept compensation.

22. The city of Houston provides a partial illustration in that it was developed with private covenants rather than zoning; the difficulty of changing land uses makes Houston's situation similar to what (we have argued) a classical liberal approach should advocate.

Chapter 6

1. See glossary.

2. The last condition embodies two shared values that are latent in the political cultures of modern democratic societies: persons are free and equal, and society should be a fair system of cooperation.

3. The conflicting private views can continue their debates, so long as they do not interfere with political life.

4. This book is based on notes for Rawls's Harvard course in political philosophy, which he reworked at the same time he was completing *Political Liberalism* (1993). Rawls was urged by his students to publish this statement, but due to illness, he was unable to complete the manuscript. It was edited for publication with his cooperation by his student, Erin Kelly.

5. We are using "method" here in a much broader and less mechanistic sense than does the advocate of the RCPM.

6. The term "reflective equilibrium" seems to have originated with Goodman (1965). Rawls (1971) brought it into ethical discourse; he later (1974) distinguished "wide" and "narrow" equilibria. Daniels (1985) popularized the term "wide reflective equilibrium" to distinguish it from the narrow reflective equilibrium of ethical intuitionists (Nielsen 1991).

7. A "WRE" is a state where all the elements outlined are in coherence; a "WRE process" is a process of seeking to move toward such a state.

8. This is a particular danger in traditional societies unaccustomed to critique. In Western liberal democratic societies, critique is such a normal part of the mainstream culture that the distinction between NRE and WRE may be blurred.

9. Mintzberg (1989) defines a professional as having (1) a general theoretical framework, (2) a tool kit of solutions (techniques), and (3) skill in (a) diagnosis and (b) application of the appropriate tools.

10. This might be called a "liberal feminist" view; it would be rejected by "radical feminists."

11. This is aside from its incoherence; it cannot be literally practiced.

12. While our pragmatic dialogical planning would advocate these two principles as a reasonable starting point, substantive principles should emerge and evolve from a WRE process.

13. For a more extensive discussion, see O'Connell (1995).

14. The problem with conversion is that there is no justification, no reason for the change, no way of evaluating it as good or bad.

15. There are still some important differences between Rawls and Habermas, but they don't have implications for the sort of planning procedure we are recommending.

Chapter 7

1. This is why the only two of his many works that we cite are those that most explicitly concern incrementalism.

2. Most planners are familiar with it (and with the RCPM response to it) through the Faludi reader (1973), which is still a very popular planning theory text (Klosterman 1992) despite its apparent obsolescence.

3. We have combined, separated, and slightly reworded some of Lindblom's original points to highlight certain elements of interest to us.

4. Lindblom acknowledges that they are difficult to disentangle in practice.

5. As a political scientist, Lindblom was more concerned with policy analysis than planning.

6. Nozick (1974) assumes this kind of hierarchical process, as do many deep ecologists.

7. Saying that planning is subject to a plethora of different rationalities amounts to the same thing as saying planing is irrational and arbitrary.

8. Although we have found much of value in Habermas's thought (Harper and Stein 1993, 1995b), at this point we differ significantly. Our approach narrows the distinction between truth and justification (which follows a WRE method). Claims to universal validity are not central to this pragmatic account.

9. Not only do ends differ, but they are in flux—for individuals, between different persons, and for purposes of public policy.

10. Note that, because the concerns of planning are broader than those of policy analysts like Woodhouse or Wildavsky, we link incrementalism as a policy and planning approach with incremental politics and with Partisan Mutual Adjustment (PMA).

11. At its *worst*, pluralism involves a PMA process in that various interest groups compete for power and influence (more or less) unconstrained by moral values, and without any critical debate regarding goals and values.

12. This is a negative label for him, because Friedmann (1987) doesn't think much of "market rationality" when it comes to allocating goods and services.

13. Of course, "crisis" and "normal" are also endpoints of a continuum.

14. As with other distinctions we have made, these terms should be viewed as end points of continua, with mixed cases in between them.

15. If the *entire* community is not converted, then one of the other two ways must be employed to deal with those who remain unconverted.

Chapter 8

1. As already argued, although its practitioners may often regard themselves as liberals, the rational comprehensive method is *not* an exemplification of liberalism. It is disqualified on the basis of its roots in utilitarianism and scientism/positivism.

2. Because our focus is on building a consensus, we emphasize areas of agreement with each of the approaches discussed. This is not to deny that there are differences between these approaches.

3. This is the case in our own province of Alberta.

4. For an extended discussion of Friedmann's first three factors, see Castells (1991).

5. Nomothetic science is science based on laws governing natural and social phenomena.

6. In a pluralistic liberal society, there must be limits to this preservation of cultural identity.

7. For an insightful critical view of corporate strategic planning, see Mintzberg (1994).

8. The analysis of internal strengths and weakness, combined with the analysis of external threats and opportunities, is often refereed to as a "SWOT" analysis.

9. Rawls himself is clear in his last work (2001) that his principles are not intended to be absolute.

10. Nielsen (1985) uses a WRE process to argue for two principles that are parallel to Rawls's but definitely different.

11. Fainstein and Fainstein (1996) see progressive and equity planning as two separate approaches—the former focusing on procedure and the latter focusing on substantive outcomes.

12. Neopragmatists tend to use a broader conception of rationality than do classical pragmatists (chapter 3), although some contemporary pragmatists still use a fairly narrow conception.

13. This quote is Friedmann's (1987) description of a "radical planner," but we find it equally applicable to our dialogical planner.

14. However, we will argue later (chapter 12) that in some contexts, certain starting points may be ill advised, as they tend to "freeze" people into adversarial positions.

15. Technically, they would be "uncertainty averse," since risk requires known probabilities, and the probabilities of different social outcomes are unknown.

16. In the economist's terms, institutional changes must be Pareto-relevant, but with the additional (non-utilitarian) condition that the redistribution must *actually* occur.

17. But note that it is the whole system that must satisfy the difference principle, not each particular situation.

18. Coordination by direct supervision is not feasible for most public organizations because they are too large.

19. Mintzberg's schema also includes the divisionalized organizational form, which coordinates via performance measures and which provides the overall structure for most governments. However, each subunit of the divisionalized organization takes one of the other forms.

Chapter 9

1. "NIMBY" is the acronym for "not in my backyard."

2. Contrary to Sandel's (1982) claim, liberalism does *not* require that we have a conception of the person that is "necessary, non-contingent and prior to any particular experience."

3. With regard to dualism, recall that we have already argued for a more pragmatic approach to dichotomies – as end points of continua that are useful for particular practical social purposes (chapters 3, 4).

4. This seems to be Klosterman's (1978) interpretation.

5. With complete abundance, principles of justice are probably unnecessary. With severe scarcity, principles of justice are not sufficient because they lack motivational power.

6. This approach is reductionistic: It assumes that morality could not be the ultimate basis of social institutions—some other (more "scientific") explanation is required. In fact, to evaluate whether mutual advantage "works," we consider whether it fits our conception of morality. Thus, at best the mutual advantage account would be explanatory; it would be coextensive with morality, not a replacement for it.

7. Habermas is critical of WRE as being too context dependent, i.e., assuming liberal democratic values. We think that it can have more general application.

8. This liberal criterion will not be universally accepted; we need to be cautious in its application (see chapter 14).

9. Friedmann (1973) originally called this approach "transactive planning."

10. This schema is an elaboration of Forester's (1989) classification of sources of misinformation (communicative distortion).

Chapter 10

1. This critique may not be explicit; it may be implicit in proposals for change.

2. In the economist's terms, a Pareto-optimal move is possible.

3. The conditions for the ideal speech situation are comprehensibility, accuracy, sincerity, and legitimacy.

4. See chapter 11 for a discussion of essentialism.

5. This is a pragmatic distinction (not an absolute dichotomy) between two related aspects.

6. We recognize that the author's key role in the case could bias her interpretation of the events.

7. Consensus is more commonly defined as "something everyone can live with," i.e., no one objects strongly enough to leave the process.

8. This account was prepared for us by Dr. Tazim Jamal, with the exception of the "evaluation" and "three-table problem" sections. These sections express our opinions, not hers.

Chapter 11

1. See Jamal (1997, 357–64) for a summary of the process, and Jamal (1997, 365–67) for vision statement and principles.

2. All of the quotes in this section are from participants, as cited in Jamal (1997), to which page numbers in brackets refer.

3. Except proper names, which we shall not discuss.

4. See glossary.

5. But a caution—such useful (and justified) new categorizations cannot be arbitrary (such as Naess [1973] proposes [Stein and Harper 1996]). They should emerge from a dialogical process (which provides the justification).

6. The citations in quotes are from a British jurist of another era, Chief Justice Matthew Hale.

7. To some degree, this tragedy may reflect the "three-table" problem discussed in chapter 10—to the extent that those who subsequently violated the spirit of the accord were not at the negotiating table.

Chapter 12

1. Of course, such limitations require substantiation, both scientific and moral.

2. Kuhn originally uses "paradigm shift" in the radical (though perhaps not the most radical) sense; his later use is more incremental.

3. For a more extended discussion of the implications of the extreme view see Stein (1994) and Harper and Stein (1996).

4. Much of this section is based on Stein and Harper 1997.

5. Much of this section is based on Harper and Stein 1993.

6. Beatley does argue an obligation to minimize any such impacts.

7. What Beatley seems to want from bio-egalitarianism is a recognition that "nature has certain inherent worth that demands respect" (1994, 129). But he doesn't need radical bio-egalitarianism to get this.

8. We are not attributing such motives to Martin and Beatley (1993) but suggest that they may find themselves in bad company if they go too far along this path.

9. We should not ignore poverty, social inequality, or racism.

Chapter 13

1. Habermas (1984) is not postmodernist in the sense we are using the term.

2. We have added "scientistic" for clarification.

3. Neopragmatists reject the scheme/content distinction: the notion that one conceptual scheme (account) is better or truer or "closer to reality" than another.

4. It is very problematic whether a government authority (particularly one providing financial support) can ever be seen as non-coercive by non-dominant cultures.

5. If advocates of WRE make this claim (which they seem to come very close to), then they have slipped into a new form of foundationalism.

6. We have argued in chapter 1 that we should retain the liberal, and discard the scientistic, aspects of the enlightenment.

7. "Strict" multiculturalism seems to be merely a new version of moral relativism and suffers from the same defects, including the contradictory acceptance of one universal value—that all values are of equal significance.

Chapter 14

1. We must be careful here. Empirical "cases" are not independent of "theory"; there is no pure (interpretation-free) description of experience.

2. As in the method of WRE.

3. See chapter 4 for a discussion of treating distinctions as continua rather than absolute dualisms.

4. See glossary.

5. Analytic statements are definitions (e.g., a sister is a female sibling); synthetic statements are contingent on empirical facts (e.g., Sue is my sister).

6. Kant postulated a trichotomy: He distinguished pure reason, practical reason, and judgment (aesthetics).

7. This conception of a radical paradigm shift is consistent with Kuhn's original intent and is still employed by some interpreters (Feyerabend 1993, Leopold 1949, Naess 1973, Livingston 1985, Taylor 1986).

8. For a more extended discussion of the implications of the extreme view, see Stein (1994) and Harper and Stein (1996).

9. Like all distinctions we make, these should be viewed as end points of continua.

Chapter 15

1. As we use "rhetorically," it means to attempt to cause someone to accept a position, in contrast to persuading them by giving good reasons.

2. We searched for an adjective here; we considered "valid," "useful," "meaningful," and "legitimate," but given Foucault's position, none of these work (as we shall argue).

3. We say "should not" because revisions to definitions *can* result in the loss of useful distinctions.

4. "Conflate" means to confuse two different meanings of a word.

5. The end of this kind of process would be a Rawlsian WRE.

6. We do not mean to make "useful" sound like an absolute, objective, outside criterion. It is itself a concept chosen with reference to all the other concepts that form part of our web of concepts and beliefs.

Chapter 16

1. There are limits to shifts in the concept of rationality or reason, e.g., the law of non-contradiction.

Glossary

ABSOLUTISM	A position that is incapable of being corrected or changed.
A POSTERIORI (or *EX POSTE*)	After experience; contingent or dependent on experience.
A PRIORI	(*in epistemology*) Before experience; not contingent or dependent on experience. *A priori* propositions do not require experience to establish their truth. Contrasts with *A Posteriori* or *Ex Poste*.
BEG THE QUESTION	To assume what you are trying to prove.
CONFLATE	To eliminate a distinction for particular purposes.
DESCRIPTIVE JUDGMENTS	Statements that give an empirical account of factual phenomena. The truth of a descriptive statement depends on empirical observation. Empirical statements are often expressed in the form of generalities. For example, we have found, as a matter of fact, that most people in London drive on the left-hand side of the street.
DESCRIPTIVE OR CULTURAL RELATIVISM	The empirical claim that different individuals, groups, or cultures have different beliefs about the world and morality.

This glossary is based on a set of definitions and explanations prepared by Laura MacKinnon. Glossary entries not found in this book are adapted from Audi (1995), Bunnin and Tsui-James (1996), or Honderich (1995).

DUALISM

A disjunctive pair in which the disjuncts are seen as oppositional (rather than as complementary) and exclusive (rather than as inclusive). **ABSOLUTE DUALISM:** Diametric opposites, associated with the idea that there is an absolute dichotomy between such contrasts as analytic/synthetic, form/content, meaning/belief, fact/value, subject/object, absolute/relative, and appearance/reality, generally with no possible in-between categories or middle ground.

ECONOMIC SYSTEM

A process by which scarce productive resources are transformed into goods and services, and allocated to consumers. Contrasts with *Political System.*

EMPIRICISM

The view that knowledge is based on experience through the five senses. Empiricism has its roots in the idea that all we can know about the world is what the world tells us; we must observe it neutrally and dispassionately, and any attempt on our part to mold or interfere with the process of receiving this information can lead only to distortion and arbitrary imagining. This gives us a picture of the mind as a "blank tablet" on which information is imprinted by the senses in the form of "sense data."

ENLIGHTENMENT

The intellectual, social, political and cultural change that occurred in Western Europe during the eighteenth century.

EPISTEMOLOGY

The branch of philosophy concerned with the nature of knowledge, its possibility, scope, and general basis.

EQUIVOCATE

To confuse two different meanings of a word.

EXTERNALITY

The unintended side effect of any action on a person (or persons) not directly involved in an original action. These effects may be on the persons themselves, on their holdings, or on unowned things (natural resources).

FALLIBILISTIC

Being open to the possibility that one's beliefs could be wrong.

FOUNDATIONALISM

The view that all knowledge rests on a foundation of indubitable beliefs from which all further statements can be inferred to produce a superstructure of known truths. Modernistic foundationalism expresses the idea that this foundation can be found in the statements of science and in our own sense experience. Medieval foundationalism was grounded in the church as the source of ultimate truth and authority.

IDEOLOGICAL DISTORTION

An idea used by Marx and critical theorists to associate ideology with false consciousness, explaining why apparently "irrational" social and economic relations are accepted, even though not in the interest of those who accept them.

IDEOLOGY

Ideas or beliefs put forward and accepted as true, which function to maintain economic and social relationships (e.g., class), when in fact the idea is illegitimate and the belief is not true. People are led by ideology to accept social arrangements that are not in their self-interest. The ideology of scientism prevents us from reaching self-knowledge and emancipation, because all our communication is systematically distorted. ("Ideology" is sometimes used in a broader sense to denote the normative justification of a political position whether or not it is legitimate or rests on true beliefs.)

INCOMMENSURABILITY

The notion that ideas, knowledge, and meaning are embedded in a particular framework of culture or scientific theory so that, in a radical sense, they cannot be translated, interpreted, or compared. For example, scientific revolutions, which involve wholesale discarding of one set of theories in favor of another, are thought typically to produce such radical shifts of meaning that the concepts employed in the theories propounded after the revolution simply cannot be expressed in terms of the concepts of prerevolutionary theory. Commitment to such an incommensurability thesis is apt to lead to a strong relativism or antirationalism.

INSTRUMENTAL VALUE

An item, idea, or action has instrumental value to the extent that it lends itself (fortuitously or by design) effectively to the achievement of some desired or valued purpose; it is that which is "good as a means to. . . ," e.g., hammers, chisels, tools of all kinds. By contrast, we think of humans as having intrinsic or inherent value.

LOGICAL POSITIVISM

A general philosophical position developed on the basis of traditional empirical knowledge (i.e., all knowledge comes from the five senses or is constructed from such knowledge) and modern logic. Logical positivism confines knowledge to science and uses verificationism to reject metaphysics, not as false but as meaningless (i.e, any claim that cannot be verified through empirical investigation is meaningless). Closely associated with reductionism and scientism.

META-NARRATIVE	An overarching explanation or story of how the world is—for example, the liberal/capitalist story of material progress through the hidden hand of the market; the Marxian drama of class conflict culminating in proletarian revolution; the Freudian plots of father–son rivalry and mother–son love; the Enlightenment's story of progress and triumph of reason. Meta-narratives attempt to derive general social principles that are precisely explanatory/predictive in the same sense as scientific laws, i.e., universally true theories. Postmodernists view meta-narratives as totalizing discourses that are imprisoning and are ultimately linked to structures of power.
METAPHYSICAL	A view that provides ultimate constituents of something, the determination of which is not found in scientific inquiry but comes from philosophical insight.
METAPHYSICAL REALISM	The view that objects and properties exist independently of the human mind; that linguistic categories, terms, or labels correspond to natural kinds "in the world"; and that language reflects (mirrors) or represents reality. Thus, the meaning of a word or sign depends on its relation to an object "in the world," an object that it signifies and to which it refers. This view requires that we be able to achieve some god's-eye perspective in order to compare language and the world to see how well it fits or how true it is.
METAPHYSICS	The branch of philosophy that tries to explain the nature of being and reality. It is concerned with the features of ultimate reality, what really exists, and what it is that distinguishes existence and makes it possible.

MODERNISM

A movement that expresses certain Enlightenment values.

(1) *Science:* The approach that produces an objective understanding through the observation of regularities. The scientific method provides a procedure for determining which regularities are causal. This method specifies a sequence of activities—observation of regularities, generalization, theorizing, hypothesis-testing, establishing scientific laws, uniting theories under general theories—that legitimize or establish empirical knowledge. For modernist Enlightenment thinkers, this is the *only* method accepted as legitimate for determining what is true. Objective knowledge about the real world is possible.

(2) *Liberalism:* The free, equal, and autonomous individual person is seen as the basic unit of society, the ultimate object of moral concern, and the ultimate source of value.

(3) *Reason:* Progress comes via rational argument—giving good reasons for what we advocate and what we oppose. Science can (and should) serve human needs and wants, if we go about satisfying them in a rational way. Action toward liberal ideals can, and should, be guided by knowledge. There is faith in progress through science and technology and faith that rational planning can produce social orders that achieve equality, liberty, and justice.

NEOPRAGMATISM

A philosophical movement embracing a form of social and practical contextualism that denies the possibility of universal conceptions of Truth or Reality. Equally denied by neopragmatists are absolute foundations of knowledge or morality. Richard Rorty initiated a return to pragmatism (drawing mainly on Dewey, Wittgenstein, Quine, and Sellars) in his 1979 book, *Philosophy and the Mirror of Nature*. Truth and meaning are to be found only in moments of specific social practices. Unlike pragmatism, neopragmatism is not rooted in empiricism, positivism, or instrumentalism.

NORMATIVE JUDGMENT

A judgment that is evaluative. It does not express an account of how things are as a matter of fact but how things ought to be. A normative judgment is intended to prescribe behavior and not to predict it. While the paradigm case of normative judgment is usually considered to be a moral/ethical judgment, normative judgments occur in all forms of discourse, e.g., economic, political, legal, scientific, aesthetic, and religious.

ONTOLOGY

The branch of philosophy that studies the ultimate constituents that make up the universe, e.g., mind, ideas, substance.

PARADIGM

A term popularized by Thomas Kuhn in *The Structure of Scientific Revolutions* (1962). It can be defined as: (1) the presuppositions, concepts, and general theories of a field; (2) the accepted procedures in that field; and (3) the constitutive rules of the community/social group that practices in the field and that accept and support these elements. A paradigm provides a framework within which theories can be tested, evaluated, and, if necessary, revised.

PARADIGM SHIFT

A "revolution" in which an older paradigm is overthrown and is replaced by a new paradigm. Kuhn argued that the empiricists were wrong regarding how scientific theory changes. Empiricists viewed theory change as an ongoing smooth and cumulative process in which empirical facts, discovered through observation or experimentation, forced revisions in theories and thus added to our ever-increasing knowledge of the world. Kuhn maintained that this view is incompatible with what actually occurs in case after case in the history of science: Scientific change occurs by paradigm shifts. See *Radical Paradigm Shift*.

PERSPECTIVALISM

The view that there is no direct experience of reality. Each of us sees the world through the filter of our own paradigm, conceptual frameworks, vocabularies, and language, so each of us lives in a different world with different rationalities, ways of knowing, and moralities.

PERSUASIVE DEFINITION

A definition put forward in order to promote a certain political or ideological position. For example, defining man as a rational, self-interested utility maximizer promotes an economic view of humans and society.

POLITICAL SYSTEM

A process (mechanism) for resolving competing interests or claims to rights via determination of government policy, i.e., action by the state. Contrast with *Economic System*.

POSITIVISM

A theory that describes the history of human thought as evolving through certain definite stages: the religious, the metaphysical, and the scientific. Scientific language is regarded as the most productive and valuable. The most extreme form is *Logical Positivism*.

POSTMODERNISM

A movement based on the critique of modernism and Enlightenment values and truth-claims. Postmodernists reject unitary definitions of truth, grand narratives of legitimation (meta-narratives), rational discourse as the sole avenue to truth, and the need for absolute foundations. Postmodernists usually argue for pluralism, relativism, and the celebration of difference.

PRAGMATISM

A philosophical movement originating in the United States in the late 1800s, partially in response to long-established ideological tendencies of European philosophy. Thinkers who shaped this movement include Charles Pierce, John Dewey, and William James. The characteristic idea of pragmatism is that efficacy in practical application—the issue of "which works out most effectively"—provides a standard for the determination of truth in the case of statements, rightness in the case of action, and value in the case of appraisals.

Pragmatism is a philosophy that stresses the relation of theory to praxis and takes the continuity of experience and nature as revealed through the outcome of directed action as the starting point for reflection. There is an emphasis on theory and praxis, knowledge and action, facts and values. Truth cannot be determined solely by epistemological criteria because the adequacy of these criteria cannot be determined apart from the goals sought and values instantiated. Values, which arise in historically specific cultural situations, are intelligently appropriated only to the extent that they satisfactorily resolve problems and are judged worth retaining. Truths are beliefs that are confirmed in the course of experience and are therefore fallible, subject to further revision. Pragmatism is distinguished from neopragmatism by its roots in empiricism, positivism, and instrumentalism.

RADICAL PARADIGM SHIFT   A fairly sudden shift to a new conceptual scheme that is unjustifiable in that it does not appeal to anything that is outside of (or independent of) the old and new paradigms (which are incompatible or even incommensurable).

REDUCTIONISM   A view that follows from scientism, empiricism, and positivism. Since the only legitimate form of knowledge is empirical, and since science is the method of determining what counts as knowledge, then anything that is not amenable to scientific investigation (such as purported facts about the mind, morality, art, religion, society) is either reduced to facts that are amenable to scientific investigation or is not counted as fact at all. The linguistic analog is that statements purported to be about mind, morality, art, religion, or society are either reduced to scientific statements or are meaningless. In philosophy of mind, reductionism is the claim that facts about mentality are reducible to physical facts (i.e., facts about matter and material processes). For example, logical behaviorism seeks to reduce mental properties by defining them in terms of behaviors and behavioral dispositions. The ultimate hope of reductionism is to provide a basic account of the universe in a language (e.g., physics) to which all other accounts can be reduced.

RELATIVISM

(*in our usage, always*) A pejorative, equivalent to what is often called normative, vicious, or ethicial relativism. It presupposes the truth of descriptive or cultural relativism (i.e., the empirical claim that different individuals, groups, or cultures have different beliefs about the world and morality).

Normative relativism holds that: (1) There are no universally valid moral principles; all moral principles are valid relative to culture. (2) If a culture accepts a particular set of beliefs (such as moral beliefs) as justified or true, then that culture is correct, right, and justified in believing that those beliefs are right and true. (3) Consequently, [normative relativism holds that] we have no right to interfere with an individual or a culture if we disagree with its beliefs, since it is right in having them.

SCIENCE

A particular paradigm that is used to describe, understand, and explain the natural world.

SCIENTISM

(*as distinguished from science*) An ideology or philosophical conception characterized by the notion that all action, thought, and knowledge can be reduced to the "objective" scientific paradigm. It claims that the only valid form of knowledge is the instrumental (scientific/technical) kind: An action is "rational" only if it is an efficient means to whatever ends have been chosen. Since only a scientific methodology is intellectually acceptable, the arts, humanities, philosophy, social sciences, and the like must adopt this methodology if they are to be a genuine part of human knowledge.

SOCIAL CONSTRUCT

Something that exists as a result of human institutions, rules, norms, thought, or intention and that would not exist independently of them. For example, baseball and elections are constructions of human thought and institutions, and their existence is dependent on them. There are entities, such as wilderness, that exist both as physical things independent of human thought and that also exist as social constructs, i.e., the way we think of nature and the value we attach to it.

Concepts are social constructs. There is much disagreement concerning what kinds of things are social constructs, with views ranging from just concepts and institutions to even the basic constituents of the physical universe. For example, to Foucault, both quarks and persons are social constructs.

SOCIAL CONSTRUCTIONISM

Analysis of "knowledge" or "reality" or both as contingent upon social relations, and as made out of continuing human practices. Social constructionists do not believe in the possibility of value-free foundations, nor do they conceptualize a clear distinction between objective and subjective, or knowledge and reality.

THICK CONCEPT

A normatively laden concept, impregnated with values.

TRANSCENDENT

Beyond the limits of time, place, or human experience; overarching and absolute.

UTILITARIANISM

An approach to morality that treats pleasure or desire satisfaction as the sole element in human good and that regards the morality of actions as entirely dependent on consequences or results for human well-being or happiness. An act is morally obligatory if and only if it produces a greater balance of pleasure over pain, or of desire satisfaction, than any alternative action available to the agent. Moral evaluation is a form of instrumental evaluation: Acts are not right or obligatory because of their inherent character, their underlying motives, or their relation to social norms and values, but because of how much overall human well-being they produce.

Utilitarianism is a consequentialist ethical theory in that it evaluates rightness and wrongness by consequences or outcomes. Generally, the right act (rule, plan, policy, or social system) is the one that maximizes the sum total of whatever is intrinsically good—usually happiness or well-being.

References

Abram, S.A. 2000. Planning the public: Some comments on empirical planning. *Journal of Planning Education and Research* 19, 4: 351–7.

Alexander, E. R. 1984. After rationality, what? A review of responses to paradigm breakdown. *Journal of the American Planning Association* 50, 1: 62–9.

___. 1986. *Approaches to planning.* New York: Gordon and Breach Science Publishers.

Allen, J. 1996. Our town: Foucault and knowledge-based politics in London. In S. Mandelbaum, L. Mazza, and R. Burchell, eds.,1996. *Explorations in planning theory.* New Brunswick, NJ: Center for Urban Policy Research. ch.16.

Allmendinger, P. 2001. *Planning in postmodern times.* London, UK: Routledge.

Andersen, J. 1997. Consensus-based land use planning: Success and failure of British Columbia's Commission on Resources and Environment's Shared Decision Making Model. Master's Degree Project, University of Calgary.

Anderson, C. W. 1979. The place of principles in policy analysis. *American Political Science Review* 73: 711–23.

Ansoff, H. I. 1965. *Corporate strategy.* New York: McGraw-Hill.

Armstrong-Buck, S. 1986. Whitehead's metaphysical system as a foundation for environmental ethics. *Environmental Ethics* 8: 241–59.

Audi, R., ed. 1995. *The Cambridge dictionary of philosophy.* Cambridge, UK: Cambridge University Press.

Austin, J. L. 1961. *How to do things with words.* Oxford, UK: Oxford University Press.

Baier, A. 1994. *Moral prejudices: Essays on ethics.* Cambridge, MA: Harvard University Press.

Banff-Bow Valley Study. 1996. *Banff Bow Valley: At the crossroads.* Report of the Banff Bow Valley Task Force.

Banff-Bow Valley Study (BBVS) Newsletter. 1995. Number 2 (May 1).

Banfield, E. 1959. Ends and means in planning. *International Social Science Journal* 11, 3. Quoted in A. Faludi, *A reader in planning theory* (Oxford: Pergamon Press, 1973).

Baum, H. 1996. Why the rational paradigm persists: Tales from the field. *Journal of Planning Education and Research* 15: 127–35.

Baynes, K.; J. Bohman; and T. McCarthy, eds. 1987. *After philosophy: End or transformation?* Cambridge, MA: MIT Press.

Beatley, T. 1994. *Ethical land use: Principles of policy and planning.* Baltimore, MD: Johns Hopkins University Press.

___. 1995. Planning and sustainability: The elements of a new (improved?) paradigm. *Journal of Planning Literature* 9, 4 (May): 383–95.

Beauregard, R. A. 1989. Between modernity and postmodernity: The ambiguous position of U.S. planning. *Environment and Planning D: Society and Space* 7: 381–95.

___. 1991. Without a net: Modernist planning and the postmodern abyss. *Journal of Planning Education and Research* 10: 189–94.

___. 2000. Neither embedded nor embodied: Critical pragmatism and identity politics. In M. Burayidi, ed., *Urban planning in a multi-cultural society.* Westport, CT: Greenwood Press. ch. 4.

Benhabib, S. 1979. Critical notice of Thomas McCarthy's "The critical theory of Jürgen Habermas." *Telos* (Summer).

Bennis, W. 1966. The coming death of bureaucracy. *Think* (Nov.–Dec.): 30–5.

Bernstein, R. J. 1992. *The new constellation: The ethical–political horizons of modernity/postmodernity.* Cambridge, MA: MIT Press.

Bish, Robert L., and H. O. Nourse. 1975. *Urban economics and public policy.* New York: Oxford University Press.

Black, A. 1990. The Chicago area transportation study. *Journal of Planning Education and Research* 10: 27–37.

Blanco, H. 1994. *How to think about social problems: American pragmatism and the idea of planning.* Westport, CT: Greenwood Press.

Bok, S. 1978. *Lying.* New York: Pantheon.

Booher, D., and J. Innes. 2002. Network power in collaborative planning. *Journal of Planning Education and Research* 21, 3: 221–36.

Bouwsma, O. K. 1986. *Wittgenstein: Conversations 1949–1951.* Indianapolis, IN: Hackett Publishing Company.

Bowles, S., and H. Gintis. 1986. *Democracy and capitalism: Property, community, and the contradictions of modern social thought.* New York: Basic Books. p.17.

Branch, M. 1985. *Comprehensive city planning: Introduction and explanation.* Chicago, IL: American Planning Association.

___. 1990. *Planning: Universal process.* New York: Praeger.

Brint, M., and W. Weaver, eds. 1991. *Pragmatism in law and society.* Boulder, CO: Westview Press.

Buchanan, M., and G. Tullock. 1962. *Calculus of consent*. Ann Arbor, MI: University of Michigan Press.

Bunnin, N., and E. P. Tsui-James, eds. 1996. *The Blackwell companion to philosophy*. Oxford, UK: Blackwell.

Burayidi, M., ed. 2000. *Urban planning in a multi-cultural society*. Westport, CT: Greenwood Press.

Calgary Herald. 1998. Take a bow: Three decades of sweat pays off with expansion pact. July 12. p. A4.

Campbell, H., and R. Marshall. 2000. Instrumental rationality, intelligent action and planning: American pragmatism revisited. Paper delivered at Planning Research 2000 Conference, London, UK.

Campbell, S., and S. Fainstein. 1996. *Readings in planning theory*. Oxford, UK: Blackwell.

Castells, M. 1991. *The informational city*. Toronto, Canada: University of Toronto Press.

———. *The rise of the network society*. Oxford, UK: Blackwell.

Cavell, S. 1964. *Existentialism and analytic philosophy*. *Daedalus* 93: 963.

Chrislip, D. D., and C. E. Larson. 1994. *Collaborative leadership: How citizens and civic leaders can make a difference*. San Francisco, CA: Jossey-Bass.

City of Winnipeg, Parks and Recreation Department. 1989. *Partners for progress*. Pamphlet.

Clarke, S. G., and E. Simpson. 1989. *Anti-theory in ethics and moral conservatism*. Albany, NY: State University of New York Press.

Cockburn, C. 1998. *The space between us: Negotiating gender and national identities in conflict*. London, UK: Zed Books.

Cohen, G.A. 1986. Self-ownership, world ownership and equality: Part II, *Social Philosophy and Policy* 3, 2: 77.

Coleman, A. 1985. *Utopia on trial: Vision and reality in planned housing*. London, UK: Hilary Shipman.

Collingwood, R. G. 1963. *The idea of history*. London, UK: Oxford University Press.

Commission on Resources and the Environment (CORE). 1993. Land-use strategy framework, goals and planning options. Draft discussion paper. Victoria, British Columbia: CORE.

Connelly, M.; T. Li; M. MacDonald; and J. Parpart. 1995. Restructured worlds/restructured debates: Globalization, development and gender. *Canadian Journal of Development Studies* 16, 3: 17–38.

Connolly, W., ed. 1984. *Legitimacy and the state*. New York: New York University Press.

Cormick, G.; N. Dale; P. Edmond; S. G. Sigurdson; and B. D. Stuart. 1996. Building consensus for a sustainable future: Putting principles into practice. Ottawa, Ontario: National Round Table on the Environment and the Economy.

Dalton, L.C. 1986. Why the rational model persists: The resistance of professional education and practice to alternative forms of planning. *Journal of Planning Education and Research* 5: 147–53.

Daniels, N. 1985. Two approaches to theory acceptance in ethics. Totowa, NJ: Rowman and Allanheld.

___. 1996. *Justice and justification: Reflective equilibrium in theory and practice.* Cambridge, UK: Cambridge University Press.

Davidoff, Paul. 1965. Advocacy and pluralism in planning. *Journal of the American Institute of Planners* 31, 6: 331–7.

Davidson, D. 1985. On the very idea of a conceptual scheme. In J. Rajchman and C. West, eds., *Post-analytic philosophy.* New York: Columbia University Press, 129–43.

___. 1987. The method of truth in metaphysics. In K. Baynes, J. Bohman, and T. McCarthy, eds., *After philosophy: End or transformation?* Cambridge, MA: MIT Press. pp. 166–83.

___. 1990. Coherence theory. In A. Malachowski, ed., *Reading Rorty.* Oxford, UK: Basil Blackwell. p. 279.

Day, J. P. 1964. John Stuart Mill. In D. J. O'Connor, ed., *A critical history of Western philosophy.* New York: Free Press.

de Saussure, F. 1986. *Course in general linguistics.* Translated by R. Harris. LaSalle, IL: Open Court.

Dear, M. 1986. Postmodernism and planning. *Environment and Planning D: Society and Space* 4: 367–84.

Derrida, J. 1982. Sending: On representation. *Social Research* 49.

___. 1989. *Limited Inc.* Evanston, IL: Northwestern University Press.

Devall, B., and G. Sessions. 1985. *Deep ecology: Living as if nature mattered.* Salt Lake City, UT: Gibbs M. Smith.

___. 1994. Deep ecology. In D. VanDeVeer and C. Pierce, *The environmental ethics and policy book: Philosophy, ecology, economics.* Belmont, CA: Wadsworth.

Dewey, J. 1920. Reprint 1950. *Reconstruction in philosophy.* New York: New American Library.

Dewey, J., and J. Tuft. 1932. *Ethics* (rev. ed.). New York: Henry Holt.

Douglass, M., and J. Friedmann, eds. 1998. *Cities for citizens: Planning and the rise of civil society in a global age.* New York: John Wiley & Sons.

Dryzek, J. S. 1993. Policy analysis and planning: From science to argument. In F. Fischer and J. Forester, eds., *The argumentative turn in policy analysis and planning.* Durham, NC and London, UK: Duke University Press. pp. 213–32.

Dworkin, R. 1977. *Taking rights seriously*. London, UK: Duckworth.

Edwards, J. 1982. *Ethics without philosophy: Wittgenstein and the moral life*. Gainesville, FL: University Press of Florida.

Etzioni, A. 1967. Reprint 1973. Mixed-scanning: A third approach to decision making. *Public Administration Review* (December). In A. Faludi, ed., *A reader in planning theory*. Oxford, UK: Pergamon.

____. 1968. *The active society*. New York: Macmillan.

____. 1993. *The spirit of community: Rights, responsibilites and the communitarian agenda*. New York: Crown Publishers.

Eyre, M., and T. Jamal. 1998. Addressing stakeholder conflicts in a Canadian mountain park. *Parks and Recreation* (September): 86–94.

Fainstein, S., and N. Fainstein. 1996. City planning and political values: An updated view. In S. Campbell and N. Fainstein, *Readings in planning theory*. Oxford, UK: Blackwell.

Faludi, A. 1973. Introduction, Part III. In A. Faludi, ed., *A reader in planning theory*. Oxford, UK: Pergamon Press. pp. 113–26.

Feyerabend, P. 1965. On the meaning of scientific terms. *Journal of Philosophy* 62: 266–74.

____. 1993. *Against method*. London, UK: Verso.

Fischer, F., and J. Forester. 1993. *The argumentative turn in policy analysis and planning*. Durham, NC and London, UK: Duke University Press.

Fischler, R. 2000. Communicative planning theory: A Foucauldian assessment. *Journal of Planning Education and Research* 19, 4: 358–68.

Fisher, R., and W. Ury. 1981. *Getting to yes: Negotiating agreement without giving in*. New York: Penguin.

Flyvbjerg, B. 1996. The dark side of planning: Rationality and "Realrationalitat." In S. Mandelbaum, S., L. Mazza, and R. Burchell, eds., *Explorations in planning theory*. New Brunswick, NJ: Center for Urban Policy Research.

____. 1998. *Rationality and power*. Chicago, IL: University of Chicago Press.

____. 2002. Bringing research to power: One researcher's praxis story. *Journal of Planning Education and Research* 21, 4: 353–66.

Foley, J., and M. Lauria. 1999. Plans, planning and tragic choices. Paper delivered at 1999 annual meeting of the Association of Collegiate Schools of Planning (ACSP), Chicago, Illinois.

Forester, J. 1987. The politics of criteria. In F. Fischer, ed., *Confronting values in policy analysis: The politics of criteria*. Beverly Hills, CA: Sage.

____. 1989. *Planning in the face of power*. Berkeley, CA: University of California Press.

____. 1990. A reply to my critics. *Planning Theory Newsletter* 4: 43–60.

____. 1993a. *Critical theory, public policy and planning practice: Towards a critical pragmatism*. Albany, NY: State University of New York Press.

____. 1993b. Learning from practice stories: The priority of practical judgment. In F. Fischer and J. Forester, eds., *The argumentative turn in policy analysis and planning*. Durham, NC and London, UK: Duke University Press.

____. 1996. How silent about politics: Pragmatism or critical pragmatism? Paper delivered at the Joint Congress of the Association of Collegiate Schools of Planning and the Association of European Schools of Planning, Toronto, Ontario, Canada.

____. 1999. *The deliberative practitioner*. Cambridge, MA: MIT Press.

____. 2001. An instructive case study hampered by theoretical puzzles: Critical comments on Flyvberg's *Rationality and power*. *International Planning Studies* 6, 3: 263–70.

Foucault, M. 1972. *Archaeology of knowledge*. Translated by A. M. Sheridan Smith. New York: Pantheon.

____. 1979. *Discipline and punish: The birth of the prison*. New York: Vintage.

____. 1980. In C. Gordon, ed., *Power/knowledge: Selected interviews and other writings, 1972–1977*. Translated by C. Gordon, L. Marshall, J. Mepham, and K. Koper. New York: Pantheon.

____. 1982. The subject and power. In H. Dreyfus and P. Rabinow, eds. *Michel Foucault: Beyond structuralism and hermeneutics*. 1st. ed. Chicago: University of Chicago Press.

____. 1983. The subject and power. In H. Dreyfus and P. Rabinow, eds. *Michel Foucault: Beyond structuralism and hermeneutics*. 2d. ed. Chicago: University of Chicago Press.

____. 1984. In P. Rabinow, ed. *The Foucault reader*. New York: Pantheon.

____. 1985. The ethic of care for the self as the practice of freedom. In J. Bernauer and D. Rasmussen, eds., *The final Foucault*. Cambridge MA: MIT Press.

____. 1987. Questions of method: An interview with Michel Foucault. In K. Baynes, J. Bohman, and T. McCarthy, eds., *After philosophy: End or transformation?* Cambridge, MA: MIT Press.

____. 1988. *Politics, philosophy, culture: Interviews and other writings, 1977–1984*. New York: Pantheon.

____. 1989. *Foucault live (interviews 1966-84)*. New York: Semiotexte.

Fraser, N. 1990. Rethinking the public sphere: A contribution to the critique of actually existing democracy. *Social Text* 25/26: 56–80.

Freeman, R. E. 1984. *Strategic management: A stakeholder approach*. London: Pittman.

Friedman, M., and R. Friedman. 1984. *The tyranny of the status quo*. San Diego: Harcourt Brace Jovanovich.

Friedmann, J. 1973. *Retracking America.* Garden City, NY: Anchor Press.

___. 1987. *Planning in the public domain: From knowledge to action.* Princeton, NJ: Princeton University Press.

___. 1989. The dialectic of reason. *International Journal of Urban and Regional Research* 13, 2.

___. 1992. Educating the next generation of planners. Paper delivered at the annual meeting of the Association of Collegiate Schools of Planning, Columbus, Ohio.

___. 1993. Toward a non-Euclidean mode of planning. *Journal of the American Planning Association* 59, 4: 482–5.

___. 1996. The new political economy of planning: The rise of civil society. Paper delivered at the Symposium in Celebration of John Friedmann. Los Angeles, CA.

___. 1998. Planning theory revisited. *European Planning Studies* 6, 3: 245–53.

Fukuyama, F. 1999. The great disruption. *Atlantic Monthly* 283, 5: 55–80.

Galloway-Cosijn, A. 1999. A theoretical framework to facilitate cross-cultural communication in the Aboriginal planning context. Environmental Design Master's Degree Project, University of Calgary, Canada.

Gauthier, D. 1978. The social contract as ideology. *Philosophy and Public Affairs* 6, 2: 130–64.

Geddes, P. 1915. Reprint 1968. *Cities in evolution.* New York: Harper and Row.

Giddens, A. 1984. *The constitution of society.* Cambridge, UK: Polity Press.

Gilligan, C. 1977. In a different voice: Women's conceptions of self and of morality. In M. Pearsall, ed., *Women and values: Readings in recent feminist philosophy.* Belmont, CA: Wadsworth. pp. 309–39.

Goodman, N. 1965. *Fact, fiction and forecast.* 2d. ed. New York: Bobbs-Merrill.

Grabow, S., and A. Heskin. 1973. Foundations for a radical concept of planning. *Journal of the American Institute of Planners* 39, 2: 106–14.

Gray, B. 1989. *Collaborating: Finding common ground for multiparty problems.* San Francisco, CA: Jossey-Bass.

Groat, L. N. 1992. Rescuing architecture from the cul-de-sac. *Journal of Architectural Education* 45: 138–46.

Habermas, J. 1971a. *Theory and praxis.* Frankfurt, Germany: Suhrkamp.

___. 1971b. Translated by J. S. Shapiro. *Knowledge and human interests.* Boston, MA: Beacon Press.

___. 1984. *The theory of communicative action.* Boston, MA: Beacon Press.

___. 1989. *The new conservatism.* Cambridge, MA: MIT Press.

___. 1992. In P. Daws, ed., *Autonomy and solidarity: Interviews with Jürgen Habermas.* London, UK: Verso.

Hampton, J. 1989. Should political philosophy be done without metaphysics? *Ethics* 99: 791–814.

Harper, T. L. 1987. Economists vs. planners? A framework for zoning debates. *Plan Canada* 27: 180–91.

Harper, T. L., and S. M. Stein. 1983. The justification of urban intervention: A moral framework. *Environments* 15: 39–47.

___. 1988. The rational planning model: The implications of its continuing dominance of planning practice. Paper delivered at the annual meeting of the Association of Collegiate Schools of Planning, Buffalo, New York.

___. 1992. The centrality of normative ethical theory to contemporary planning theory. *Journal of Planning Education and Research* 11, 2: 105–16.

___. 1993a. Normative ethical theory: Is it relevant to contemporary planning practice? *Plan Canada* (September): 6–11.

___. 1993b. Response to Charles Hoch's commentary. *Journal of Planning Education and Research* 12: 93–5.

___. 1994. Neopragmatism and planning. Paper delivered at the annual meeting of the Association of Collegiate Schools of Planning, Phoenix, Arizona.

___. 1995a. Classical liberal (libertarian) planning theory. In S. Hendler, ed., *Planning ethics: A reader in planning theory, practice and education.* New Brunswick, NJ: Center for Urban Policy Research. ch.1.

___. 1995b. Contemporary procedural ethical theory and planning theory. In S. Hendler, ed., *Planning ethics: A reader in planning theory, practice and education.* New Brunswick, NJ: Center for Urban Policy Research. ch.3.

___. 1995c. Out of the post-modern abyss: Preserving the rationale for liberal planning. *Journal of Planning Education and Research* 14, 4: 233–44.

___. 1995d. Review of F. Fischer and J. Forester, "The argumentative turn in policy analysis and planning." *Journal of Planning Education and Research* 14: 3, 228–9.

___. 1996. Post-modern planning theory: The incommensurability premise. In S. Mandelbaum, L. Mazza, and R. Burchell, eds., *Explorations in planning theory.* New Brunswick, NJ: Center for Urban Policy Research. ch. 20.

Hart, H. L. 1973. Rawls on liberty and its priority. *University of Chicago Law Review* 40: 551–5. Reprinted in H. L. Hart (1983), *Essays in jurisprudence and philosophy* (Oxford, UK: Oxford University Press).

Harvey, D. 1989. *The condition of postmodernity.* Oxford, UK: Basil Blackwell.

Healey, P. 1993. Planning through debate: The communicative turn in planning theory. In F. Fischer and J. Forester, eds., *The argumentative turn in policy analysis and planning.* Durham, NC, and London, UK: Duke University Press.

___. 1997. *Collaborative planning.* London, UK: Macmillan.

Hendler, S., ed. 1995. *Planning ethics: A reader in planning theory, practice and education.* New Brunswick, NJ: Center for Urban Policy Research.

Hoberg, G. 1993. Environmental policy: Alternative styles. In Michael M. Atkinson, ed., *Governing Canada: Institutions and public policy*. Toronto, Canada: Harcourt Brace Jovanovich Canada Inc. ch. 10.

Hoch, C. J. 1984. Doing good and being right: The pragmatic connection in planning theory. *Journal of the American Planning Association* 50, 3: 335–45.

___. 1985. Make no large plans. *Plan Canada* 25, 3 (September): 80–7.

___. 1988. Letter to Krumholz. Cited in N. Krumholz and J. Forester, *Making equity planning work: Leadership in the public sector*. Philadelphia, PA: Temple University Press. p. 250.

___. 1992. The paradox of power in planning practice. *Journal of Planning Education and Research* 11: 206–15.

___. 1993. Commentary on "The centrality of normative ethical theory to contemporary planning theory." *Journal of Planning Education and Research* 12: 93.

___. 1994. *What do planners do?* Chicago, IL: Planners Press.

___. 1996. Planning theorists taking an interpretive turn need not travel on the political economy highway. Paper presented at the Joint Congress of Association of College Schools of Planning/AESOP, Toronto, Canada.

Hodge, G. 1986. *Planning Canadian communities*. Toronto, Canada: Methuen.

Hollis, M. 1970. Reason and ritual. In B. Wilson, ed., *Rationality*. Oxford, UK: Blackwell.

Honderich, T., ed. 1995. *The Oxford companion to philosophy*. Oxford, UK: Oxford University Press.

Howe, E. 1994. *Acting on ethics in city planning*. New Brunswick, NJ: Center for Urban Policy Research.

Hummel, R. P. 1977. *The bureaucratic experience*. New York: St. Martin's Press.

Huxham, C., ed. 1996. *Creating collaborative advantage*. London, UK: Sage.

Huxley, M. 2000. The limits to communicative planning. *Journal of Planning Education and Research* 19, 4: 369–78.

Huxley, M., and O. Yiftachel. 2000. New paradigm or old myopia? Unsettling the "communicative turn" in planning theory. *Journal of Planning Education and Research* 19, 4: 333–42.

Ignatieff, M. 1998. *Isaiah Berlin: A life*. London, UK: Random House.

Innes, J. 1995. Planning theory's emerging paradigm: Communicative action and interactive practice. *Journal of Planning Education and Research* 14, 3: 183–89.

___. 1996. Planning through consensus building: A new view of the comprehensive planning ideal. *Journal of the American Planning Association* 62, 4 (Autumn): 460–72.

Innes, J., and D. Booher. 2000. Public participation in planning: New strategies for the 21st century. Institute of Urban and Regional Development. IURD Working Paper Series. Paper WP-2000-07. November 1.

Innes, J.; J. Gruber; M. Neuman; and R. Thompson. 1994. Coordinating growth and environmental management through consensus building. Berkeley, CA: California Policy Seminar.

Jacobs, H. M. 1995. Contemporary environmental philosophy and its challenge to planning theory. In S. Hendler, ed., *Planning ethics: A reader in planning theory, practice and education*. New Brunswick, NJ: Center for Urban Policy Research. ch. 8.

Jamal, T. 1997. Multi-party consensus processes in environmentally sensitive destinations: Paradoxes of ownership and common ground. Ph.D. dissertation, University of Calgary.

Jamal, T.; S. M. Stein; and T. L. Harper. 2002. The politics and metaphysics of multi-stakeholder processes in tourism-environmental conflicts. *Journal of Planning Education and Research* 22: 164–77.

James, W. 1972. *Pragmatism and the meaning of truth*. Cambridge, MA: Harvard University Press.

Jameson, F. 1984. Postmodernism, or, the cultural logic of late capitalism. *New Left Review* 146: 57.

Kant, Immanuel. 1783. Reprint 1956. Translated by H. J. Paton. *Groundwork of the metaphysics of morals* [*The moral law*]. London, UK: Hutchison.

Kaufman, J. L. 1990. Forester in the face of planners: Will they listen to him? *Planning Theory Newsletter* 4: 27–39.

Kaufman, J. L., and H. M. Jacobs. 1987. A public planning perspective on strategic planning. *Journal of the American Planning Association* 52, 1: 21–31.

Klosterman, R. 1978. Foundations for normative planning. *Journal of the American Institute of Planners* 44, 1: 51–69.

___. 1992. Planning theory education in the 1980s: Results of a second course survey. *Journal of Planning Education and Research* 11, 2: 130–40.

Kolb, D. 1992. *Postmodern sophistication: Philosophy, architecture and tradition*. Chicago, IL: University of Chicago Press.

Krumholz, N., and J. Forester. 1990. *Making equity planning work: Leadership in the public sector*. Philadelphia, PA: Temple University Press.

Kuhn, T. S. 1970a[1962]. *The structure of scientific revolutions*. 2nd ed. Chicago, IL: University of Chicago Press.

___. 1970b. Reflections on my critics. In I. Lakotas and A. Musgrave, eds. *Criticism and growth of knowledge*. Cambridge, UK: Cambridge University Press.

Kymlicka, W. 1987. Liberalism and communitarianism. Paper prepared for the annual meeting of the Canadian Philosophical Association at McMaster University, Hamilton, Ontario, Canada.

___. 1989. *Liberalism, community and culture.* Oxford, UK: Clarendon Press.

Lauria, M., ed. 1995. Planning theory and political economy: A symposium. *Planning Theory* 15: 3–115.

Lauria, M., and R. K. Whelan. 1995. Planning theory and political economy: The need for reintegration. *Planning Theory* 14, 1: 8–33.

Lefebvre, H. 1991. *The production of space.* Oxford, UK: Blackwell Publishers.

___. 1996. *Writings on cities.* Oxford, UK: Blackwell Publishers.

Leopold, A. 1933. The conservation ethic. *Journal of Forestry* 31: 634–43. Cited in E. P. Odum (1974), *Environmental ethics and the attitude revolution.*

___. 1949. *A Sand County almanac, and sketches here and there.* Oxford, UK: Oxford University Press.

Leroi, A. M. 1997. The name of the beast. Review of J. Roger, *Buffon* (Ithaca, NY: Cornell University Press), in *London Review of Books* 19, 24 (December 11): 3.

Liggett, H. 1991. Where they don't have to take you in: The representation of homelessness in public policy. *Journal of Planning Education and Research* 10: 201–08.

Light, A., and E. Katz, eds. 1996. *Environmental pragmatism.* London, UK: Routledge.

Lilla, M. 1998. The politics of Jacques Derrida. *New York Review of Books* (June 25): 36–41.

Lindblom, C. E. 1959. Reprint 1973. The science of "muddling through." *Public Administration Review* (Spring). In A. Faludi, ed., *A reader in planning theory.* Oxford, UK: Pergamon Press. pp. 151–70.

___. 1979. Still muddling, not yet through. *Public Administration Review* (November): 517–26.

Livingston, J. 1985. Moral concerns and the eco-sphere. *Alternatives* 12, 2: 3–9.

___. 1986. Ethics as prosethics. In P. P. Hanson, R. Bradley, and S. Duguid, eds., *Environmental ethics: Philosophical and policy perspectives.* Burnaby, British Columbia, Canada: Simon Fraser Institute for the Humanities. pp. 69–82.

Locke, J. 1967 (1690). Second treatise. In P. Laslett, ed., *Two treatises on government.* New York: Cambridge University Press.

Lye, J. 1993. Contemporary literary theory. *Brock Review* 2, 1: 90–106.

Lyotard, F. 1987. The postmodern condition. In K. Baynes, J. Bohman, and T. McCarthy, eds., *After philosophy: End or transformation?* Cambridge, MA: MIT Press.

MacIntyre, A. 1977. Utilitarianism and the presuppositions of cost-benefit analysis: An essay on the relevance of moral philosophy to the theory of bureaucracy. In K. Sayre, ed., *Values in the electric power industry.* Notre Dame, IN: University of Notre Dame Press. pp. 217–37.

Mandelbaum, S. 1979. A complete general theory of planning is impossible. *Policy Science* 11: 59–72.

___. 1990. Deserving communities. Paper delivered at the annual meeting of the Association of Collegiate Schools of Planning, Austin, Texas.

___. 1991. Telling stories. *Journal of Planning Education and Research* 10: 209–14.

___. 2000. *Open moral communities*. Cambridge, MA: MIT Press.

Mandelbaum, S.; L. Mazza; and R. Burchell, eds. 1996. *Explorations in planning theory*. New Brunswick, NJ: Center for Urban Policy Research.

Margerum, R. D. 2002a. Evaluating collaborative planning: Implications from an empirical analysis of growth management. *Journal of the American Planning Association* 68, 2: 179–93.

___. 2002b. Collaborative planning: Building consensus and building a distinct model for practice. *Journal of Planning Education and Research* 21: 237–55.

Martin, E., and T. Beatley. 1993. Our relationship with the earth: Environmental ethics in planning education. *Journal of Planning Education and Research* 12, 2: 117–26.

McCarthy, T. 1991. *Ideals and illusions: On reconstruction and deconstruction in contemporary critical theory*. Cambridge, MA: MIT Press.

___. 1994. Kantian constructivism and reconstruction: Rawls and Habermas in dialogue. *Ethics* 105, 1 (October): 62.

McConnell, S. 1981. *Theories for planning*. London, UK: Heinemann.

McDougall, G. 1990. Planning theory: Constructing an agenda for 1992. *Planning Theory Newsletter* 4: 93–100.

Meyerson, M., and E. C. Banfield. 1955. *Politics, planning and the public interest: The case of public housing in Chicago*. Glencoe, IL.: Free Press.

Milroy, B. 1990. Critical capacity and planning theory. *Planning Theory* 4: 12–18.

___. 1991. Into postmodern weightlessness. *Journal of Planning Education and Research* 10: 181–87.

Mintzberg, H. 1989. *Mintzberg on management*. New York: Free Press.

___. 1994. *The rise and fall of strategic planning: Reconceiving roles for planning, plans, planners*. New York: The Free Press.

Mulgrew, A. 1995. Critical planning theory and its application: Steen Community Centre. Practicum Project, University of Winnipeg, Canada.

Mumford, L. 1938. *The culture of cities*. New York: Harcourt and Brace.

Murphy, J. P. 1990. *Pragmatism from Peirce to Davidson*. Boulder, CO: Westview Press.

Naess, A. 1973. The shallow and the deep, long-range ecology movement: A summary. *Inquiry* 16: 95–100.

___. 1992. The encouraging richness and diversity of ultimate premises in environmental philosophy. *The Trumpeter* 9, 2 (Spring): 53-62.

Neuman, M. 1998. Does planning need the plan? *Journal of the American Planning Association* 64: 208–20.

___. 2000. Communicate this! *Journal of Planning Education and Research* 19, 4: 343–50.

Neurath, O. 1973. *Empiricism and sociology.* Boston, MA: D. Reidel Publishing.

Nielsen, K. 1979. Some theses in search of an argument: Reflections on Habermas. *National Forum* 69:1, 27-31.

___. 1981. A rationale for egalitarianism. *Social Research* 48: 2.

___. 1982. On needing a moral theory: Rationality, considered judgements, and the grounding of morality. *Metaphilosophy* 13: 97–116.

___. 1983. Emancipatory social science and social critique. In D. Callahan and B. Jennings, eds., *Ethics, the social sciences, and policy analysis.* New York: Plenum. pp. 113–57.

___. 1985. *Equality and liberty: A defense of radical egalitarianism.* Totowa, NJ: Rowman and Allanheld.

___. 1991. *After the demise of the tradition: Rorty, critical theory, and the fate of philosophy.* Boulder, CO: Westview Press.

___. 1996. *Naturalism without foundations.* Amherst, NY: Prometheus Books.

___. 1998. Liberal reasonability a critical tool? Reflections after Rawls. *Dialogue* 37: 739–59.

Nietzsche, F. 1968 (1901). *The will to power.* New York: Vintage Press.

Norris, C. 1990. *What's wrong with postmodernism: Critical theory and the ends of philosophy.* Baltimore, MD: Johns Hopkins University Press.

Nozick, R. 1974. *Anarchy, state and utopia.* New York: Basic Books.

___. 1989. *The examined life: Philosophical meditations.* New York: Simon and Schuster.

Nussbaum, M. 1994. Feminists and philosophy. *New York Review of Books.* October 20.

___. 1997. *Cultivating humanity: A classical defense of reform in liberal education.* Cambridge, MA: Harvard University Press.

O'Connell, S. 1995. Rawlsian planning theory. In S. Hendler, ed., *Planning ethics: A reader in planning theory, practice and education.* New Brunswick, NJ: Center for Urban Policy Research. ch. 2.

Odum, E. P. 1974. Environmental ethics and the attitude revolution. In W. T. Blackstone, ed., *Philosophy and the environmental crisis.* Athens, GA: University of Georgia Press.

Osborne, D., and T. Gaebler. 1992. *Reinventing government.* Reading, MA: Addison-Wesley.

Papineau, D. 1992. In the steps of the dodo. *The New York Times Book Review.* October 4.

Parekh, B. 2000. *Rethinking multiculturalism*. London, UK: Macmillan.

Parsons, T. 1937. *The structure of social action*. New York: McGraw-Hill.

Passmore, J. 1985. *Recent philosophers*. London, UK: Duckworth.

Perks, W. T., and L. I. Kawan. 1986. Strategic planning for small-town community development. *Alberta Journal of Planning Practice* 5: 28–45.

Peters, T. J., and R. H. Waterman. 1982. *In search of excellence*. New York: Warner Books.

Phelps, E. S., ed. 1973. *Economic justice*. Baltimore, MD: Penguin Books.

Premfors, R. 1993. Knowledge, power and democracy: Lindblom, critical theory and postmodernism. In H. Redner, ed., *An heretical heir of the enlightenment: Politics, policy and science in the work of Charles E. Lindblom*. Boulder, CO: Westview Press.

Putnam, H. 1981. *Reason, truth and history*. Cambridge, UK: Cambridge: Cambridge University Press.

———. 1987. *The many faces of realism*. LaSalle, IL: Open Court.

———. 1990. *Realism with a human face*. Cambridge, MA: Harvard University Press.

———. 1992. *Renewing philosophy*. Cambridge, MA: Harvard University Press.

———. 1994. *Words and life*. Cambridge, MA: Harvard University Press.

———. 1995. *Pragmatism*. Oxford, UK: Blackwell.

Putman, R. D. 1993. *Making democracy work: Civic traditions in modern Italy*. Princeton, NJ: Princeton University Press.

Quine, W. V. O. 1953. *Two dogmas of empiricim*. Cambridge, MA: Harvard University Press.

———. 1960. *Word and object*. Oxford, MA: Technology Press.

———. 1961. On what there is. In Willard V. Quine, *From a logical point of view: Nine logico-philosophical essays*. 2d ed. New York: Harper and Row.

———. 1969. Natural kinds. In Willard V. Quine, *Ontological relativity and other essays*. New York: Columbia University Press. pp. 114–38.

———. 1990. *Pursuit of truth*. Cambridge, MA: Harvard University Press

Rawls, J. 1971. *A theory of justice*. Cambridge, MA: Harvard University Press.

———. 1974. Independence of moral theory. *Proceedings of the American Philosophical Association* 49.

———. 1980. Kantian constructivism in moral theory. *Journal of Philosophy* 77, 9: 544.

———. 1985. Justice as fairness: Political not metaphysical. *Philosophy and Public Affairs* 14, 3: 223–51.

———. 1987. The idea of an overlapping consensus. *Oxford Journal of Legal Studies* 7, 1: 1–25.

___. 1993. *Political liberalism*. New York: Columbia University Press.

___. 2001. *Justice as fairness: A restatement*. Cambridge, MA: Harvard University Press.

Reder, M. 1947. *Studies in the theory of welfare economics*. New York: Columbia University Press.

Redner, H. ed. 1993. *An heretical heir of the enlightenment: Politics, policy and science in the work of Charles E. Lindblom*. Boulder, CO: Westview Press.

Rees, W. 1995. Achieving sustainability: Reform or transformation? *Journal of Planning Literature* 9, 4: 343–61.

Reuter, W. 2002. The complementarity of discourse and power in planning. *AESOP Prize Papers in Planning*. Bristol, UK: Association of European Schools of Planning.

Rittel, H. W. J., and M. Webber. 1973. Dilemmas in a general theory of planning. *Policy Sciences* 4: 155–69.

Robinson, I. M., ed. 1972. *Decision-making in urban planning*. Beverly Hills, CA: Sage Publications.

Rorty, R. 1979. *Philosophy and the mirror of nature*. Princeton, NJ: Princeton University Press.

___. 1980. A reply to Dreyfus and Taylor. *Review of Metaphysics* 34: 39–46.

___. 1982. *Consequences of pragmatism*. Minneapolis, MN: University of Minnesota Press.

___. 1985. Solidarity or objectivity? In J. Rajchman and C. West, eds., *Post Analytical Philosophy*. New York: Columbia University Press. pp. 3–19.

___. 1989. *Contingency, irony and solidarity*. Cambridge, UK: Cambridge University Press.

___. 1990. The priority of democracy to philosophy. In A. Malachowski, ed., *Reading Rorty*. Oxford, UK: Basil Blackwell. p. 279.

___. 1991a. Cosmopolitanism without emancipation: A response to John Francois Lyotard. In Richard Rorty, *Objectivity, relativism and truth: Philosophical papers*. Vol. 1. Cambridge, UK: Cambridge University Press. pp. 211–22.

___. 1991b. *Essays on Heidegger and others: Philosophical papers*. Vol. 2. Cambridge, UK: Cambridge University Press.

___. 1995. Philosophy and the future. In H. J. Saatkamp, ed., *Rorty and pragmatism*. Nashville, TN: Vanderbilt University Press. pp. 97–205.

Rosa, M. 1995. Goods and life forms: Relativism in Charles Taylor's political philosophy. *Radical Philosophy* 71 (May–June): 20–26.

Rousseau, J. J. 1768. *Du contrat social, ou principes du droit politique*. Reprint 1968. *The social contract*. New York: Hefner.

Rowland, W. 1999. *Ockham's razor: A search for wonder in an age of doubt*. Toronto, Canada: Key Porter.

Ruse, M. 1994. The struggle for the soul of science. *The Sciences* (Nov./Dec.): 39.

Sager, T. 1994. *Communicative planning theory*. Aldershot, UK: Avebury.

___. 1998. Comment on "Pragmatic incrementalist planning in post-modern society: A normative justification." *Planning Theory* 18: 3–28.

Sandel, M. J. 1982. *Liberalism and the limits of justice*. Cambridge, UK: Cambridge University Press.

___. 1996. *Democracy's discontent: America in search of a public philosophy*. Cambridge, MA: Harvard University Press.

Sandercock, L. 1998a. *Towards cosmopolis: Planning for multicultural cities*. London, UK: Wiley.

___, ed. 1998b. *Making the invisible visible: Insurgent planning histories*. Berkeley, CA: University of California Press.

___. 2000. When strangers become neighbours: Managing cities of difference. *Journal of Planning Theory and Practice* 1, 1: 13–20.

Sandercock, L., and A. Forsyth. 1990. Gender: A new agenda for planning theory. *Planning Theory* 4: 61–92.

Schaar, J. H. 1984. Legitimacy and the modern state. In W. Connolly, ed., *Legitimacy and the state*. New York: New York University Press.

Schmermann, S. 1998. Swords into plowshares (Review of Uri Savir, 1997, *The process: 1,100 days that changed the Middle East* [New York: Random House]. *New York Review of Books* (June 7).

Schön, D. 1983. *The reflective practitioner: How professionals think in action*. New York: Basic Books.

Scruton, R. 1979. The aesthetics of architecture. Princeton, NJ: Princeton University Press.

___. 1990. *The philosopher on Dover Beach*. Manchester, UK: Carncanet Press.

Shklar, J. N. 1986. Injustice, injury, and inequality: An introduction. In F. S. Lucash, ed., *Justice and equality here and now*. Ithaca, NY: Cornell University Press.

Simon, H. A. 1945. *Administrative behaviour*. New York: Free Press.

Skinner, B. F. 1971. *Beyond freedom and dignity*. New York: Knopf.

Smart, J. J. C. 1972. *A system of utilitarian ethics*. Melbourne, Australia: University of Melbourne Press.

Smith, N. 1996. The role of Expo86 and BC Place in economic and social restructuring of Vancouver's False Creek. Master's Degree Project, Faculty of Environmental Design, University of Calgary.

Sober, E. 1993. *Philosophy of biology*. Boulder, CO: Westview Press.

Soja, E. J. 1989. *Postmodern geographies*. London, UK: Verso.

Spitler, G. 1982. Justifying a respect for nature. *Environmental Ethics* 4: 255–60.

Stein, S. M. 1973. The ontological status of social institutions. Ph.D. thesis, University of Calgary.

___. 1994. Wittgenstein, Davidson and the myth of incommensurability. In J. Couture and K. Nielsen, eds., *Reconstruction in philosophy: New essays in metaphilosophy*. Calgary, Alberta, Canada: University of Calgary Press.

___, and T. L. Harper. 1996. Planning theory for sustainable development. *Geography Research Forum* 16 (December).

___, and T. L. Harper. 1997. Pragmatic incrementalist planning in post-modern society: A normative justification. *Planning Theory* 18: 3–28.

___, and T. L. Harper. 1998. Conceptions of the environment: Political not metaphysical. Paper delivered at the Annual Congress of the Association of European Schools of Planning in Portugal, July 1998.

___, and T. L. Harper. 1999. A pragmatic role for deep ecology. Paper delivered at the annual meeting of the Association of Collegiate Schools of Planning in Chicago, Illinois (November); also delivered at the annual Congress of the Association of European Schools of Planning in Bergen, Norway (July).

___, and T. L. Harper. 2000. The paradox of planning in a multi-cultural society: A pragmatic reconciliation. In M. Burayidi, ed., *Urban planning in a multi-cultural society*. Westport, CT: Greenwood Press. ch. 5.

___, and T. L. Harper. 2005. Rawls's "Justice as fairness": A moral basis for contemporary planning theory. *Planning Theory* 4, 2: 147–72.

Stephens, M. 1994. Jacques Derrida. *New York Times Magazine* (January 25).

Stockland, P. 1998. Lyons is roaring. *Calgary Herald* (July 12), p.A5.

Stout, J. 1988. *Ethics after Babel*. Boston, MA: Beacon Press.

Susskind, L.; S. McKearnen; and J. Thomas-Larmer. 1999. *The consensus building handbook: A comprehensive guide to reaching agreement*. Thousand Oaks, CA: Sage.

Sutcliffe, A. 1981. *Towards the planned city*. Oxford, UK: Basil-Blackwell.

Taylor, C. 1986. Foucault on freedom and truth. In D. C. Hoy and M. Foucault, *Foucault: A Critical Reader*. Oxford, UK: Blackwell.

___. 1989. *Sources of the self: The making of modern identity*. Cambridge, MA: MIT Press.

___. 1991. *The malaise of modernity*. Concord, Ontario, Canada: Anansi Press.

___. 1994. The politics of recognition. In A. Gutman, ed., *Multiculturalism: Examining the politics of recognition*. Princeton, NJ: Princeton University Press.

Taylor, P. W. 1986. *Respect for nature: A theory of environmental ethics*. Princeton, NJ: Princeton University Press.

Tett, A., and J. M. Wolfe. 1991. Discourse analysis and city plans. *Journal of Planning Education and Research* 10: 195–200.

Tewdwr-Jones, M., and P. Allmendinger. 1998. Deconstructing communicative rationality: A critique of Habermasian collaborative rationality. *Environment and Planning A* 30: 1975–89.

Tully, J. 1995. *Strange multiplicity: Constitutionalism in an age of diversity.* Cambridge, UK: Cambridge University Press.

Verma, N. 1993. Revisiting rationality in planning: Pragmatic planning theory. Paper delivered at the annual meeting of the Association of Collegiate Schools of Planning, Philadelphia, Pennsylvania.

Wachs, M. 1985. Introduction. In M. Wachs, ed., *Ethics in planning.* New Brunswick, NJ: Center for Urban Policy Research.

Walzer, M. 1986. The politics of Michel Foucault. In D. C. Hoy and M. Foucault, *Foucault: A Critical Reader.* Oxford: Blackwell.

———. 1987. *Interpretation and social criticism.* Cambridge, MA: Harvard University Press.

Warren, K. J. 1990. The power and the promise of ecological feminism. In D. Van DeVeer and C. Pearce, eds., *The environmental ethics and policy book: Philosophy, ecology, economics.* Belmont, CA: Wadsworth.

Weber, M. 1946. *From Max Weber: Essays in sociology.* H. Gerth and C. Mills, eds. and translators. Oxford, UK: Oxford University Press.

———. 1947. *Theories of social and economic organization.* Glencoe, IL: Free Press.

Weisbord, M., and 35 coauthors. 1992. *Discovering common ground: How Future Search Conferences bring people together to achieve breakthrough innovation, empowerment, shared vision, and collaborative action.* San Francisco, CA: Berett-Koehler Publishers.

White, S. K. 1991. *Political theory and postmodernism.* Cambridge, UK: Cambridge University Press.

Whorf, B. 1956. In J. B. Carroll, ed., *Language, thought, and reality: Selected writings of Benjamin Lee Whorf.* Cambridge, MA: MIT Press.

Williams, B. 1972. *Morality: An introduction to ethics.* New York: Harper and Row.

———. 1985. *Ethics and the limits of philosophy.* Cambridge, MA: Harvard University Press.

———. 1991. Terrestrial thoughts, extra-terrestrial science. *London Review of Books* 13, 3 (Feb. 7): 12–13.

Winch, P. 1958. *The idea of a social science.* New York: Humanities Press.

———. 1970 (1964). Understanding a primitive society. *American Philosophical Quarterly* I: 307–24. In B. Wilson, *Rationality.* Oxford: Blackwell.

Wisdom, J. 1965 (1951). *Gods.* In A. Flew, ed., *Logic and language.* Garden City, NY: Doubleday.

Wittgenstein, L. 1958. *Philosophical investigations (Philosophische Untersuchungen)*. 2d. ed. Oxford, UK: Basil Blackwell.

___. 1969. *On certainty (Uber Gewissheit)*. New York: Harper and Row; Oxford, UK: Basil Blackwell. Edited by G. E. M. Anscombe and G. H. von Wright.

Wood, M. 1982. Planning, justice and the public good. In P. Healy, G. McDougall, and M. Thomas, eds., *Planning theory: Prospects for the 1980's*. Oxford, UK: Pergamon Press. pp. 68–80.

Woodhouse, E. J., and D. Collingridge. 1993. Incrementalism, intelligent trial-and-error, and the future of political decision theory. In H. Redner, ed., *An heretical heir of the enlightenment: Politics, policy and science in the work of Charles E. Lindblom*. Boulder, CO: Westview Press.

Yiftachel, O. 1999. Planning theory at the crossroads. *Journal of Planning Education and Research* 18, 3: 67–9.

Yiftachel, O., J. Little, D. Hedgcock, and I. Alexander. 2001. *The power of planning: Spaces of control and transformation*. Dordrecht, the Netherlands: Kluwer Academic Publishers.

Young, I. M. 1996. *Difference as a resource for democratic communication*. Toronto, Canada: University of Toronto Press.

Index

A

Aalborg Project, 273, 276–7
Abram, Simone, 162, 163
absolute dualism, 67–8
access and power, 159–60
action-oriented planning, xviii
Administrative Behavior (Simon), 20
ADR. *See* alternative dispute resolution
advocacy planning, 137–8, 160
Age of Reason, 4
Alberta, Canada, 199, 202
Alexander, Ernest, 33
Algerian War, 110–11
Allen, J., 272
Allmendinger, Philip, xi, 76, 174, 177, 282–3
alternative dispute resolution (ADR), 185–6
anarchy, 271–2
Andersen, J., 194, 197
Anderson, C. W., 27
Armstrong-Buck, Susan, 219
Austin, J. L., 234
autonomy, 83, 94–5

B

Baier, A., 278
Banff, Canada, 202
Banff-Bow Valley Study (BBVS), 202–6, 213–4, 218
Banfield, Edward C., 15, 20, 33, 34, 119
Baum, Howell S., 38, 39
BBVS. *See* Banff-Bow Valley Study
Beatley, Timothy, 224, 228, 239
Beauregard, Robert A.
    liberal democracy, 245

multiculturalism, 246, 253
postmodernism and planning, 75, 76, 78
theoretical reflection, 12
truth and reason, 68
Berlin, Isaiah, 84
Bernstein, Richard J., 48, 49, 61, 282
Blanco, H., xvii
Booher, D., 160
Borges, Jorge Luis, 66
Bouwsma, O. K., 53
Brezinski, Zbigniew, 30
British Columbia, Canada, 94
Buffon, Georges de, 217
bureaucracy
    alternatives to bureaucracy, 152–4
    bureaucratic claim, 35–6
    bureaucratic creep, 154
    bureaucratic organization, 36–7
    critique of, 115–6
    described, 5, 35
    key concepts, 36
    function and dysfunction, 37–8
    type of organization, 153
    underlying concepts, 37
Burnham, Daniel, 44, 168

C

Calgary, Canada, 167, 193, 200
Calgary Herald, 193, 194
California, 198
California State University, 198
Campbell, H., 177
Canmore Growth Management Strategy, 199–202

Cariboo-Chilcotin, Canada, 196
case studies, 190
   Banff-Bow Valley Study, 202–6
   Canmore Growth Management Strategy, 199–202
   Committee on Resources and the Environment, 194–8
   Growth Management Consensus Project, 198–9
   Steen Community Centre, 191–2
   Victoria Park, 193–4
Castells, Manuel, 167
categories, 215
Cerda, Ildefons, 168
charity, 71
Chomsky, Noam, 68
Chrislip, David, 17, 186–7, 260
civil society, 86–7
classical liberalism, 82–4. See also liberalism
Cleveland, Ohio, 138, 143, 155
Cockburn, Cynthia, 164–5, 187, 216
coercion, 130
Cohen, G. A., 85, 87, 88, 178
Coleman, A., 26
collaborative leadership, 186–7
collaborative planning, 185
Collingwood, R. G., 27
Committee on Resources and the Environment (CORE), 194–8
common ownership, 87–8
communicative and critical rationality, 16
communicative planning
   action, xvi, 139–40, 144
   civil society, 87
   consensus, production of, 163–6
   described, xvi
   dialogical planning approach and, 135, 137
   intellectual roots, 96
   narrowness of
      derivative theory, 166–7
      image, need for, 167–8

      spatial/physical forms, 167
      theory, lack of grand,168
      vision, lack of, 168–9
   political liberalism, 82
   positivistic approach, 256
   power, ignoring, 157–8
      caution regarding, 162
      macro theory, lack of explanatory, 160–1
      relation to state, 161–3
      vs. persuasion, 158–60
communicative rationality, xv, 6, 16, 115, 139
communism, 84
communitarian, 96, 174–6, 180
community and liberalism, 174–6
compassion/care, 87
consensus
   building, 187
      democratic processes, 189–90
      gender, 189
      inclusivity, 189
      outcomes, 188
      peacemaking, 189
      planners' roles, 188
      public interest, 188
      representation, 187
      shared values, 180
      social capital, 188
   incrementalist element, 121, 131
   overlapping, 97, 99, 148, 246–8
   production of, 163
      conflicting interests, 163
      hierarchical contexts, 163
      values and concepts, 163–4
   relativism and incommensurability, 273–4
   seeking, 113–5, 127
      identification of "interest" representatives, 213–4
      shared categories and principles, 214–5
   superficial —, 164
      dynamic process, 164–5
      flexible, nonhierarchical process, 165–6
conservatism and dialogical planning, 178–9

contemporary liberalism. *See also* liberalism
  autonomy, 94–5
  described, 94
  evolution of, 81
  ideological distortion, 95–6
  institutions and procedures, 95
  intellectual roots, 96–7
  vs. classical liberalism, 82–4
control and power, 160
conversation, 56
CORE. *See* Committee on Resources and the Environment
Coventry, England, 28
conversion, 130
Creation of Adam (Michelangelo), 3
critical interpretation, xix, 110–2, 144–5, 281
critical rationality, xvi, 6, 16, 135, 187
critical theory, 112–5
criticism, purpose of, 183
critique, practical, 284
cultural differences, interpretation of, 249–51

D
Dalton, L. C., 27, 38
Daniels, N., 103
Davidoff, Paul, xvii, 156, 160
Davidson, Donald
  charity, principle of, 278
  conceptual differences, 105
  language, 58
  neopragmatism approach, 49, 61, 282
  scheme and content, 51–2
Dear, M., 48, 68, 72, 75, 78
decision making
  incrementalism and, 32
  public, 31–2
deconstructionist
  issues raised by, xxii
  postmodernism and planning, 75, 76
  truth and reason, 70, 71, 72
deep ecologists, 228–30, 233–6
definitions in planning process, 221–2

democratic
  democratic processes, 189–90
  socialism, 149
  tradition and incrementalism, 126–127
Derrida, Jacques
  foundationalism, 64, 78
  ideas drawn from, 10
  intellectual root of postmodernism, 47–9
  meaning and ambiguity, 66, 67
  names vs. descriptions, 217
  normalization approach, 242
  planning theory, 78
descriptions versus names, 217
developmentalism, 241
Dewey, John
  consensus building, 187
  fact and values, distinctions between, 54
  planning process steps, 135–6, 156
  pragmatic alternative, 49
  tradition, criticism of , 265
  trust, 279
Dialogical Planning
  attributes, 142–7
  strengths, 282
dialogical planning approach
  attributes, 142
    communicative, 144
    critical, 144–5
    incremental, 145
    liberal, 143
    planner roles, 146–7
    political, 145–6
    pragmatic, 143–4
  contemporary liberal planning approaches
    communicative active planning, 139–40
    non-Euclidean planning, 138–9
    progressive/equity planning, 137–8
    social learning, 137
    strategic planning, 141–2
    TAMED planner, 140–1
  critiques and questions, 157

communicative approach ignores power, 157–62
consensus, production of, 163–6
modernist approach, 169–78
narrow approach, 166–9
radicalism and, 178–82
described, xvi, 135
environmental planning, organization of, 152, 155–6
alternatives to bureaucracy, 152–4
bureaucratic creep, 154
precursors, 135–6
insights from, 282
practice of, 185
cases, 190–206
collaborative leadership, 186–7
consensus building, 187–90
principled vs. interest-based negotiation, 185–6
procedural aspects
planning issues, 148
Wide Reflective Equilibrium applied to planning, 147–8
substantive elements
natural resources, 152
negative externalities, 151
private property, 151
social institutions, 149
urban planning, 151–2
wealth, 149–50
success, factors contributing to, 207–8
différance, 47–8, 70
discourse and power, 160
Diversity of Life, The (Wilson), 237
dualisms, 67–8, 258
Dupuy, Michael, 203

E
East Kootenay, Canada, 197
ecological dominance, 205
ecologists and justification of position, 233
borrowing words, 235
conforming to existing values, 234

enhancing existing values, 234
environmental crisis, 235–6
reductionism, 234
Einstein, Albert, 8
Enlightenment, 3, 46, 170–1, 241
entrepreneurial organization, 153
environmental crisis, 235–6
epistemology, practical, 32–3
equality, 7, 82–3, 108
equity planning, 111, 116, 137–8
essentialism, 54, 216
ethical theory, 97, 102
Etzioni, Amitai, 119, 128–9

F
fair system of cooperation, 7
fallibilism, 64
Faludi, Andreas, 33, 119, 125–6
Fascists, 82
feminists
analysis accepted in other cultures, 249
incrementalism and, 130
interpretation of
Derrida, 48
Rorty, 58
issues raised by, xxii
liberalism and, 82
narrow equilibrium, 106
normative approach, 180
postmodern, 260
rejection of modernism, 10
respect for other narratives, 243
Fischer, F., 16
Fischler, Raphaël, 159, 184, 263, 269
Fisher, Roger, 127, 185
flexibility in planning process, 221
Flyvbjerg, Bent
Aalborg Project, 273, 276–7
communicative approach and power, 158
Forester's critique of work, 270
naming, 215
power and control, 160
Forester, John

approaches to planning, xviii, 190

argumentative turn in planning and policy, 16

autonomy, 94

bureaucratic environment, 155–6

communicative action planning, 144, 161, 167, 256

conservatism of Wide Reflective Equilibrium, 178

critical pragmatism, xvii

critique, 145

dialogical planning approach, 156, 282

ideological distortion, 30

incrementalism, 120

interpretation of, xix

liberalism, 143

planners' roles, 187

planning, relation to state, 162

power and persuasion, 158, 160, 270

practical action, xvi, 33

progressive planning, 113, 116, 137–8

skillful planners, 262

theoretical reflection, 14

trust, 280

Foucault, Michel

approach to planning, 265–75

consensus-seeking, 114

contrast with Habermas, 275–6

critical school, xvii

dialogical planning approach, 180, 184

ideas drawn from, 10, 48, 77

intellectual root of postmodernism, 45–7

interpretation of, xix

naming, 215

normalization approach, 242

power

abuses, 61, 77, 78, 157–60, 246

external theory of, 270–1

meaning of, 266–9

philosophical approach to, 282

two senses of, 269–70

vocabulary of, 58, 265–6

foundationalism

characterization of modernism, 5, 63–5

dialogical planning and, 170

incrementalism and, 120, 122–3, 130, 132

rejection of, 228

frameworks, shared, 8, 222

free-market system, 86–7, 88

Freud, Sigmund, 281

Friedman, M., 10

Friedman, R., 10

Friedmann, John

communicative planning, 168

conservatism of Wide Reflective Equilibrium, 178

criticism of Lindblom, 127

dialogical planning approach, 156, 179, 180–2, 282

incrementalism, 128–129

institutional planning, failure of, 10

interpretation of, xix

liberalism, 82

non-Euclidean planning, 138–9

planner roles, 146

planning crisis, view of, 11

pragmatism, xvii

public interest, 188

RCPM, 27, 38

social learning, 116, 136–7

Fukuyama, F., 175

G

Gaebler, Ted, 10

Gauthier, David, 178

gender and consensus building, 189

Giddens, A., 156, 273

Gilligan, C., 181

GMS. *See* Growth Management Strategy

goals

alternative, 34

articulation, 34–5

Godel, Kurt, 9

Goebels, Joseph, 233

good articulation, 34–5

Goodman, N., 55, 103, 105

government
  legitimate roles, 8
  restrictions on the coercive powers, 7
  role in protection of liberty, 7
Grabow, S., xvii, 179
Growth Management Consensus Project, 198–9
Growth Management Strategy (GMS), 200–1
Gruber, Judith, 187, 198

H

Habermas, Jürgen
  bureaucracy, critique of, 115–6
  civil society, 87
  communicative and critical rationality, 16, 61, 139–40, 187
  communicative planning, xvii, 96
  conception of rationality, 28–9
  conservatism of Wide Reflective Equilibrium, 178
  contrast with Foucault, 275–6
  critical theory, 112–15
  dialogical planning approach, 180, 184, 282
  differences, views on, 76
  dominant culture, 242
  foundationalism, 170
  ideological distortion, 29, 95–6, 251
  interpretation of, xix
  liberal democratic notions, 64
  Narrow Reflective Equilibrium, 249
  power and persuasion, 158, 160
  pragmatic elements, 61, 143
  progressive planning, 137–8
  rational person, dialogical approach and, 173–4
  RCPM practice, 15
  Rorty's similarity to, 56
  scientism, 5, 24, 255, 281
  social theory, 123
  utilitarianism, 26
Hampton, J., 97
Hart, H. L. A., 108–9

Harvard Negotiation Project, 186
Harvey, David, 75
Healey, Patsy
  collaborative planning, 17
  communicative planning, 139–40, 144, 167
  consensus planning, 103
  dialogical planning approach, 156, 282
  new practices and institutions, 260
  planning defined, xvii
Hegel, Georg, 131
Heskin, A., xvii, 179
hierarchical planning, 163, 221
Hoch, Charles J.
  approaches to planning, 190
  communicative planning, 167
  critical interpretation, 112, 138, 260
  deliberative planning, 17
  dialogical planning approach, 156, 179, 282
  failure of modern RCPM, 9, 38, 39
  joint partnership of theory and practice, 262
  postmodern insight and planning, 78
  pragmatism, xvii
  role of philosophy in planning, 12
holism, 227, 289n. 5
Houseman, Eugene, 168
Howe, Elizabeth, 39
Hummel, Ralph P., 115–16, 155
Huxley, Margo, 162, 163, 167, 173

I

ideological distortion, 27, 29–30, 112–15, 249–51
ignorance, veil of, 101
impersonality, 36
inclusivity and consensus building, 189, 194, 202
incommensurability, 71–2, 273–4
incrementalism
  change and, 128
    innovation/big steps, 128–30

legitimizing big breaks, 130–1

described, xvi

decision making and, 32

dialogical planning, 145, 169–70

justification and practice, xvi

liberal democratic tradition, 126–7

   consensus-seeking processes, 127

   critique, 128

Lindblom's original, 118–120

postmodernist critiques, 121

   foundationalism, 122–3

   meta-narrative, 123–4

   neopragmatism, 124–5

   progress and legitimation, 124

   rationality, 125

   test of knowledge, 125–6

pragmatic, incremental approach, 227–8

   chosen principles, 229–30

   necessity of change, 228–9

reconstruction of, 120–1

individual, authentic, 236–7

Industrial Revolution, 4

Innes, Judith

   communicative planning, 139–40, 144, 167

   consensus building, 16–17, 187, 198

   dialogical planning approach, 156, 282

   new practices and institutions, 260

   planners' roles, 187

   power and persuasion, 160

   practical action, xvi, 33

   pragmatism, xviii

   reflective equilibrium, 103

innovation, 285

innovative, 139

innovative organization, *153*

instrumental/technical rationality, *6*, 23. *See also* rationality

insurgent planning, 140–1, 181–2

intelligibility, 260–1

"interest" representatives, 213–4

interest-based negotiation, 185–6

International City Managers Association, 37

J

Jamal, Tazim, 199, 202, 213–4

James, William, 49

Jefferson, Thomas, 6, 112

Jesus, 112

joint ownership, 87–8, 262

Justice as Fairness: A Restatement (Rawls), 102

justice, principles of, 101–2, 138

justification

   cause and, 230–1

   incrementalism and, 123

   modernist planning, 7–8, 74

   planning requires—, 7

   public—, 100–1

K

Kant, Immanuel, 73, 85, 102, 170, 257–8

Kekule, Friedrich August, 131

Kissinger, Henry, 30

knowing-in-action, 13, 14

knowledge, test of, 125–6

Kolb, D., 98

Krumholz, Norman

   bureaucratic environment, 155–6

   equity planning, 111, 117, 138

   liberalism, 143

   theoretical reflection, 14

Kuhn, Thomas

   incrementalism, 129, 131

   paradigm shift, 17, 58, 224–7, 232–3

   pragmatism, 61, 261

   scientific view, 9, 55, 111, 126, 236

Kymlicka, Will, 171

L

labeling, problems with

   dominant approach and, 241–2

   essentialism, 216

   naming, 215

laissez-faire capitalism, 149

language

incommensurability, 71
meaning and ambiguity, 66
radical paradigm shifts and, 226–7, 261
Rorty's views, 58–9
structures existence, 278
Larson, Carl, 17, 127, 186–7, 260
law, rule of, 7
leadership, collaborative, 186–7
legitimation, 261–2
Leopold, Aldo, 224, 234, 238
liberal planning approaches
    communicative active planning, 139–40
    non-Euclidean planning, 138–9
    progressive/equity planning, 137–8
    social learning, 137
    strategic planning, 141–2
    TAMED planner, 140–1
liberalism
    classical — vs. contemporary — , 82–4
    community and, 174–6
    critical liberal perspective
        contemporary liberalism, 94–7
        critical interpretation, 110–12
        Habermassian critique of bureaucracy, 115–16
        ideological distortion, 112–15
        political liberalism, 97–102, 107–10
        Wide Reflective Equilibrium, 102–7
    described, xvi, 6, 81–2
    dialogical planning, 177–8
    modernist planning, 6–7
    natural resources
        limited positive rights, 89–90
        Lockean proviso, 87–8
        more reasonable proviso, 88–9
    negative externalities, regulation of, 90–1
    negative natural rights, 84–5
        civil society, 86–7
        minimal state, 86
        property, 85–6
    normative values, xvi
    notion of the person, 171

liberty, 7, 108
limited positive rights, 89–90
Lindblom, Charles
    decision making, views on, 31–2
    dialogical planning approach, 156, 180
    incrementalism, 118–32
    pragmatism, xvii
linguistic philosophy, 50
Livingston, John, 224, 235
Locke, John, 6, 86, 87–8, 89, 92
logical positivism, 22, 24. *See also* positivism
London, England, 25
Los Angeles, California, 28, 71
Lyons, Glen, 193, 194
Lyotard, Jean-Francois, 10, 77, 123

M

macro theory, lack of explanatory, 160–1
Madison, James, 37
malice, 72
management science, 20
Mandelbaum, Seymour J.
    communicative planning, 169
    plurality and different frames, 74
    positivistic approach, 256–7, 282
    RCPM view, 33, 156
    strategy of agreeing to disagree, 105, 117
Margerum, Richard D., 186, 190, 209
Marshall, R., 177
Marx, Karl, 112, 270
Marxism, 5, 65, 82, 244, 281
Mawson, Thomas, 168
McCarthy, Thomas, 174, 267
McKearnen, S., 190
McNamara, Robert, 15
meta-narratives
    defined, 5
    dialogical planning, 170
    incrementalism, 123–4, 132
    replacement approach, 243, 244
    theory and, 65

Meyerson, Martin 15, 33, 34, 119
Michelangelo, 3
Mill, John Stuart, 27, 216
Milroy, B., 68, 77, 160
minimal state, 86
Mintzberg, Henry, 37, 142, 152
modernist planning
  background, 20
  bureaucracy, 35
    bureaucratic claim, 35–6
    bureaucratic organization, 36–7
    function and dysfunction, 37–8
    underlying concepts, 37
  crisis in, 8
    challenges to authority of science, 8–9
    nature of, 11–12
    paradigm shift, 9–11
    practice without theory, 15–16
    role of theoretical reflection, 12–15
  described, 3–4
    justification, 7–8
    liberalism, 6–7
    rationality, 6
    science, 4
    scientism, 4–6
  dialogical approach, 169
    community and liberalism, 174–6
    foundationalism, 170
    incrementalism and neopragmatism, 169–70
    liberal values bias, 177
    liberalism, 171, 177–8
    meta-narrative, 170
    rationality and, 173–4
    Rawls's principles and, 172–3
    relative framework, 176
    Wide Reflective Equilibrium, ethnocentricity of, 176–7
  ideological critique
    concealing the normative, 30–1
    evasion of responsibility, 31
    ideological distortion, 29–30

  philosophical bases
    objectivity, 27–8
    positivism, 22, 24
    rationality, 23–4, 27–9
    scientism and reductionism, 24–6
    utilitarianism, 22–3, 26–7
  practical critical critique
    practical epistemology, 32–3
    public decision making, 31–2
  rational comprehensive planning model, 21
    critique of, 24–9
    defenses of, 33–5
    justification, 21–2
    perseverance of, 38–9
  responses to
    neopragmatism and pragmatism, 60–1
    neopragmatism, intellectual roots of, 50–60
    postmodernism, 44
    postmodernist challenge, 43–4
    postmodernism, intellectual roots of, 45–9
    pragmatic alternative, 49–50
moral concerns, 236–7, 259
Moses, Robert, 168
Mulgrew, Angela, 191
multicultural trap
  core tension, 244
  cultural differences, interpretation of, 249–51
  described, 240–1
  paradox of, 246
  postmodern critiques, 241
    dominant approach attacked, 241–2
    other narratives, respect for, 243
    replacement approach provided, 242–3
  reconciliation, pragmatic process of, 251–3
  strict, 297n. 7
  useful distinctions, 244
    external and internal perspectives, 244–5

wide and narrow reflective equilibria, 245–6

Mumford, Lewis, 136, 137, 156

N

Naess, Arnie, 227–8, 232–3

naming
  described, 215
  descriptions vs., 217
  new names, 218

Narrow Reflective Equilibrium (NRE), 104–6, 110, 147, 245–6, 249

natural resources
  dialogical planning and, 152
  limited positive rights, 89–90
  Lockean proviso, 87–8
  more reasonable proviso, 88–9

negative externalities, regulation of, 90–1

negative natural rights, 84–5
  civil society, 86–7
  minimal state, 86
  property, 85–6

negotiation, 198

neopragmatism
  alternative, 216–7
    names vs. descriptions, 217
    new names, 218
    to postmodernism, 49–50
  classical pragmatism, 60–1
  consensus building and, 187
  described, xvi
  incrementalism, 124–5, 169–70
  intellectual roots of, 50–60
  philosophical orientation, xvi, 282
  planning, 143–4, 276–8
  postmodernist, 64
  rights and, 83–4
  Wide Reflective Equilibrium and, 176

Neuman, Michael, 166–7, 168, 187, 198

Neurath, Otto, 122, 227

New York City, New York, 25, 115

Newton, Isaac, 9

Nielson, Kai, 178, 251

Nietzsche, Fredrich, 45, 77

NIMBY. *See* not in my backyard

non-Euclidean planning, 138–9

normalization approach, 242

normative
  concealing, 30–1
  described, xviii
  focus, xx–xxii
  non-Euclidean planning, 139

not in my backyard (NIMBY), 163, 295n. 1

Notre-Dame de Paris, 3

Noumena, 73

Nozick, Robert
  autonomy, 95
  conservatism of Wide Reflective Equilibrium, 178
  free-market system, 86
  limited positive rights, 88, 90
  natural rights, 61, 84–5, 108
  utilitarianism, 26

NRE. *See* Narrow Reflective Equilibrium

Nussbaum, Martha, 48

O

objectivity, 27–8

Olmsted, Frederick Law, 168

operations research. *See* management science

organizational environment (of planning), 152, 155–6
  alternatives to bureaucracy, 152–4
  bureaucratic creep, 154
  precursors, 135–6

Osborne, David, 10

Oslo peace process, 222–3

overlapping consensus. *See* consensus, overlapping

Oxford, England, xv

P

Papineau, David, 237

paradigm shift
  ecologists and justification of position, 233

borrowing words, 235
conforming to existing values, 234
enhancing existing values, 234
environmental crisis, 235–6
reductionism, 234
justification and cause, 230–1
moral vision, 236
authentic individual, 236–7
pragmatic, incremental approach, 227–8
chosen principles, 229–30
necessity of change, 228–9
radical —
justification, 226
language and, 226–7
nature of, 225–6
supporting, 231–3
sustainability, challenge of, 224–5
Parker, Barry, 168
Parsons, Talcott, 22
Partisan Mutual Adjustment (PMA), 121, 127, 128
peacemaking and consensus building, 189
Peirce, Charles Sander, 49
perspectivalism, 43
persuasion and power, 158–60
Peters, Tom, 10
philosophical bases of RCPM
objectivity, 27–8
positivism, 22, 24
rationality, 23–4, 27–9
scientism and reductionism, 24–6
utilitarianism, 22–3, 26–7
philosophy of planning, 12–3
Plan for Chicago (Burnham), 44
planning. *See also* modernist planning
changing approaches to, *18*
contrasting approaches, 263–75
defined, xvii–xix, 5
emerging approach, 16–19
issues, 148
liberalism and —
classical — vs. contemporary — , 82–4
described, 81–2

natural resources, 87–90
negative externalities, regulation of, 90–1
negative natural rights, 84–5
urban planning, 91–93
philosophy of, 12–3
postmodernist, 75–8
Planning in the Face of Power (Forester), 160
planning organizations, 152–4
planning practice and planning theory, 258–9
application to practice, 262
critical reflection on practice, 259–60
evaluation of new practices, 260
intelligibility, 260–1
legitimation, 261–2
generation of new practices, 260
joint partnership, 262
planning process, 197, 221–3
planning profession, 3, 5–6
planning professional
as technical expert 6
legitimacy of, 13
reductionist, 33
rejection of theory
positivistic approach, 255–7
pragmatic approach, 257–8
problem with theory, 254–5
roles, 106, 146–7, 187–8, 192
talk of, 10, 15–6
TAMED, 140–1
Wide Reflective Equilibrium and, 106
Planning Programming and Budgeting
Systems (PPBS), 15
Plato, 112, 255
pluralism, 97–8, 246–7, 253
plurality, 73–4, 120
PMA. *See* Partisan Mutual Adjustment
political
dialogical planning and, 145–6
non-Euclidean planning, 139
political liberalism
defined, 82, 95
dialogical planning and, 143, 177–8
justice, principles of, 101–2

metaphysical vs., 100
overlapping consensus, 99
private and public realms, 98–9
private property, 151
public justification, 100–1
rationality and reasonableness, 100
Rawls's ethical theory, 97, 102, 237
substantive implications of, 107–8, 110
  basic liberties, 109
  concretizing the principles, 108–9
  primary goods, 109–110
political utilitarianism, 23. *See also* utilitarianism
positivism
  approach, 255–7
  critique of, 24
  described, 5, 22
  incrementalism and, 120
  limited rights, 89–90
  practice without theory, 15
postmodernism
  challenge, 43–4
  critique of dominant culture, 241–2
  described, 44
  intellectual roots of, 45–9
  themes, 63
    dualisms, 67–8
    foundationalism, 63–5
    incommensurability, 71–2
    justification, 74
    meaning and ambiguity, 66–7
    meta-narrative and theory, 65
    planning, 75–8
    plurality and different frames, 73–4
    relativism, 72–3
    truth and reason, 68–70
poverty, 30
power, 157–8
  caution regarding, 162
  external theory of, 270–1
  macro theory, lack of explanatory, 160–1
  meaning of, 266–9

persuasion and, 158–60
  forms of, 159–60
relations, 77–8, 155, 179
  relation to state, 161–3
two senses of, 269–70
vocabulary of, 265–6
PPBS. *See* Planning Programming and Budgeting Systems
practical action approach, xvi
pragmatic incrementalism. *See* incrementalism
pragmatism. *See* neopragmatism
Premfors, R., 125
principled negotiation, 185–6
principles, universal
  in planning process, 221–2
  search for, 213
    abstract, 219–20
    consensus-seeking processes, 213–15
    labels, 215–16
    neopragmatic alternative, 216–18
    planning processes, recommendations for, 221–3
  validity, 172
priority, 108
process design, 202
professional organization, *153*
professional protocol, 6, 20, 38
progressive planning, 113, 116, 137–8
property, 85–6, 151
property-owning democracy, 149
public decision making, 31–2
public forum, 198
public good, 7, 11
public housing, 26
public interest, 11, 27, 188
public planning
  definition, xviii
  rationale for, 283
Putnam, Hilary
  comments on Derrida, 48
  dualism, 68
  fact and value, 54–5

meaning and ambiguity, 67
narrow and wide reflection, 105
neopragmatism, 49, 51, 61
rejection of sharp practical/theoretical distinction, 64
scientism, 55
truth and reason, 70
Putnam, Robert, 186, 218, 248

Q

Quine, Willard van Orman
fact and value, 51, 54, 67
meaning and ambiguity, 66, 72
meta-narrative and theory, 65
neopragmatist, 49, 61
pragmatic approach, 257

R

radical interpretation, 285
radical paradigm shift
justification, 226
language and, 226–7
nature of, 225–6
supporting, 231–3
radicalism and dialogical planning
conservativism, 178–9
insurgent planning, 181–2
radical planning, 179–80
status quo, support of, 179, 180–1
Rational Comprehensive Planning Model (RCPM)
critique of, 24–9, 118–20, 183
defenses of, 33–5
described, 21
dialogical planning and, 136
incrementalism and, 125, 127, 132
justification, 21–2
meta-narratives, 65
non-Euclidean planning, 138
perseverance of, 38–9
practice, 15
scientism, 5
theoretical reflection, 13

Rational Decision Model, 15
rational planning. *See* modernist planning
rationality
described, 69, 70
dialogical planning, 173–4
incrementalism and, 125
modernist planning, 6
objectivity and, 27–9
philosophical base, 23–4
political liberalism, 100
types of, 6
Rationality and Power (Flyvbjerg), 270
Rawls, John
community and liberalism, 174–6
dialogical planning, 172–3, 282
ethical theory, 96, 97–110, 116, 120, 149
interpretation of, xix, xx
Justice as Fairness: A Restatement, 102
liberalism, 82, 83, 126, 143, 171
moral perspective, 92
natural resources, 152
negative externalities, 151
neopragmatism, 61
overlapping consensus, 148
political liberalism, 95, 237
principles, universal validity, 172
private property, 151
progressive/equity planning, 138
rational self-interest, 173
reasonableness, xxi, 127, 135, 173
Theory of Justice, A, 102
utilitarianism, 26
wealth, distribution of, 149–50
Wide Reflective Equilibrium, xx, 55, 62, 178, 247–8, 281
RCPM. *See* Rational Comprehensive Planning Model
reality, 56–8
reason and truth, 68–70
reasonableness, 100, 125, 127, 135, 173, 283–4
reconciliation, pragmatic process of, 251–3
reductionism, 35, 234

reductionist planner, 33
reflection-in-action, 14
reflective choice, 7
regional planning process, 136
relativism, 72–3, 273–4. *See also*
 multicultural trap
religion, 3–4
representation issues, 205
representative democracy, 5
representatives, "interest," 213–14
responsibility, evasion of, 31
Reuter, Wolf, 160
Richardson, T., 168, 170, 174
rights, 83. *See also* negative natural rights
Rittel, H., 209, 286
Roman Catholic Church, 4
Roosevelt, Franklin D., 112
Rorty, Richard
 abstract universal principles, 220
 analytic philosophy, 50, 51
 consensus-seeking, 115
 conversation, 56
 description of Foucault's views, 46
 incrementalism, 130–1
 justification, 58
 language games, vocabularies, and
  descriptions, 58–9, 265
 neopragmatist, 49, 61, 227
 philosophical theory, 261, 282
 radical conceptual change, 231–3
 social hope, 276
 theory, 58
 truth and reality, 56–8, 279
Rosenberg, Alfred, 233
Rousseau, Jean-Jacques, 7
routine, 36
Rowland, W., 3

S

Sacramento, California, 198
Sager, Tore, 16, 169, 170
Sandercock, Leonie
 approaches to planning, 190

cities of difference, 165
dialogical planning approach, 156,
 181–2, 280, 282
insurgent planning—TAMED planner,
 140–1
postmodern paradigm, xvi, 76
radical planning, 179
rationality, 6
Sartre, Jean-Paul, 110–11
Saussure, Ferdinand de, 47, 71
Schaar, J. H., 116
Schön, Donald, 13, 14
science
 challenges to authority of, 8–9
 ecological dominance, 205, 236
 modernist planning, 4
 test of knowledge, 126
scientific rationality. *See* rationality
scientism
 described, 55, 255
 ideological distortion, 113
 incrementalism and, 120
 modernist planning, 4–6, 281
 reductionism and, 24–6
Scruton, Roger, 28, 248
shared frameworks. *See* frameworks, shared
Simon, Herbert A., 15, 20, 119
Sistine Chapel, 3
Skinner, B. F., 230
slum, 26, 30, 34
social benefits, 27
social capital, 186, 188
social concerns, 33
Social Democrats, 82, 178. *See also*
 contemporary liberalism
social engineering, 20
social hope, 46, 276, 287
social institutions, 149
social learning, 116, 136, 137, 139, 179
social science, 5, 20
social theory, xviii, 121, 123
Soja, E. J., 75
specialized vocabulary. *See* planning
 professional, talk of

Spitler, G., 238

stakeholders. *See* "interest" representatives

state socialism, 149

Steen Community Centre, 191–2

Stockland, P., 193

Stout, J., 258

Strategic Arms Limitation Talks, 186

strategic planning, 141–2

strengths, weaknesses, opportunities,
     threats (SWOT), 10, 16, 142, 286n.
     13, 294n. 8

structuralist, 66

Susskind, L., 190

sustainability, challenge of, 224–5

SWOT. *See* strengths, weaknesses,
     opportunities, threats

T

TAMED planner, 140–1, 289n. 1

Taylor, Charles, 159, 274

technical activist. *See* traditional technician

technical rationality/instrumental, 6

Tewdwr-Jones, M., 174, 177

theoretical reflection, role of, 12–15

theory, rejection of
  by planners
    positivistic approach, 255–7
    pragmatic approach, 257–8
    problem with theory, 254–5
  planning theory and planning practice,
       258–9
    application to practice, 262
    critical reflection on practice, 259–60
    evaluation of new practices, 260–2
    generation of new practices, 260
    joint partnership, 262

Theory of Justice, A (Rawls), 102

thick concepts, 285n. 20

Thomas-Larmer, J., 190

Thompson, Robert, 187, 198

three-table problem, 206

thresholds, 32

Throgmorton, James, 282

tipping points. *See* thresholds

tolerance, 7

traditional technician, 38, 287n. 19

trust, 53–4, 56, 87, 222, 278–80

truth and reason, 68–70

"Two Dogmas of Empiricism" (Quine), 51

U

universal planning approaches, 240

universal principles. *See* principles,
     universal

Unwin, Raymond, 168

urban planning
  dialogical planning and, 151–2
  liberalism and, 91–3

urban politics, 155

urban renewal, 26, 30, 33, 107

Ury, William, 185

U.S. Defense Department, 15

utilitarian
  critique of RCPM, 26–7
  described, 5
  incrementalism, 120
  negative externalities, regulation of, 91
  philosophical base, 15, 22–3
  power and, 271

V

values
  conforming to existing — , 234
  consensus production and, 163–4
  enhancing existing — , 234
  moral, 87
  shared, 180

Vancouver Island, Canada, 196

Verma, N., xvii

victimhood, 272

Victoria Park, 193–4

vision, 287

vocabulary
  choice of, 59–60
  multiculturalism and, 249–51
  of power, 265–6

specialized. *See* planning professional,
    talk of

W

Wagner, Robert F., 168
Walzer, M.
    communitarian philosopher, 96, 282
    conservatism of Wide Reflective
        Equilibrium, 178
    critical interpretation, xix, 281
    external and internal perspectives, 244
    incrementalism, 128
    liberalism, critical interpretation of, 110–2,
        116, 144
    neopragmatist, 61
    theoretical reflection, 14
    utilitarianism, 26, 272
Waterman, Robert, 10
wealth, 149–50
Webber, M., 209
Weber, M., 35
welfare state capitalism, 149
West Kootenay-Boundary, Canada, 196
Why Do Planners Plan? (Hoch), 260
wicked problems, 286
Wide Reflective Equilibrium (WRE)
    alternative dispute resolution, 186
    application of, xx
    communicative action planning, 140, 167
    consensus through, 121, 124, 164
    conservatism, 178–9
    contemporary liberalism, 97
    conversation, 56
    described, xx, 102–7
    dialogical planning and, 143, 144, 161,
        184
    ethnocentricity of, 176–7
    examples, 106–7
    foundationalism, 170
    inclusivity, 189
    incrementalism, 128, 129
    meta-narrative, 65
    meta-narrative and theory, 65

multicultural trap and, 245–6, 247–8
natural resources, 152
negative externalities, 151
neopragmatic resolution, 15
planning, and, 147–8
pragmatic view, 61, 62, 281
procedural approach, 102
    internal and external perspectives,
        103–4
    narrow and wide reflection, 104–6
    planner's professional role, 106
    reflective equilibrium, 103, 106–7
progressive/equity planning, 138
reconciliation and, 252
scientism, 55
use of, 209
Williams, B., 26, 247
Wilson, E. O., 237
Wilson, Woodrow, 37
Winch, P., 98
Winnipeg, Canada, 191
Wittgenstein, Ludwig
    abstract universal principles, 219
    essentialism, 54
    family resemblances, xix, 217
    foundations, 52–3
    incrementalism, 131
    justification, 74
    language, 71, 264, 278
    neopragmatism approach, 61, 282
    paradigm shifts and language, 226
    pragmatist, 49, 51
    theory, 53
    trust, 53–4
    truth and reason, 57, 69–70
World War II, 20
WRE. *See* Wide Reflective Equilibrium

Y

Yiftachel, Oren, xvii, xviii, 160, 167

Z

zoning, 91–3, 152